The Promise Keepers

To
Jerry & Earlene Claussen

The Promise Keepers

Essays on Masculinity and Christianity

Edited by DANE S. CLAUSSEN

McFarland & Company, Inc., Publishers
Jefferson, North Carolina, and London

Library of Congress Cataloguing-in-Publication Data

The Promise Keepers : essays on masculinity and Christianity / edited by Dane S. Claussen.
    p. cm.
    Includes bibliographical references and index.
    ISBN 0-7864-0700-X (library binding : 50# alkaline paper) ∞
    1. Promise Keepers (Organization)   I. Claussen, Dane S., 1963– .
BV960.P76   2000
267'.23—dc21   99-38799
                                                             CIP

British Library Cataloguing-in-Publication data are available

©2000 Dane S. Claussen. All rights reserved

No part of this book may be reproduced or transmitted in any form or by any means, electronic or mechanical, including photocopying or recording, or by any information storage and retrieval system, without permission in writing from the publisher.

Manufactured in the United States of America

McFarland & Company, Inc., Publishers
   Box 611, Jefferson, North Carolina 28640
   www.mcfarlandpub.com

Acknowledgments

Several individuals have been helpful—all in different ways—in the initiation, writing, editing or production of this book. I begin with thanks to Professor Carol J. Pardun, now at the School of Journalism and Mass Communication, University of North Carolina–Chapel Hill, who first encouraged me to research Promise Keepers' media coverage when we both were at the A.Q. Miller School of Journalism and Mass Communications, Kansas State University, and who continues to have great faith in both the importance and the quality of my work. My master's thesis, which she directed, ultimately led to this book.

Professor Michael Eidenmuller of Northwestern State University of Louisiana (author of Chapter 7), and George L. Daniels, a graduate student at the Henry W. Grady College of Journalism and Mass Communication, the University of Georgia, gave encouragement and help. Professor Robert D. Linder of Kansas State University and Professor Randy Balmer of Barnard College, Columbia University, expressed enough confidence in me and this project to agree early to write the Conclusion and Introduction, respectively, to this book.

Professor Glen T. Cameron, now the Maxine Wilson Gregory Chair in Journalism Research and director of the Center for Advanced Social Research at the University of Missouri–Columbia, facilitated my work on this book and another one during spring quarter 1998 at the University of Georgia. Professor Elizabeth "Elli" Lester Roushanzamir, of the Grady College at UGA, tried diligently to prevent the two books from interfering too much with my doctoral program's schedule, and she largely succeeded.

Professor Andy Kavoori of the Grady College, University of Georgia, provided helpful comments on the Preface, and numerous scholars have provided the same on my master's thesis and conference papers about Promise Keepers, the mythopoets, or the Men and Religion Forward Movement of 1911–12.

I owe an inestimable debt to Elizabeth A.R. Boleman-Herring, publishing editor at the Literate Chigger, Ink, Pendleton, S.C., who was a thorough, quick and witty (only in the margins, that is) line editor, as well as a true friend; of course all remaining faults in the text are my responsibility alone. And finally, thanks and an apology to my relatives (particularly my parents) and friends (just a few of whom are Phil Comer, Paul Featheringill, Christopher Lane, and especially Suttichai "Tom" Chuvessiriporn) whom I either neglected or subjected to some of my most stressful moments in 1998, all of which they cheerfully withstood.

Athens, Georgia
Summer 1999

Contents

Acknowledgments   v
Preface   xi

INTRODUCTION   *by Randy Balmer*   1

CHAPTER 1   Keeping the Promise of the Moral Majority?
A Historical/Critical Comparison of the Promise Keepers
and the Christian Coalition, 1989–98
by Andrew Quicke and Karen Robinson   7

CHAPTER 2   The Religious Roots of the Promise Keepers
by Michael J. Chrasta   20

CHAPTER 3   Upstaging the Masons: The Promise Keepers
and Fraternal Orders
by Paul Rich and Guillermo de los Reyes   29

CHAPTER 4   The Price of Admission? Promise Keepers'
Roots in Revivalism and the Emergence of Middle Class
Language and Appeal in Men's Movements
by Michael A. Longinow   42

CHAPTER 5   Are Promises Enough? Promise Keepers
Attitudes and Character in Intensive Interviews
by George N. Lundskow   56

CHAPTER 6   Sacred Male Space: The Promise Keepers as
a Community of Resistance
by Don Deardorff   76

CHAPTER 7   Promise Keepers and the Rhetoric of Recruitment: The Context, the Persona, and the Spectacle
by Michael E. Eidenmuller   91

CHAPTER 8   Identification and Invitation as Competing Rhetorics in the Promise Keepers Movement
by Robert A. Stewart   102

CHAPTER 9   Promising to Be a Man: Promise Keepers and the Organizational Constitution of Masculinity
by Robert A. Cole   113

CHAPTER 10   Exodus and the Chosen Men of God: Promise Keepers and the Theology of Masculinity
by David S. Gutterman   133

CHAPTER 11   The Promise Keepers' Use of Sport in Defining "Christlike" Masculinity
by Becky Beal   153

CHAPTER 12   Onward Broken Soldiers: A Rhetorical Analysis of the Atlanta Promise Keepers Clergy Conference
by John D. Suk   164

CHAPTER 13   Ecumenical Promise Keepers: Oxymoron or Fidelity?
by J. Lynn Reynolds and Rodney A. Reynolds   175

CHAPTER 14   Reading a Promise Keepers Event: The Intersection of Race and Religion
by Billy Hawkins   182

CHAPTER 15   Keep the Faith and Go the Distance: Promise Keepers, Feminism, and the World of Sports
by Randy Balmer   194

CHAPTER 16   Building a Social Evangelical Organization: The Lincoln Bedroom or Oval Office Model?
by Bryan W. Brickner   204

CHAPTER 17   The Irresolvable Tension: *Agape* and Masculinity in the Promise Keepers Movement
by Kevin Healey   215

CHAPTER 18 Silencing the Voice of God: Rhetorical
Responses to the Promise Keepers
by Colleen E. Kelley   226

CHAPTER 19 Liberated Through Submission? The Gender
Politics of Evangelical Women's Groups Modeled on the
Promise Keepers
by Tanya Erzen   238

CHAPTER 20 Who Are These Guys? The Promise Keepers'
Media Relations Strategy for "Stand in the Gap"
by Ken Waters   255

CHAPTER 21 They Just Don't Get It! Promise Keepers'
Responses to Media Coverage
by L. Dean Allen II   269

CHAPTER 22 "So Far, News Coverage of Promise Keepers
Has Been More Like Advertising": The Strange Case
of Christian Men and the Print Mass Media
by Dane S. Claussen   281

CONCLUSION Will the Promises Be Kept?
by Robert D. Linder   308

About the Contributors   325

Index   327

Preface
by Dane S. Claussen

Before I introduce the various chapters in this book, I want to provide a short history of how I became interested in the Promise Keepers and why I ultimately chose to edit this book.

In late 1995, while deciding on a master's thesis subject, I was familiar with but not very knowledgeable about the mythopoetic men's movement (best known for Robert Bly's *Iron John*) and Promise Keepers, and the Million Man March had just been held. I was curious about how these three phenomena were similar, and equally curious about how they were different. Coverage in the popular media was not very helpful. It seemed that the mythopoetic men's movement had received overwhelmingly cynical, sarcastic, and satirical coverage, while Promise Keepers (hereafter PK) was receiving what I thought to be surprisingly favorable coverage. The Million Man March received favorable coverage for its attendees and not-so-favorable coverage of its primary organizer, Louis Farrakhan.

If the media were giving the benefit of the doubt to PK, as Gerald Seib (1997) later wrote, why hadn't they done the same for mythopoetism? After all, if mythopoetism seemed silly to whose who didn't think it was sexist, it also should have struck those same individuals as harmless, perhaps even unnewsworthy. Moreover, unlike PK and perhaps even the March, all agreed that mythopoetism had no explicit political agenda.

The question of media coverage was not in itself enough to inspire me to research media coverage of men's movements. But all of the political, religious, psychological, cultural, journalistic, gender-related and other questions raised by the men's movements were. Thus my thesis and later this book.

As the manuscript for this book was being completed, the only mass market book about PK yet published was Ken Abraham's *Who Are the Promise Keepers? Understanding the Christian Men's Movement*, published in early 1997. Abraham is a PK insider, writing articles for *New Man* (formerly PK's official magazine), and his book is essentially a promotional piece for PK. Although national indexes list numerous other pamphlets, manuscripts and small press or self-published books on PK, the only other significant work on PK has been *Promise Keepers: Another Trojan Horse*, by Phil Arms. It is a fundamentalist critique of PK that charges PK with not being conservative enough. At least three other books currently are in progress (one by Michael Eidenmuller and one by Bryan Brickner, both contributors to this volume), but it obviously would be premature to compare and contrast them with this one. Other scholarship has been limited to a few journal articles (one of which is reprinted here), various unpublished conference papers and several articles in mainstream—not academic—periodicals.

This book attempts an in-depth interpretive analysis of PK, its historical antecedents, its media coverage, and its contextual placement within the issues of gender, race, media coverage, national politics and other spheres.

Contributors were located through programs of conferences at which papers on Promise Keepers had been given; through widely circulated national requests for chapter proposals; through database searches of theses, dissertations, books, and articles; and through personal networking. Selection of contributors was primarily based on the importance and inherent interest of their proposed chapter subjects as well as their expertise. Selection also included an effort to minimize duplication of material in the book. The degree to which contributors might support or reject the Promise Keepers played no role in the selection process, although in one instance a chapter proposal was rejected because its faith-based arguments and conclusions ignored or rejected widely accepted social science research findings about American society.

Contributors have been drawn from a wide variety of disciplines, and they have approached their essays from different theoretical and methodological orientations. Readers of this book will likely find parts that they agree with, parts that they disagree with, and hopefully much to stimulate debate. It may be assumed that the book's text includes many individual assumptions, hypotheses, interpretations, and conclusions with which I disagree, but which I have included anyway for the sake of publishing a broader cross-section of scholarship.

Randy Balmer's Introduction provides a brief overview of what this volume demonstrates overall, and makes many key points. Following the Introduction, the first four chapters attempt to establish a historical context for Promise Keepers. Andrew Quicke and Karen Robinson's Chapter 1 evaluates the claim that PK is a "third wave" among new Christian political organizations, following the Moral Majority and the Christian Coalition; they conclude that PK is, as it claims, not political. In Chapter 2, Michael J. Chrasta argues that questions of PK's religious identity can be answered by locating its roots in the Vineyard, Calvary, and "Jesus" movements of the 1970s and 1980s; Chrasta is aware that his is a new interpretation and that readers may disagree. In Chapter 3, Paul Rich and Guillermo de los Reyes discuss some similarities and differences between PK and historical fraternal orders such as the Masons. They explore the motivations of those who belong to men's organizations, and ultimately express hope that the impetus behind PK may eventually be good news for traditional men's groups. In Chapter 4, Mike Longinow looks at Promise Keepers through the lens of late 19th century and early 20th century Protestant revivals, particularly those led by Billy Sunday and other Muscular Christians, as well as the Men and Religion Forward Movement, which sought men who had socioeconomic clout.

In Chapter 5, George Lundskow seeks the basis of the relationship between PK leaders and PK participants, with an emphasis on theories of authoritarianism. In Chapter 6, Donald Deardorff II posits that PK is a community of resistance for its participants, who have experienced negative images of men, isolation, role confusion and other issues that have made them feel alienated in U.S. society. In Chapter 7 Michael Eidenmuller analyzes how PK's rhetoric synthesizes "sacred" and "secular" vocabularies into a unifying vision of religious motive and action, and how PK copes with critical "exigencies" that challenge it as an organization. He concludes that it is a postmodern religious organization that may be demonstrating the forms religion may or must assume in an emerging global social order.

In Chapter 8, Robert Stewart shows how PK uses men's identification with various aspects of its organization to effectively build and maintain itself, but how these same sources of identification appear to PK detractors actually to cultivate biases of gender and race. Stewart concludes that use of "invitational rhetoric" by PK would not change its relationship with its critics and that they may simply have to agree to disagree.

In Chapter 9, Bob Cole analyzes PK texts to demonstrate that the organization restores social acceptability to patriarchal hierarchy and privilege. He offers a monolithic definition of what it believes are men's biblically dictated characteristics, and argues that men's potential is unrealized because of assaults on their manhood by women and "society." Cole finds many PK positions to be hypocritical, illogical or inconsistent.

In Chapter 10, David Gutterman analyzes PK's responses to increasingly fragile individual and group identities; he concentrates on prophetic narratives and a "theology of masculinity," both of which lie within the particularly American historical tradition and have profound political implications. In Chapter 11, Becky Beal explains how PK literature uses sport to promote a specific style of masculinity and male leadership that it calls "Christlike." Through critical feminist analysis, she details how sport is used to link masculinity with superior leadership, to develop images of male superiority, and then to rally men around those images.

In Chapter 12, John Suk analyzes sermons given at PK's Fan Into Flame pastors convention in Atlanta, and finds that nearly every keynote preacher portrayed pastors not so much as revival leaders, but as broken, hurting men at serious risk of failing their churches, families and God. Speakers tried to give pastors strategies for accomplishing revivals but were not successful in reaching that goal, Suk concludes.

In Chapter 13, Lynn and Rodney Reynolds report the results of a survey that asked PK men about their beliefs on particular theological issues, such as the infallibility of Scripture, a literal creation account, and the virgin birth. They find that there are no significant differences among members of differing denominations, and that PK men generally are tolerant of Protestants with different beliefs. The Reynoldses conclude that PK is an ecumenical organization.

In Chapter 14, Billy Hawkins explores PK's 1996 racial reconciliation theme, Breaking Down the Walls; he finds that although PK provides familiar, comfortable settings to begin addressing the racial and religious issues that have given rise to barriers, limited strategies are engaged for those barriers' destruction. In Chapter 15, Randy Balmer puts into historical context PK's usage of both military and sport metaphor, which are found throughout the history of Christianity. He concludes that such images are not benign, however, as they help PK vigorously enforce rules and combat feminism underneath a facade of "benevolent patriarchalism."

In Chapter 16, Bryan Brickner develops the theory that PK is not part of traditional evangelism like Billy Graham's organization, nor part of new evangelism like Pat Robertson. Instead, Brickner argues, PK has forged "social evangelicalism"—a way to socially and morally change society without succumbing to a political agenda—that starts with men reconciling their relationships with their God, wives, children, families, friends and coworkers. In Chapter 17, Kevin Healey addresses PK's goal of *agape* ("universal love") by analyzing a key PK book and an electronic PK community on the Internet; he finds that PK's religious ideology creates a warlike discussion around the issues of gender and sexuality similar to fundamentalism, and that this prevents achievement of agape.

In Chapter 18, Colleen Kelley provides and analyzes evidence of PK's efforts to occupy a "rhetorical high ground" by defining for itself terms such as fatherhood, family, morality, faith and even God. She contrasts PK's successes in this sphere with the National Organization for Women's mostly unsuccessful attempts to reframe PK as an ultraconservative front for the Religious Right; PK has been more successful, Kelley concludes, because NOW has not founded its arguments in biblically based, "God-term" ideographs. In Chapter 19, Tanya Erzen details and analyzes the relationships of PK rhetoric and that of Christian women's organizations, such as Chosen Women, Women of Faith, Suitable Helpers and others.

In Chapter 20, Ken Waters examines PK's media and public relations strategies, giving rare insight into how PK avoided becoming a "spokes-group" for the Christian right and how efforts by PK helped ensure increased and more favorable media coverage. Waters concludes that conservative and fundamentalist Christian groups can learn about communication strategies from PK, including that national media journalists used to covering politics seem to have no frame of reference about the religious aspects of other Americans' lives.

In Chapter 21, Dean Allen explores and analyzes PK men's predisposition of skepticism and even hostility towards the news media. He attributes it to dichotomous thinking that views the world in terms of polar opposites, and explains how such thinking is spiritualized, leading PK men to label those opposed to them as instruments of evil. Allen finds that such phenomena are consistent with Hunter's descriptions of an American culture war.

Chapter 22 is my own. I point out how PK has received significantly more media coverage than other men's organizations, and that, contrary both to expectations based on theory and to PK men's complaints, media coverage has been overwhelmingly favorable. I suggest numerous possible explanations—including PK's deemphasis on certain hot-button issues, and the limitations of U.S. journalism's standards and practices—for PK's generally favorable media coverage; I also make suggestions about how media coverage of PK could be more complete and more interesting.

Finally, Robert D. Linder caps the book with an insightful Conclusion, drawing out the major conclusions of this book—the most notable of which is, plainly, that PK is many different things to many different people—and highlighting the essays that he finds most important, as well as offering his own thoughts on PK.

Subjects not addressed in any detail in this book include PK's expansion into other countries; its internal operations (with regard to finances, personnel or other issues); its relationship to other current Christian men's organizations; the experiences of mass media workers who have covered PK; politicians' perspectives; fundamentalist attacks; the positions on PK held by religions and denominations that are not conservative Christians; the experiences of gay men and gay men's relatives who participate in PK; PK's accountability groups; and the organization's unusual emphasis on close male friendship ("vital relationships"). Nor will the reader find extensive research based on ethnographies or autobiographies of PK men or their female relatives. All of these are topics for another book, another day. Meanwhile, it is my hope that the reader will find useful information and much to ponder in the pages that follow.

References

Abraham, K. (1997). *Who are the Promise Keepers? Understanding the Christian men's movement.* New York: Doubleday.

Arms, P. (1997). *The Promise Keepers: Another Trojan horse.* Houston, TX: Shiloh Publishers.

Claussen, D. S. (ed.) (1999). *Standing on the promises: The Promise Keepers and the revival of manhood*. Cleveland, OH: Pilgrim Press.

Seib, G. (1997, September 10). A man's march: Behaving right, or going right (Capital Journal). *The Wall Street Journal*, A24.

Introduction
by Randy Balmer

Promise Keepers was the Rorschach test of the 1990s. Analysts of every stripe—and there was no shortage of analysts—saw in this men's mass movement almost anything, or at least whatever they wanted to see. Apologists regarded it as a religious revival, a moment of racial healing, and an important movement reminding men of their God-given responsibilities. Detractors saw Promise Keepers as frontal assault on homosexuality and feminism and as a tool of the Religious Right. Historians saw precedents in the ritual tradition of ancient Israel, in the religious awakenings of the eighteenth and nineteenth centuries, and in the camp meetings of the antebellum frontier. Marxists pointed to the movement's appeal to middle-class sensibilities and its commodification in T-shirts, audiocassettes, books, and trinkets. Politically minded analysts identified Promise Keepers as yet another front in the so-called culture wars of the 1990s. Cultural historians cited precedents in fraternal orders—with initiatory rites and the stadium replacing lodge rooms as a place to reaffirm one's masculinity—and in various manifestations of muscular Christianity.

Other observers noted how Promise Keepers, founded by the head football coach at the University of Colorado, drew on various theological and cultural metaphors: sports, militarism, pilgrimage, the soft-breasted male of the Iron John movement. Some saw it as a field day—or a time of testing—for ethnographers and for journalists, who molded the story to fit their own purposes and whose stories, in turn, may have been molded by the organization's high-powered public relations machinery. Still others commented on the opportunism of Promise Keepers—coming to prominence at a moment when conservatives were decrying divorce rates, paternal irresponsibility, and the demise of the nuclear family. Some liberal (or mainline) Protestants criticized Promise Keepers for their slavish biblical literalism on the issue of gender roles and expressed a suspicion about the movement's message, all the while neglecting to provide their own message to beleaguered American males.

Many of these interpretations of the Promise Keepers movement (or variations thereof) appear in this volume, the arguments elaborated and fortified with the requisite evidence. The nature of a Rorschach test, of course, is that there is no "right" answer, and this applies as well to Promise Keepers. There are elements of truth to all of these interpretations. Yes, Promise Keepers has its roots in previous evangelical revivals and in the various manifestations of muscular Christianity throughout American history. Although Bill McCartney, head of the movement, insisted that Promise Keepers was apolitical, he was one of the forces behind the passage of Amendment 2 in Colorado, which sought to limit civil rights for gay men and lesbians. McCartney must be judged (at least in part) by the company he keeps, and his close association with leaders of the Religious Right belie his protestations of political insouciance. Finally, although the National Organization for Women hardly clothed itself in glory with its screeds against Promise Keepers, feminists were doubtless correct to see the movement as a reassertion of patriarchalism and a protest against feminism.

* * *

Because the movement has been so extensively analyzed, it is tempting to believe that everyone understands all of the terminology associated with it. Recognizing that that may not be the case, I offer here a brief lexicon covering "evangelicalism," "muscular Christianity," and "Promise Keepers," three terms that appear repeatedly in these essays:

EVANGELICALISM

Evangelicalism, the most influential social and religious movement in American history, grew out of the eighteenth-century fusion of the remnants of Puritanism with continental Pietism, a movement that emphasized the importance of warm-hearted religion, not merely intellectual assent. That combination erupted in two religious conflagrations, the Great Awakening of the 1730s and 1740s, and the Second Great Awakening in the decades surrounding the turn of the nineteenth century. Those Awakenings, in turn, stamped North America with revivals and with a zeal to reform society according to the norms of godliness. As it evolved in the American context, evangelicalism acquired two general characteristics: first, a belief in the centrality of a conversion or "born again" experience as the criterion for entering the kingdom of heaven; second, a proclivity to take the Bible seriously to the point of interpreting it literally, from Genesis and the account of creation to Revelation, which most evangelicals see as a roadmap for understanding the impending apocalypse and the end of time.

Beneath that large umbrella of evangelicalism are several strains: fundamentalists, who take their name from a series of pamphlets published between 1910 and 1915; pentecostals, who believe in the gifts of the Holy

Spirit, including divine healing and speaking in tongues; holiness people, who emphasize the importance of spiritual discipline and godly living; and charismatics, who seek spiritual renewal within denominations that, on the whole, look askance at the pentecostal gifts. Contrary to popular perceptions, evangelicals can be found at both ends of the political spectrum; while the media in recent years have focused on the various elements of the Religious Right, evangelicalism also claims a vigorous political left wing.

MUSCULAR CHRISTIANITY

The term "muscular Christianity" originated in a review of Charles Kingsley's novel, *Two Years Ago*, published in Britain in 1857. The reviewer took exception to the book's celebration of heroic Christian activity. The term was pejorative, but it stuck and came to be associated with masculine expressions of piety and with various initiatives designed to make Christianity more attractive to men. The background for such efforts is the fact that women have far outnumbered men in church adherence ever since the late seventeenth century. Reformers and revivalists at various moments throughout American history have tried to redress that imbalance, and the appeals to men have taken many forms. The Revival of 1857-58, also known as the Businessmen's Awakening or the Prayer Meeting Revival, targeted men engaged in business and commerce. Dwight Moody and Billy Sunday fashioned their messages to appeal to men, with Sunday taunting his male auditors to "be a real man" and give their lives to Christ. Around the turn of the twentieth century a flurry of books—Charles Sheldon's *In His Steps*; *The Masculine Religion*, by Carl Case; *The Manhood of the Master*, by Harry Emerson Fosdisk; and John Pierce's *The Masculine Power of Christ*—all purveyed a Christianity shorn of Victorian sentimentalism so that it might appeal to men.

In the twentieth century muscular Christianity has often employed the language of sports and athletics. The Men and Religion Forward Movement of 1911-12, for instance, used rallies and display ads in the sports sections of newspapers to appeal to men, and such groups as Athletes in Action and the Fellowship of Christian Athletes routinely uphold Christian athletes as paragons of masculine piety. Promise Keepers stands very much in this tradition of muscular Christianity.

PROMISE KEEPERS

On March 20, 1990, Bill McCartney, head football coach at the University of Colorado, and his friend Dave Wardell were traveling to a meeting of the Fellowship of Christian Athletes in Pueblo, Colorado. In the course of their conversation, they came upon the idea of filling Colorado's Folsom Stadium with men dedicated to the notion of Christian discipleship. This vision spread to a cadre of seventy-two men, who engaged in fasting and prayer in support of the notion.

Over four thousand men showed up for the first gathering, and by July 1993 McCartney's original vision had been fulfilled: Fifty thousand men piled into Folsom Stadium for singing, hugging, and exhortations to be good and faithful husbands, fathers, and churchgoers. These men were asked to make seven promises that would commit them to being better at all these roles. Promise Keepers is unabashedly an evangelical organization; witness its purpose statement and statement of faith:

> Promise Keepers is a non-denominational, Christ-centered ministry dedicated to uniting men through vital relationships to become godly men who influence their world. Using God as our model, a Promise Keeper chooses to reflect the trustworthy nature of his Lord and to exhibit integrity. Our character should reflect utter sincerity, honesty, candor, no artificiality, no shallowness and no empty promises.
>
> • We believe that there is one God, eternally existing in three persons: the Father, the Son, and the Holy Spirit.
>
> • We believe that the Bible is God's written revelation to man, and that it is verbally inspired, authoritative, and without error in the original manuscripts.
>
> • We believe in the deity of Jesus Christ, His virgin birth, sinless life, miracle, death on the cross to provide for our redemption, bodily resurrection, and ascension into heaven, present ministry of intercession for us, and His return to earth in power and glory.
>
> • We believe in the personality and deity of the Holy Spirit, that He performs the miracle of the new birth in an unbeliever and indwells believers, enabling them to live a godly life.
>
> • We believe that man was created in the image of God, but because of sin, was alienated from God. That alienation can be removed only by accepting through faith God's gift of salvation which was made possible by Christ's death.

By 1996 the organization, Promise Keepers, had an annual budget in excess of $115 million and offices in thirty-two states and provinces throughout North America. In 1995 more than one million men attended twenty-two rallies at sports stadiums across the country, and on October 4, 1997, Promise Keepers conducted a mass rally, called Stand in the Gap: A Sacred Assembly of Men, on the Mall in Washington, D.C. The movement quickly faded, however; by February of the following year Promise Keepers announced that it would lay off its entire staff and rely on volunteer labor, although an infusion of donations resuscitated the movement several months later.

* * *

One final observation. If Promise Keepers was the Rorschach test of the nineties, any analysis was rendered even more difficult by the fact that Promise Keepers was an extraordinarily protean movement, with shifting strategies and messages. Those who have studied the rhetoric of Promise Keepers in its early years, for example, find a noticeable softening in the later stages. Promise Keepers, while purporting to shape public attitudes, was also remarkably adept at responding to criticism and to public sentiment. But that, alas, is another time-honored characteristic of evangelicalism.

Chapter 1

Keeping the Promise of the Moral Majority? A Historical/Critical Comparison of the Promise Keepers and the Christian Coalition, 1989–98

by Andrew Quicke and Karen Robinson

When Pat Robertson was defeated in his bid for the nomination as Republican candidate for the Presidential election of 1988, and when the Rev. Jerry Falwell closed the offices of the Moral Majority, academics and critics proclaimed the collapse of the Christian Right (Bruce, 1988). It is true that the first wave of the Christian Right organizations had died, but the second wave represented by the Christian Coalition (CC), and an apparent third wave, represented by the Promise Keepers movement (PK), were just emerging. Our thesis is that the Christian Coalition was primarily a political organization, in contrast to the primarily socio-religious Promise Keepers. We define a "political organization" as one concerned with political issues and affecting legislation, even though it may not endorse political candidates. We define a "socio-religious organization" as one concerned with relationships, both familial and inter-cultural, as well as the promotion of religious values. As we write in mid-1998, about 10 years after the first collapse of the Christian Right, both the CC and PK are short of funds. But to proclaim their demise would be premature, since both organizations seem likely to continue into the new century, or be reborn under new names and new leadership.

This chapter compares the origins and growth of each organization, and then analyzes their historical development according to the four criteria of the political "institutionalization" of the Christian Right developed by Dr. Matthew Moen (1994, pp. 351–353) of the University of Maine. Using these criteria, we assess the extent to which the PK and CC movements achieved financial stability by building a genuine membership base. Then, we seek to measure the extent to which they appealed to constituencies broader than their own immediate supporters. Finally, we question the degree to which the two movements established a more inclusive rhetoric, and we assess how far they were oriented to grassroots political activity.

During the 1990s, the pro-family movement remained "predominantly and frankly almost exclusively a white, evangelical Republican movement with a political center of gravity centered in the safety of the suburbs" (Kurtz, 1996, p. A32). Many who generalized about the Promise Keepers suggested that PK was simply another component of the Christian Right as a political movement. But the evidence shows that the identity of the Promise Keepers is more complex, and is profoundly linked with a religious rather than a political inspiration, even though the past actions of PK leaders indicate a more political position than that of PK itself. For purposes of clarity we will use the Moen (1992) socio-theological definitions to identify the groups comprising PK. "*Evangelicals* are identified by belief in traditional morality, mission work, and individual commitment to Christ. *Fundamentalists* are identified by those beliefs plus a literal interpretation of the Bible. *Pentecostals* embrace some or all of the views of evangelicals and fundamentalists, and also stress gifts of the Holy Spirit, such as speaking in tongues. *Charismatics* are essentially Pentecostals from traditionally 'mainline' denominations, such as Methodists" (p. 162).

The Promise Keepers movement began on a car journey between Boulder and Pueblo, Colorado, on March 20, 1990. Bill McCartney, head football coach at the University of Colorado, and his friend, Dr. Dave Wardell, assistant professor of Physical Education, were driving to Pueblo to attend a Christian Athletes banquet. As they talked, they decided to start a new religious movement for men (Abraham, 1997). Each man had experienced the "born again" experience of conversion to belief in Jesus Christ and the second rebirth experience of "being filled with the Holy Spirit," both expected experiences for full members of a charismatic Vineyard Fellowship Church. All of the early Promise Keepers leadership was strongly influenced by a "charismatic group of Vineyard churches that feature emotionally charged services, rock music and ... power evangelism" (Swomley, 1997, p. 8). PK president Randy Phillips, chief executive and cofounder Bill McCartney, and cofounder James Ryle are all members of the Valley Vineyard Fellowship in Boulder, a church that teaches the aggressive power evangelism principles of the late Rev. John Wimber. These principles include strongly charismatic beliefs in spiritual healing, "signs and wonders," and accountability groups where men are held responsible to one another for all their actions: business, marital and sexual.

The first and third promises of a Promise Keeper are primarily religious, and closely allied to the teachings of the Vineyard churches. The last four promises are concerned with societal ethics. The religious/individual ethics are as follows: "1. Trust in Christ; 2. Form a few close male friendships; 3. Practice moral and sexual purity" (Abraham, 1997, p. 35). The societal ethics are "4. Love your wife and children; 5. Support your local church; 6. Overcome racial and denominational prejudice; 7. Encourage men to do likewise" (Abraham, 1997, p. 35). The PK aims are generalized: "Promise Keepers is a Christ-centered ministry dedicated to uniting men through vital relationships to become Godly influences in their world" (PK web site). As one journalist commented: "Promise Keepers is purely non-political or quintessentially political, according to your politics" (Wagner, 1997, 10). We suggest that any socio-religious organization such as PK, concerned with cultural change, will develop in various ways, and should be regarded as neither political or non-political, but "pre-political."

The growth of Promise Keepers was spectacular: 70 men shared the coach's vision, and the first PK conference in Boulder in July 1991 drew 4,200 participants. "That swelled to 727,000 in 1995, and 1.1 million last year" (Phillips, 1997, p. 52). And when a similar number gathered in Washington on a single Saturday in October 1997, the press suddenly took an even greater interest in a movement that seemed to some journalists to have come from nowhere.

Though PK is avowedly non-political, its cofounder has a record of taking up right-wing political positions. McCartney was much more than simply a prominent football coach who led the Colorado Buffaloes to victory in a 1990 national collegiate football competition. He was already well known for his outspoken mixing of sports and Christianity. The Jewish Anti-Defamation League had attacked McCartney for using his tax-funded university position as a Christian pulpit; the American Civil Liberties Union had threatened the University of Colorado with a lawsuit. He had already proclaimed homosexuality "an abomination against God," and had publicly supported a Colorado state ballot question that refused to provide for gay rights and drew the fire of gay-rights supporters. However, though McCartney, as a former Catholic, is clearly opposed to abortion, PK has no official policy on it, though it is a subject that is usually of particular importance to the Christian Right. Another controversial issue is the absence of women at all PK rallies; they are simply not invited. The National Organization for Women (NOW) has been predictably outraged. NOW President Patricia Ireland said, "Promise Keepers have created a false veneer of men taking responsibility, when they really mean taking charge. Their targets are women, lesbians, gay men and anyone who supports abortion rights or opposes an authoritarian, religiously-based government" (Hetherly, 1997, p. 14). Less easy to attack has been McCartney's stand on racial issues, in which he stands out as one of the most ardent advocates of racial integration within the entire Religious Right.

If the birth of Promise Keepers came about due to a conversation between two sports enthusiasts, by contrast, the Christian Coalition was born during a conversation between two political enthusiasts, Pat Robertson and Ralph Reed, at an inaugural dinner for George Bush in January 1989 (Reed, 1994). Its origins at a political dinner colored the growth of the Christian Coalition as much as the origins of Promise Keepers were colored by its inception on the way to a religious dinner. Ralph Reed, then a doctoral candidate at Emory University, was a veteran campaigner for the Republican Party. Reed was introduced to a group of Robertson's former political supporters in Atlanta in September 1989, and soon set up his headquarters in the old Robertson campaign headquarters in Chesapeake, Virginia. Starting with no financial backing, Reed set out to organize grass-roots support for the new-born Christian Coalition in every precinct and state in the United States. As he told *Time*, "You have to organize, organize, organize, and build and build, and train and train, so that there is a permanent vibrant structure of which people can be part" (Birnbaum, 1995, p. 28).

Reed is an evangelical Christian, having experienced conversion at an Assemblies of God (Pentecostal) church in Maryland in September 1983. His monthly letters to CC members, cosigned by Pat Robertson, always contain references to the Almighty, but in deference to Jewish supporters, do not mention the name of Jesus Christ. This omission would be unthinkable in a PK meeting. Reed seems to have been a realist from the start. Not for him the mass emotion of stadium rallies, with the tears of forgiveness that led a journalist writing for the *New Republic* to call PK followers the "Promise weepers" (Rosin, 1997, p. 11). No one cries at CC rallies; Reed is always very pragmatic about his political professionalism and sees no conflict between that and his religious beliefs. He wrote, "What does it mean to be a person of faith in the political arena?" and concluded that it was no different from being a Christian in any other occupation. "Politics is a contact sport. I have a job to do, and it involves trying to advance my agenda. But I never hit below the belt" (Reed, 1986, p. 24).

The growth of Reed's Christian Coalition was less spectacular than that of Promise Keepers. The early months were slow; the Christian Coalition only gained public attention when, in June 1990, it took out full page advertisements in the *Washington Post* and *USA Today*, demanding the end of "taxpayer-funded pornography funded by the National Endowment for the Arts" (Reed, 1996, p. 133). In 1991, the Coalition's membership was less than 51,000; the following year, membership had quintupled to 250,000, and the budget was $8.5 million. At the 1992 Republican National Convention in Houston, one quarter of the 105 members of the platform committee were Christian Coalition supporters who helped the Republican Party publish "the most conservative pro-family platform in the party's history" (Reed, 1996, p. 137). By 1993, the membership topped 450,000; by 1996, it was a claimed 1.5 million (Gerner, 1995, p. 16).

Having briefly sketched the origins of the two movements, we must now assess them according to the fourfold criteria of the political institutionalization of the Christian Right proposed by Moen (1994). We begin with seeking to answer how far the two movements had achieved financial stability by building a genuine membership base.

ACHIEVING FINANCIAL STABILITY

Promise Keepers notes that it is not a membership or dues-paying organization, but is rather a group of Christian men who are encouraged to become more active in their faith and in their local churches (PK web site). But despite lacking a subscription, Promise Keepers' financial base grew faster than that of the Coalition. By 1994, the PK budget was $26 million, and it employed a staff of some 150 people. One year later, the budget had nearly tripled to $64 million and staff members had grown to 300. Most of this money came from conference registration fees. Donations were only $8.6 million, but merchandise sales showed a healthy $14 million in sales. By 1996, the budget had grown to $97 million and the paid staff numbered more than 360 (Swomley, 1997, p. 13). Thousands of other unpaid personnel helped staff the big stadium rallies. All rallies were by ticket entrance only, and tickets cost between $60 and $80. However no charge was made for the "Stand in the Gap" Washington rally, and the central PK organization soon found itself heavily in debt as a result. Lacking a proper subscription membership base, and dependent on big rallies for its income, PK had insufficient reserves for the rumored $9 million cost of the Washington rally. In March 1998, cofounder Bill McCartney dismissed all permanent staff, claiming that in the future the work of Promise Keepers would be handled by volunteers only. But in April 1998, 315 staff were rehired after PK received $4 million in donations.

In contrast, the Christian Coalition built a strong subscription base for its membership. All members were expected to contribute, and were encouraged to make monthly $20, $30 or $50 gifts. By 1994, the Coalition claimed a nearly $22 million income, 96 percent of these monies coming from "public support," as the Coalition termed it. The level of subscription income remained high, but when an estimated $26 million income in 1996 fell to a modest $17 million in 1997 after Ralph Reed left the Coalition, stringent economies were introduced.

The Christian Coalition applied in 1989 for tax-exempt status as a nonprofit "social welfare" organization, as classified in the IRS code section 501c.4. This classification is different from the Political Action Committee (PAC), whose financial activities are strictly scrutinized. The Coalition's classification gives it wide latitude to produce voter guides, lobby public officials and suggest particular legislation, but it cannot engage in partisan politics and all Coalition literature states that "the Christian Coalition is not affiliated with any political party and does not endorse any candidate" (CC donation forms, April 1998).

The Coalition suffered what may become a serious financial reverse when, in July 1996, the Federal Election Commission, a body consisting of three Republicans and three Democrats, launched a civil lawsuit in a U.S. District court alleging that the Coalition had illegally aided various Republican political campaigns in the 1990, 1992, and 1994 elections. The case, based partly on complaints from the Democratic National Committee, continued at the time of this writing in 1998. As academic commentator Justin Watson points out, "If the court finds against the Christian Coalition, it could be fined and prohibited from engaging in similar activities in the future" (Watson, 1997, p. 65). Some have believed it significant that in March 1998 the Christian Broadcasting Network was fined by the IRS for its political activities in connection with Pat Robertson's bid for the presidency in 1988; the Coalition's future bears close watching.

Appealing to a Broader Constituency

In order to become a grass-roots movement, Promise Keepers used a two-pronged approach, holding large rallies in football fields and also working through small groups in existing churches of many different denominations. "Ultimately, PK wants to have a key man in each of the nation's 400,000 churches, using the military ideas of discipline and male bonding in small groups" (Swomley, 1997, p. 9). In one of his most telling admissions, Bill McCartney said, "The goal is to go into every church, whether they like us or not" (Swomley, 1997, p. 9). PK leaders want to expand their movement considerably, both in the United States and overseas.

One of the broader constituencies PK would like to reach is the armed forces, so the organization hired military officers, such as Special Services Lieutenant-Colonel Chuck Stecker, to help it organize in the Armed Forces. While preaching to a group of military chaplains in Atlanta, Stecker said, "I believe with all of my heart that the military structure that we know and love so well is perfect for the accountable relationship that God is calling us to in Promise Keepers" (Swomley, 1997, p. 8). Since active participation in the local church is one of the seven PK promises, local groups led by a "key man" meet weekly to check out every aspect of members' behavior. These "key men" report to "area ambassadors," who in turn report to headquarters. The PK structure is therefore a top-down hierarchical structure, like that of most Pentecostal churches, and democratic accountability is noticeably absent: a small self-perpetuating group of men run every aspect of PK, from its theological position to its finances and personnel (Swomley, 1997).

Since the membership of 400,000 churches in America could provide huge growth for Promise Keepers, the leadership has spent large sums trying to woo the clergy of America, whatever their denomination. In 1996, Promise Keepers held a clergy conference in Atlanta that may have been the largest and most comprehensive such conference ever to convene in the United States. Promise Keepers spent $4 million in scholarships and expenses to get 39,000 ministers to attend the clergy conference, plus an additional $14 million for field ministry before, during and after the conference. Great emphasis was put on the attendance of black ministers, and many were generously subsidized to attend.

Speaking on behalf of the Conference of Catholic Bishops' Secretariat for Family, Laity, Women and Youth, Catholic spokesman Rick McCord said that he was "concerned about PK's potential for leading men away from the Catholic parishes to evangelical congregations, as well as its teaching on male 'headship' and its 'prejudice and discrimination against homosexuals'" (Rabey, 1996, p. 46). Promise Keepers' attitude towards Catholics and the Catholic church continues to be warm, despite a historical antipathy to Catholics by many Protestant churches, especially Baptists. By encouraging Catholic involvement, the PK appeals to a much wider constituency than that of the traditional Pentecostal, charismatic and fundamentalist churches.

Since the sixth promise of a Promise Keeper is to overcome racial as well as denominational prejudice, McCartney has made commendable efforts to reach out to African Americans. In 1993, when other high-profile Christian ministries were avoiding this topic as being too sensitive, McCartney spoke out on racial reconciliation at rallies in Indianapolis, Boulder, Anaheim, and Portland, Oregon, even though his remarks were greeted with icy silence. One black man commented on the Portland Meeting: "I never thought in my lifetime that I would hear a white man say what's said here today" (Abraham, 1997, p. 128). McCartney's stand has brought results: at the Washington "Stand in the Gap" PK rally in October 1997, a *Washington Post* poll reported the rally was 80 percent white, 14 percent black and 2 percent Asian (Maxwell, 1997, p. 62).

When we turn to consider the Christian Coalition's attempts to reach a broader constituency, we must remember that Pat Robertson, its founder, has always benefited from Catholic and African American support for his "700 Club" daily religious talk show. The Christian Coalition tried to appeal to a broader constituency than that of the Moral Majority, and went out of its way to court the Catholic vote. The first big opportunity for working with Catholics came with the 1992 elections to the New York school board. Reed realized early the emergence of significant opposition to certain sex education programs, and helped the Catholic Archdiocese of New York to distribute 100,000 voter guides to some 213 Catholic parishes in Manhattan, Staten Island and the Bronx. Another half-million voter guides were distributed to over 2,000 New York City churches, as well as synagogues. The results were gratifying: 51 percent of all Coalition–backed candidates were successful, though many of the Coalition school board candidates had never stood for election before (Gerner, 1995, p. 28).

Catholics have no denominational problems in agreeing with the original five-fold purposes of the CC as described by Reed: "1. Training Christians for effective social action; 2. Combating anti-religious bigotry; 3. Alerting Christians of issues and legislation on a timely basis; 4. Speaking out for pro-family values in the media; 5. Representing people of faith at every level of government" (1996, p. 13). Conscious of the need to institutionalize the participation of Catholics within the Coalition, Reed formed the Catholic Alliance in October 1995. He hoped this action would boost Catholic membership to two million members by the end of the decade (Reed, 1995, p. 219). But only 30,000 joined in the first year, and some Catholic bishops would not allow Christian Coalition and Catholic Alliance literature to be distributed in their churches. The Catholic Alliance became a separate corporation in September 1996, with its own all–Catholic board of directors.

Significant cooperation with Jewish and African American communities had long been another of Reed's aims. In 1996, he appointed the Rev. Earl Jackson, a well-known conservative African American minister, to be national liaison officer to black churches. When arsonists destroyed many black churches in the South in 1996 and 1997, the Christian Coalition raised $750,000 from churches on its mailing list to be given to the "Save the churches" fund.

Establishing a More Inclusive Rhetoric

Since PK rhetoric had never been political, the rhetoric did not change significantly as the movement grew. But important changes of emphasis occurred, in that anti-homosexual and anti-feminist rhetoric was abandoned. Reporter John Leo of *U.S. News and World Report* noted that the liberal media were generally positive about the PK "Stand in the Gap" Washington rally. He commented, "Cynicism defused. The main reason, I think, was the racial angle. Even cynical media elitists are reluctant to attack white guys who confess their sins, condemn racism, and reach out to blacks, particularly when so many of the white guys come from churches that historically dragged their heels on racial justice or tried to impede it. PK's total absence of anti-gay and antifeminist rhetoric played a role too" (Leo, 1997, p. 16). NOW's on-line bulletins lamented the fact that "despite NOW's best efforts to expose the Promise Keepers through the media, the information aired is overwhelmingly positive" (1997, p. 16); Claussen (1996) found that PK's print media coverage had been mostly positive since the organization's founding.

The Christian Coalition's use of more inclusive rhetoric widened considerably in the aftermath of the Bush defeat in 1994. Ralph Reed dubbed the new strategy "casting a wider net" (Reed, 1994, p. 225). So it was that the CC played down the abortion issue, and developed positions on taxes, crime, government waste, health care, education and economic security. Two years later it was difficult to show that the CC policy of casting a wider net had worked. A 1996 survey showed that only 7 percent of voters thought of themselves as members of the "religious right" (Pew Research Center, 1996, p. 5). A 1996 election day poll conducted by the Voter News Service showed that at least 17 percent of voters claimed to be members of the Religious Right. While a better figure, it was still a long way short of Reed's claim that one third of the electorate comprised "pro-life and pro-family voters" (Edsell, 1995, p. 6).

Orienting Concerns to Grassroots Activity

When we investigate Promise Keeper's orientation to grassroots political activity, there is nothing to report, since the movement has rejected such activity. This overt rejection has led left-wing critics of PK to argue that all organizations have a political agenda, whether or not they are aware of it. Radical author Michael Kimmel discerns "increasingly ominous signs of connections between Promise Keepers and far right religious organizations such as Focus on the Family, Christian Coalition, and the Campus Crusade for Christ" (1997, p. 46). Kimmel quotes McCartney as saying, "We are going to war as of tonight. We have divine power; that is our weapon. We will not compromise. Wherever truth is at risk, in the schools or legislature, we are going to contend for it. We will win" (1997, p. 46). In disagreement with Michael Kimmel, we suggest that this language owes more to religious inspiration than political intent, and that PK was still a "pre-political" movement in 1998.

In the Christian Coalition, we discern a pattern of grassroots political activity from the very inception of the organization. Political scientist Matthew Watson stated that "grassroots activism has been one of the most consistent themes of the Christian Coalition" (Watson, 1997, p. 65). Reed charged the Christian Right with having been wrong to concentrate its activities in Washington during the 1980s, because it should have been concentrating on the grassroots activists. He said, "The real battles of concern to Christians are in the neighborhoods, school boards, city councils, and state legislatures" (Watson, p. 63). Reed has provided a structure for the Coalition that is highly decentralized, and works through a network of state affiliates, each of which is incorporated in its own state with its own legal identity, with its own tax-exemption from the IRS. Rather like a franchise operation, the CC Board of Directors provides each affiliate with an operating charter that must be renewed annually. Reed proudly claimed in 1995, "We're the McDonald's of American politics" (Birnbaum, 1995, p. 28).

Other organizations within the Christian Right had begun to pay more attention to local activism from the late 1980s on, but the genius of the Christian Coalition approach was to give selected issues, some local, some national, the spotlight of nationwide attention. The attack on the National Endowment for the Arts in 1991 and the concentration on the School Board elections in New York in 1993 both showed Ralph Reed to be a shrewd political operator who far outshone his colleagues in other sectors of the Christian Right. The power of local Christian Coalition groups redoubled. In 1996, Reed told the National Press Club that "there are an estimated 2,000 religious conservatives who now serve on school boards, city councils, state legislatures and in Congress" (Reed, October 22, 1996).

Critics of the Christian Coalition have accused it of undermining democracy through grassroots "stealth campaigns." Reed has emphatically rejected this, stating, "We believe pro-family candidates should run unapologetically on who they are and what they believe because the public share their viewpoint" (Innerst, 1994, p. A1). Seven years later, the Christian Coalition's grassroots organization remains very strong. As Pat Robertson said in a private meeting to some 100 Coalition activists in Atlanta in September 1997, "We've got a playbook at the Christian Coalition. It is very simple. We're the only ones who are executing it and it's called precinct organization. There are 175,000 precincts in the country, and we wanted 10 trained workers in each of them. That's about [enough] to take the nation ... when you get down to the school board races and the city council races and the legislative races ... [a] few thousand votes makes the difference.... So if you have a couple thousand people, you can do wonderful things" (Robertson Delivers, 1997).

CONCLUSION

To sum up, it seems clear from the foregoing that the Promise Keepers, when compared with the Christian Coalition, are more of a socio-religious than a political organization. One priest-journalist sees them as "but the latest expression of revivalism or evangelical Protestantism ... because they flow directly from local Protestant wellsprings. The Promise Keepers share the American ethos, and are understood by the American people, especially since revivalist imagery is so familiar" (Woods, 1997, p. 18). The fears of feminists and humanists that the Promise Keepers' underlying goal is "the creation of an ultraconservative, authoritarian nation segregated along gender lines that merges church and state, and returns men to the helm of all political and religious institutions" (Hetherly, 1997, p. 14) does not seem to be borne out by the facts.

Promise Keepers do not fulfill the Moen (1994) criteria of the political institutionalization of the Christian Right: PK has not achieved financial stability by building a genuine membership base and, in 1998, seemed to suffer from insufficient funding. While PK attempted to appeal to a broader constituency by using more inclusive rhetoric, and downplaying its opposition to homosexuality, its success in attracting African Americans has been limited, and by its own rules it has wholly excluded women. Finally, at no stage did PK either endorse or achieve grassroots political activity.

In contrast, the Christian Coalition meets all the Moen criteria: it achieved a genuine membership base that raised as much as $26 million in 1996, and still collected some $15 million in 1997. Ralph Reed, by downplaying abortion and developing a comprehensive political program entitled "The Contract with the American Family," did indeed adopt more inclusive rhetoric. From its earliest days the Christian Coalition was strongly oriented towards grassroots political activity.

Can we guess what the future of the two movements will be? Despite predictions that the Christian Coalition would survive a challenge to its tax-exempt status by the Federal Election Commission, it did not. Replacing a leader as effective as Ralph Reed has been difficult; should the Coalition lose Pat Robertson as well, its future may be bleak. At the present time, despite its claimed party political neutrality, it looks set to play an important part in supporting the Republican Party in the next elections.

To predict the future of a movement as complex as that of Promise Keepers is more difficult. Any movement that grew so fast may shrink equally rapidly, as have many 19th and 20th century revival organizations and movements. The Men and Religion Forward Movement of 1911-12 was planned to last less than a year (Smith, 1987) and, in any event, may not have been feasible year after year as a national organization. But the local cell structure of Promise Keepers could give it a strong base, and PK might become a large part of the men's movement in the new century. The contrast between the aims and the achievements of Promise Keepers and the Christian Coalition suggests that they fulfill different needs, the one primarily socio-religious and the other primarily political, and that neither movement is likely to replace the other.

References

Abraham, K. (1995). *Who are the Promise Keepers? Understanding the Christian men's movement.* New York: Doubleday.

Birnbaum, J. H. (1995, May 15). The gospel according to Ralph. *Time 145*, 28–35.

Bruce, S. (1988). *The rise and fall of the Christian right.* New York: Oxford University Press.

Christian Coalition. (1998, April). Donation form. Chesapeake, VA: Author.

Gerner, George W. (1995, May 5). Catholics and the religious right: We are being wooed. *Commonweal 122*, 15–20.

Hetherly, M. (1997 Sept.-Oct.). PK publicity and production: Between the lines and behind the scenes. *The Humanist 57*, 14–18.

Innerst, C. (1994, April 13). Parents labeled religious fanatics for fighting schools: Schools learn ways to pin labels on potential foes. *Washington Times*, A1.

Kimmel, M.S. (1997, March-April). Promise Keepers: Patriarchy's second coming as masculine renewal. *Tikkun 12(2)*, 46–50.

Kurtz, H. (1996, November 3). Clinton ad counters Christian Coalition's voter guide. the *Washington Post*, A32.

Leo, J. (1997, Nov. 3). Men behaving well. *U.S. News and World Report 123*, 16.

Maxwell, J. (1997, Nov. 17). Will the walls fall down? Promise Keepers draws a "bead" on the "giants" of racism, family breakdown, and church disunity. *Christianity Today 41*, 62–65.

Moen, M. (1992). *The Christian right and Congress.* Tuscaloosa, AL: University of Alabama Press.

Moen, M. (1994, Fall). From revolution to evolution: The changing nature of the Christian right. *Sociology of Religion 55*, 345–357.

Oldfield, D.M. (1996). *The right and the righteous.* Lanham, MD: Rowman and Littlefield.

Pew Research Center (1996, June 25). *The diminishing divide ... American churches, American politics.* Washington, DC: Author.

Phillips, A. (1997, Oct. 6). Christian men on the march: A movement preaching male dominance angers feminists. *Macleans's 110*, 52–53.

Promise Keepers (February 24, 1998). Promise Keepers: Men of integrity [Homepage of Promise Keepers]. Available:http://www.promise keepers.org [April 21, 1998].

Rabey, S. (1996, April 29). Where is the Christian men's movement headed? Burgeoning Promise Keepers inspire look-alikes. *Christianity Today 40*, 46–49.

Reed, R. (1994). *Politically incorrect: The emerging faith factor in American politics.* Dallas, TX: Word Publishing.

Reed, R. (1996). *Active faith: How Christians are changing the soul of American politics* New York: Free Press.

Reed, R. (1996, Oct. 14). How people of faith are changing the soul of American politics. Speech to the National Press Club, Washington, DC. *The Washington Post*, A31.

Robertson delivers pep talk to coalition. (1997, Oct. 8). *Christian Century 114*, 865–866.

Rosin, H. (1997, Oct. 27) Promise weepers: The right embraces sentimentality. *New Republic 217*, 11–12.

Smith, G. S. (1987). The Men and Religion Forward Movement of 1911–1912: New perspectives on evangelical social concern and the relationship between Christianity and Progressivism. *Westminster Theological Journal 49*, 91–118.

Swomley, J. M. (1997, Sept.-Oct.). Storm troopers in the culture war. *The Humanist 57*, 8–13.

Wagner, David. (1997, Sept. 29). Blessed are the Promise Keepers. *Insight on the News 13*, 10.

Watson, J. (1997). *The Christian Coalition: Dreams of restoration, demands for recognition.* New York: St. Martin's Press.

Woods, W. J. (1997, Dec. 13). Promise Keepers: How should Catholics respond? (Reflections on the Protestant evangelical movement and its challenge to Catholics). *America 177*, 18–20.

CHAPTER 2

The Religious Roots of the Promise Keepers

by Michael J. Chrasta

Observing the Promise Keepers movement from the perspective of America's cyclical religious awakenings distinguishes it in two important contexts. The movement functions as a link in a unique "revival sequence" begun in the 1960s, on the one hand, while the sequence itself marks a terminal phase in a much larger cycle—America's Fourth Great Awakening. This context is important because it challenges several popular interpretations of the Promise Keepers—that they were the political offspring of the Religious Right, or catalysts for revivals, or desperate fundamentalists engaged in one last counteroffensive against the feminists (see, for example, Kimmel [1997] or Conason et al. [1996]).

In the late 1920s, as mainline churches were in decline, signs of vigorous new life were appearing in the Pentecostal wing of American Protestantism (Handy, 1960, p. 14). In 1929, a second-generation Pentecostal named J. Elwin Wright convened the first meeting of the New England Fellowship (NEF). With the motto, "In essentials, unity; in non-essentials, liberty; in all things, charity," this non-sectarian association sought the renewal of all churches for the purpose of world evangelism (Evans, 1991, pp. 9–10). Wright, it seems, had his finger on the pulse of a new awakening:

> A movement of great proportions and mighty possibilities is in the making. It is not the expression of one person or one group. No man, no organization, can rightfully boast of creating this movement. It is a thing of supernatural origin.... It is a movement back to apostolic standards of faith and practice [qtd. in Evans, p. 13].

Through conferences, evangelistic meetings, and radio programs, Wright united pastors throughout New England and later became integral to the formation of the National Association of Evangelicals in 1942, a powerful coalition backing religious conservatives in the culture wars of the 1990s (Evans, pp. 116–117).

2. The Religious Roots of the Promise Keepers

The NEF, the rapid growth of Pentecostal churches such as the Assemblies of God and the Church of the Foursquare Gospel, along with the simultaneous emergence of new ministries by William Branham, Kathryn Kuhlman and Oral Roberts, announced that a new awakening was occurring. It developed in a series of waves and troughs—dramatic infusions of the spirit followed by quieter periods of organization and the development of infrastructure. The contours of the larger waves are well known; the healing revivals of the late 1940s and the charismatic movement of the 1960s marked major phases of the cycle and served to pass on the revival fire from a previous wave to a wider, more inclusive audience.

The late 1960s marked the final stage in the unfolding of this awakening. From 1967 to 1971 a cluster of revivals broke out in several different geographical theaters of the country. Two of those centers, Costa Mesa, California, and Ann Arbor, Michigan, then quickly matured into major charismatic communities with large national teaching ministries.

Following these, and in several ways incorporating elements of both, was a powerful church renewal movement spearheaded by an association of churches known as the Vineyards. Led by a former rock musician named John Wimber, the Vineyards were among the most dynamic churches in America in the 1980s, their influence extending into every major nation. It was this movement, a renewal movement wholly in line with J. Elwin Wright's original vision, that was crucial to the formation of the Promise Keepers in 1990.

The leadership core of the Promise Keepers—Bill McCartney, the founder; Randy Phillips, the President; and James Ryle, McCartney's pastor and a frequent conference speaker—were converted within a few years of one another in the early 1970s, during an event historians have mistakenly called the Jesus Movement. Movements were fashionable in those days—civil rights, anti-war, and so on—so when thousands of young Christians suddenly appeared on Southern California's beaches, editors in the secular press were quick to name another, not realizing they were seeing the latter stages of a much older phenomenon—an outbreak of spontaneous religious revivals.

Well before *Look* magazine announced the emergence of the Jesus Movement in 1971, revivals had already erupted in Costa Mesa, Seattle, Ann Arbor and Wilmore, Kentucky (Smith, 1972, p. 97; Enroth & Ericson, 1972, pp. 119, 203; Coleman, 1970, p. 9). A few early observers thought the events in these areas might be related; a popular Jesus People spokesman, Duane Pederson, for example, considered the activity in Seattle and Costa Mesa part of the same Jesus phenomenon, as did a few others, but in the end historians settled for a far more fractured narrative (Pederson, 1971, p. 83).

They gave the name "Jesus Movement" to the centers of religious activity on the West Coast, later applying it in general to the upsurge of religious interest across the nation. The Ann Arbor revival, because it was a part of a larger Catholic phenomenon, became an element in the "Catholic Charismatic Renewal," while the revival at Asbury College in Wilmore essentially was ignored by all but Asbury students and faculty (Enroth, 1972, p. 232; Sullivan, 1988, p. 112).

Separating the three might be justified sociologically, but not historically, for these revivals were far more alike than different. Calvary, Asbury and Ann Arbor were classic revivals of place, regional "watering holes" so to speak, that attracted the spiritually thirsty and generated powerful ministries for months, even years, afterward. Each was thought to have been begun due to a move of the Spirit, and each replicated itself in other regions. All three revivals appealed to the same constituency—young people—and manifested the same cross-denominational unity typical of revivals in the past.

From May 1968 on, Chuck Smith's Calvary Chapel of Costa Mesa was known as a spiritual hot spot. No other center in the movement was doing what Calvary was doing—attracting young people by the thousands to its church services and baptizing hundreds of people in the waters at Corona del Mar. As one veteran reporter put it, Calvary was the place "where more people were being won for Christ than anywhere" (Vachon, 1972, p. 83).

It started in 1968 when Smith teamed up with a hippie turned Christian evangelist named Lonnie Frisbee. Both were outsiders. Smith, an iconoclast looking to throw off 17 years of dead denominationalism, sought to return the church to basics—solid Bible teaching combined with the ministry of the Holy Spirit. Frisbee, an unchurched drug addict from Haight-Ashbury, shared Smith's inclusive vision for the church, but was a more forceful advocate for the ministry of the Spirit (Balmer, 1994, pp. 674, 689).

Frisbee was the evangelist and Smith the teacher; Frisbee brought in the young people literally by the thousands, and Smith, dedicated as he was to the laity, built them up. The numbers tell the story: 8000 baptisms and 20,000 conversions in two years (Smith, 1972, p. 97) and, by the mid-1970s, 30,000 people calling Calvary Chapel their church home (Wuthnow, 1988, p. 193).

As Calvary was booming, a similar revival was underway in Ann Arbor. As a result of reading David Wilkerson's *The Cross and the Switchblade*, easily the single most effective salvation narrative of the entire Fourth Awakening, a number of Catholics at Duquesne University and Notre Dame experienced the Pentecostal baptism in the Spirit and began speaking in tongues (O'Connor, 1971, p. 62). Soon afterward, "spirit-filled" members from those communities moved to Ann Arbor and formed a unique ecumenical community called the Word of God—the same community with which Bill McCartney would enjoy a "warm fellowship" prior to his moving to Colorado (McCartney, 1990, p. 116).

Led by Steve Clark, a Yale graduate, and Ralph Martin, an agnostic philosophy major converted in 1964, the community quickly distinguished itself as a center of ecumenical charismatic activity and church renewal. It hosted national and regional conferences, developed an influential magazine, *New Covenant*, and devised a popular training manual and series of seminars for instruction in the spirit-filled life (O'Connor, 1971, p. 62; Hocken, 1988, p. 128).

The Calvary and Ann Arbor communities were remarkably similar. Both were sparked by third-generation Pentecostals whose denominations had experienced tremendous growth at the beginning of the awakening cycle: Smith came from the Church of the Foursquare Gospel, and Wilkerson from the Assemblies of God. Both became large influential centers of charismatic activity, developed important teaching and music ministries, and became templates for a host of other churches and prayer groups nationwide.

Both communities would also figure prominently in the next phase of the sequence, the Vineyard movement of the 1980s and 1990s. Kenn Gulliksen, a former Calvary Chapel pastor, started the Vineyards in 1974, later merging them with John Wimber's church, Calvary Chapel of Yorba Linda, in 1982, keeping the Vineyard name but ceding the leadership to Wimber. At the time, Wimber's fellowship was still enjoying a huge revival sparked two years earlier by Lonnie Frisbee. Adding an estimated 1,700 new converts to the church in four months, Frisbee's revival was the catalyst for the signs and wonders ministry for which Wimber would soon become famous (Wimber, 1986, p. 26).

Along with Gulliksen, nearly 30 Calvary Chapel pastors joined Wimber's Vineyards in 1982, thus making Wimber the overseer of a movement with an unusual pedigree—it was a new revival movement led by an essentially Calvary Chapel core (Miller, 1997, p. 49). So striking were the differences between the two that some observers believed Wimber's movement was a new "Third Wave" of revival phenomena in this century (Wagner, 1983, p. 5).

A key difference was Wimber's openness to the Spirit. While still a Calvary Chapel pastor, Wimber was having the kinds of spiritual experiences Smith was seeking to contain. "God began manifesting himself in lots of ways," Wimber told his congregation in 1978. "We began to see healings, we began seeing people filled with the Holy Spirit ... and it sounded just like the Bible. It just blew my mind" (Wimber, 1978).

Signs and wonders like these became normative in the church renewal movement Wimber was soon to lead. The titles of his books indicated the direction such renewal would take: *Power Evangelism* and *Power Healing* told how the unchecked power of the Spirit could become a means of winning the lost as well as a tool for planting new churches (Wimber, 1986, p. xix).

Wimber soon found himself at the center of a convergence movement of the kind that often occurs after revivals break out. Each new wave of the Spirit must be harnessed in some kind of institutional structure before it can spread. *The Voice of Healing*, Gordon Lindsay's magazine for healing evangelists in the 1940s, served that purpose, as did the Full Gospel Businessmen's chapters of the 1950s, and the regional and national charismatic conferences later. Each served to organize and unify various "streams" from recent revivals (Harrell, 1975, pp. 53, 148; Hocken, 1988, pp. 135–138).

In the 1980s and 1990s, Wimber was bringing together not only many of the various constituencies that comprised the earlier Jesus Movement, but also many streams from the entire Fourth Awakening cycle. Pentecostals, Neo-Evangelicals, Fundamentalists, and Protestant and Catholic Charismatics, were all brought together at various times under the Wimber umbrella (Perrin, 1989, p. 74–75).

In 1994, Wimber's Vineyards spawned the "Toronto Blessing," a worldwide revival that began in a small Vineyard in Toronto, then spread to nearly two-thirds of the 500 North American Vineyards, eventually igniting revival meetings in hundreds of other churches outside the Vineyard fold at home and abroad ("Ministry Matters," 1995, p. 18). Revival phenomena not seen since the 19th century outbreak at Cane Ridge—shaking, jerking, shrieking, and falling down in the power of the Spirit—were a distinctive feature of Toronto, and one of its most publicized aspects. A new refreshing was at hand, and everyone, it seemed, was talking about revivals.

The Promise Keepers movement, three years old by this time, was a movement that matured in the penumbras of Toronto. Remarkably, both movements had ties to the Vineyards. McCartney was a member of James Ryle's Boulder Vineyard, and Randy Phillips had been a Vineyard church planter in the late 1980s. All three were speakers at the first regional Promise Keepers conference, which featured music by Tom Stipe, pastor of the Denver Vineyard, the largest in Colorado. Wimber himself later observed that the movement was "very much out of the ethos of our [Vineyard] hearts and our desire to serve the Lord in what he's doing" (Wimber, 1995).

This history is important for the challenge it poses to popular interpretations of the Promise Keepers at the time—that they emerged from the Religious Right, as critics have argued, or that they were revivalists, as the Promise Keepers themselves have claimed (Allen, 1997, pp. 10, 13; Conason, Ross, & Cokorinos, 1996, p. 16). The political charge fails because of the Promise Keepers' unmistakable link with the Vineyards, while the revivalist charge fails because Promise Keepers meetings were of an entirely different order than those occurring in Toronto, or in any other Vineyard, for that matter.

With Toronto-style revivals breaking out across North America at the same time the Promise Keepers were on the rise, it is easy to see why McCartney and other Promise Keepers leaders often couched their mission in revivalist terms. At their meetings, however, there were no signs and wonders, baptisms in the spirit, miraculous healings or deliverances. Men were not coming under the spirit and then setting out to start new communities as they did in the Calvary and Vineyard phases of the sequence.

The huge stadium events that eventually became the hallmark of the movement looked more like old-fashioned tent meetings than classic religious revivals. Most of the content was straightforward evangelical stuff—the salvation message, Billy Graham style, with the traditional altar call; ubiquitous Bible teachings, and plentiful exhortations to moral and sexual purity. Oddly enough, McCartney created a kind of ersatz revivalism—a coalition of religious, ethnic, and spiritual leaders who used contemporary revival language to define what essentially was a very traditional evangelical message.

The religious elements of that coalition—the Fundamentalists, Evangelicals, and Charismatics—clearly presented problems for those attempting to define the movement. Coverage by the secular press, for example, consistently emphasized the fundamentalist elements, giving rise to the notion that the entire movement was either a fundamentalist campaign or an exercise in muscular Christianity.

This error is easily seen in a 1993 statement Tony Evans made urging men to take back their role as head of the household:

> Sit down with your wife and say something like this: "Honey, I've made a terrible mistake. I've given you my role. I gave up leading this family, and I forced you to take my place. Now I must reclaim that role." ... I'm not suggesting that you ask for your role back, I'm urging you to take it back [Evans, 1994, p. 79].

Evans, a graduate of the fundamentalist Dallas Theological Seminary and a popular speaker at Promise Keepers conferences, became famous for this statement, easily the most quoted remark of any Promise Keepers leader, including McCartney, and this remark became the standard by which the entire movement came to be judged.

The Promise Keepers, however, were not backward-looking Fundamentalists, Toronto-style revivalists, nor some clandestine offspring of the Religious Right. They were a coalition *containing* Fundamentalists, a movement birthed *in* a season of revivals, a movement with *religious*, rather than political, origins. Theirs was a classic reform movement, the kind that develops when revived men try to remedy a perceived social problem, in this case, a pervasive and destructive cultural malaise brought on by a crisis of masculinity in American men.

The earliest Promise Keepers meetings support this view, for at them McCartney stressed objectives from which he never strayed. Speaking at a June 1991 regional meeting in Denver, McCartney made it clear that although he was interested in renewing men and churches, ultimately his target was American society itself:

> Don't you know what kind of society we have today? It's an effeminate society. It doesn't raise men—it doesn't raise vibrant, energized men who are proud and unashamed of the gospel of Jesus Christ [McCartney, 1991a]!

If the men could be revived, McCartney argued, the church could be renewed, and then the social and cultural conditions he was describing could be reversed. But men had to wake up and take responsibility for the condition of their homes. That did not mean reasserting social power over wives, as Evans had stressed; it meant accepting responsibility for their half of the spiritual role both parents were obligated to perform—praying for their children, for example, or teaching them standards of moral behavior. This meant the men would have to be men of integrity. It meant they would have to become promise keepers (McCartney, 1991a).

Later that July, McCartney reiterated his call for renewed Christian men, but then defined his mission more precisely as a quest for justice. After studying Micah 6:8 and related texts, he explained, he was amazed to find that Biblical justice was a relational concept: "When Almighty God thinks of justice he immediately thinks of people," McCartney told his audience. "His concern is for mankind" (McCartney, 1991b).

Justice, then, was simply the restoration of broken relationships—with the fatherless, the widow, and the orphan, but also with the black, Hispanic, and Native American. If there were any motive central to the entire Promise Keepers ministry—the big stadium events, the Atlanta rally for the nation's pastors, the 1997 Stand in the Gap assembly in Washington, DC—it would be McCartney's desire to promote justice, *defined as reconciliation*, in all spheres of a man's life.

It is this motive, along with this movement's place in recent religious history, that ultimately reveals the identity of the Promise Keepers. McCartney's overarching goal is the restoration of his country. He would accomplish this according to a logic that has inspired many a reformer: men shape the families and churches that shape the nation. McCartney's vision, and his achievement, was the creation of an army of grassroots social reformers—revived Christian men united in a pan-evangelical coalition who hoped to renew the church and ignite a social reform campaign of the domestic sphere.

Conclusion

With the death of John Wimber in 1997, Chuck Smith nearing retirement, and the churches they founded hardening into denominations—at a time when new revivals were erupting across America—the cycle that was America's Fourth Great Awakening came to a close.

In blood and in spirit, the Promise Keepers were intimately a part of this cycle: in blood, because the movement they formed was intricately woven into the sequence closing out this era; in spirit, because religious leaders in the sequence overall—Frisbee, Smith, Wimber, and McCartney—were all religious outsiders engaged in some way with church reform.

Viewing the Promise Keepers in this particular historical context lays a great many questions of identity to rest, as we have seen, but it might also serve to engender new questions. McCartney's coalition, for example, is a curious phenomenon. Given its diversity, can one expect to find different, perhaps even competing, assumptions about masculinity? Would the fundamentalist construction, for instance, differ significantly from a charismatic one? If so, can these differences be traced to specifically religious elements? And what might be the consequences for the movement as a whole, or for the construction of masculinity itself, if one faction were to withdraw or gain hegemony?

Given its link to recent revivals as well as its identity as a social reform campaign, Promise Keepers presents a rare opportunity to address one of the most enticing questions in all revival literature—whether revivals do in fact lead to social reform. Countless Promise Keepers accountability groups have sprouted up across America, where, once a week, men get together in homes, churches, or restaurants to hold one another to specific standards of moral behavior. Are these groups working? Have marriages improved; are wives and children happier because their husbands and fathers attend these meetings?

Questions such as these are sure to remain relevant even long after the corporate forms of the Promise Keepers organization have faded. Evangelicals have always been great synthesizers, and the ministries and movements for which they have been known are remarkable for their easy adaptability, their genius for reinventing themselves. Promise Keepers will survive because the vision driving them has been so synthetic. They will survive because, in the dawn of a new awakening, more than a million Christian men suddenly discovered a mission, a masculinity, and more importantly, a *momentum* in a time of great crisis.

References

Allen, L.D. II (1997, January). Breaking down the wall? *Church and State* 50(1), 10–13.

Balmer, R., & Todd, J.T. (1994). Calvary Chapel, Costa Mesa, California. In J. P. Wind and J. W. Lewis (eds.), *American Congregations* (pp. 663–698). Chicago: University of Chicago Press.

Coleman, R. E. (ed.) (1970). *One divine moment*. Old Tappan, NJ: Fleming H. Revell.

Conason J., Ross, A., & Cokorinos, L. (1996, October 7). The promise keepers are coming: The third wave of the religious right. *The Nation 263*, 11–19.

Enroth, R. M., & Ericson, E. E. (1972). *The Jesus people: Old-time religion in the age of Aquarius*. Grand Rapids, MI: Eerdman's.

Evans, E. (1991). *The Wright vision: The story of the New England Fellowship*. Lanham, MD: University Press of America.

Evans, T. (1994). Spiritual purity. In A. Janssen & L.K. Weeden (eds.), *Seven promises of a promise keeper* (pp. 73–81). Colorado Springs, CO: Focus on the Family.

Handy, R.T. (1960, March). The American religious depression, 1925–1935. *Church History XXIX*(1), 3–16.

Harrell, D. (1975). *All things are possible: The healing and charismatic revivals in modern America*. Bloomington, IN: Indiana University Press.

Hocken, P. (1988). Charismatic movement. In S. M. Burgess & G. B. McGee (eds.), *Dictionary of Pentecostal and Charismatic movements* (pp. 130–160). Grand Rapids, MI: Zondervan.

Kimmel, M. (1997, March–April). Promise Keepers: Patriarchy's second coming as masculine renewal. *Tikkun 2*, 46–50.

McCartney, B. (1990). *From ashes to glory*. Nashville: Thomas Nelson.

McCartney, B. (1991a, June 11). Being a promise keeper. *Where are the men?* Regional Meeting, Denver First Church of the Nazarene [Videotape].

McCartney, B. (1991b, July). Blessing the family and blessing the fatherless. *Where are the men?* Statewide meeting, Colorado University Events Center [Videotape].

Miller, D.E. (1997). *Reinventing American Protestantism*. Berkeley, CA: University of California Press.

Ministry Matters. (1995, March/April). *Ministries Today 13*, 17–18.

O'Connor, E.D. (1971). *The Pentecostal movement in the Catholic church*. Notre Dame, IN: Ave Maria Press.

Pederson, D. (1971). *The Jesus people*. Glendale, CA: Regal Books.

Perrin, R. D. (1989). *Signs and wonders: The growth of the Vineyard Christian Fellowship*. Unpublished doctoral dissertation, Washington State University.

Smith, C. (1972). *The reproducers: New life for thousands*. Glendale, CA: Regal Books.

Sullivan, F.A. (1988). Catholic charismatic renewal. In S.M. Burgess & G. B. McGee (eds.), *Dictionary of Pentecostal and Charismatic movements* (pp. 110–126). Grand Rapids, MI: Zondervan.

Vachon, B. (1972). *A time to be born*. Englewood Cliffs, NJ: Prentice-Hall.

Wagner, C.P. (1983, July/August). A third wave? *Pastoral Renewal 8*(1), 1–5.

Wimber, J. (1978, April 30). Concepts of faith. In *Series on Colossians* [Audiocassette #9032, Side A].

Wimber, J. (1986). *Power evangelism*. San Francisco, CA: Harper and Row.

Wimber, J. (1995, July 12). *Leading a committed people*. Vineyard Pastor's Conference, Anaheim [Videotape].

Wuthnow, R. (1988). *The restructuring of American religion*. Princeton, NJ: Princeton University Press.

Chapter 3

Upstaging the Masons: The Promise Keepers and Fraternal Orders

by Paul Rich and Guillermo de los Reyes

Concern about declining membership is widespread in the world of fraternal orders but at the same time, the Promise Keepers have emerged, who have been euphorically hailed as "the largest and most important men's movement in the United States today" (Abraham, 1997, p. 2). As will be seen, a certain irony is obvious in this as far as the Freemasons and other long-extant men's groups are concerned. The success of the Promise Keepers seems to confirm that, despite centuries of activity, American men's lodges are still unknown and misunderstood by large segments of the general public.

Bill McCartney founded Promise Keepers to gather men together with a platform of "utter sincerity, moral soundness, honesty, and candor, with nothing artificial and no empty promises." Their rallying cry would be "a man of integrity is a man who keeps his promises," expounded in stadiums at massive rallies, which, in 1996, drew 1.1 million men. Meeting speakers emphasize the male role, claiming that men have been "emotionally emasculated" and need to take back their leadership position in family life (Niebuhr, 1997, p. 5; Abraham, 1997, p. 20).

Some of this sounds familiar to members of organizations such as the Masons, Odd Fellows, Pythians, and other orders. Whatever else may be said about Freemasonry and its imitators, their rituals clearly emphasize the importance of a promise. In fact, the seriousness with which Masonic obligations are undertaken has gotten the fraternity into hot water, at least since the Morgan Affair and the Anti-Masonic Party activities of the early 19th century. So, there is a bittersweetness that, after such a contentious history of debate over the oaths of fraternalism, a new movement should be filling the bleachers with men eager to proclaim their seriousness in fulfilling commitments. (At least a few Promise Keepers are interred with their lapel buttons and have A PROMISE KEPT etched on their memorial stones [Abraham, p. 200].)

Although the Promise Keepers like to emphasize their uniqueness and are closely associated with evangelical Christianity, they also have a relation to a number of past movements discussed in this volume, including not necessarily Christian men's groups of the 1980s and, in particular, to the mythopoetic men's movement, one of whose inspirations was the bestselling book by Robert Bly, *Iron John* (Allen, 1995, p. 12). Bly might be described as a male chauvinist version of Joseph Campbell. He is a clever manipulator of mythology who has created a wise old man and mentor, Iron John (Bly, 1990; Don't Miss This One!, 1994). If you see your neighbor half-naked and dabbed in war paint, the chances are he has been impressed by Bly's arguments (Rotundo, 1993, pp. 288–289). Dane S. Claussen (1997) has written:

> Quite a few specific observations about American society, and quite a few pieces of advice or direction for PK men are almost identical to the mythopoetic men's movement of the late 1980s and early 1990s, which is associated with Robert Bly, Sam Keen, Shepherd Bliss, Michael Meade and others. On one hand, crediting the mythopoetic men's movement for raising certain questions or providing certain answers might make PK more appealing to men other than evangelical Christians. PK is on the offensive with evangelical Christianity, not on the defensive, and of course the mythopoetic movement hardly had an image of being mainstream or popular; more generally, PK no doubt feels that either they came up with all of their ideas independently or at least that they don't need or want to give any credit to others.

Although the Promise Keepers and the mythopoetic "Iron Men" have attracted considerable attention, if people are again looking for ritual to enhance their gender identity, Freemasonry and like groups may benefit. Despite recent reverses, in the United States no other fraternity approaches Masonry in size and assets. While the Masons currently have approximately 2,000,000 members, the Odd Fellows have been reduced to 300,000. The Knights of Pythias have only 60,000 members and the Red Men number only 20,000. The Elks claim 1.5 million, but they have virtually converted their lodges into entertainment centers (Putney, 1993, p. 185), as have the Moose with 1.8 million and the Eagles with 1.1 million members (World Almanac, 1995, p. 575). The heyday of the ritualistic secret societies in the United States was in the last part of the 19th century, when an estimated 235 new orders were invented (Putney, 1993, p. 179). Most of them have vanished. Given the disastrous drops in membership, men's fraternal orders increasingly have been regarded as a lost cause. As Putney explained:

> How successful were fraternities in emulating the progressive mainstream? To what extent did they leave behind their Victorian origins,

entering the 20th century taut, trim and full of practicality? The answer depends on the lodge. Elks, for example, proved wonderfully adept at purging themselves of unwanted ritual. To quote one Elk historian, "The apron went in 1895. The 'secret password' expired in 1899. The badge and grip died natural deaths in 1902 and 1904, respectively. The test oath and a few other extraneous things disappeared and the Elks began to be themselves and look less like a cross between the Masons and a college fraternity. Partially as a result of their staying contemporary, Elk membership grew from 826,825 in 1923 to 1,611,139 in 1976. Elk lodges likewise grew in number from 1,470 to 2,200. Other orders fared less favorably. Particularly hard hit were those orders for whom ritualism remained an integral part. Thus Red Men and Knights of Pythias both lost 67% of their membership between 1923 (their peak year) and 1940.

But "lost cause" may prove to have been a premature verdict, at least with regard to the Masons. For one thing, ways to counteract the bad effects of the fatherless household are needed. Bly quite rightly states: "Thousands and thousands of women, being single parents, are raising boys with no adult man in the house." He says, "Women who were raising sons alone were extremely alert to the dangers of no male model. One woman declared that she realized about the time her son got to high-school age that he needed more hardness than she could naturally give. But, she said, if she made herself harder to meet that need, she would lose touch with her own femininity" (Bly, p. 17). This sounds very much like what the Promise Keepers are talking about.

But the fuss over the alleged decline of masculinity and its unfortunate consequences may cause anthropologists and sociologists to yawn. Every generation seems to rediscover the same wheel. At the start of the 20th century members of the Ecole Sociologique in Paris, including Emile Durkheim, Arnold van Gennep, Lucien Lévy-Bruhl and Emile Doutté were convinced of the importance of ritual in sustaining a male identity: "Initiation, more than any other body of knowledge, has suffered throughout history from the fate of continually being forgotten and having to be rediscovered" (Henderson, 1979, p. 11). Bly asserts:

> There is male initiation, female initiation, and human initiation. In this book I am talking about male initiation only.... We have defective mythologies that ignore masculine depth of feeling, assign men a place in the sky instead of earth, teach obedience to the wrong powers, work to keep men boys, and entangle both men and women in systems of industrial domination that exclude both matriarchy and patriarchy.

He draws heavily on what he alleges is North American Indian tradition in his suggestions for men staging "new" initiation rituals that will "free" them of this supposed female domination (Bly, p. x). But when the authors presented a preliminary paper on Bly and Iron John to the 1995 meetings of the Popular and American Culture Associations, a Native American in the audience vehemently denied that Bly understood Native American customs, and expressed considerable resentment over what she considered his harsh treatment of Native rituals. In any case, alas for the Improved Order of Red Men, who are virtually extinct! Perhaps if they had held on just a little longer, the enthusiasm for Bly would have helped them.

The Promise Keepers would be uncomfortable being included in any category that lumped them with Bly's converts, let alone the Masons or Red Men. But one characteristic these groups share is an assertive masculinity, something that has met with mixed reviews. Not everyone would agree that what the world needs is to unleash the male ego through uninhibited male-only ceremonies. In fact, the Promise Keepers are now being stalked by Equal Partners, a Brooklyn-based organization whose head, the Rev. David Dyson, claims that "The Promise Keepers' movement undermines the equality of women in family, church, and society" (Niebuhr).

Although Masonry is itself controversial, a case may be made that it has considerable intellectual content and makes more of a contribution to civil society in several respects than do many more recently founded movements. When Freemasonry is compared to the mythopoets and to the Promise Keepers, the allegations that it is extremist as regards gender issues look ill-informed. Teaching restraint is one of the objects of Freemasonry: a non-Mason scholar comments, "Men devised experiences that helped transform the impulsive passions of the boy into the purposeful energies of the man" (Rotundo, p. 21). The lodge room, with its formal etiquette and sense of decorum, is a far cry from drums in the woods or vast stadium rallies.

Mary Ingham in her book, *Men: The Male Myth Exposed*, holds that the male search for gender affirmation "stems largely from insecurity, the need to try and prove that they are male and that they are strong, because they lack the inner ego strength to feel it." As far as she is concerned, the end result is to "add another layer of insensitivity" (Ingham, 1984, p. 114). The leaders in the new movements—the Promise Keepers certainly—show little awareness of this or much sign of being aware that they are reinventing the wheel. Bly remarks, "Men's clubs and societies have steadily disappeared" (Bly, p. 16), but fails to address, for instance, that many such organizations were devoted to the "harnessing of passions" and included domesticating groups such as debating clubs and literary societies.

While the disappearance of men's organizations is lamentable because "only men can initiate men, as only women can initiate women" (Bly, p. 35), he claims to have found the solution in ceremony and ritual. He asserts that American salvation can occur via ritual (although apparently he is unaware of ritual's political aspects [Kertzer, 1988, p. 2]) and that "the ancient practice of initiation then—still very much alive in our genetic structure—offers a third way through, between the two 'natural' roads of manic excitement and victim excitement. A mentor or 'male mother' enters the landscape. Behind him, a being of impersonal intensity stands, which in our story is the Wild Man, or Iron John" (Bly, p. 36).

Any discussion with Promise Keepers about the issues their program raises is complicated by the fact that they and like new movements are to an extent ahistorical, which is to say they are largely unacquainted with the long history of male fraternalism or believe that it is irrelevant to their activities. But as Doty (1986) wrote, even before the Promise Keepers were conceived, "Ritual in the usual formal sense can be viable only in a community possessing strong communal bonds; given the lack of such bonds today, many commentators have predicted the complete dying off of rituals in the future or have redefined the classical concepts to make them applicable to civil religion or to other ritualistic aspects of modern life" (p. 94).

The truth is that very little is new under the patriarchical sun; as Bateson (1995, p. 31) wrote most pointedly: "Too many women are still being told that glamour following childbearing is the single route to honorable adulthood, that marriage leads to living 'happily ever after.'" To put it plainly, the discovery that ritual is important to mark the stages of life is not an exciting discovery to fraternalists; neither is the observation that marks of transition into adulthood—such as mundane drivers' licenses, college diplomas, or even first communions, bar mitzvahs, or confirmations—will not do (Prior, 1993, *passim*).

The question asked for centuries about the Masons might as well be asked about the Promise Keepers, which is whether or not we need "wilderness and extravagance" to sustain masculinity (Bly, p. 55). Bly claims we moderns are troubled because "having abandoned initiation, our society has difficulty in leading boys toward manhood.... These blockages we have to add to our explanation of why we have so many boys and so few men. The main reason I think is our own ignorance of initiation, and our dismissal of its value" (Bly, p. 182). His suggestion that new initiations must be invented has been taken up. It is now possible to purchase do-it-yourself manuals for initiating youths into manhood (see, for example, Weiner [1992], who also pays little attention to fraternal society initiations). Whether they represent an improvement on the Masonic third degree remains to be seen.

Renewed interest in male ceremonies—illustrated by the stadium rallies of the Promise Keepers—may be viewed in part as a reaction to women's demands for equality. Women protesters have intruded into Promise Keepers' meetings with signs proclaiming "Real Men Don't Dominate Women" and hired airplanes to tow banners reading "Promise Breakers Not Promise Makers." Dressed as a man, one woman infiltrated a meeting (Masons might reflect on the eavesdropping women of the 18th century) and was relieved to find that the Promise Keepers were using the women's restrooms as well as the men's, and thus she could relieve herself in a private booth (Abraham, p. 1). An often-quoted excerpt from a key text, *Seven Promises of a Promise Keeper*, urges men to sit down with their wives and inform them, "Honey, I've made a terrible mistake. I've given you my role. I gave up leading this family, and I forced you to take my place. Now I must reclaim that role" (Evans, p. 79).

That any attack on women is intended would be denied by the proponents of the new groups. The Promise Keepers, for example, state, "There's nothing to substantiate those criticisms. We often find the people who are leveling those charges have never been to a conference and heard what was said" (PK spokesman Mark DeMoss, quoted in Niebuhr). Nevertheless, the appeal is clearly to a desire to reaffirm male values.

Whatever the reasons for their popularity, initially the Promise Keepers made remarkable progress. Starting from scratch in 1991, the budget rose to $26 million in 1994, to $65 million in 1995, and to $115 million in 1996. The enormous stadium "shows" required use of the contents of 11 tractor trailers. By 1996, PK had a paid staff of 400 and a promising line of Promise Keeper CDs, coffee mugs, and shirts.

But these expenditures must be put in perspective. Despite the decline of fraternal numbers, American men's groups remain very powerful in financial terms. The Promise Keepers have only a fraction of the financial underpinnings of the Shrine (which has a larger endowment than that of Harvard University) or of even one state Masonic grand lodge such as those in California and Pennsylvania.

Much of the Promise Keepers rhetoric concerns what, to a Mason, would appear to relate to the more general issues of male bonding, the place of male mentoring and, of course, taking obligations seriously. In the case of the Promise Keepers, official and unofficial web sites (see, for example, http://www.newmanmag.com/) emphasize—as do the lodges—the need for having an inner circle of a few brothers with whom male concerns may be shared. Yet those who are enthusiastic about the Promise Keepers appear to have little patience for rites of other groups (Abraham, p. 2).

These movements reflect in part the "confused, insecure, anxious, 'makeshift males'" in American society, as well as the "absence of the social institutions which have served in the past as initiations into manhood" (Segal, 1990, p. 131). Women are to be relegated to the home while the men are out celebrating their maleness. Women will be surprised to learn how, once again and despite feminist lobbying (Acker, 1992, p. 567)—at least according to Martin Green (1993, p. 145) in *The Adventurous Male* (1993)—"politics is a male group phenomenon" (see also Tiger, 1970).

Thus an old theme in American culture, male initiation and bonding, has replaced the New Age emphasis in the 1970s and 1980s on a male liberationism emphasizing freedom from masculine roles. (The New Age is a curious amalgam of rather old pseudo-sciences such as astrology, the tarot, and pyramid power; some Masonic writers, such as Henry R. Evans, have straddled the line by writing about Masonry and what we today term the New Age; 1970s men's conferences, however, focused on divorce and alimony rights, parenting, job situations, sexual fulfillment and, especially, gay rights [Dubbert, 1979, p. 286]). But moonbeams are out, and raw meat is decidedly in. Rolling in the dust, flaying the flesh, and rooting in the cinders are preferred to sharing domestic chores with one's Significant Other. What is curious is that all of this has gone on without any reference to some of the oldest of all male movements. One commentator sees the Masonic lack of relevance as reflecting a longterm change in the Craft: "In the American revolutionary period, Freemasonry was nearer its medieval beginnings and was more a mystical brotherhood than essentially the social lodge it became after widespread persecution of Masons in the nineteenth century" (Ferguson, 1988, pp. 130–131).

The newest new idea then is the *old* idea: that men now should enhance their maleness through collective ritual. In the *New York Times*, Professor Hal Foster of Cornell University has described this development as a "celebration of the masochistic man." He relates it to the growth of "the cult of abjection," with an oscillation between sensitivity and sadism, adding: "God save the women who get caught in between" (Foster, 1994, p. A17).

Masons may have distinct feelings of *déjà vu* about this renewed interest in reaffirming masculinity. Even non–Mason Claussen (1997) pointed out that

> Questions invariably asked of PK and sometimes commented on by critics or experts have been: Is PK sexist? Is it racist? and Is it homophobic? I think these are proper questions, but the media have almost completely overlooked what is perhaps PK's most unusual message: that American men should form with other men close friendships of a type that most American men admit they don't have and perhaps have never had (friends with whom you openly discuss your most private fears, faults, problems, etc.) because of varying combinations of competitiveness, homophobia, superficiality, etc.

That *déjà vu* is not surprising because Masons, after all, certainly know something about male initiations. As Dumenil (1984, pp. xii–xiii) explained,

> One of the major activities was the performance of various esoteric rituals. Heavily infused with religious symbolism and allegories, the rituals emphasized man's relationship to god, the inevitability of death, and the hope for immortality. Masonic literature, in which authors debated the nature of Masonry's religious content, further underlines the sacred quality of the order and also illuminates the

controversies over faith that characterized late nineteenth-century America.

Freemasonry and kindred societies have played a major role in the life of the American male; Allen pointed out that "white males take understandable pride in their organizations: the New York Yacht club, the Mafia, the Lions Club of Chillicothe, Ohio, and the Holy Roman Empire are only four of them."

The reputation of Masonry as masculinity par excellence seems fairly well deserved. Rotundo (p. 203) explained:

> The rituals of the Masons and other orders completely dominated lodge meetings, and they were focused in great measure on men's feelings about women. In particular, these rites dwelt implicitly on men's discomfort with their female-dominated upbringing and expressed the wish for an all-male family—a wish that was fulfilled both in the outcome of the ritual and in the fact of lodge membership.

Carnes (p. 118) earlier had concluded:

> An examination of fraternal literature suggests how difficult it was for men to break away from their mothers and to renounce the restricted gender role associated with female domesticity. Poems, guidebooks, and novels consistently endorsed maternal nurture and criticized wives, even though one purpose of such publications was to mitigate wives' opposition to the orders.... Fraternal ritualists and writers confirmed that maternal attachment had left a deep and enduring emotional imprint.

The librarian and archivist of the Grand Lodge of New York, William D. Moore (1993), p. 125, wrote:

> The lodge room then can be understood as a place in which masculine values which were disappearing in the outside world were preserved. It was a theater in which millions of American men entertained each other by acting out morality plays, and a hallowed space where the same men found spiritual meaning and perpetuated what they unconsciously recognized as a disappearing social order.

However, while Freemasonry partly was and still is about initiation and male bonding, its rituals deal with more than that. The lodges developed through a long process and hence have an authenticity and sophistication that the shamanist characteristic of the new male initiatory cults lacks. For example, Masons' interest in Doric and Ionian architecture is a considerable distance from mythopoets' use of percussive instruments, spirit animals, and the writings of Carlos Castaneda. In fact, Masonry has an illustrious intellectual pedigree: "Musicians, architects, writers, theorists, philosophers, and even Churchmen (of many persuasions) of the time joined Masonic Lodges in numbers, and there can be no doubt that Freemasonry not only offered many of the finest minds of the Enlightenment something not available in other organizations (including the Church), but attracted the loyalty and interest of an astonishing number of significant historical figures, and unquestionably influenced aspect of endeavor in an age of fecund creativity" (Curl, 1991, p. 9).

Masonic ritualism is predicated on the idea of advancing the candidate from a lower to higher enlightenment—with, hopefully, a parallel transcending of man's animal nature. That is part of the theme in Mozart's Masonic opera, *The Magic Flute*. Masonry generally has presented itself as opening the door to philosophical and intellectual knowledge. In contrast with the representation of initiation as deprivation and violence, Freemasonry does not "haze" the candidate. The Craft displays considerable evidence of its Enlightenment roots and is neither a Fraternity Row house for adolescent adults nor a sort of ritualistic astrology (Rich, 1994b, p. 100).

The teachings include innumerable injunctions to temperance and prudence, along with the imparting of considerable common sense. When this is considered in conjunction with the usually formal lodge room where the degree is communicated, and the fact that the officers are often in black tie, one sees the argument that a considerable difference in sophistication exists between Masonry and the Promise Keepers (Carnes, p. 119). While both are concerned with metaphor and myth, their sources and intent are altogether different (Danile, 1994, p. 65). The Promise Keepers would concur, because the Christian Right's view of Freemasonry is one of profound suspicion. The major point that bears repeating is that whatever criticisms may be leveled regarding its syncretistic religious influence and misuse by politicians, Masonry has along with its nonsense some intellectual content and is considerably different from many cults that are feeding on the world's current insecurities (Taylor, 1975, p. 115).

The renewed interest in having some separate ceremonial activities for men and women has more manifestations than are embodied by Promise Keepers. For example, women's colleges and sororities have returned to favor. For that reason, one is tempted to suggest that there could be a revival in sight for interest in the older fraternal orders, especially if the leadership of those orders demonstrates a sensitivity to change. It is hard to believe that *nouveau*, ahistorical rites will be preferred to those that have been tested and retained over time.

The degrees worked by the older fraternal orders and in particular by Freemasonry represent a legacy of wisdom. Everyone's great-grandfather seems to have been a Red Man or Tall Cedar or Elk. The extinction of this tradition would mean the loss of a significant part of American history and the mythological lifework of hundreds of thousands of individuals. Like old road maps, "They may be crude and they may be out of date, but even a crude map gives more guidance in reaching one's goals than does striking out on a random walk" (Inglehart, 1990, p. 422). The old rituals as maintained by the fraternal lodges represent the fruit of social interplay over many years and hence have a content that recently contrived movements cannot replicate (Meltzer, Peters, and Reynolds, 1975, p. 35).

The desacramentalism or deritualization of society has exacted a price, and the success of the mythopoetic and Promise Keepers movements shows that this has become a concern. As Eliade (1987, pp. 205–206) noted, "Strictly speaking, the great majority of the irreligious are not liberated from religious behavior, from theologies and mythologies. They sometimes stagger under a whole magico-religious paraphernalia, which, however, has degenerated to the point of caricature and hence is hard to recognize for what it is. The process of desacralization of human existence has sometimes arrived at hybrid forms of black magic and sheer travesty of religion."

But if people do feel this lack of gender identity in their lives, particularly the lack of initiatory ritual to mark the transition into adulthood (Eliade, pp. 208–209), the use of existing ritual systems would seem preferable to the mentorship of Bly's Wild Man and his rituals, an image that Bly himself admits turns off many.

The efforts of many Masonic bodies to regain relevance by sponsoring blood drives and visiting hospitals indicates an abdication of belief in the ritual role of the fraternity. But helping people to find their identity through ritual is surely just as important as some of the charities that the fraternity has adopted in its search for popularity. In conversation with Joseph Campbell, Bly obliquely asked Campbell to define ritual. Campbell replied, "A ritual is a situation that puts the individual not only in touch with, but in place of, being the agent of a power that is not out of his intention at all. He has to submit to a power that's greater than his own individual life form." Campbell criticizes the way in which a sense of myth has vanished from religion.

Bly agrees, complaining, "I'm a Protestant, and of course, in the Protestant churches we've gone even farther in removing the tremendum. We don't have any statues of the Virgin. I was in church in California the other day and there was nothing living in the entire church, and yet we were reading texts that talked about the holiness of the meaning" (Cousineau, 1990, pp. 191–192). Those who do not wax enthusiastic about stadium religion, but recognize that the Promise Keepers have arisen out of a genuine need, will want to consider the long history of fraternalism in America (see, for example, Burnard [1995], writing about the 1691–1776 period). Without descending into psychological labyrinths, it is possible to acknowledge that, along with a belief in the equality of the sexes and a recognition that being macho is not the epitome of personality development, one can have conviction for *a legitimate case for male and female rites of passage and separate ritual observances* (Allen, p. 12). Masonry recognized this long ago with the creation of sister orders; the degree of Heroine of Jericho was being conferred by the 1830s (Allyn, 1835, p. 177).

Women as well as men have felt a need to rediscover ritual and to use it to maintain a gender identity (Doty, pp. 101–102). Viewed historically, gender rites are always part of a society. The Promise Keepers are part of a continuing phenomenon (Dubbert, 1979, pp. 287–288), which is illustrated by several essays in this book. Scoffers at formal gender ritualism still pursue rituals that they hope will provide their ideal of social identity and interaction (Doty, p. 98).

It should be possible to have gender rites without gender prejudice. A re-examination of those organizations that served earlier generations and are still with us could be useful (Rich, 1994a, pp. 45, 50). "Human beings are dreaming, myth-bearing creatures," wrote theologian James Luther Adams, "and our myths are our bane as well as our blessing: they are the harbingers of damnation as well as of salvation, of disease as well as of healing, of the demonic as well as of the daimonic, of abject pessimism as well as of indomitable optimism" (Adams, 1986, p. 228). He might also have added, of boundless controversy; as Henningsen (1998) wrote recently, "Freemasons are the original promise keepers. We may not get the media recognition, but we surely have been in the forefront of promisekeeping for centuries."

References

Abraham, K. (1997). *Who are the Promise Keepers? Understanding the Christian men's movement.* New York: Doubleday.

Acker, J. (1992). Gendered institutions: From sex roles to gendered institutions. *Contemporary Sociology 21,* 565–569.

Adams, J.L. (Beach, G.K. [ed.])(1986). *The prophethood of all believers.* Boston: Beacon Press.

Allen, H. (1995, January 2–8). The year of the white male. *Washington Post* (National Weekly Edition), 12.

Allyn, A., & "A traveller in the United States" (1835). *A ritual, and illustrations of Free-Masonry, and the Orange and Odd Fellows' Societies.* England: Devon.

Bateson, M.C. (1995, May-June). Holding up the sky together. *Civilization 2*(3), 29.

Bly, R. (1992). *Iron John: A book about men.* Shaftesbury, England: Element.

Burnard, T. (1995). A tangled cousinry? Associational networks of the Maryland elite, 1691–1776. *The Journal of Southern History 61,* 17–42.

Carnes, M. (1993, September). Iron John in the Gilded Age. *American Heritage* 44, 37–45.
Claussen, D.S. (1997, October 5). Promise Keepers Rally: Historical Roots. In *Popular Culture & American Culture Associations/H-Net Discussion* (H-PCAACA@H-NET.MSU.EDU).
Cousineau, P. (ed.)(1990). *The hero's journey: The world of Joseph Campbell.* New York: HarperCollins.
Curl, J.S. (1991). *The art and architecture of Freemasonry: An introductory study.* London: B.T. Batsford.
Danile, J. (1994). *Scarlet and the beast: English Freemasonry, mother of modern cults, vis-à-vis mystery Babylon, mother of harlots.* Tyler, TX: JKI Publishing.
Don't miss this one! (1994, March). *The Plumbline*, Scottish Rite Research Society 3(1), 4.
Doty, W.G. (1986). *Mythography: The study of myths and rituals.* Tuscaloosa, AL: The University of Alabama Press.
Dubbert, J.L. (1979). *A man's place: Masculinity in transition.* Englewood Cliffs, NJ: Prentice-Hall.
Dumenil, L. (1984). *Freemasonry and American culture, 1880–1930.* Princeton, NJ: Princeton University Press.
Eliade, M. (1987 [1957]). *The sacred and the profane: The nature of religion.* San Diego, CA: Harcourt Brace.
Evans, T. (1994). Spiritual purity. In A. Janssen & L.K. Weeden (eds.), *Seven promises of a Promise Keeper*, pp. 73–81. Colorado Springs, CO: Focus on the Family.
Ferguson, M. (1988 [1982]). *The Aquarian conspiracy: Personal and social transformation in the 1980s.* London: Paladin Grafton Books.
Foster, H. (1994, December 30). Cult of despair. *The New York Times*, A17.
Green, M. (1993). *The adventurous male: Chapters in the history of the white male mind.* University Park, PA: Pennsylvania State University Press.
Henderson, J.L. (1979 [1967]). *Thresholds of initiation.* Middletown, CT: Wesleyan University Press.
Henningsen, G.A. (1998, Spring). Who are the Promise Keepers? *The Voice of Freemasonry* 10(1), 3.
Ingham, M. (1984). *Men: The male myth exposed.* London: Century Publishing.
Inglehart, R. (1990). *Culture shift in advanced industrial society.* Princeton, NJ: Princeton University Press.
Kertzer, D.I. (1988). *Ritual, politics and power.* New Haven, CT: Yale University Press.
Meltzer, B.N., Peters, J.W., & Reynolds, L.T. (1975). *Symbolic interactionalism: Genesis, varieties and criticism.* Boston: Routledge & Kegan Paul.
Moore, W.D. (1993). Masonic Lodge rooms and their furnishings, 1870–1930. *Heredom, The Transactions of The Scottish Rite Research Society* 2, 125.
New man: Proclaiming life to men. Available: http://www.newmanmag.com.
Niebuhr, G. (1997, August 2). Converts and critics for a men's group. *The New York Times*, 5.
Prior, K. (1993). *Initiation customs.* New York: Tomson.

Putney, C. (1993). Service over secrecy: How lodge-style fraternalism yielded popularity to men's service clubs. *Journal of Popular Culture 27*, 179–190.

Rich, P. (1994a). Comment on C.N. Batham's "The Origin of Freemasonry." *Ars Quatuor Coronatorum, Transactions of Quatuor Coronati Lodge No. 2076, Volume 106 for the Year 1993*, 45, 50.

Rich, P. (1994b). Comment on James W. Daniel's "Pure—and accepted Masonry: The craft and the extra-craft degrees, 1843–1901." *Ars Quatuor Coronatorum, Transactions of Quatuor Coronati Lodge No. 2076, Volume 106 for the Year 1993*, 100.

Rotundo, E.A. (1993). *American manhood: Transformations in masculinity from the revolution to the modern era*. New York: BasicBooks/HarperCollins.

Segal, L. (1990). *Slow motion: Changing masculinities, changing men*. New Brunswick, NJ: Rutgers University Press.

Taylor, G.R. (1975). *How to avoid the future*. London: Secker & Warburg.

Tiger, L. (1970). *Men in groups*. New York: Vintage.

Weiner, B. (1992). *Boy into man: A fathers' guide to initiation of teenager sons*. San Francisco: Transformation Press.

Willis, R. (1994). New shamanism. *Anthropology Today 10*(6), 16–18.

The World Almanac and Book of Facts 1995 (1995). "Associations and Societies." Mahwah, NJ: Funk & Wagnalls.

Chapter 4

The Price of Admission? Promise Keepers' Roots in Revivalism and the Emergence of Middle Class Language and Appeal in Men's Movements

by Michael A. Longinow

"Where's the beer?" yells Barry, described as a balding middle-ager at Three Rivers Stadium entering his first Promise Keepers rally. "We don't need any beer to get rowdy this weekend," says an athletic-looking buddy as he throws an arm across Barry's shoulders (Abraham, 1994, p.1). Barry has his answer; he enters the event. From there, the Promise Keepers victory story seems to unfold seamlessly. Christianity, so it's said, is not only applicable to real men, but actually belongs in places like Three Rivers Stadium—or any stadium. Never mind that in a majority of 1990s evangelical churches those singing loudest in the pews and choir stalls are women. Men, who belong in church too, are conspicuously absent, and it is this tragic imbalance that largely drives the Promise Keepers.

Men need Jesus to do their jobs—in the office as well as at home with their wives and children. But to get 1990s men into solid faith commitment and eventually back to Sunday worship, the Promise Keepers believe, takes an appeal as outrageous as high-decibel Friday-night hymn-singing on an infield full of men. If Promise Keepers' pattern be fully followed, it would also seem to involve front-page news coverage, slick magazines devoted to Christian men's success stories, a fully-functioning web site, and even men's New Testaments laced with four-color photos of pro-athlete Christians testifying to the Christian faith. For the Promise Keepers, it all fits. Christianity's message applies to women, but should be applicable as well to the successful 1990s man.

Yet hidden beneath this picture hides a deeper question. What kind of men choose to become Promise Keepers? Beer, slick programs and, indeed, mere admission to most 1990s professional sporting events cost money. So do Promise Keepers stadium rallies, running up to $60 a ticket prior to the 1997 decision to make these rallies a low-cost (or no-cost) proposition (Woodard, 1998, p. 32; *Promise Keepers*, 1998, p. 254.) Once inside, the cost of shirts, mugs, tapes, and other Promise Keepers paraphernalia adds to the bottom line. In the view of some, their economics comprised a quiet but nagging criticism of this intricately-organized movement from the very beginning. But another question also began surfacing: Was Promise Keepers an upper middle-class phenomenon? To become, in fact, an ideal husband and father did one need credit card approval? Even with cost aside, Promise Keepers' 1990s appeal to upwardly-mobile American men has seemed, at best, a tricky bow to middle-class culture. The question is whether it can be otherwise in a masculine culture increasingly skeptical of organized religion. One 1997 *Wall Street Journal* special edition asked whether truly successful American businessman can return at all to committed faith after a deep immersion in the marketplace (Miller, p.W1).

Such were the sorts of questions, both from within and without the popular media, being asked a century before Bill McCartney's vision for promise-keeping men — a time when the problem of luring reticent men back to Christian faith and practice had rung a similar note of alarm. For American men of the late 1800s, the solution to church non-involvement had become more complex than simply getting them back to church. The church would have to go to them. Indeed, the idea of church as organized religion was under siege (Latourette, 1975, pp. 1263–1265). For men to return, it seemed, would require that the church connect with them on several levels. Self-image was just one of those levels — one which, in the booming industrial age, had stiff ties to men's occupations and careers outside the home. The appeal would happen not within the confines of pew-lined, stained-glass sanctuaries, but in the public sphere: at newsstands, on billboards, and in the day-to-day banter of men with men in the marketplace.

The men's movement of the late 19th and early 20th century was a movement much needed. Although women have always outnumbered men in American churches, 100 years ago it seemed that men were staying away from Protestant evangelical churches and camp meetings in droves. "Where are the men?" asked one Christian writer in 1890, suggesting that rather than taking time for church, men who were "not in the penitentiary are at the Odd Fellows Hall, or at the Grange or at the Club House, or attending a meeting of this or that order" (Bridgman, 1890, p. 391). In their place were the women — often teachers and mainstays of local church functions — who, in the words of Henry Ward Beecher, were "ordained to perform many things much better than man, on account of ... superior delicacy of organization and keenness of perception" (McLoughlin, 1968, p.18). Boosted by such revivalist preachers as Charles Finney, women not only outnumbered men in many

Protestant churches, but had taken over men's former role as spiritual initiators (Hardenbrook, 1987, p. 58–59). Such clout would propel women into leadership in other areas of society, ranging from social reform to political lobbying (Rendell, 1985, p. 77). Yet the absence of men from American churches raised serious questions about the future of evangelical Protestantism—and American culture as a whole. What had kept the men away? Was muscular Christianity what they needed? Study of this question is tied up in greater questions of how Protestant Christianity in America provided a foundation for gender identity, acquisition of cultural values, and the emerging role of the middle class. As support for more thorough analyses of Promise Keepers in this volume, the present study will deal with men's movements in 19th- and early 20th-century evangelicalism in particular. Its leaping-off point, however, will be 18th century Methodism, with its penchant for powerful media and the use of popular education to shape cultural identity for Christian faith in society.

Promise Keepers, by definition, has been a non-denominational movement. Listed fifth in the organization's list of Seven Promises is one asking that a man be "committed to supporting the mission of the church by honoring and praying for his pastor, and by actively giving his time and resources" (Who are the Promise Keepers?, 1997). While this statement includes no denominational signification, its language—using such terms as "church" rather than parish, and "pastor" rather than priest—has been fleshed out in other Promise Keepers literature to place the movement solidly within mainstream conservative evangelicalism—well-distanced from both ultra-conservative fundamentalists and the leftist fringes of Christian denominations. This, despite Promise Keepers founder Bill McCartney's own roots in Roman Catholicism and his participation in the controversial charismatic-oriented Vineyard movement (Abraham, 1997, p.124). And despite Promise Keepers' middle-of-the road doctrinal stance, its overall approach—from the stadium-packing structure to the emphasis on music, preaching and public repentance—must be seen as revivalist, following a pattern seen in the camp meeting movement of the 18th and 19th centuries. Camp meetings, as a movement, were popularized by Methodists in this country (Sweet, 1965, pp. 129–130) but carried over into other denominations as well (McLoughlin, 1959, p. 22) and in the 18th and 19th centuries dotted the map from coast to coast, roughly following the paths of circuit-riding evangelists.

But campmeetings were less a function of location than of community. They were people—that network of men and women, boys and girls—willing to gather faithfully from June to September each year under big-top style tents or open-air tabernacles, at varying distances from urban centers. In the camp meetings, music, preaching and Christian literature and media coalesced in a common theme of revivalist socio-religious experience (Jones, 1974, pp. 15–16). Rules of membership in camp meeting culture were simple:

regular attendance and a public expression of a genuine experience of faith. Preaching was ferocious; singing was robust; repentance was up front and personal. Francis Asbury, a camp meeting promoter, found them so intense that he rarely slept during the several days they lasted (Hatch, 1989, p. 49). At camp meetings, toddlers learned about God, young people found their mates and the elderly conferred about leaving this life (McPheeters, 1940, p. 3). In all, they were times of learning and becoming cultured, sanctuaries for those ministering and those ministered unto. "These holiness camp meetings are great Bible schools," wrote revivalist editor and evangelist Henry Clay Morrison in 1924. "The holiness camp meeting is one of the greatest means of a powerful propaganda in this nation" (Morrison, 1924, p.1).

To understand Promise Keepers' roots in Methodist revivalism, one must see that the success of early Methodism, a movement that helped shape evangelism, sprang from the power of words—words emanating primarily from pulpits but also on the printed page. Revivalism, by definition, was spiritual power preceded, accompanied or followed by narrative image—images often rooted in the commonest of cultures. Americans, perhaps more than any other people in the 1800s, needed images to guide their vision forward. Robert Baird, in a nod to this tendency, argued in 1849 that "a state of continuous awakening was the normal condition of the church" in this country and proved it—some might say helped define it—through articles in his periodical (Smith, 1980, p. 45). This linkage of image with experience flew like a refreshing wind in the face of a more heavily-structured, socially-stratified Calvinist determinism of thought and faith that had pervaded New England Protestantism. With revivalists, the streams of God's power to change human hearts and behavior were as unpredictable as the floods and trickles of human interaction within cultures. "Methodism did not suppress the impulses of popular religion, dreams and visions, ecstasy, unrestrained emotional release, preaching by blacks, by women, by anyone who felt the call," notes historian Nathan Hatch, adding that between 1776 and 1850, more African Americans became Christians in 10 years of Methodist preaching than in any given century of Anglicanism. Under Methodist revivalism, more church members were added to this denomination than to any other between the Revolutionary War and the mid-1800s. By the mid-19th century, one in 15 Americans (1.5 million out of 23 million) belonged to a Methodist church (Hatch, 1994, pp. 5–6).

Methodism's revivalist power has been described by Victor Turner as liminal, or transcendent of cultural structures by means of a quiet disorderliness "in which the ordinary rules of the world do not apply" (Mathews, 1993, p. 23). What animated revivalist communication was an image of change that began within individuals, spread to entire societies and deeply affected their way of life. Revivalist communication was a language of courageous hope for the future (Schneider, 1994, p.150). American revivalists had no fear of disrupted routine except where it squelched an ear to the Spirit. It drew life, through the 18th and early 19th centuries, from circuit-riding preachers—such as Francis Asbury—whose saddlebags were more often stuffed with literature than luggage in treks over thousands of miles to take Christ's power of expectant faith to the frontier (Hatch, 1989, pp. 81–86). By the 1890s, revivalist communication had begun developing unbroken links to media and popular education—each in its own way a voice for cultural interaction throughout the changing American continent (Sweet, 1993, p. 11). From such popular education a growing middle class within American society crafted a mirror of itself that would influence how both men and women viewed themselves, and the opposite gender, for generations.

Historians of religion and its culture have argued that the varieties of media among American Christians after the Revolutionary War—ranging from newspapers to doctrinal broadsides—sprang from an information-shift from clergy to laity (Hall, 1930, p. 240; Hatch, 1989, pp. 125–126; Nord, 1993, p. 241). The gospel of Jesus Christ, as it was advanced in the New World, was aimed at all the people rather than merely at clergy, as had been the case in Europe (Noll, 1992, p. 7). Through the late 18th century and much of the 19th, American Protestant churches used print media, building on a strong oral culture, to innovatively and strategically empower their members for service and leadership (Gilmore, 1982). They did so using—as Polanyi would put it—symbols of cultural language through text and shared meaning (1958, p. 61). Part of this shared meaning contributed to a re-shaping of an image of manliness within the culture of American families and shifting socioeconomic structures of the East as well as the expanding frontier.

Men in 18th-century New England were seen as manly if they derived pleasure—and showed requisite skill—as the chief authority figures in home and family. Such leadership was considered not only biblical and socioreligiously proper, but intensely practical. Male leadership in the home was second only to male leadership of the local church. The power of the colonial economy and the sociocultural foundation for daily life—stretching into the early years of the early Republic—derived from these two institutions. Farms, shops, trades, and early industry were homegrown and well-supported by laws and custom (Rotundo, 1993, pp. 11–13). The local churches served as an unseen guide to decision-making and policy that governed state-house and poorhouse. By 1800, the economic base of the spreading nation, as well as the theology of the churches along the new frontier, was changing. Men had turned to pursuing self-fulfillment in a less family-centered workplace and had begun to seek more advanced forms of educational attainment—each of these less and less conducive to an active home-life through the 18th and 19th centuries. By 1896 and Woodrow Wilson's famous "Princeton in the Nation's Service" speech, scientific knowledge and free inquiry were being heralded as genuine pursuits for men at the dawn of a new century (Marsden, 1992, p. 19).

4. The Price of Admission?

For practicing American Protestants in 1900—many of whom were women—the dawn of a new century was a time of fragmented reality not only as regards Christian doctrinal concepts but for cultural definitions as well. The fragmentation was perhaps most visible on the printed page. Between the Civil War and the turn of the century, more types of publications appeared on newsstands and in mailboxes than ever had been thought possible (Mott, 1950). One set of words had helped shape a conservative track for Protestantism in public life, but another set had at the same time contributed disturbing questions about the Christian faith as well (Marty, 1984, pp. 337–339). "Like no other class in history, mid–Victorians dealt in words," notes Burton Bledstein (1978). "A man was his 'word' and the words others used about him" (pp. 70, 73). And the popular word about men through the 19th century was less and less church-oriented. Men were more often described in terms of their workplace, even when that meant the edges and not the center of the marketplace or the halls of political power. Indeed, Boorstin (1965, pp. 115–116) notes that the term "businessman" came into parlance in a 19th-century effort to create a public sphere for men in an urban marketplace. And whereas in the 18th century man's noble struggle—one from which he drew male identity—was for independence of home and family, the equally noble struggle of 19th-century man was for self-identity in a competitive marketplace and on a shrinking continent. A real man, after 1850, had to win. It didn't matter how. And, whereas in the 18th century a man's home had been his castle—often in a village setting where he knew his neighbors—men in modernizing 19th-century America increasingly had lost touch with their boyhood homes and ended up in unfamiliar places, facing inhuman market forces producing inhumane conditions in which a man, it seemed, had to sell his soul for sheer survival. In such a world, real men taught their sons to be fighters—winners in the marketplace, on the ball field, on the battlefield (Rotundo, 1993, pp. 244–245). The boy's mother could teach him to care about others and about God in the process—if he was still listening. But more than likely, the young man's attention was on the marketplace of ideas in the images he could find there of himself in an age of adventure.

It was here, in the marketplace, that the men's movement began gaining momentum. Its first stirrings were not with men but with boys. Such was only natural: the very notion of boyishness versus manhood in 19th-century popular culture was a crucial distinction. Who could be a hero? In answering the question the press, again, had their place. Men could be boys and boys could be men but, as Henry David Thoreau put it, the brash spoken word was to be distinguished from the "consciously learned" written word of seasoned adult males. Boys played in the streets; men aspired to control those streets (Rotundo, 1993, pp. 20–21). As social instruction for the new generations of male-cultural aspirants, muscular Christianity books began emerging in the 1880s highlighting the place of men in Christian culture, among them Hughes' *The Manliness of Christ* (1880), Conant's *The Manly Christ: A New View* (1904), Case's *The Masculine Religion* (1906), Mahan's *The Harvest Within* (1909), Fosdick's *The Manhood of the Master* (1911), Pierce's *The Masculine Power of Christ* (1912), Wayne's *Building the Young Man* (1912), Smith's *A Man's Religion* (1913), White's *The Call of the Carpenter* (1913), and Barton's *The Man Nobody Knows: A Discovery of the Real Jesus* (1924).

Dwight Lyman Moody, a shoe salesman turned revivalist preacher, began his ministry in the 1860s by collecting wayward young men off the streets and packing them into Sunday School classes. Eventually, Moody—who never gave up his manly business-like approach—would become president of the Chicago YMCA. Through international YMCA links, Moody would tour Scotland in the 1870s and become a world figure in evangelicalism through a Scottish revival sparked by his preaching (Marsden, 1980, pp. 33–34). Though Moody would retain his concern for youth and eventually build ties to the Student Volunteer Movement, his later ministry turned to adults—both male and female—in the late 19th century. Moody's theology was more notable in the oratory of his crusades than in any systematic treatise, and although preaching against "Sunday newspapers" because he said they broke the Sabbath, he nonetheless believed strongly in the need for reading. Moody's ministry produced its own books, magazines and other literature—these taking their place alongside other media aimed at framing the notion of revival for lay Americans (p. 35). By this and many other means, men had begun reentering churches again by the early 1900s—both as youths and as curious adults. Revival in these years struck an inviting tone for men, spinning off as it did an accompanying media image.

Men who on Sunday morning would not darken the door of a church, apparently would reach for some reading matter over Sunday morning coffee. Charles Sheldon's *In His Steps,* a late 19th-century fictional account of revival, included appeals to women, but must be seen as clearly aimed at wayward men—men at work. The wild popularity of Sheldon's parable stems perhaps from its strategic attacks on palisades of 19th-century socioeconomic power— within limits. The story's clergyman hero begins in a small, nondescript rural community and ends up in Chicago, a Midwestern socioreligious hub often associated with cultural change in the 19th century. In one scene, a minister confronts a pair of armed muggers with the proposition, "Suppose I found good jobs for both of you? Would you quit this and begin all over?" (Sheldon, 1982, p. 158). One of the richer men in the story commits suicide in a tragedy of white-knuckled grasping for material power—power that had seduced and corrupted him. Men who come to revived faith, in Sheldon's story, turn their attentions away from wealth toward helping the poor, but never totally lose their place in educated, middle-class society. Indeed, the means for reaching the poor of the inner city comes through the benevolence of an upper middle-class benefactor. The hard-driving editor of a prominent daily newspaper chooses not to quit his job but to keep it, turning his writing and editing toward only what Jesus would, and "creating a force in journalism that in time came to be recognized as one of the real factors of the nation to mold its principles" (Sheldon, 1982, p. 187)—for those capable by training or culture of reading a newspaper, of course. That group, with notable exceptions, was predominately male through much of the 19th century (Leonard, 1995, p.29).

Sheldon's call to men, with its decidedly middle-class tenor, bespoke a movement of evangelism and discipleship aimed at men that bears much resemblance, with some key differences, to the Promise Keepers movement. The Men and Forward Religion Movement of 1911–1912 brought 1.5 million men together in stadium-like events that drew both urban and rural participants in scores of cities. It was a movement driven by scientific management techniques, elaborate staff-training and an uncanny media savvy (Claussen, 1998b) that launched the message of religion to men across barriers of denomination and class (McLoughlin, 1959, p. 396). Though some have pointed to a crisis of feminized Christianity (Bederman, 1989, pp. 436–437) or the combination of early 20th-century urban problems, Progressive politics, and the Social Gospel (Smith, 1987; Claussen, 1997, 1998a) as the explosive force behind this movement, its real force can rather be seen as an outgrowth of a long-building desire among American men for the community of male culture of which 19th century competitive social structures had deprived them. Men came into revivalist services because raw capitalism made them lonely—fed up with overdose-quantities of self-service that modern culture and the marketplace had fed them (Marty, 1984, p. 319). They were also tired of the mirrors (perhaps smoke and mirrors would be a better metaphor) toward which they had been directed by the status-conscious framers of middle-class culture. What men had entered the marketplace to find—a map for identity on which they could plan their hopes—turned out to have given misleading directions. The system that had driven them to succeed had fed off their insecurities (Bledstein, 1978, p. 102). If a man won at the game of business, what did it get him except the need to distance himself from potential adversaries? No one, nothing, was to be trusted, including a man's own heart. The isolation was torturous (Hardenbrook, 1987, pp. 44–55).

By 1900, many American men apparently sensed that at the core they could know themselves only in linkage with other men—and with God. As one writer put it, stirring was a "consciousness that God is with us, that life is packed with His meaning, that ... the energies of the and impulses of the Spirit are pressing out the manhood of this time into paths of service...." (Thompson, 1911, p. 1). Men's revival movements were not the only means to fraternal linkage, of course. Victorian Freemasonry and other secret societies of the 18th and 19th centuries had brought men together in a spiritual bond that transcended marketplace isolation and acted as a kind of alter-ego for rising evangelicalism (Carnes, 1989, pp. 31–33). The difference, however, in the revivalistic fervor of Christian men's movements was a deeply appealing hope—a way back to healing for broken masculine image. Kneeling before God, men could come shoulder to shoulder in common repentance, as opposed to toe-to-toe in marketplace combat. In the revivalist doctrine of the men's movements, no one was to be excluded. How could they be? Their ticket in was experience of God—experience whose combined autonomy and commonality fed the hungry masculine soul in ways that secular 19th-century culture could not.

Men in the 19th century had valid criticisms of the evangelical churches they'd abandoned, Washington Gladden had once commented in the late 19th century. But they should return anyway, the theologian warned, for to stay away from church was a move that harmed the very fabric of their manhood. "There are faculties and powers of my nature that are but scantily exercised or cultivated in my daily work," argued Gladden. "And Sunday is the time and Church is the place for the care of these higher interests" (1885, pp. 68–69). With such appeals, Gladden joined a host of other prominent clergy in the years before 1910 in helping build a middle-class base of support for the work of Fred B. Smith, head of the YMCA's Religious Work Department, in creating the Men and Forward Religion Movement.

Much like Promise Keepers, the Forward Movement was as memorable for what it did—assembling men from virtually every Christian denomination on the continent—as for how it went about its task. As one historian put it, "The movement took a year to plan and another year to execute" (McLoughlin, 1959, p. 396). The MRFM event in each major city was a week-long series of forums, conferences and public religious meetings that featured speakers as diverse as William Jennings Bryan, Gipsy Smith, Jane Addams, Washington Gladden, Charles Stelzle and Raymond Robbins. The movement had many faces: to some it was an evangelistic campaign, to others a social-service campaign, to still others a rallying cry for men who had abandoned church work and Christian service. If nothing else, the Forward Movement was well organized. The Movement's New York headquarters structured its planning of nationwide events in corporate style and the staff consisted of executive committees and subcommittees, with strategies and sub-strategies. The marketing's execution was tactical and brash, with managers employing press agents nationwide, press releases, press conferences, billboards, lighted signs and newspaper advertisements set in sports pages (Bederman, 1989, pp. 441–443). Workers attended nightly "institutes" that trained them in precise duties; lay people were schooled in Bible Study, Boy's Work, Community Extension, Evangelism, Missions and Social Service (p. 444).

That the movement exceeded all expectations, drawing attendees in 76 cities and 1,083 small towns across the nation, is not surprising. Something

4. The Price of Admission?

about these events made men drop their guard and link arms. Men's groups from virtually every Protestant denomination, 10 denominational brotherhoods, the International Sunday School Committee, the Gideons and the YMCA boosted the events (Bederman, 1989, p. 432). Besides the powerful appeal of revivalist commitment—a force that had been brewing within much of Protestantism through the late 19th century—Christian service served as a force that drew men together. "Men who receive a blessing at it will too gladly work in connexion with it," wrote one men's revivalist in the late 19th century (Watts-Ditchfield, p. 45).

Perhaps more surprising than how quickly it grew is how quickly the Men and Religion Forward Movement seemed to fade from view. Although disbanding MRFM as a national organization following its final event—New York City's Christian Conservation Congress of 1912—had been part of the original plans, MRFM leaders also called for the organization's work to continue through local committees. Apparently this plan failed almost completely; the only post–1912 local committee about which much evidence survives is Atlanta's, perhaps because it became highly controversial (Kemp, 1993; Kuhn, 1993). By 1914, the MRFM was essentially already forgotten (McLoughlin, 1959, p. 397), fading into the background behind other Social Gospel and then fundamentalist movements and organizations. Whereas prior to 1900 Protestant evangelism had been preeminent, men reborn to service of the church after 1900 seemed more intent on helping others. Some criticized post–1900 evangelism as works-oriented—too involved with the outer person and less in tune with the soul. Society seemed more important than individuals in this approach to men and Christian service. Indeed, Walter Rauschenbusch claimed the Men and Religion Forward Movement had "made social Christianity orthodox" (Bederman, 1989, p. 456). Had something gone wrong? Or had the movement got it right from the beginning? Similar questions arise about Promise Keepers, whose commitment to multiracial peace has been a hallmark of the movement. Did the Men and Religion Forward Movement win the argument for the civic responsibilities of manly Christians? Did Billy Sunday and other Muscular Christians win the argument for a manly Christian faith? Apparently, neither MRFM nor the Muscular Christians won the argument for significantly increased church attendance by men.

Have the Promise Keepers won these arguments now? Should social service be the real goal of a Christian man? Or should his efforts be toward evangelism? Perhaps the win-loss metaphor—tied as it is to the stadium venues of late 20th-century revivalism—is less than helpful. The point, in reality, is that the men are there at all—and that significant personal change seems to be happening among them along the way. Rather than gladiators in an arena, Smith chided, "The social message and the individual message are not foreign, are not antagonistic, are not pitted one against each other" (Smith, 1911,

p. 155). The revivalism of the 19th century framed a door through which men could return to Christian commitment and the work of the church in the early 20th century. In their public repentance, men found a deeply appealing freedom from bondage to self-absorption. Once inside their new faith commitment, whatever cultural market position they held became a tool for helping those less fortunate—physically or spiritually. Did middle class values matter to reaching 20th-century men? Of course, Smith would say. Could they become a preoccupation and a distraction? Certainly, Smith would agree.

But in a telling anecdote, Smith recalled a fiery rebel student from the University of Minnesota who had told him that one of the chief liabilities of modern life was the notion of religion and the supernatural. One day, at the close of a service, Smith felt a hand clasp his in a crowd. There, with trembling lips, stood the Minnesota student saying, "Mr. Smith, it's all right with me." The student had seen a boyhood friend in the service do something that gripped him in his masculine soul. "When I saw that man, whom I had known from my very boyhood, rise before an audience of men to confess his personal need of God, I said in my heart, 'That is supernatural. God is in this place.'" Male culture would not become less complex, nor the barriers against entry or re-entry to the Christian faith less formidable at the close of the new century; but the language men might use for speaking of Christian commitment—whether labeled as promises or pretense revealed—had become richer for having, yet again, navigated the powerful currents of American revivalism.

References

Abraham, K. (1997). *Who are the Promise Keepers? Understanding the Christian men's movement*. New York: Doubleday.

Barton, B. (1924). *The man nobody knows: A discovery of the real Jesus*. Indianapolis, IN: n.p.

Bederman, G. (1989, September). The women have had the charge of the church work long enough: The Men and Religion Forward Movement of 1911–1912 and the masculinization of middle-class protestantism. *American Quarterly 41*, 432–465.

Bledstein, B.J. (1978). *The culture of professionalism: The middle class and the development of higher education in America*. New York: W.W. Norton and Company.

Boorstin, D. (1960). *The image: A guide to pseudo-reality in America*. New York: Atheneum.

Boorstin, D. (1965). *The Americans: The national experience*. New York: Vintage Books.

Bridgman, H.A. (1890, April). Have we a religion for men? *Andover Review 7*, 388–396.

Carnes, M.C. (1989). *Secret ritual and manhood in Victorian America*. New Haven, CT: Yale University Press.

Case, C.D. (1906). *The masculine religion.* Philadelphia: American Baptist Publication Society.

Claussen, D.S. (1997, Oct. 2–3). *Surveys of the Men and Religion Forward Movement, 1911–12: A case study of the social survey movement's status as historical footnote.* Paper presented at the Southern Association for Public Opinion Research annual conference, North Carolina State University, Raleigh, NC.

Claussen, D.S. (1998a, April 24–25). *The historical significance of the Men and Religion Forward Movement, 1911–12: An interdisciplinary look at one Social Gospel organization.* Paper presented to the Conference on the Social Gospel, Colgate Rochester Divinity School, Rochester, NY.

Claussen, D.S. (1998b, Aug. 3–8). *United States print mass media coverage of the Men and Religion Forward Movement, 1911–1917.* Paper presented to the Religion and Media Interest Group, Association for Education in Journalism and Mass Communication annual convention, Baltimore, MD.

Conant, R.W. (1904). *The manly Christ: A new view.* Chicago: Author.

Fosdick, H.E. (1911). *The manhood of the master.* New York: Association Press.

Gilmore, W.J. (1982, April). Elementary literacy on the eve of the Industrial Revolution: Trends in rural New England, 1760–1830. *Proceedings of the American Antiquarian Society 92.*

Gladden, W. (1885). *The young men and the churches; Why some of them are outside, and why they ought to come in.* Boston: Congregational Sunday School and Publishing Society.

Hall, T.C. (1930). The religious background of American Culture. Boston: Little, Brown.

Hardenbrook, W.M. (1987). *Missing from action: Vanishing manhood in America.* Nashville: Thomas Nelson.

Hatch, N.O. (1989). *The democratization of American Christianity.* New Haven: Yale University Press.

Hatch, N.O. (1994, October 7) The puzzle of American Methodism (Bartlett Lecture, Yale University). *Methodism and the shaping of American culture, 1760–1860* conference proceedings, Asbury Theological Seminary.

Hughes, T. (1880). *The manliness of Christ.* Boston: Houghton Mifflin.

Jones, C.E. (1974). *A guide to the study of the Holiness Movement.* Metuchen, NJ: Scarecrow Press.

Kemp, K.W. (1993). *Asa Griggs Candler: An Atlanta life.* Unpublished doctoral dissertation, Georgia State University.

Kuhn, C.M. (1993). *"A full history of the strike as I saw it": Atlanta's Fulton Bag and Cotton Mills workers and their representations through the 1914–1915 strike.* Unpublished doctoral dissertation, University of North Carolina at Chapel Hill.

Latourette, K.S. (1975). *A history of Christianity: Reformation to the present, Vol. II* (Revised Ed.). San Francisco: Harper and Row.

Leete, F.D. (1912). *Christian brotherhoods.* Cincinnati, OH: Jennings and Graham.

Leonard, T.G. (1995). *News for all: America's coming of age with the press.* New York: Oxford University Press.

Mahan, A.T. (1909). *The harvest within: Thoughts on the life of the Christian.* Boston: Little, Brown.

Marsden, G.M. (1992). The soul of the American university. In Marsden, G.M., and Longfield, B.J. (eds.), *The secularization of the academy*. New York: Oxford University Press.

Marty, M.E. (1984). *Pilgrims in their own land: 500 years of religion in America*. New York: Penguin Books.

Mathews, D.G. (1993). *Evangelical America: The Methodist ideology*. Nashville: Abingdon Press.

McLoughlin, W.G. (1959). *Modern revivalism: Charles Grandison Finney to Billy Graham*. New York: The Ronald Press Company.

McLoughlin, W.G. (ed.)(1968). *The American evangelicals, 1800–1900*. New York: Harper Torchbooks/Harper & Row.

McPheeters, J.C. (1940, Sept. 25). Camp Sychar. *The Pentecostal Herald 52*.

Miller, L. (1997, April 10). Can you go back? More professionals return to church or synagogue: Having it all isn't enough. *The Wall Street Journal*, W1.

Morrison, H.C. (1924, June 25). Great Bible school with revival power. *The Pentecostal Herald 36*.

Mott, F.L. (1950). *American journalism: A history of newspapers in the United States through 260 years: 1690–1950*. New York: Macmillan.

Noll, M. (1992). *A history of Christianity in the United States and Canada*. Grand Rapids, MI: Eerdmans.

Nord, D.P. (1993). Systematic benevolence: Religious publishing and the marketplace in early nineteenth-century America. In Sweet, L.I. (ed.), *Communication and change in American religious history*. Grand Rapids, MI: Eerdmans.

Pierce, J.N. (1912). *The masculine power of Christ, or Christ measured as a man*. Boston: The Pilgrim Press.

Polanyi, M. (1958). *Personal knowledge: Towards a post-critical philosophy*. Chicago: University of Chicago Press.

Promise Keepers to lay off paid staff. (1998, March 11). *The Christian Century 115*, 254–255.

Rendell, J. (1985). *The origins of modern feminism*. Houndsmill, England: Macmillan.

Rotundo, E.A. (1993). *American manhood: Transformations in masculinity from the revolution to the modern era*. New York: Basic Books.

Schneider, A.G. (1993). From democratization to domestication: The transitional orality of the American Methodist circuit rider. In Sweet, L.I. (ed.), *Communication and change in American religious history*. Grand Rapids, MI: Eerdmans.

Shedd, C.P. (1934). *Two centuries of student Christian movements: Their origin and intercollegiate life*. New York: Association Press.

Sheldon, C. (1982). *In his steps*. Old Tappan, NJ: Fleming H. Revell/Spire Books.

Smith, F.B. (1911). The evangelistic emphasis. Ch. 15 in *Men and religion*. New York: Young Men's Christian Association Press.

Smith, F.B. (1913). *A man's religion*. New York: Association Press.

Smith, G.S. (1987). The Men and Religion Forward Movement of 1911–1912: New perspectives on evangelical social concern and the relationship between Christianity and Progressivism. *Westminster Theological Journal 49*, 91–118.

Smith, T.L. (1980). *Revivalism and social reform: American Protestantism on the eve of the Civil War*. Baltimore: Johns Hopkins University Press.

Sweet, L.I. (1993). Communication and change in American religious history. In Sweet, L.I. (ed.), *Communication and change in American religious history*. Grand Rapids, MI: Eerdmans.

Sweet, W.W. (1965). *Revivalism in America: Its origin, growth and decline*. Gloucester: Peter Smith, 1965.

Thompson, F.L. (1911). Men and Religion: The program. In *Men and religion*. New York: Young Men's Christian Association Press.

Watts-Ditchfield, J.E. (c. 1900). *Fishers of men: or, How to win the men*. London: Charles Murray and Company.

Wayne, K.H. (1912). *Building the young man*. Chicago: A.C. McClurg.

White, B. (1913). *The call of the carpenter*. Garden City, NY: Doubleday, Page.

Who are the Promise Keepers? (1997, October 24). Available at web site http://ftp.vix.com/menmag/pkdescr.html.

Woodard, J. (1998, March 9). The gates open, out go the staff. *Alberta Report/Western Report 25*, 32.

CHAPTER 5

Are Promises Enough? Promise Keepers Attitudes and Character in Intensive Interviews

by George N. Lundskow

When I began my research on the Promise Keepers, I discovered a near total dearth of field or quantitative research, and a plethora of speculation. This situation made finding a starting point more difficult. My first task was to attend a stadium conference as a participant observer, which I did on May 29, 1997, at Kansas City's Arrowhead Stadium. I also traveled to Washington, DC, in October, 1997, for Stand in the Gap, along with about 700,000 other men. I spoke with men and women in two counter demonstrations at Stand in the Gap—one sponsored by the National Organization for Women, and one by the Lesbian Avengers. However, these efforts served only to scratch the surface, because my goal was to understand the PK men at the level of personal character, where their basic behavioral and attitudinal tendencies reside. I developed an interview protocol and questionnaire, and conducted 22 intensive interviews with PK men; five with PK wives. Before I discuss the methods in more detail, I should mention that after the first two or three interviews, it became apparent that the mass conferences are, in fact, a secondary aspect of the Promise Keepers. As officially stated (Promise Keepers web site):

> Promise Keepers is not merely a series of stadium events, but rather, a year-round outreach to men through the local church. PK is not a membership or dues-paying organization, but is part of a larger movement of Christian men becoming more active throughout their local churches. Furthermore, PK is not a political or partisan organization, nor is it affiliated with any denomination. Finally, Promise Keepers does not promote a self-help or self-improvement philosophy, but encourages men to commit every aspect of their lives to Jesus Christ.

Indeed, the first interviews revealed that participation at the local level, especially through what the men call "accountability groups" or "sharing groups," constitutes PK's core. The conference is only one moment in the overall process of spiritual renewal and "living the life of Christ." In response, I altered my interviews to inquire about the small groups. In the end, I interviewed 18 men from four different groups, four men who did not belong to a group, and five wives.

INTRODUCTION

My own experience at the Kansas City rally and Stand in the Gap suggests that, although certain patriarchal elements are present, PK defies such simple categorization. After the first few interviews, especially, I discovered that in order to understand the men who comprise the Promise Keepers, one must understand the men in their accountability groups and other social relations where they construct their notions of "a godly man" and a "servant-leader."

A lack of empirical evidence and an abundance of polemics has led to many generalizations lacking substantiation. One belief is that PK offers a sort of sanctuary where men can be boys, and enjoy the simple and clearly defined gender roles, morality, innocence and camaraderie of youth. The rally and movement allow men to shed responsibility by submerging in something greater than themselves, yet also dominate those of lesser status than themselves, namely, women and children (Diamond, 1995; Gilbreath, 1995; Kimmel, 1996; Messner, 1997; Minkowitz, 1995; Shapiro, 1995; Van Biema, 1995). In particular, Kimmel (1996) identifies the Promise Keepers as muscular Christians, concluding that "the enormous response to the Christian men's organization called the Promise Keepers is a testimonial to the sustained drawing power of a muscular Christian vision" (Kimmel, 1996, p. 313). Arriving in the United States from England, the American brand of muscular Christianity originally overlapped with Christian socialism and sexual liberation (Hall, 1994), promoting a sense of masculinity based on physical fitness, faith and integrity of character. However, the early 1900s' Billy Sunday, the most prominent of American muscular Christians, was a social conservative and a fundamentalist. Although PK retains the emphasis on integrity and some fundamentalist values (e.g. reading the Bible literally), they never had the socialist or emancipatory sexual values (PK believes in sex only within a heterosexual marriage). Thus, Kimmel relies on analogy rather than empirical evidence to support this conclusion.

Similarly, Messner (1997) speculates about what PK men believe, again with no data, to assert that the Promise Keepers "can be viewed ... as organized and highly politicized antifeminist and antigay backlash" (Messner,

1997, p. 35). He reaffirms this conclusion with a chart (p. 91) that locates the PKs as the most extreme of the antifeminist backlash movements—well beyond even the mythopoetic men's movement. Messner condemns the stadium rallies through the impressions of a colleague (Coakley, 1993), and the impressions of one reporter at one rally (Sahagun, 1995), neither of whom offers research questions or an analytical regimen. As proof that PK adherents in general seek to dominate their families and rub out the "feminizing" influences in our society, Messner cites Beal and Gray (1995), who performed a content analysis of PK leader texts. They conclude that the official message or, as they call it, the "hegemonic discourse" is "the reassertion of a natural hierarchy of authority" (Beal and Gray, 1995, p. 79). Although this is, arguably, one aspect of PK doctrine, my interview data reveal that the men have multiple interpretations of this message, and none of them held the unyielding attitude of domination that Messner claims. The Beal and Gray study cannot tell us whether PK men actually internalize the apparently dogmatic and severe dicta in the official message. Even if we accept that the message is overwhelmingly patriarchal, we cannot automatically conclude that this is the primary reason, or even an important reason, that men are drawn to the stadiums.

THEORY

The men seem to be brought together in common identity and purpose by their shared attributes, or what we might call *social* character, not the idiosyncrasies of individual psychological traits. Thus, the goal is to construct an overall picture of character traits PK men share in common, because it is these traits that enable them to relate to each other. It also consists of the commonly shared meanings, expressions and symbols that anchor individuals to a social group. It includes all the references a person uses to interpret the world, and to communicate with other similarly minded people.

What common references unite the Promise Keepers in shared meaning? Throughout the current newspaper and magazine editorials and polemics, one consistent theme stands out: that PK men are simply dupes who respond to familiar calls of patriarchal domination and macho posturing. They are, in effect, men willing to submit to something they perceive as more powerful than themselves, and who in turn seek to dominate their wives and children. As Fromm (1936, 1994, [1941] 1994, [1973]) and Adorno et al. (1950) called it, PK men exhibit an *authoritarian character*.

In the simplest terms, authoritarianism is the desire to submit to anyone or anything perceived as stronger, and to dominate and control anyone or anything perceived as weaker. It is a measure of character or, in other words, a measure of basic tendencies that influence how a person perceives the world, and how he responds to it. Authoritarian character results from feelings of insecurity and low self-esteem. Since many claim that PK assuages feelings of emptiness and lack of direction, it seems logical to assess whether the PK men reach fulfillment primarily through authoritarian relationships, or through their opposite, the productive relationship, or through both in combination.

After Fromm's initial 1936 conceptualization, and the subsequent Berkeley studies published as *The Authoritarian Personality* in 1950, numerous studies have applied the theory to different populations, on a variety of issues, using different methods. For example, a series of studies examined right-wing attitudes and political affiliation (Eysenck, 1954; Eysenck and Coulter, 1972; Eysenck and Wilson, 1978). Others found correlation between ethnocentrism, nationalism, and anti-feminist views among those who support the fascist Centrumpartij (Hagendoorn and Janssen, 1983; Raaijmakers et al., 1985; Meloen et al., 1988). Yet others, such as the extensive Altemeyer (1997, 1988, 1981) and Lederer (1993) research, found more generally that authoritarian character influences many aspects of life, not political views alone. Thus, character in general shapes preferences and decisions regarding many facets of life, including the relationship of an individual to a mass movement—and a leader such as Bill McCartney.

METHODOLOGY

My methodology follows from the psychoanalytic tradition, which Connell summarizes as the "intensive" study of people in their social relations, "one person at a time. It involves the decoding of personal meanings in an extraordinarily fine-grained way" (Connell, 1994, p. 16). In practical application, the intensive interview allows access to the deeper feelings and especially the context in which people hold particular beliefs or experience certain emotions. As the interview continues, the researcher balances between "concern for the person and critique of what the person says" (Connell, 1994, p. 16). This does not mean cold detachment, but rather an intensive discussion with the subject, a back-and-forth discourse through which the interviewer interacts both as a human being and as a skeptical scientist.

For this reason, the interviewer must share some common references with the subject in order to facilitate communication and, ultimately, critical analysis. Common references build an ethnographic process that cannot be quantified, and which always involves a degree of uncertainty. As McCracken (1988, p. 18) argues, "the investigation cannot fulfill qualitative research objectives without using a broad range of [the researcher's] own experience, imagination, and intellect." As Schatzman and Strauss (1973, p. 69) say, the "researcher believes everything and nothing simultaneously," and

McCracken (1988) and Mishler (1986) designate the researcher as an "investigative instrument" who stands in an appropriate social position from which to facilitate understanding, yet still maintains an appropriate scientific "distance" through critical awareness (Neuman, 1994, p. 342). The goal is to become an insider, or at least pass for one, without losing sight of the role as researcher. I would claim acceptance on the grounds that I obtained extensive interview time with each respondent, in which we discussed serious and emotional issues, but also that each man provided me with a list of other men I might approach for an interview, several suggested that I speak with their wives, and one man insisted on paying for my lunch. Two asked me to join them in prayer at the end of the session. All invited me to call them again if I had anything further to discuss.

I conducted all interviews face-to-face, except for three which, because of travel distances, were conducted over the phone. From a total of 22 interviews to date, using snowball sampling, I gathered approximately 48 hours of discussion during the period October 15, 1997, to April 24, 1998. The sample includes 20 white men and 2 black men. As Neuman (1994, pp. 367–358) indicates, field interviews use "theoretical sampling," by which the interviewer chooses the sample size according to theory requirements that develop before and during time in the field conducting interviews. With this in mind, I finished at 22 because I had interviewed men from four different accountability groups, and several who are not part of a group.

Occupations included truck driver, pastor, physician, attorney, government classified employee, building maintenance supervisor, corporate executive, graduate student, self-employed salesman and sports team mascot. They ranged in age from 22 to 57. All lived in suburban neighborhoods. All were raised in religious households, in the sense that their parents more or less regularly attended church and taught their children that a relationship with Jesus Christ the savior is the most important goal in life—except for one man who was reared a Jew and later converted to Christianity, and an evangelical pastor who decided in his 30s to leave his Catholic roots.

Findings

Are the Promise Keepers patriarchal? Are they authoritarian? As with all questions we might ask, the answers depend in part on the definition of patriarchy, which I here define as a situation in which a man holds an authoritative relationship over a woman or his wife, that the woman's identity is centered on the man and, in general, men are seen as the "measure of all things." The woman becomes the "Other," not a person in her own right, but simply a non-male. Although these notions are present to an extent, other more egalitarian impulses also mitigate the patriarchal tendencies. The PK men see themselves as "servant-leaders," which is not about domination, but rather:

> No, no, it's not about dominating or controlling somebody at all. Servant-leadership for me means serving and leading together, that sometimes you need to lead if you know better or have more experience or something, and other times, say if my wife knows better, then I become the servant, but either way, you are serving the Lord or serving your family.... One of the biggest problems is the sin of selfishness, so when you start working only for yourself, that's when you get into trouble.

Other men expressed the idea this way:

> If a man becomes a servant of the Lord, or humbles himself and becomes a servant to his family, this is not the same as a slave or a robot. Women do not become slaves because they are working for their family. This whole thing about servant leadership is knowing when to be a leader and when to be a follower; it requires awareness and knowledge and one thing that men have real problems with—sensitivity.

> I learned that the way to go is two people working together as one, as partners.

The servant-leadership idea does include some elements of demarcated gender roles that follow conventional (and some might say patriarchal) lines:

> My wife is great at figuring out what a person is really all about. I mean, she can just hear me tell her about what is going on at work, and she doesn't even have to be there and she can tell me exactly what somebody's motives are, what they're after. It's the same at parties, anywhere. She definitely has a lot more intuition than I do.

They commonly spoke of women having more intuition, being more sensitive to unspoken feelings or motivations. This is the familiar belief that women are more emotional and intuitive, men more material and logical. But at the same time, the men became involved in Promise Keepers because the organization allows them to share feelings in a men-only environment that they find more comfortable and conducive to the sharing of difficult emotions. They hope to return to their families as more sensitive and dedicated husbands and fathers. On this point, several men echoed the following:

> For the first time, I was at stadium with a bunch of guys, and I didn't see all the swearing, and fighting, and drinking that you normally see at a stadium. It was so different it felt strange at first, but it also made me more comfortable.

> I didn't know what to expect, but eventually I got more comfortable and, for the first time in a long time, I cried. I didn't really know why, but there was so much inside, so much pain in me and a lot of the other guys, that it helps to get it out and in the company of men. Once you learn to let down the pretensions, you start to get a sense of what's really important. I suppose that is why I cried, because it hit me that I had spent so much time doing the wrong things.

Like what kind of things?

> Gosh, there's so much, like spending all night at home on the phone with business associates rather than with my wife and kids, like watching TV, like worrying about making more money, more than you need even to live comfortably.

All the men are married with children, yet many have wives who did and will again (when the children are old enough) work outside the home. Although most believe that it is the woman's place to stay home with the children, they also see this as a matter of choice, one choice among many in life:

> Nobody can have everything they want in life, although I think Bill Gates might be getting close [laughs]. If a woman wants a career, that's fine. If she wants children that's fine, too. Some women can manage both, but it's best if both the husband and wife talk it over. I don't think women are better automatically at raising children because it takes both parents to raise healthy children, but somebody has got to be there with the kids and somebody has got to work, and I know housework is work, but I mean work for money. I think some people aren't prepared for raising kids and maintaining a career. The important thing is to talk it over BEFORE [his emphasis] you have kids.

This shows a certain sensitivity to the woman's life and her interests, even if the general preference is the conventional nuclear family model of a husband and wife with 2.5 children and a husband who works outside the home. Still, I did not encounter the "barefoot and pregnant" attitude that some writers seemingly imply. For many men, involvement with PK has brought them closer to their families, in deed as well as in thought.

> There was time when I was doing that, just going home and watching TV. My wife and I spend a lot more time talking now, because once you realize how far apart you are, and how far you have to go ... it just hit me when I was with my brothers [at the stadium conference] and man, I just broke into tears when I realized that I have not been responsible in my marriage the way God intends. One of the best things they [the Promise Keepers] ever did for me, and it might

sound silly, but it was just to turn off the TV. But you have to want to change, or you can find a whole bunch of ways to escape dealing with important things and escape talking to your wife.

I was on the wrong side for a long time. Before I got involved with the Promise Keepers, I would yell and swear at my wife, I would ignore my son, who lives in California, I would get belligerent at work and with customers. I started drinking more; man, I was just lost. My behavior wasn't in a godly image, and it wasn't even practical. It definitely brought me closer to my wife, and I got myself into counseling to control my anger, because the Promise Keepers helped me to see how important and precious my family is.

The wife of one man said:

> For the first time in years, we went on a vacation, just the two of us, and [name deleted] was really enjoyable company. I'm glad he started going to the conferences, because it definitely made him a better person. Before he went the first time, I thought it would be another boys' club type thing; I was skeptical, because I thought it would be another excuse to get out of the house and sit around with the boys, but it has really helped our relationship.

In what ways?

> Like we do things together, even just going to McDonald's is nice because we actually talk to each other, about how we feel, about our hopes for our children. And as far as the children go, [name deleted] has made a real effort to talk with them and spend time together. We definitely do things more as a family, and as I think back, I don't know if we ever really had that from the beginning. Since my husband has been going to the Promise Keepers, we have both been more aware of our problems, and how to deal with them.

Through all the interviews, the testimony reinforces over and over that the Promise Keepers inspired the men basically to sit down with their wives, to deal with problems and, especially, to accept humility. As one man put it:

> If you can admit to your wife, "I was wrong," this is different than saying, "Well I guess you're right." The Promise Keepers have taught me that humility is important. Men need to say "I was wrong" when they're wrong and accept that responsibility. Sometimes, and it might be embarrassing, but sometimes your kids might be right, and you need to say to them the same way, "You're right, and I was wrong." If you aren't honest to yourself, and honest with your family, and admit your faults, that kind of pride will bring you down.

These factors construct a family man servant-leader, and the men ascribe various and diverse interpretations to the notion of the man as the household "head," "leader," or "decision-maker":

> Leader of the family just means that you take responsibility, that you consider what your wife and children need ... it doesn't mean you do whatever you want and it's not about giving orders.... Sometimes you have to tell your kids what to do, but that's because they look up to you and you need to be there to provide guidance ... so it's not about orders, but about responsibility.

Honesty, humility and responsibility are certainly important in a relationship, but how much leeway should a person have? What about intimate decisions, when a person holds very different views, the premise for which is a different moral system? What about a woman's right to choose an abortion? All agreed that abortion is a sin and, really "when you think about it, it's murder," although some also distinguished between "killing an unborn child" and "murdering" an unborn child. On this issue, they are decidedly conservative, yet aside from the distinction mentioned, they also show ambivalence to an extent:

> I'm against abortion, but I also understand how difficult it is to carry a child to term because my wife just had a baby, and I at least have an idea of what it's like to carry a child to term, but I don't pretend to really know what it feels like, but it can be tough. So when I hear someone say that a woman who has been raped should still have her child, I want to tell that person, "Why don't you try carrying her child full-term!"

Ambivalence in this sense refers sociologically to the tendency to feel different and often opposing emotions about some issue or experience. This often manifests as the inability to formulate an exact position, but true ambivalence refers to conflict within a person at the level of character disposition, rather than simply the failure to make a decision.

Along with abortion, homosexuality is one of the most significant issues for the men. Overwhelmingly, they see it as a misguided or a "bad choice," or something somebody might do for fun to experiment with something different. It's important to understand that the men view the world through scripture, and although they acknowledge scripture can be contradictory at times, they say it also has clear prohibitions of certain beliefs and behaviors—one of which is homosexuality:

> Yes, I think homosexuality is a sin, and I think most Christians in their hearts know it is too. But if they [gays] want to be part of the

5. Are Promises Enough?

> Promise Keepers, or to be a Christian, then I have no problem with that. Everybody sins and that is one they have to deal with but I have my sins too. Everybody sins... Jesus Christ is the only man without sin. You know, I believe that God created men and women to love one another and to join through marriage, but gosh, I'm not perfect so who am I to judge somebody else?

I asked, "How would you feel if an openly gay teacher was instructing your child?" and was told by one man, after he asked for clarification:

> I have no problem with it if they're teaching, let's say, math or science or something. I don't think they should talk about sexuality, but parents have the responsibility of teaching their children about sex, so I would say that it's inappropriate for schools to teach sex education anyway.

None of the men advocated that society persecute gays or bar them from employment. They generally expressed sympathy for the "sinners." Again, even though the PK men condemn homosexuality, they also acknowledge their own sins and are not willing to judge others, much less advocate discrimination or persecution. In fact, the PK men I interviewed overwhelmingly expressed a distaste, if not outright rejection, of attempts to politicize Christian morality.

The mass media often seem to assume a friendly collusion between all Protestant organizations, regardless of their focus or orientation. So I asked the men about organizations such as the Christian Coalition or Moral Majority. As one man said:

> If we take abortion again, I know the Christian Coalition and Operation Rescue think abortion is a sin, so to an extent I support them, but still, you've got to be really careful trying to turn Christian values into political action. There's a couple of reasons why I am not comfortable with it. One is that you have to enter the political arena, which is full of power games and dishonesty, and so on. The other reason is related to that, because it means you have to lower yourself to their tactics, and you can see it with Operation Rescue. I saw on the news once this Operation Rescue woman holding up a fetus in a glass jar. If she really believes this is one of God's children that was murdered, why was she displaying it like that? What I mean is you start to get into dirty tactics to make your point, and then you start to degrade yourself and to offend God.... One thing I like about the Promise Keepers is they go to great lengths to not take political stands.

Another man said that he didn't like the Christian Coalition because it takes an issue and "run with it until you lose track of why the issue was important in the first place." In general, the interviews show that the men believe that politics involves corruption and power, and a Christian will eventually become corrupted and power hungry if he participates long enough. Moreover, I think the men's dislike for politics comes from their faith being a matter of personal conversion and commitment; it is not something that should be institutionalized. As mentioned, for the most part, their faith and their involvement with the Promise Keepers resides in their small groups, and their personal relationship with God. The mass conferences are only a means of getting men together. Albeit in brief, I have presented a sketch of what the PK men believe in their daily lives. How they construct meaning and order brings us to our analytical categories and the question of authoritarianism.

ANALYSIS

As mentioned, I did not choose authoritarianism capriciously, but because, as a theory, it addresses issues that seem central to understanding who the men are and how they see the world. Fromm ([1973] 1994, [1970] 1996, [1941] 1994, 1936) creates a basic distinction between the authoritarian character and the anti-authoritarian, or productive, character. The former demonstrates suspicion towards anything unfamiliar, a predilection for rigid and dogmatic views, usually expressed in terms of morality, and hostility or aggression towards anyone who deviates from this rigid moral code. The productive character exhibits curiosity, critical awareness, a patience and desire to "explore" the world's complexities, and tolerance for different opinions and lifestyles. The productive character may also actively struggle to change the world so as to improve conditions for people beyond his-/herself or reference group, whereas the authoritarian struggles to preserve the status quo (conventionalism), or only to benefit his/her own reference group. Overall, the authoritarian submits to anyone or anything perceived as more powerful and therefore superior, and dominates anyone or anything perceived as weaker and therefore inferior. So long as relationships are seen as a matter of stronger or weaker, authoritarians see hierarchy as the most meaningful social order, and equality as nonsensical, if not contemptible. It is important to keep in mind that these are tendencies, not absolutes, and most people exhibit a combination of authoritarian and anti-authoritarian characteristics.

Promise Keepers men embody a moderate level of conventionalism. As detailed above, they have a fixed notion of what constitutes a proper family, and any deviation, such as same-sex relationships, or sex outside of marriage, is considered sinful. However, they do not show tendencies toward authoritarian aggression, which we might expect to manifest as a desire to limit legally same-sex marriages or lobby for other legal constraints on personal decisions (such as the right to choose an abortion). Still, given their dislike of turning what they see as religious (and therefore personal) issues into a political agenda, they would not necessarily vote based on moral issues. The men are also hesitant to judge other people, and in this respect show tolerance. After all, the conversion to a godly life, to live the life of Christ is, in accordance with their Protestant foundation, a matter of personal conversion. A believer may bring the Word to other people, but conversion must be sincere, from the heart. Thus, compelling people to live a certain way that is not sincere avails nothing.

Often, the notion of authoritarian conventionalism includes a tendency to view people in terms of two groups—us and them. This tendency is present, as in the following:

> For some people, it might be hard for them to understand why we live our life the way we do, and why all of us go to the stadiums in search of Christ, and why we go to church. I think if a person doesn't understand, it's because they have not let Jesus Christ into their hearts, but I also think that God calls all men, and he has a purpose for all of us.

The division is clearly neither rigid nor absolute, but they still draw a line between the saved and the damned. Certain lifestyles, especially homosexuality, are not acceptable, although the men universally expressed concern for, rather than hostility against, gay men. This shows a degree of tolerance, yet it is blunted by the belief that homosexuality is "wrong" and a sin. The result is ambivalence, though perhaps leaning towards tolerance.

We also see here the presence of anti-authoritarian tendencies, that all men (and some made a point of saying that women are also called) should live the life of Christ. So, some people are saved and others are not, but the possibility of salvation exists for everyone. Those outside will not understand until they "surrender themselves to the Lord." Thus God calls for submission, and a degree of obedience, but He also helps us in return and guides us to a better life and salvation hereafter. He is a benevolent master and our relationship with Him is reciprocal. The men derive both inspiration for productive action, such as getting closer to their families in sincere ways, and the sense of certainty that submission to a perceived superior power provides.

This introduces the possibility of authoritarian submission. The call to "submit" and "surrender" to Christ permeates PK rhetoric (analyzed elsewhere in this volume) and appeared repeatedly during both conferences I attended. The men spoke of their own faith in similar terms, yet also expressed the notion that surrender will "fill you with the joy of the Lord" and "He will guide you through life on the path He has chosen." At the same time, the men are not overly mystical or simply submissive, simply waiting for a leader to deliver the orders:

> Once Jesus comes into your life, you can do all those things you wanted to do, but you've got to be willing to accept that motivation and purpose. God doesn't lift your hands, or activate your mind; He just provides the ability and the opportunity, but you've got to recognize it and act on it.

Authoritarian submission necessitates that the follower perceive something as superior in an ultimate or supernatural sense, before which a person can only bow down in submission. This "power" may be a real person, an inanimate object, or even an idea such as the nation, the flag, the cause, and so on. In all cases, the "power" is socially constructed, in that its supernatural qualities, above and beyond any real qualities, exist in the minds of the believers, and they submit accordingly. For example, the men in general think highly of Bill McCartney, but all see him as still a man and they do not idolize him:

> I think he's a great man, a man chosen by God. One thing that's interesting is that God didn't choose someone like Jerry Falwell, and He didn't choose Jimmy Swaggert, but in His divine wisdom He chose Coach McCartney.

Others saw Bill McCartney on a more mundane level:

> He's a tremendous organizer, but I don't think he was ready to handle the kind of pressure that you get when you organize something on a national level, especially something like the Promise Keepers, that grew so rapidly. In my own experience, I have been discouraged by all the egotism that developed, and I don't think Bill was ready for that.

In this testimony, we see that McCartney is perceived as skilled in some areas, but also fallible, a mixture of real human qualities. Another man expressed his opinion of McCartney similarly, although with emphasis on a different fallibility:

> Bill McCartney is a football coach, and he talks like it and thinks like it.... I don't think he really considers what the ramifications of what he says will be—he's just like, "Let's get these guys together, and then let's get these type of guys together," and so on. He's trying to do too much, and it's becoming unfocused.

Bill McCartney is, then, a leader—and even a great leader—but still just a man. One of the respondents said: "But eventually I think the Promise Keepers will exist as a network of local accountability groups and men's ministries in local parishes. There probably won't be the big assemblies anymore, so I imagine that Coach will go on to something else." The men in general see McCartney as a great organizer, but not as a spiritual leader.

Just as authoritarian submission requires the component of the superior force, and the exclusiveness of "us" versus "them," it also evokes an evil counterpart to the moral defenders (us)—the Evil Them—the moral violators. The desire to persecute moral violators and "the weak" forms the basis of authoritarian hostility and aggression. But none of the men called for persecution or even restrictions on gay men. Although they condemn the gay lifestyle, they have nothing against gay men as people. This fairly moderate attitude does not suggest the presence of strong authoritarian aggression, and it follows logically from the fact that the men don't see McCartney as an infallible and absolute master. Similarly, they do not see anyone or any grouop as an evil and absolute threat. I found some reservations (see also Allen, this volume) and misconceptions about the mass media (but see Claussen, 1996; Claussen, this volume; Waters, this volume), expressed as follows, when I asked: why do you think the media so readily misrepresents the Promise Keepers?

> I think it's a combination of things. Most reporters don't really understand what a godly life is about, or why someone would devote their life to Christ. I think a lot of reporters are raised or educated on the East Coast, or on the West Coast, and they don't really know what's going on outside their own circles of contacts.

(In fact, most reporters were not raised or educated on the East or West coasts [Weaver & Wilhoit, 1996].) I also asked: do you think they have their own agenda?

> No, I mean other than selling newspapers, no. It's a sad state of affairs today, but it seems like people are most interested in scandal and sensationalism.

The most absolute view that I encountered concerned the theory of evolution, which one man said he was very familiar with because his degree was in biology. He believes "there is no proof that evolution is true. I mean, if somebody could bring proof forward and show me, then I might believe it but, until then, I can't accept it." I asked: If there is not evidence, why do you think it's so widely taught?

> I think teachers either don't believe in the Word of God anymore, or they're not allowed to teach creationism. I understand that to an extent, because they need scientific proof that you don't get with faith but, if you did, I guess it wouldn't be faith anymore [smiles]. So, there are probably different reasons, depending on which school or area of the country we're talking about.

Again, we do not see evidence of one-sided authoritarian tendencies, but rather a mixture of tendencies, both for and against. Knowledge is seen as a matter of faith, but also, knowledge requires evidence. Society may have forces, such as the media and education, that work against a Christian, but not for conspiratorial reasons. Instead, various personal beliefs and formal rules come into play. The media, the educational system, and other institutions are not inherently evil, but perhaps beholden to non-Christian values. As one man said, " If a person pursues money and power, you can be sure the truth will not be told unless it makes money or brings them power." This suggests an awareness of real-world problems and relationships as opposed to a reliance on supernatural explanations.

One strongly anti-authoritarian theme stands out markedly. All the men embrace the notion of "racial reconciliation," that men of all races must put aside their racist beliefs and come together under the Lord. At the Kansas City conference, one speaker urged the men:

> It is not enough to tolerate men of other races; we must embrace our brothers of all races, and challenge racism wherever you encounter it. It is not enough to simply avoid racist jokes, but you must challenge those who laugh at racism, and tell them they are violating the gospel, they are violating the Word of the Lord. This might mean that you will have to intrude on their comfort zone, but this is serious business.

I read this statement to the men, and they all agreed that it was a good idea. One man worked as a volunteer in the inner-city for three years after he retired from a tire business, and told me:

> It was difficult sometimes, because you see all these young people in trouble with drugs or violence, and it breaks your heart to go back there day after day and see the poverty and the violence. Satan is having a field day in our inner cities, and we need to stand with our black brothers to end this suffering. I'll tell you this, though, that was some of the most satisfying work I have ever done, because you can see people light up with the hope that the days ahead will be better. We've got to make some real changes to end Satan's rule in our inner cities.

Even though the respondent expresses his perceptions of poverty, violence and other social problems in terms of "Satan," and he literally believes that Satan is responsible, he believes the solution lies in our actions, in what we do as a society.

Another man used the old adage that "faith without works is dead" and that social problems require a social solution through human action (although the knowledge and inspiration come from God). Furthermore, racism is a barrier created by men that prevents us from solving problems and drawing nearer to God, so it's time for men to unmake racism. The problem involves both a moral/spiritual choice, and a will to take action against harm to others, both a personal and social problem.

Another distinctly anti-authoritarian trend relates to the willingness to perpetrate violence or aggression. When asked if there is anything a man should be willing to fight for, none of the men provided an immediate answer, and many could cite no particular cause that warranted violence or aggression in all cases. More commonly, I found the men reluctant to use violence:

> That's a tough question, because killing is a huge step. If you kill someone, they're gone, and I think each person you kill must take a little bit of you with him. The Bible says Thou Shalt not Kill. I suppose I could defend myself with violence if necessary but to march off and kill somebody, I really don't know if I would be able to do that.

Although the respondent is concerned about violating a higher commandment, he also notes that violence is dehumanizing and, eventually, a person may lose all human emotion and sensitivity. In any case, the stakes are high when it comes to taking another life and the men were not eager to do so, nor could they readily think of a reason when it would be appropriate.

I asked: What about spanking children or other forms of corporal punishment?

> You have to be real careful about that. Let's say, for example, that I see my youngest son [age 8] hitting another child in an aggressive way, or for selfish reasons. In that case, I think a spanking would be helpful to show him, "Well, how do you like getting hit?" It's important, though, to talk through why he got the spanking. Physical punishment is always wrong if the parents do it because they don't want to bother with a more appropriate punishment, and by that I mean one that fits the crime, so to speak. If a child tells a lie, he doesn't deserve to be hit, but the parents should expose the lie, and take the time to show how lying can hurt other people, and how it diminishes your character.

Many of the men made similar statements, although several also said they never hit their children. One man said that "the ability to inflict pain means that you have power over someone, and you must be extremely careful how you use it." On this issue, the men seem to be struggling with a willingness to think through conventional beliefs, yet only incrementally. They do not totally abandon the conventional wisdom of "spare the rod, spoil the child" but they do not automatically view the parent as right and perfect compared with the child. I asked, What are the most important values that children should learn? The following represents a typical answer:

> They should learn honesty, the ability to be humble, to be generous, to walk with Jesus, and they should learn to laugh and enjoy life. I hope that parents, including myself, will work harder so their children feel free to laugh.

None of the men mentioned discipline, respect, obedience, or anything of the sort. The closest answer was "to recognize Jesus Christ as the savior and accept His purpose for you," but otherwise the men seem rather mild-mannered. Overall they expressed the notion, in various ways, that controlling anger and finding non-destructive outlets for frustration is crucial to living a life pleasing to God. The PKs are not Puritans, even though they are against sex outside of marriage. Life is something to enjoy but, as with most things, best in moderation.

Conclusions

Overall, my interviews suggest that the Promise Keepers are low in the area of authoritarian aggression and submission, while low to moderate in the area of conventionalism. The ramifications of these findings are important. The men also exhibit productive tendencies, and at least accept that the model nuclear family they seek may not be realistic and certainly not the fantasy from *Leave It to Beaver*. In any case, they are willing to examine critically their own lives, and make changes in accordance with the needs and feelings of their families. They vacillate between the security of formulaic conventionalism, and the need for personal growth.

First, this is not virulent movement that threatens the rights of others. Nor does it seem likely that the PK constituency would join with the Christian Coalition or other similar groups that more aggressively condemn nonconventional lifestyles and seek to shape policy using (fundamentalist and intolerant) versions of Christian values. Neither the Promise Keepers leadership nor enthusiasts want to politicize the movement, because the call is to revive faith within the hearts of men, not to enact policy as a means to force morality on others.

Second, I learned that meeting in small groups within the local parish or community is one of the most important aspects of being a Promise Keeper, and these accountability groups are nothing new. In this light, Promise Keepers appears far less extremist and more a revival of tradition. This is not a fundamentalist revival, but a movement of middle-class men with middle-class sensibilities—everything in moderation. Their faith is central to their lives but they are not willing to persecute or in other ways attack other people in the name of faith. Faith provides the inspiration to deal with the tasks of the day, not to attack others.

Third, the movement contains many positive and humanitarian aspects, so I am forced to agree with the self-proclaimed "lesbian leftie" Suzanne Pharr (1996, p. 29), who concluded that "the Promise Keepers are not the patriarchal monsters we thought they were." This does not excuse any troubling patriarchal elements, but neither do the men want mindlessly to dominate their families.

The PK men I interviewed hold moderately conservative views because their underlying character, though it evidences an ambivalent disposition as a result of conflicting values, has productive tendencies that override authoritarian tendencies. They are moderate because their character directs them away from extremism. They would not likely be receptive to aggressive doctrine that condemned some group or sought to control the lives of others. Unless the men were to experience a sudden and considerable economic decline with little hope of improvement, any residing authoritarian tendencies will likely remain in the background.

References

Adorno, T., Frenkel-Brunswik, E., Levinson, D.J., & Sanford, R.N. (1950). *The authoritarian personality.* New York: Norton Company.

Altemeyer, B. (1981). *Right-wing authoritarianism.* Winnipeg: University of Manitoba Press.

Altemeyer, B. (1988). *Enemies of freedom: understanding right-wing authoritarianism.* San Francisco: Bass Publishers.

Altemeyer, B. (1997). *The authoritarian specter.* Cambridge, MA: Harvard University Press.

Beal, B., & Gray, J. (1995). *Bill McCartney and the Promise Keepers: Exploring the connections among sport, Christianity, and masculinity.* Paper presented at the annual meeting of the American Alliance for Health, Physical Education, Recreation, and Dance, Portland, OR.

Claussen, D.S. (1996). *United States print mass media coverage of two men's movements: Robert Bly, Iron John, and the mythopoets, and Bill McCartney and the Promise Keepers.* Unpublished master's thesis, Kansas State University, Manhattan.

Coakley, J. (1993). *The Promise Keepers national men's conference: The cutting edge?* Unpublished manuscript, University of Colorado at Colorado Springs.

Connell, R.W. (1994). Psychoanalysis on masculinity. In Brod, H., & Kaufman, M. (eds.), *Theorizing masculinities.* Thousand Oaks, CA: Sage Publications.

Diamond, S. (1995, December). The new man: The Promise Keepers are on the road to stardom. *Z Magazine,* 16–18.

Eysenck, H.J. (1954). *The psychology of politics.* London: Routledge and Kegan.

Eysenck, H.J., & Coulter, T.T. (1972). The personality and attitudes of working-class British communists and fascists. *Journal of Social Psychology 87,* 59–73.

Eysenck, H.J., & Wilson, G.D. (1978). *The psychological basis of ideology.* Lancaster, England: MTP Press.

Fromm, E. (1936). Sozial-Psychologischer Teil. *Studien über Authorität und Familie.* Paris: Alcan.

Fromm, E. (1994 [1941]). *Escape from freedom.* New York: Henry Holt and Co.

Fromm, E. (1994 [1973]). *The anatomy of human destructiveness.* New York: Henry Holt and Co.

Fromm, E., & Maccoby, M. (1996 [1970]). *Social character in a Mexican village.* New Brunswick, NJ: Transaction Publishers.

Gilbreath, E. (1995, February 6). At awakening: Promise Keepers' ambitious agenda for transforming Christian men. *Christianity Today,* 21–28.

Hagendoorn, A., & Janssen, J. (1983). *Turn to the right.* Ambo, Netherlands: Baarn.

Hall, D.E. (ed.)(1994). *Muscular Christianity: Embodying the Victorian age.* New York: Cambridge University Press.

Kimmel, M.S. (1996a). *Manhood in America: A Cultural History.* New York: The Free Press.

Kimmel, M.S. (1996b, March-April). The struggle for men's souls. *Tikkun 11*(2), 15–17.

Lederer, G. (1993). Authoritarianism in German adolescents: Trends and cross-cultural comparisons. In *Strength and weakness: The authoritarian personality today.* New York: Springer-Verlag.

McCracken, G. (1988). *The long interview.* Newbury Park, CA: Sage Publications.

Meloen, J.D. (1993). The F-scale as a predictor of fascism: An overview of 40 years of authoritarianism research. In *Strength and weakness: The authoritarian personality today.* New York: Springer Verlag.

Meloen, J.D. and Middendorp, C.P. (1991). Authoritarianism in the Netherlands: The empirical distribution in the population and its relation to theories on authoritarianism. *Politics and the individual 1*(2), 49–71.

Meloen, J.D., Hagendoorn, L., Raaijmakers, Q., & Visser, L. (1988). Authoritarianism and the revival of political racism: Reassessments in the Netherlands of the reliability and validity of the concept of authoritarianism by Adorno et al. *Political Psychology 9,* 413–429.

Messner, M. (1997). *The politics of masculinity: Men in movements.* Thousand Oaks, CA: Sage Publications.

Minkowitz, D. (1995, November-December). In the name of the father. *Ms. Magazine,* 64–71.

Mishler, E.G. (1986). *Research interviewing: Context and narrative.* Cambridge, MA. Harvard University Press.

Neuman, W.L. (1994). *Social research methods: Qualitative and quantitative approaches.* Boston: Allyn and Bacon.

Pharr, S. (1996, August). A match made in heaven. *The Progressive 60* (8), 28–30.
Raaijmakers, Q., Meeus, W., & Vollebergh, W. (1985). Extreme political views of high school students. *Transcripts of the First Dutch Conference of Political Psychology*. Nijmegen, Netherlands.
Sahagun, L. (1995, July 6). Christian men's movement taps into identity crisis. *The Los Angeles Times*, p. A1.
Schatzman, L., & Strauss, A.L. (1973). *Field research: Strategies for a natural sociology*. Englewood Cliffs, NJ: Prentice Hall.
Shapiro, J.P. (1995, October 2). Heavenly promises. *U.S. News and World Report 119*(13), 68–70.
Van Biema, D. (1995, November 6). Full of promise. *Time*, 62–63.
Weaver, D.H., & Wilhoit, G.C. (1996). *The American journalist in the 1990s: U.S. news people at the end of an era*. Mahwah, NJ: Lawrence Erlbaum Associates.

CHAPTER 6

Sacred Male Space: The Promise Keepers as a Community of Resistance

by Don Deardorff

Promise Keepers—though often referred to as "weekend weepers" by both supporters and detractors—are seen by many Americans as the dangerous, extreme right wing of the nation's burgeoning men's movements. Feminists quickly condemned the organization as a patriarchal group of reactionaries bent on preserving traditional family structures and gender roles that reaffirm male power and female submission. Novosad (1996) wrote that PK espouses a "vision of a radical Christian patriarchy," which exhorts men "to reassert male dominance in the family" and "to take their rightful place as society's leaders." Noted sociologist Kimmel (1997) calls the movement "the Second Coming of patriarchy," which "excludes women and gay men and lesbians from the table of humanity" in a way that is reminiscent of past "repressive and censorious voices of theocratic authoritarianism." Theologian Swomley (1996) admits that PK makes a strong case for the biblical argument against racism, but adds that "when laudable teachings on racism are mixed with reactionary teachings about women, gays, and sexuality, the result is less than laudable." Even Christian feminists such as van Leeuwen (1997a) have retained a healthy degree of skepticism. She recognizes the need for a men's movement and is especially amenable to one that is Christian in nature. But she accuses PK of practicing a "soft patriarchy," one that generally works for the betterment of women to some degree, but which ultimately supports male ascendancy. While critics remain watchful of this increasingly powerful band of Christian knights, it is perhaps a bit too early to pass judgment.

PK men see themselves as harbingers of the word of God, men who have the ultimate answers for all that ails the American male. They promise to recommit men to their wives and families, establish spiritual healing among men who have strayed from the laws of God, heal the wounds of racism in a nation with a bleak racial history, and much else. And PK is a young organization with ambitious goals and several noble intentions.

Between these two opposing interpretations of PK, what seems clear to me is that most men join not for nefarious reasons, but because they see the organization as a refuge, a place where they can cope with alienation that they feel on several fronts. PK gives American men what they have not had in a long time, if ever: a supportive community in which they can resist harmful stereotypes, outdated myths and traditions, confusing new mores, spiritual isolation and neglect, and both subtle and overt forms of discrimination. For most members, it is a place of safety, hope and empowerment. The question is whether or not the group can transcend its white, male, middle-class roots, and bear fruit for men and women of divergent backgrounds and beliefs.

An Ignominious History

Ritualized resistance has always been the male way of coping with fear and alienation precipitated by cultural changes. The problem is that rarely has it been a noble resistance. Instead, men's groups have traditionally sought to deal with change in a reactionary manner designed to bolster masculine hegemony, to retrench male power in a way that accommodated new political or social realities. This process has left an understandable legacy of distrust and paranoia regarding male organizations and movements. For instance, historian E. Anthony Rotundo (1993) recounts men's late-18th century transition from a masculine identity based on community and family service to one based on individual conquest in the capitalist marketplace. As the industrial revolution slowly forced men away from the family farm toward the industrial workplace, the dominant notion of manhood was reconfigured to fit the new economic conditions. Manhood had existed in the embodiment of what Rotundo calls the "community man," a man who functioned as the spiritual leader of an agrarian family unit that was largely self-sufficient and, though clearly deferent to its patriarchal leader, was quite egalitarian in the sense that each family member played a vital role in sustaining prosperity. Yet, in the late 18th century "men were using manliness with new meanings, [and] they were creating a new society based on the free expression of traditional manly passions—assertiveness, ambition, avarice, lust for power. The forces of community and tradition failed in their struggle to contain personal ambition, and the claims of the individual self appeared in all realms of a man's life with growing legitimacy." This new masculine individualism allowed men to adapt male needs and values to a new economic context, but its maintenance had dire consequences for women. As husbands became the chief breadwinners, wives lost their role as partners within a stable family unit as well as any chance to define the rules and regulations of the fast expanding professional world their husbands were entering. Instead, they became the exclusive caretakers of the home. Their function was no longer economic, but moral. They existed as caretakers for the state and guardians of the masculinity of the men who would run that state. As Rotundo writes, "By preserving the sense of common social virtue, women were allowing men to pursue self-interest. The new, moral womanhood made the new, individualistic manhood possible."

The years between 1880 and 1920 roughly mark another period of profound cultural change for men. For instance, mass production made men into interchangeable assemblers, resulting in a loss of individual identity through work. The closing of the western frontier symbolized an end to the rugged individualism that had characterized American manhood for more than a century. But the greatest threat, by far, to the American man was the American woman, who was beginning to move out of the home and into the workplace, the political arena, the athletic field, and leadership positions in the church. Clyde Griffin (Carnes & Griffin, 1990) writes that "the expanding demands of women created a confusing 'crisis in masculinity' which has yet to be resolved. By the turn of the century the New Woman's insistence on public recognition deprived men of their traditional role, and her assertiveness made them feel less manly."

The male response to these changes took several forms, but all of them had in common the desire for the creation of male space in which traditional masculinity could be maintained. For instance, cultural studies scholar Michael Oriard (1993) argued that football's popularity at the turn of the century can partly be attributed to masculine angst. He contends men used the gridiron as a sacred space in which to reestablish the idea that courage, grace under pressure, leadership, physical conquest and the ability to overcome adverse conditions were integral to a brand of masculinity essential to a nation that depended on male soldiers, captains of industry and heads of state. Crucial to football culture, of course, was that—while the men took center stage—the women cheered from the sidelines in the supporting role. Oriard writes, "Gender concerns played a major role in assuring football's acceptance despite its patent dangers. Without football, masculine anxiety might have been more acute. The outcry against football brutality was great, but concern over the possibility of an emasculated American manhood greater."

Another response involved male retreat into fraternal lodges, which grew at an unprecedented rate during the Victorian period. Social historian Carnes (1990) documented how men found comfort in lodges that reaffirmed male strength and models of leadership, and whose activities had important implications in the workplace. The fraternities, made up largely of middle-class white men who had the most to lose from decline of masculine privilege, had a powerful symbolic function: the removal of men from the female authority of the hearth and the recognition that only male brothers could properly nurture and advise other men. Carnes writes that young men were drawn to these orders, "where they repeatedly practiced rituals that effaced the religious values and emotional ties associated with women." Of course, the brotherhood also had an important economic function in that it promoted anti-female solidarity among professional men, and therefore helped exclude women from the workplace. It was not only paternal and fraternal connections that were cemented through ritual, but also business associations. As Carnes confirms, "By emphasizing a surrogate father's benevolence and love, the ritual made it easier for the initiate to identify with the masculine role; by accepting him into the family of patriarchs, the ritual enabled him to approach manhood with greater self-assurance."

Naturally, religion was another area in which men tried to reassert traditional gender roles. Though women had outnumbered men in the pews of America's churches since the Colonial era, men did not attempt to change radically the face of religion in the country until female influence in the nation's churches began to assert itself in the directions of temperance, women's suffrage, entrance into the work force and increased decision making within churches. In short, when women were no longer content to be the moral buttress of hegemonic masculinity, but were instead interested in using their positions in churches to become more equitable partners in American success, men began to organize male-only evangelical movements. As van Leeuwen (1997b) points out in an article called "Weeping Warriors," these new men's organizations were, to some degree, about energizing men spiritually. But, they also were, to a lesser degree, about stemming female power and bolstering male power, which, after all, was and is the cornerstone of hegemonic masculinity: "The male-directed religious campaigns of the early 1900s were thus a frank attempt to inject a counterdose of masculinity, suitably redefined for a corporate age, into a church life now perceived as overly effeminate and woman dominated." But van Leeuwen's (1997b) profile of the Men and Religion Forward Movement of 1911-12 as an organization that "promoted a kind of muscular, individualistic Christianity in response to men's loss of independence and accountability in the corporate world" is highly dubious. Gary Scott Smith (1987), for instance, has shown quite convincingly that MRFM was in fact a noble experiment whose main goal was to galvanize male support behind popular social reforms. Still, van Leeuwen's analysis underscores the fact that the legacy of such male movements, even when they have good intentions and results, is one characterized by mistrust. It is this legacy that Promise Keepers is forced to combat.

MEN IN CRISIS

While the history of men in groups certainly necessitates a healthy degree of skepticism regarding Promise Keepers, one point on which group members and their detractors can agree is that men have been and continue to be "in crisis." That is, their life experience in the postmodern world has left them with an acute sense of alienation. Some feel disdain for their jobs; some are isolated from their families; some are spiritually bankrupt; some are confused about their relationships with women; some feel trapped by social expectations or outdated myths and traditions; some feel distanced from themselves. The reasons for alienation may be complex and highly subjective, but the condition exists, and is perhaps the main reason for the existence and popularity of Promise Keepers.

One of the main causes of male confusion is that men can no longer rely on traditional roles to understand who they are and how they should behave. In many ways, this is a positive development. Men always have been conditioned to earn their manhood via an unhealthy objectification of woman as the "other" against whom man was to measure his masculinity. Sadly, men have never had any definition of what it means to be a man. Instead, they have accepted the vague notion that a man is someone who does the opposite of whatever a woman might do. A man could, for instance, display manliness by performing well as a sports star, military hero, sexual athlete, intellectual, adventurer, power broker, or in other roles that featured male achievement in a realm from which females were either excluded or allowed to function only as objects or as moral support.

It is comforting that these roles are crumbling. Sexual harassment suits are forcing men to behave better. Talented women athletes, courageous female soldiers and astronauts, and successful business women and brain surgeons have forced men to reevaluate what had been single gender arenas in which one proved one's manhood. Still, even positive change can be painful and disillusioning. Men have had to ask themselves what it means to be a man. Even honorable duties such as the breadwinner role seem to be disappearing as a way that men can gain a sense of manhood. Most wives and mothers now work outside the home, sometimes earning more than the husbands. As Samuel Osherson (1986) writes in *Finding Our Fathers*, "Today, when a wife goes to work, ... the man is less able to turn to traditional sex roles and expectations. He is often put back in touch with feelings of helplessness and powerlessness."

But what are men to do? Some men seek refuge in traditional masculine myths, but usually wind up confused when they begin to see how normative patriarchal codes, which they were told would make them strong men, actually sabotage their personal and family lives. For instance, in *No Less a Man: Masculinist Art in a Feminist Age*, Doug Robinson (1994) explains the dangers of the myth of the capitalist hero, the industrial conqueror who has financial and political power. He is "the strong, silent warrior who ignores pain ... suppresses emotion, stands alone ... in order to overcome impossible odds and rise from success to success." As Robinson points out, this ethos has allowed men to succeed in business, but its costs have far outweighed its benefits. Men are beginning to see the stupidity of sacrificing relationships with wives and children for material success, especially when the stress and work required to gain that success leads to a significantly shorter, less fulfilling life. Men are recognizing that the hero myth "remains one of the most dehumanizing aspects of capitalism," one in which "the typical modern hero dies in his 50s of a massive coronary." One of the main problems with the hero myth is that it fails to allow men to embrace anything that has feminine connotations. Because this includes child rearing or, indeed, any nurturing practice, it has estranged men from their families. Joe L. Dubbert (1979) confirms in *A Man's Place: Masculinity in Transition* that "it was not something 'respectable males' caught up in the masculinity syndrome would do voluntarily.... To men who operated out of the old stereotype, it was better not to get too close to children for fear of being unmanly." Finally, men are waking up to the fact that they have distanced themselves from the joys of rearing children for fear of being stigmatized as unmanly, and they are questioning why they have done this and what alternatives exist for them.

The lack of a single unified masculine myth is one of men's problems. "It [masculinity] has no essence, no central core" (Easthope, 1990). It is composed of several myths and models of manhood that are overtly contradictory and that are subtly pushed at men every day in films, television programs, songs, newspapers, magazines, novels and advertisements. Men are encouraged to be the athlete, the cowboy, the tough guy, the violent avenger, the law man, the lover, the wild man, the cynic, the new age man, the comic, the intellectual man of taste and the sensitive guy. Men can't possibly be all of these, but popular culture remains insistent that they try. More and more, men are recognizing that, in trying to play out these roles, they often wind up hurting themselves and others. In *The Masculine Mystique*, Andrew Kimbrell (1995) points to alarming statistics that show just how much this schizophrenic process hurts men. For instance, men may be the macho gender, but the result is that "men's life expectancy has dropped dramatically as compared with women's over the last several decades." Men may revel in their ability to conquer others, but the result is that men make up 94% of all prisoners in the United States, and are "victimized by violent crime at a 63% higher rate than women." Kimbrell notes that boys are eight times more likely than girls to suffer from hyperactivity and twice as likely to be diagnosed with autism. Men and boys are over-represented when it comes to committing suicide, experimenting with alcohol and drugs, flunking out of school, being homeless, losing custody of their children in divorce hearings and getting seriously injured on the job. Many men can relate to Kimbrell's sobering statistics because they see on the news every night the results of failed masculine templates. Many can relate because they see the results played out in their own lives.

Understanding the Power of the Promise Keepers

The question still remains as to what men can actually do about this dilemma. In the past, men and women were able to look toward religion when life became too complex to understand. However, postmodern philosophy—with its emphasis on an existence free of definitive meaning and a world that features multiple, ever-changing, purely subjective truths—has permeated American culture, causing many men to lose faith in conventional religion. Sam Keen (1992), men's spiritualist and author of the highly acclaimed *Fire in the Belly*, said, "In the sixties, we had a militant revival of this new age religion and we had a very reactionary group trying to preserve traditional American values. Now, you pick up a copy of *Common Ground* or its equivalent in any of the big cities and there are 400 listings of different kinds of spiritual options—everything from UFOs to crystals to Zen to different forms of meditation." Most of these spiritual options have not fulfilled men; they have not provided men with a supportive community with behavioral norms that address men's alienation. For many men, that is exactly what Promise Keepers has done.

Over the last 10 years, several scholars have attempted to explain the power of intentional communities to those who feel alienated from mainstream society. Laird Sandhill, a member of Missouri's Sandhill Farm for 18 years, writes, "Community gives people linked with other individuals the leverage to express themselves and find answers that make sense in a sustainable way" (Forsey, 1993). Sociologist Stuart Hall (1993) argues in *Resistance Through Rituals: Youth Subcultures in Post-War Britain* that communities provide a controlled space where those who feel marginalized by the dominant culture can negotiate an effective resistance to the confusion they experience within that culture's discourse. Hall refers to this community as a "theater of struggle," in which the subordinate class manufactures "a repertoire of strategies and responses—ways of coping as well as resisting" (1993). For many men, the main attraction of Promise Keepers is that it provides them with a community where being a man is valued and where the reality of male repression is taken seriously. As Kenneth Clatterbaugh (1997) confirms, one of the main premises of the group is that "it is tough to be a man, especially a Christian man. Christian men face not only the sexual temptations of a permissive society but they also face the risks of living in a society that is hostile to their Christian values." While it is true that the organization insists that men have failed God and their families, and thus are in dire need of change, it provides them with supportive male connections and friendships with which to make the much needed transformations. Indeed, the seventh covenant professed by the men who attended Washington's Stand in the Gap rally in October 1997 was, "We covenant by your grace to pursue vital relationships with a few other Godly men for the purpose of encouraging one another toward love and good deeds" (Promise Keepers, 1997). The second promise of the group calls upon each member to "pursue vital relationships with other men, understanding that I need brothers to keep my promises" (Clatterbaugh, 1997). Each member is encouraged to "go back to his own community and find a 'faith partner' with whom he can share his fears, sins and secrets. It is about men becoming accountable to one another and keeping their promises" (Clatterbaugh, 1997). As noted sociologist Michael Messner (1997) writes, "The sense of relief at being given permission—by thousands of other men, in the masculine environs of a football stadium—to relax one's masculine posturing with one's self and with other men appears to be a great draw for men who attend the Promise Keeper events." If, as communications researchers Julia T. Wood and Christopher Inman (1993) conclude, "Men, more than women, appear to regard practical help, mutual assistance, and companionship as bench marks of caring," it is not surprising that men who feel isolated from themselves and from other men find Promise Keepers to be a nurturing environment that gives them strength and confidence. As group member David Smith (1997) confirms, "It's like one big group therapy session. Men are free to express themselves because they know they won't be laughed at. They'll be supported by other men who are in the same boat. We have no other outlet."

Within this supportive community, many of men's deepest fears and doubts are addressed. For instance, men, as well as women, continue to question why life matters at all. What is the meaning of work and family? Why should I be a good person? Do our actions, good or bad, actually matter? Does life have an ultimate meaning? Much of postmodern thought says no. At best, a pluralistic society offers several equally viable "truths," most of which are constructed to carefully avoid declarations of absolute truth for fear of stepping on the beliefs of others. It seems to be fashionable to be in search of truth, but arrogant and dangerous to insist that one has found it. Still, as James Dittes (1985) contends, "To be masculine is to be spiritual." This condition has left men in search of the kind of transcendent meaning that organizations such as Promise Keepers provide.

As the Stand in the Gap rally began, the men were asked to meditate on the following Bible verse from 2 Chronicles, which was included in the program syllabus: "If my people, which are called by my name, shall humble themselves, and pray, and seek my face, and turn from their wicked ways; then will I hear from heaven, and will forgive their sin, and will heal their land" (Habecker, 1997). Implicit in this passage and many others like it that were recited by the throngs at the revival is the idea that an entity called God is omnipotent, has given humanity rules to live by, and will punish or reward an individual based on his or her ability to follow those rules. For the duration of a Promise Keepers rally, life is not random series of incomprehensible events, but is instead purposeful and understandable. Men are encouraged to repent of their sins, to accept Christ as the savior through whom they can gain forgiveness for their misdeeds, and to follow Christ's teachings about how to live on Earth. The fact that God has a purpose for the life of each man in attendance is vitally important to the rally's rhetoric. The men read in their manuals, "When men are cleansed they can be usable to God. All of us desire significance. Our hope is in God. Our future is His" (Habecker, 1997). Men not only find a purpose for their lives on Earth as servants of God who are supposed to use their talents for God's glory, but also see that an ultimate reward, entrance into Heaven, is received for committing one's life to Christ. With hundreds of thousands of men affirming the truth of this world view, the entire rally, like all PK functions, created a powerful text that reaffirmed the universe as a meaningful place, governed by the laws and grace of a divine ruler, in which these men could play a crucial part if they could only believe it. As Smith (1997) affirms: "If you were confused about your role as a man when you got there, you had to be sure by the time you left. This is an organization which encourages men to be strong, Christian men whose lives are dedicated to being Christ-like."

While reaching out to single men, PK is particularly concerned with addressing the needs of husbands and fathers. Specifically, the group seems to have the function of rescuing these men from the uncertainty of the male role within the contemporary marriage in a way that is tremendously empowering. Messner (1997) writes, "This assertion of men's responsibility to seize the reins of family leadership is a key to understanding the appeal of Promise Keepers to men." Indeed, men are told that God wants them to be strong leaders in their homes, both as financial breadwinners and as domestic caretakers. The group's fourth official promise is that its members will assume the responsibility of building "strong marriages and families through love, protection and biblical values" (Clatterbaugh, 1997). Biblical values are the key part of this because they are seen as representative of God's absolute truth. Society may leave men confused about what to do within the family unit, but PK uses the Bible to shatter that confusion with explicit dictates that leave no doubt in men's minds as to what is expected of them. For instance, Ephesians 5:22-29 is a staple at PK rallies: "Wives, submit to your husbands as to the Lord. For the husband is the head of the wife as Christ is the head of the church.... Husbands, love your wives as Christ loved the church and gave himself up for her to make her holy ... and blameless. In this same way, husbands ought to love their wives as their own bodies" (New International Version, 1984).

Critics argue that verses such as this one are merely excuses for reestablishing male power over women, but most group members take the words as a clear mandate for men to take responsibility for creating an atmosphere that empowers their wives and children. The fourth covenant at the Stand in the

Gap rally was, "We covenant by your grace to love and serve our wives and children; we commit to give them first priority in our prayers and schedules.... Where we have used our masculinity against others, we now commit to honor all women and value all human life through our words and our actions" (Promise Keepers, 1997). This is what many Promise Keepers attempt to do. Many contend that it has changed their lives, insisting that this type of leadership through humble servitude is doubly liberating. Not only does it give men a directive from on high about how to be husbands and fathers, but it also gives them an entirely new definition for manhood. Harmful notions of excessive competition, sexual conquest and self advancement are replaced by Christ-like characteristics of servanthood, self-sacrifice and humility.

Ironically, many men find strength and power in this new version of manhood. David Warren (1997), who attended the Stand in the Gap Rally but does not consider himself a "member" of Promise Keepers, says, "Many people think the organization is designed to make men dominant over women. That is clearly not the case. The emphasis is on mutual submission, on a softer version of manhood that allows men to be good servants to their wives. Many men find this very powerful. It can only be good for us." While some call the organization sexist, it is clear that most members believe they are doing their part to battle sexism by forging healthy definitions of masculinity.

If Promise Keepers encourages married men to believe that it is good for them to be strong leaders, it is equally adamant that all men, by following the teachings of Jesus Christ, can be noble, important servants of God on Earth, men who have dignity and purpose. In the face of so many relatively negative and disabling images of men in popular culture, the insistence that men can and should think of themselves positively is one of Promise Keepers' most important functions. Consider the disturbing picture of the American male found in even a cursory glance at popular television shows in the 1990s. Whether one watches Homer Simpson's ignorant and abusive parenting; Al Bundy's sexist, pubescent diatribes; Tim Taylor's childish obsession with power tools that he is, of course, too goofy to operate effectively; the boorish, selfish, inconsiderate nature of the male characters on shows such as *Men Behaving Badly*; or the outlandish immorality and stupidity of two outcasts named Beavis and Butthead, it is clear that men and boys have an image problem in contemporary America.

Recently, a few scholars have written about the negative side of male representations in popular culture. Roger Horrocks' *Male, Myths and Icons: Masculinity in Popular Culture* (1995), for instance, argues that if men aren't being portrayed as laughingstocks, they are cast as outcast heroes who can make sense of their world only through violence (*Rambo*), as outlaws whose warped sense of manhood forces them to prey on society because they cannot live within accepted mores and rules (*Goodfellas*), or as incompetent males who are so inept that they continually sabotage themselves and those they influence at every turn (*Four Weddings and a Funeral*).

Promise Keepers provides a space in which men can resist embodying these images. Within the boundaries of the organization, men don't have to feel as though they are stupid and somehow bereft of civility, but neither must they be the rugged individualist, the ultra-masculine hero who is out of touch with himself and society. As Smith (1997) says, "We were certainly forced to confront sin, but the emphasis was on the fact that we could be better, that we had to be because God expects that of men. Christ died for us because we have value and purpose." Not only does Promise Keepers provide a space for this kind of resistance, but it also provides a role model in Jesus Christ, whose actions are presented as being infallible and uplifting for all people. For instance, if men are portrayed as unreliable, weak perpetrators of crime, the PK men are encouraged to be spiritual warriors who pledge to "become men of integrity, relying on your word and Christ in us," so that "when faced with moral, ethical, and sexual temptations, we commit to ask you for help that we might do the right thing" (Promise Keepers, 1997). If men today are portrayed as violent beings who are out of step with healthy communities, PK men are encouraged to follow the commandments of Jesus, who told his disciples to turn the other cheek instead of seeking vengeance, to forgive instead of casting blame, to love one's enemy as well as one's neighbor, to prevent feuds, and to do unto others as one would have others do unto him.

In short, if contemporary culture suggests that men are the problem, PK suggests that men are also the solution. The power of this for PK men is astounding. Warren (1997) affirms that "while men have failed in the past, Promise Keepers insists that each man could and should be better because of his recommitment to Jesus Christ." Within PK, as long as one understands that being a man is tantamount to living out the Christly values of nonviolence and community service while boldly protecting one's family and community, it is good to be a man.

Not only is it good to be a man, it is good to be a man of any race or ethnicity. While the organization is still composed primarily of white, middle-class men, one of its main goals is to reach men of all races, many of whom labor not only under the general yoke of masculine instability discussed in this chapter, but who, because of their race, suffer under culturally specific masculine templates. For instance, in his book *Cool Pose: The Dilemmas of Black Manhood*, Richard Majors (1993) describes the "hard," often combative and uncaring attitude adopted by inner-city black males as a defense against racism and other environmental conditions that make prosperity a seemingly unattainable goal. Majors writes that the desire to be tough and prove one's manly worth in the face of this repressive culture leads to gang violence, crime and other activities that irrevocably damage these boys and men. PK has made a special effort to minister to minority males—to give them a masculine alternative. In 1997, for instance, the organization sponsored a four-day summit in which 100 Latin-American clergy and laity met with Promise Keepers administrators to facilitate Hispanic involvement in the organization. Other summits were held with Asian American, Native American, and African American religious leaders (Kennedy, 1997).

Though still few in number, some minority men are responding and finding in Promise Keepers the strength to redefine themselves in more positive terms or to cope with spiritual problems. Led by Chicago minister Raleigh Washington, minority representation on Promise Keepers' administrative team is now up to 30 percent. Washington has said, "We are seeing more men of color. There is a gradual increase, and we are now beginning to do some intentional things that are going to bring about even more of an increase" (Abraham, 1997). If the organization's commitment to help men of all races develop a healthy sense of masculinity is beginning to help minority men, its commitment to attack racism on all levels seems to be empowering white males, inspiring some to question their attitudes on race and to redirect their actions. Gregory Belliveau (1997), a professor of English who attended the rally with his father and brothers, was moved by the emphasis on racial healing: "There was a major emphasis on reconciliation. We were in diverse groups praying for forgiveness for our racism. African Americans, Asian Americans, Native Americans all praying to end racism. It wasn't just a bunch of white guys. It was men from all races, coming to grips with the racism in their lives. It was tremendously powerful." Promise Keepers set the ambitious goal of destroying racism in churches by the year 2000 when it planned to meet in Detroit for a second Stand in the Gap rally. By all admissions, it has a long way to go. But for many men, no matter what their racial or ethnic identity, PK is providing a refuge from unhealthy masculine paradigms and a way to heal past divisions.

Not only does Promise Keepers provide a forum in which its men can heal divisions with other men, the organization also acts as a powerful arena in which men confront their worst character flaws, termed sins, so that they can become stronger individuals with a higher sense of self-esteem. As mentioned, Promise Keepers commit to "spiritual, moral, ethical, and sexual purity" (Clatterbaugh, 1997). Anyone who watched the Stand in the Gap Rally on television saw hundreds of thousands of men lying prostrate on the ground, praying for forgiveness for their sins and for the strength to turn away from behavior that had hurt them, their families and communities. Sexism, racism, intolerance, anger, pride, alcoholism, neglect and selfishness were a few of the ills that were addressed by the rally's featured speakers. As a sign of their contrition and commitment to be better men, the men uttered in unison the following prayer (Habecker, 1997):

> God our father, we kneel before you guilty of sin. As a group, we have failed to reflect your glory to those in our families and to others around us. We have been preoccupied with our own concerns. We have ignored or even resented the needs of others.... We are not very good at owning up to sin. For so long we have practiced shifting the blame or denying reality. Today we stop! One by one, we acknowledge our sins before you. Each one of us has his own list of offenses before a holy God. We do not compare ourselves by our neighbor's standard, but by your standard. You said, "Be holy as I am holy." We invite your conviction in each area of our life. Not only will we address our sin, but we pledge to seek forgiveness and reconciliation with those we have sinned against. Amen.

As Warren (1997), professor of Biblical Studies at Cedarville College, said, "It reminded me of the Old Testament, where Jewish men were required to go to Jerusalem to repent and make sacrifices to the Lord. Those gatherings must have been similar to the Washington event in spirit. In both cases, it was nothing but repentance, praise and commitment." For many of the Promise Keepers, this atmosphere of repentance and redemption for the good of all is enough to inspire change. As Warren says of his experience, "It is a very powerful text. I was moved to address some of the flaws in my life, and I know of many men who say that the rally has helped them change for the better. I don't know how it could be anything other than positive."

Perhaps the greatest endorsement of the potential of Promise Keepers to help men be better men comes from Sandi Entner (1997), whose husband and sons are regular attendees of Promise Keepers events: "My sons loved it and felt a real impact. My one son can hardly express the changes it has made in his life in words. And, he's very wordy. It's been misconstrued by women who don't understand that loving leadership is a far cry from control."

Conclusion

The concept of resistance is hardly new. For centuries marginalized groups have used intentional communities nobly to resist their oppression. Of course, men who have held considerable power also have used such communities to resist cultural changes that, while liberating for marginalized groups, threatened their own power. Obviously, this type of masculine resistance inspired by fear is ignoble. Considering our penchant—not without some justification—for thinking of men as privileged and powerful, it is difficult for many Americans to understand why a group of modern men, especially one largely composed of white, middle-class men, needs such a community. To PK men, their organization is attractive primarily because it allows them to resist alienation that they feel on a number of levels. For them,

Promise Keepers does not have the nefarious, reactionary elements of past male refuges. Instead, the organization has the function of helping them combat negative images of men, discrimination against men, isolation from other men, women and themselves, personal problems (sin), racial and ethnic division, spiritual desiccation, and role confusion as husbands, fathers, friends and workers. Promise Keepers' effectiveness in the eyes of the organization's members seems beyond question. Ultimately, however, the question is this: Is this just another form of male resistance to threats against masculine privilege, or is this a movement inspired by God or, at least, by positive motivations that will help men redefine themselves in a manner that is beneficial not only for men, but for society in general? It is a young organization that, in early 1998, already faced serious financial difficulty. Only time will reveal its true character.

References

Abraham, K. (1997). *Who are the Promise Keepers? Understanding the Christian men's movement.* New York: Doubleday.

Belliveau, G.K. (1997, April 14). Personal communication.

Carnes, M., & Griffin, C. (1990). *Meanings for manhood: Constructions of masculinity in Victorian America.* Chicago: University of Chicago Press.

Clatterbaugh, K. (1997). *Contemporary perspectives on masculinity: men, women, and politics in modern society.* Boulder, CO: Westview Press.

Dittes, J. (1985). *The male predicament: On being a man today.* San Francisco: Harper & Row.

Dubbert, J.L. (1979). *A man's place: Masculinity in transition.* Englewood Cliffs, NJ: Prentice-Hall.

Easthope, A. (1990). *What a man's gotta do: The masculine myth in popular culture.* Boston: Hyman Books.

Entner, S. (1997, April 14). Personal communication.

Forsey, H. (1993). *Circles of struggle: Community alternatives to alienation.* Philadelphia: New Society Publishers.

Habecker, E.B. (1997). *Stand in the Gap: A sacred assembly of men.* Washington, DC: American Bible Society.

Hall, S. (1993). *Resistance through rituals: Youth sub-cultures in post war Britain.* London: Routledge.

Horrocks, R. (1995). *Male myths and icons: Masculinity in popular culture.* New York: St. Martin's.

Keen, S. (1992). *Fire in the belly.* New York: Bantam.

Kennedy, T., & Tapia, A. (1997, June 16). Candor, repentance, mark the PK Latino summit. *Christianity Today 41(7),* 58–59.

Kimbrell, A. (1995). *The masculine mystique.* New York: Ballantine Books.

Kimmel, M.S. (1997, March). Promise Keepers: patriarchy's second coming as masculine renewal. *Tikkun 12(2),* 46–53.

Majors, R. (1993). *Cool pose: The dilemma of black manhood.* New York: Simon & Schuster.

Messner, M. (1997). *The politics of masculinity: Men in movements.* Thousand Oaks, CA: Sage Publications.

New International Version Bible. (1984). Grand Rapids, MI: Zondervan Publishing House.

Novosad, N. (1996, August). God squad: The Promise Keepers fight for a man's world. *The Progressive 60(8),* 25–30.

Oriard, M. (1993). *Reading football: How the popular press created an American spectacle.* Chapel Hill, NC: University of North Carolina Press.

Osherson, S. (1986). *Finding our fathers: The unfinished business of manhood.* New York: Free Press.

Promise Keepers. (1997, November). *D.C. Covenant* (9 paragraphs). Promise Keepers Net. Available: http://www.promisekeepers.org/manual/sitg/covenant.htm.

Robinson, D. (1994). *No less a man: Masculinist art in a feminist age.* Bowling Green, OH: Bowling Green University Press.

Rotundo, E.A. (1993). *American Manhood: Transformations in masculinity from the revolution to the modern era.* New York: Basic Books.

Smith, D.R. (1997, April 15). Personal communication.

Smith, G.S. (1987). The Men and Religion Forward Movement, 1911–12: New perspectives on evangelical social concern and the relationship between Christianity and Progressivism. *Westminster Theological Journal 49,* 91–118.

Swomley, J. (1996, January). Promises we don't want kept (Watch on the Right). *The Humanist 56(1),* 35–38.

van Leeuwen, M.S. (1997a). Servanthood or soft patriarchy? A Christian feminist looks at the Promise Keepers movement. *The Journal of Men's Studies 5,* 233–259.

van Leeuwen, M.S. (1997b, November-December). Weeping warriors. *Books & Culture 12,* 9–11.

Warren, D. (1997, April 14) Personal communication.

Wood, J.T., & Inman, C.C. (1993). In a different mode: Masculine styles of communicating closeness. *Journal of Applied Communication Research 21,* 279–295.

Chapter 7

Promise Keepers and the Rhetoric of Recruitment: The Context, the Persona, and the Spectacle

by Michael E. Eidenmuller

The advent of the Promise Keepers represents one of the most remarkable chapters in the story of late 20th-century evangelicalism. Broadly conceived, PK is an uninstitutionalized, centrally-organized collectivity that has emerged to bring about a program of change over a sustained period of time. Its purpose responds to a profound sense of disease within the American social order, a sense that may be extended to include the problem of social fragmentation generally, and of religious fragmentation in particular.

PK's "vision" targets specifically audiences historically divided by religious preference, doctrinal orientation and liturgical custom. That PK has succeeded on a national level in procuring the allegiance of these audiences in the span of a few years is, by most accounts, phenomenal. And as with all movement phenomena, PK has relied extensively on rhetoric to attract and mobilize followers (Stewart et al., 1994). For the purposes of this chapter, rhetoric should be understood as those symbolic acts or processes by which disinterested audiences become partisan and divided audiences enter into substantial communion (Burke, 1969). This definition, while restrictive, is sufficient for the purposes of acounting for rhetorical phenomena discussed below. As Cheney (1991) and others have well shown, rhetoric remains an indispensable tool for inducing organizational allegiance within and across divergent interest communities.

The means by which PK moved from the status of "mere idea" to full-blown evangelical movement is this chapter's subject. More specifically, this chapter argues that the growth of PK, especially during its incipient stage, may be attributed to three rhetorical factors whose combination well served the movement organization's recruiting efforts. I begin by examining the geo-ideological context in which PK developed. Next, I discuss the role played by PK co-founder Bill McCartney's prior public persona in attracting recruits to PK. I then consider the significance of PK's signature recruiting vehicle, the stadium event. Finally, I offer some implications suggested by this analysis as regards the nature and function of evangelical rhetoric in a postmodern, fragmented society.

THE GEO-IDEOLOGICAL CONTEXT

Nestled in the foothills of the picturesque Rocky Mountains, Boulder is widely known as a culturally diverse and ideologically progressive community. The city is studded with numerous exhibits, galleries, coffeehouses, cafes, bistros and bed-and-breakfasts (Boulder Convention and Visitors Bureau, 1997). Boulder's inhabitants are relatively young, racially homogenous and affluent. The median age is 29, and the vast majority (90 percent) of Boulder's residents are white (Boulder Chamber of Commerce, 1997). The median Effective Buying Income (EBI) hovers around $30,000 (Boulder Chamber of Commerce, 1997).

Approximately one-third of Boulder's residents are students at the University of Colorado (or "CU"), the state's generally liberal, premier institution of higher education. The 1992 Colorado University Club Guide indicates that the campus has housed an impressive array of liberal, even radical, activist groups. Among these are CU World Citizens, Feminist Alliance, Lesbian/Bisexual/Gay/Community Alliance, Students for Sane Nuclear Policy and Students for Reproductive Freedom. All told, and in the words of one commentator, Boulder "has the look and feel of a European community, seemingly far removed from society's problems" (Teitcher, 1992, p. C-1).

While Boulder is understandably considered a community unto itself, it is also part of a larger geographical area known as the "front range." This area extends from Fort Collins in the north to Pueblo in the south, and encompasses the communities of Denver and Colorado Springs. Importantly, the communities comprising this area are home to some of evangelicalism's most powerful ministries and parachurch organizations. James Dobson's Focus on the Family ministry, the International Bible Society, Compassion International, Athletes in Action International, Youth for Christ and Navigators—to name just a few—are headquartered within 90 minutes' drive of Boulder. Indeed, more than 70 evangelical ministries are located in Colorado Springs alone.

Consequently, it is not unreasonable to speculate on the existence of a network of relationships, interpersonal and organizational, by which conservative religious ideology is channeled along the range and into Boulder. In a telephone conversation with me on May 20, 1998, PK national spokesperson

Steve Chavis confirmed that a loosely-knit personal network exists and probably did at the time of PK's advent. Chavis added that PK's early development was aided substantially by Dobson's radio ministry as well as by the contributions of individuals variously associated with evangelical organizations along the front range. Add to this the half dozen or so evangelical ministries located on CU campus proper and the several large evangelical churches located in Boulder itself, and one begins to suspect that the pigeonholing of the community as liberal is not so clear cut.

When asked how PK could possibly have started in a place such as Boulder, Chavis responded that it was "God's way of expressing his sense of irony." Alternatively, and God's humor notwithstanding, Boulder is part of a geoideological context uniquely situated in ways that favor the confluence of incompatible ideological interests. More strongly, the communities in and around Boulder form a curious—and potentially volatile—synthesis of liberal and religiously conservative elements, however uniformly progressive the surface image may appear.

As is often the case with small communities that contain relatively large universities, Boulder's identity is in no small part associated with (and reactive to) that of its university. One of the readily available sources for promoting a university's public identity is through its athletic programs. In 1982, the University of Colorado hired as head coach the unheralded Bill McCartney to rescue its football program from a decade of mediocrity. It was a decision that would prove catalytic in bringing to the surface the area's underlying ideological tensions.

The Persona of Bill McCartney

In retrospect, Bill McCartney was a fitting candidate to fill the role he was about to assume. Consistent with Boulder's profile, he was young, white and professionally ambitious. Yet, he made no secret of his evangelical religious convictions, or of his intent to make those convictions a part of his coaching practices. PK co-founder Dave Wardell (1997) said that McCartney publicly affirmed those convictions in no uncertain terms during his inaugural meeting with the Colorado Board of Regents. Specifically, McCartney declared that both his leadership and the program would be committed to the "lordship of Jesus Christ."

McCartney's early job performance was anything but promising. In his first three years, McCartney's teams lost three out of every four games they played. Supporters were quick to point out that the coach had been singularly responsible for improving the visibility and integrity of the program within Colorado. Player dropout rates were down and player graduation rates were up. Some local writers, however, initially circumspect in their criticism, began to question openly the priorities of a coach whose recruits were more notable for their religious character than for their athletic talent.

It was clear, then, from very early on in his tenure at Colorado, that McCartney was a perfect target for a particular kind of criticism whose rhetorical character was beginning to take the form of a tension between "private" religious conviction and "public" professional performance. McCartney felt the tension deeply. In his 1995 autobiography, he makes no secret of his desire to win the respect of his peers, his players and the community of Boulder. But he also desires to remain faithful to his religious convictions. His early years as Colorado coach were pivotal for McCartney, because they would foreshadow how his identities as college football coach and evangelical Christian would be managed in ways favorable to his recruiting purposes.

About this time, McCartney began focusing on the task of recruiting national-caliber athletic talent. During his years as an assistant football coach at the University of Michigan, McCartney often appealed to that program's long-standing tradition of excellence to win recruits (McCartney, 1995). CU's program had little to offer by comparison. As a result, McCartney was forced to consider alternative strategies to secure the commitment of potential candidates. The strategy he chose represented, in McCartney's (1995, pp. 192–193) own words, "a whole new perspective" on the business of recruiting:

> Colorado is a beautiful setting. The state, the community, the university, all beautiful. Yes, there's the reputation of being a "party school," but that's not so bad. There are lots of parties there. Lots of things to do. Lots going on. A fun place to play football and go to school. I sold those things: a fresh start, a revitalization. And I told these youngsters they could be a factor in turning the program around; in bringing it to another level.

This discourse reveals two important principles of McCartney's recruiting strategy. At a basic level, McCartney's appeal associates a select geographical location with a new life-beginning. The rhetorical process is one of identification in which the promise of a change of scenery is associated with the promise of individual and corporate (i.e., CU's football program) change. To further the logic of the process, one finds an implicit conflation of the aesthetic quality of the scene with that of CU's football program. It is not just any kind of change that is being offered, but an attractive one. And so the quality of the scene becomes an entailment for the quality of the football program, thereby translating the latter into a thing of potential beauty in its own right.

The principle also responds to questions that potential recruits may have had about McCartney's religious priorities. At first, McCartney's acknowledgement of CU's party reputation is cast in familiar normative terms. To characterize a school's party reputation as "not so bad" is to say that it is a lesser evil, one among any number of others that might be encountered.

Immediately following this, however, McCartney relocates the normative standard within the scene itself. That is, it is the terms and conditions of the scene that set the standard for judgment; and the nature of the CU scene is simply that it offers "lots of parties ... lots going on." In other words, parties are all part of the scenic package and should be judged as such. The implication is that McCartney's recruits could expect to receive a certain level of tolerance, perhaps even support, from their "Christian" coach concerning certain extra-curricular activities.

The second feature addresses the program's problem of tradition. Where a foundation does not exist, it must be built. If McCartney's recruits would not be heirs to an established tradition of excellence, they would be its benefactors.

The rhetorical turn here is seen in the negotiation of time itself. Past events, rather than acting as points of reflection, as those that necessarily shape the here and now, become insubstantial shadows in the light of present opportunity. The turn is completed through a process of identification in which the marginalization of the program's beleaguered past co-participates with one's own individual past. In essence, McCartney is offering potential recruits a new identity. This identity affords a means of isolating the "self" from places and experiences located in the past, possibly a troubled past, in favor of experiencing new ideas and lifestyles in an environment in which both change and "fun" are natural. Moreover, it is an identity that grants recruits a privileged role in producing positive, lasting change.

Finally, the strategy makes overtures toward an ironic future, wherein adherents will have earned the "right to possess" that part of time they must presently relinquish—that is, the past. In this way, McCartney sought to manage the tension between his identity as college football coach and evangelical Christian in ways favorable to his recruiting purposes. And although the strategy at times left him feeling like "one of those cultists or a brush salesman" (McCartney, 1995, p. 193), it was a compromise with which he was evidently willing to live.

Analogies between McCartney's efforts to attract college athletes and PK's attempts to attract followers are readily evident. Both situations entailed rhetorical constraints in which appeals to a long-standing tradition of winning teams were unavailable. In both cases, the choice was made to target the properties of the scene as motivating ingredients toward participation in the program's larger vision.

In the case of PK, it was the stadium event that offered a new and invigorating locale, presently removed from the trappings of the past, of the old identity. Promotional videos of PK stadium events depict a fun, even celebratory (or party) atmosphere for audiences to partake of (cf. Wimber, et al., 1995). Early PK literature presents the stadium event as a unique opportunity "to recapture the spiritual climate" (McCartney, 1992, p. 11), and to seek "God's favor for a national revival" (Phillips, 1994, p. 6). The stadium event thus provided a point of identification linking a select geographical location with a new life-beginning. At a time when PK was still relatively young, the implicit message was that new recruits would bear a privileged responsibility as God's chosen initiators for the new program, ultimately becoming the benefactors of nationwide revival.

McCartney's recruiting efforts as college football coach were eminently successful. His teams went on to achieve national prestige, winning several Big Eight championships and a share of the mythic national championship in 1990. During this period, McCartney won a host of major coaching awards and thereby secured a privileged position within college football's elite coaching ranks. But if McCartney's persona was established at one level (as successful college coach), it remained a source of ongoing criticism and speculation at another.

In 1985, the American Civil Liberties Union charged McCartney with holding mandatory prayer meetings for his players and granting preferential treatment (i.e., playing time) to those players who concurred with the coach's religious views. Although McCartney vehemently denied the charges of favoritism, he made no apologies concerning his religious views, nor his desire to see those views openly expressed in "voluntary" team prayer meetings. Media reports of player unrest and misconduct served further to heighten the perception of McCartney as one caught in an intractable struggle between his religious and professional identities.

In 1989, two events, coupled with their subsequent media portrayal, transformed the rhetorical character of McCartney's persona from one of public interest to that of public spectacle. First came the reports that McCartney's daughter, Kristi, had conceived a child out of wedlock. The father had been identified as Sal Aunese, McCartney's prize recruit and the starting quarterback for the CU football team. Denver's *Westword*, an alternative newsweekly, published an article, "CU Football Players Score! But Coach Bill McCartney is the loser" (Claussen, 1996, p. 40). The cover of that same newsweekly read, "The Sinning Season: CU Coach Bill McCartney keeps the faith—and gets a grandson fathered by his star quarterback" (McCartney, 1995, p. 52).

In an important sense, these portrayals actually undermined the very dichotomy they meant to underscore. Opposition to McCartney generally had been framed within a public versus private context. As Denver attorney and local ACLU representative Judd Golden said, "I don't care if [McCartney] takes every Sunday off to hit the bully pulpit. He can wear a collar around the house for all I care. He just needs to keep it out of the football program" (Teitcher, 1992, p. C-1). In choosing to publicize this incident, however,

Westword demonstrated that a person's religious values were very much a public matter. The issue was not whether one's religious values should be integrated into one's public identity, but rather how those values were to be characterized in relation to that identity.

The second event was as devastating to the community as the former had been to McCartney. In September of that same year, Sal Aunese died of cancer. A public memorial service was held at the University. Two thousand members of the community and a host of local and regional dignitaries—including then Colorado Governor Roy Romer—came to pay tribute to the young man. Incredibly, Aunese had become a "born again" Christian shortly before his death. In a letter written to his teammates, Aunese exhorted them to "strive only for victory each time we play, and trust in the Lord for He truly is the way!" (McCartney, 1995, p. 63). The players subsequently dedicated the year to Aunese. They would finish the regular season with an 11–0 record and a number one ranking.

While McCartney had long been the target of criticism, 1989 marked a decisive turn in the way his persona was characterized, as well as the effect that characterization would have on the community. Subsequent episodes involving McCartney's public stand on abortion and homosexuality evoked thousands of letters both in support of and against him. If McCartney's persona divided a community, it also seems apparent that it became an important source of attraction for thousands of men in the community for whom McCartney cut a heroic figure on the religious side of the divide.

On the one hand, McCartney was an affluent, white male who commanded respect in a profession heralded for its cultural popularity—a profession, too, that offered numerous points of identification around cultural notions of masculinity. On the other hand, McCartney's failures were the failures of many evangelical men who struggled to manage the competing interests germane to their professional and religious identities. It was this prior public persona that gained McCartney access to speak in churches in and around the Boulder area where most of the initial recruiting occurred. It was the package of beliefs McCartney embodied that gave him, particularly among male audiences, the credibility to speak as a leader of and among men. And it was this persona that cut a sympathetic figure for males who saw in McCartney's real life their own successes and failures and were persuaded that the battle was worth going public over in a community seemingly hostile to the very idea. Finally, it was this prior public persona that would prove to be pivotal in warming local audiences to the concept of appropriating Boulder's public event centers for expressly religious purposes.

REAPPROPRIATING THE PUBLIC SPECTACLE

While McCartney's prior public persona supplied an initial and important impetus for attracting recruits, it was that persona's relationship to the larger vision of CU's football program that attracted audiences to early PK stadium events. Owing to the efforts of both McCartney and the media, the meaning of CU football had been subject to competing modes of interpretation for some time. Lurking behind each game lay the specter of transcendent significance in which each victory or loss could be held up for judgment framed in religious terms. For some, CU victories were "God's victories." For many others, bringing religion into the program was tantamount to committing sacrilege against all that the team, the program, indeed the community, represented.

Media opposition originally targeted McCartney's coaching tactics, but failed largely in proportion to the coach's on-field success. Later efforts targeted McCartney's personal life. The apparent strategy was to discredit the coach's religious beliefs, and thereby divorce any positive identification between those beliefs and CU football.

Whether the strategy was successful in eliminating any connection to religion from the CU football program is largely irrelevant to this analysis. What is relevant is that important groundwork had been laid toward the construction of a public spectacle that was primarily religious in meaning. Whatever else they may have symbolized, early PK stadium events represented a zealous show of support for and participation in the public expression of religious values. McCartney's persona thus became a principal target of identification in what was perceived by sympathizers as a legitimate attempt to reappropriate Boulder's public event centers for religious purposes.

It is hardly surprising, then, that PK's first official public event, held at Fulsom's Event Center, found a number of attendees wearing CU football T-shirts. Nor is it surprising that subsequent conventions, held at CU's football stadium, featured speeches from current and former CU football players. The bouncing of beach balls around the stadium, call and response chants from opposite sides of the stadium, extended versions of "the wave" and prolonged verbal outbursts prominent at these events are behaviors much more readily associated with fan activity at CU football games than with religious gatherings. Audiences were never more vociferous than when McCartney, who always has the last word at these events, took the stage (Wardell, 1997).

The battle against the enemies of public religious expression in Boulder was waged in the locations where numerous other culturally-significant battles had been fought (and usually won) by "Coach Mac." In claiming the stadium for its own purposes, Promise Keepers capitalized on the notion that holding a religious event in a place designated for secular public spectacle represented a kind of occupation, even a "takeover" of such a space. And with that takeover came all the culturally unifying power with which public spectacles are endowed.

This explains why PK places so much emphasis on filling entire stadiums. Victory, on some level, is a game of numbers in which individual weakness and failure are proportionately subverted in relation to the corporate worth of the community—which has come to be measured, in substantial degree, in terms of sheer numbers. As long as large numbers of people attend its events, PK's leaders and audiences must believe that an important, if symbolic, victory has occurred; when attendance at regional events dropped dramatically in 1997 from 1996, PK leaders anxiously offered various explanations. It is a sense of community, and of community victory, that provides an ideological (and psychological) impetus toward PK's eventual national expansion.

In sum, Promise Keepers' early recruiting efforts benefited greatly from the nexus of three rhetorical factors: 1) a geo-ideological context characterized by a potentially volatile wellspring of divergent interests and ideas; 2) PK co-founder Bill McCartney's prior public persona and its zealous representation of the legitimate public expression of religious faith; and 3) the allure of the public spectacle, reappropriated for religious ends.

Conclusion

I must acknowledge that this essay explains only in part PK's recruiting success. Other factors undoubtedly contributed to the process. The development of a sophisticated system of recruitment and recruiting officers ("Key Man" and "Ambassador" ministries) operating at the grass roots level certainly has done much to expand the scope of PK influence. It is also probable that women, wives of men who have become Promise Keepers, play an important role in motivating their husbands to attend PK stadium events (Dager, 1995). Even so, it is difficult to conceive of PK being as successful, as quickly, absent the factors discussed in this essay.

One example may be seen in a relatively recent turn of events. In 1997, PK suffered a 28 percent decline in stadium event attendance figures. As a result, the organization dismissed—in two waves—hundreds of employees and closed a number of state offices, leaving uncertain its future status. In mid-1998, Promise Keepers still was in the process of reorganizing its economic and religious priorities.

Clatterbaugh (1995; 1997) has predicted that Promise Keepers will soon fade from view in the manner of its evangelical predecessors. PK believes it is fighting a battle to recover a culture that is economically and morally weighted against it. Society, Clatterbaugh contends, is changing its preferences and prejudices at a clip faster than PK can negotiate them.

For those who subscribe to the vision, however, Promise Keepers is not the last hue and cry of a battle lost, but rather a resounding trumpet call to a war newly discovered. Theirs is a rhetoric of restoration, of restoring fathers to their sons, husbands to their wives, men to their churches and, ultimately, a nation to its God. In the main, Promise Keepers may be said to represent evangelicalism's frontline response to the postmodern problem of unity and diversity.

As a case study in the rhetoric of recruitment, this analysis suggests that movement-organizations of the evangelical variety must continue to draw much of their rhetorical sustenance from "secular" cultural symbols of identity and authority. It is a synthesis that is at once a strength and a liability. For although an evangelical rhetoric that uses such symbolic resources is sure to attract attention, it also may render its subscribers beholden, perhaps unconsciously, to the underlying sociocultural tendencies to which that rhetoric responds. Put another way, PK's rhetorical efforts may be perpetuating some of the maladies they mean to redress.

This is evidenced in PK's promise of relatively simple solutions to fairly complex social problems by recourse to symbolically enhanced productions and experiences. It is evidenced in the consumerist orientation to signs and signifiers that attempt to construct "vital relationships" with others by drawing dramatic attention to themselves. It is evidenced in the arbitrary reappropriation of cultural symbols of power and authority, a process in which the Scriptures themselves become part of the morass of de-historicized, de-authorized fragments of meaning, full of sound and fury, signifying almost anything and thereby signifying almost nothing.

Perhaps most paradoxically, it is seen in a signature recruiting device principled on the notion of commitment whose rhetorical means spectacularize, and thereby render most meaningful, the experience of the dramatically-situated moment. It is a paradox of commitment whose habits are informed by rhetorical fixes and transformative experiences, sensationally-styled and perpetually recycled. Rhetorically considered, Promise Keepers' fate lies not so readily in the "power of a promise kept" as it rests in the power of a rhetoric purchased.

References

Boulder Chamber of Commerce. (1997). Demographics [Brochure]. Boulder, CO: Author.
Boulder Convention and Visitors Bureau. (1997). Boulder, Colorado USA. [Brochure]. Boulder, CO: Shelly Helmerick & Jill Mills.
Burke, K. (1969). *A rhetoric of motives*. Berkeley, CA: University of California Press.
Chavis, S. (1998, May 20). Telephone interview.
Cheney, G.E. (1991). *Rhetoric in an organizational society*. Columbia, SC: University of South Carolina Press.
Clatterbaugh, K. (October, 1995). Whose keepers, what promises? *M.E.N. Magazine*. [On-line]. Available: http://www.vix.com:80/menmag/pkclattr.htm.
Clatterbaugh, K. (1997). Promise Keepers: An evangelical Christian men's movement. In K. Clatterbaugh (ed.), *Contemporary perspectives on masculinity:*

Men, women & politics in modern society (pp. 177–193). Boulder, CO: Westview Press.

Claussen, D.S. (1996). *United States print mass media coverage of two men's movements: Robert Bly, Iron John and the mythopoets, and Bill McCartney and the Promise Keepers.* Unpublished master's thesis, Kansas State University, Manhattan.

Dager, A.J. (1995, July). Promise Keepers: Is what you see what you get? *Media Spotlight*, 1–24.

McCartney, B., et al. (1992). *What makes a man?* Colorado Springs, CO: NavPress.

McCartney, B. (1995). *From ashes to glory* (Rev. ed.). Nashville, TN: Thomas Nelson, Inc.

Phillips, R. (1994). Seize the moment. In A. Janssen & L.K. Weeden (eds.), *Seven promises of a Promise Keeper* (pp. 1–12). Colorado Springs, CO: Focus on the Family Publishing.

Stewart, C.J., Smith, C.A., & Denton, R.E. (1994). *Persuasion and social movements (3rd ed.)*. Prospect Heights, IL: Waveland Press Inc.

Teitcher, A. (1992, December 26). Colorado's coach has followers buffaloed. *The San Diego Union-Tribune*, p. C-1.

Wardell, Dave. (1997, August 28). Telephone interview.

Wimber, T. (producer); Franklin, P. & Hancock, J. (directors). (1995). *The next step: From the stadium to the small group*. [Videotape]. Available from Promise Keepers Production in association with IMSProductions, Colorado Springs.

CHAPTER 8

Identification and Invitation as Competing Rhetorics in the Promise Keepers Movement
by Robert A. Stewart

> America is in the midst of a culture war that has and will continue to have reverberations not only within public policy but within the lives of ordinary Americans everywhere.... Our most fundamental ideas about who we are as Americans are now at odds [Hunter, 1991, pp. 34, 42].

The reason for the culture war of which Hunter writes is a clash of oppositional worldviews within our society, which pits divergent ideologies against each other. On one side is a liberal ideology that espouses the preeminence of individuals' self-determination and the equal value of multiple truths. On the other side is a conservative ideology that views individuals as responsible to a higher authority who represents ultimate truth and reason. The vast difference in worldviews maintained by these opposing ideologies produces an incongruity in approaches to issues of mutual interest. Neither side, for example, places a high value on the *act* of abortion, but one side touts the value of a woman's choice to have an abortion while the other side argues that the woman's right to choose is nullified by the value of the individual life and soul of the unborn child. Consequently, the two sides fail to arrive at a common understanding of the issue—adherence to their respective ideologies prohibits receptivity to the other's perspective. The result is misunderstanding, lack of tolerance and, sometimes, violence.

Currently, the clash between liberal and conservative worldviews is nowhere better exemplified than in the Promise Keepers movement and critical responses to it. The ideologies involved are conservative Christianity and secularism. PK claims to be a "Christ-centered ministry dedicated to uniting men through vital realtionships to become godly influences in their world" (PK web site). The movement is seen by its mostly secular critics (yet other critics have emerged, including Christians both more moderate and more fundamentalist than PK) as a direct, almost militant challenge to the political and social progress made on behalf of women in the past and present generation. Some say it is a movement toward Christian-male domination with the aim of subjugating women to gain control of families, communities and, through an implicit political agenda, society at large (e.g., Cooperman, 1997; Stodghill, 1997).

Critics use PK's expressed mission statement against the movement. Whereas PK claims to promote principles and actions that will foster positive inter- and intragender relationships, detractors say the principles and actions promoted by Promise Keepers actually stifle productive relationships and understanding between the sexes. Similarly, whereas Promise Keepers claims to promote principles and actions that will foster greater inter-racial and inter-denominational unity, critics contend that the imagery used in Promise Keepers' messages of unity actually promotes restrictive hierarchical structures that further disadvantage the already disadvantaged.

These different ideological takes on the gender and cultural issues involving the Promise Keepers movement offer meaningful opportunities for communication studies. This chapter's purpose is to show that PK employs features of Burkeian identification to seek transformation in Christian men's gender and cultural roles. It is argued that these strategies, although effective for influencing hundreds of thousands of Christian men with the Promise Keepers message, fail with the movement's detractors because to them it actually cultivates the gender and racial biases out of which the movement wants men to be transformed. Finally considered is whether Promise Keepers might gain more positive acclaim from critics if its message were presented using features of an invitational rather than traditional rhetoric.

EVIDENCE OF OPPOSING WORLDVIEWS

At issue for PK's critics is not least the message that Christian men need to gain their leadership role in the home. Perhaps the most-often—and now too-often—quoted such message is that written by Pastor Tony Evans in his chapter in an early Promise Keepers book:

> Sit down with your wife and say something like this: "Honey, I've made a terrible mistake. I've given up my role. I gave up leading this family, and I forced you to take my place. Now I must reclaim that role."... I'm not suggesting that you ask for your role back, I'm urging you to *take* it back [Evans, p. 79].

As sociologist of religion Robert Wuthnow observed, "When religious discourse enters the public sphere—when it becomes public rhetoric—we confront another compelling reason for trying to understand it: Some of it seems to affront common sensibilities so deeply that we find it difficult even to focus on what is being said" (1988, p. 320). Feminists and many liberal Christians alike find Evans' comments clearly indicative of a mentality and move toward right-wing Christian masculine superiority.

Critics also cite passages of scripture Promise Keepers uses as foundational text for its cause. One example is from Paul's letter to the Ephesians: "Wives, submit to your husbands as to the Lord. For the husband is the head of the wife [and] wives should submit to their husbands in everything." This notion of wives submitting to their husbands is in fact what draws the preponderance of critics' ire to Promise Keepers. The National Organization for Women argues that the principle of wifely submission highlights PK's intent "to force wives back under the patriarchal thumb" (McDonald, 1997, p. 28).

Members and supporters of the Promise Keepers movement attempt to counter charges of macho domination by arguing that detractors misunderstand their message of submission. The movement asserts that the gender roles it espouses are based on a Christian worldview in which leadership is equated with service, or servanthood. The admonition to husbands, therefore, is to lead their families, thus serving them, not by controlling them. Wives of movement participants have been reported as saying that although final decisions in their households often are made by their husbands, the wives make equal contributions to the decision-making process in the home. Feminist critics, especially, see this suggestion of servant leadership as paradoxical, a ruse to cover up an agenda of agitation and control.

Evident in all this is a clash of opposing worldviews that is sharply manifested in the discourse of both sides. Basically, PK's opponents charge that the movement is on a sociopolitical campaign to avert the many advances made on behalf of women and feminism in the past two or three decades. Supporters of Promise Keepers retort that the movement's mission is a spiritual one aimed at improving life in Christian homes by strengthening the relationships among men and God, their families, and other men. This impasse presents Promise Keepers a Catch-22, as religion columnist and Christian academic Terry Mattingly puts it: "One side believes that traditional Christianity can heal the wounds in homes today; the other is convinced that Christian tradition is the root cause of the suffering" (1997, n.p.).

Promise Keepers' Use of Identification

The Burkeian notion of *identification* helps shed some light on the nature of the ideological impasse surrounding Promise Keepers. Identification occurs in at least four forms in religious discourse: identification between the speaker and audience, between what is familiar and unfamiliar to the audience, between individual and group, and between what is sacred and what is secular (Palinkas, 1989).

Identification Between Speaker and Audience. The messengers of Promise Keepers are men to whom other men can easily relate. From the movement's founder—former collegiate football coach Bill McCartney—to each of its rally speakers, the men who carry the Promise Keepers message share stories that strike at the hearts and life experiences of their listeners. They speak of marital difficulties, job loss, financial stress, troubles with teen children, and apathy toward matters spiritual. Stories about such issues give the speakers *ethos* with their mass audiences vastly heterogeneous regarding several demographic factors but wholly unified with respect to having similar problems, needs, and expectations in life. Central to the Promise Keepers message is the essentiality of Jesus Christ in transforming men's lives. The *ethos* established for the speakers in their identification with their audiences contributes significantly to the success of their message. For example, "McCartney's failures—and his willingness to own up to them—give him a certain authenticity with PK men who recognize that God has always found greater use for flawed, broken men whose hearts seek after Him than for sanctimonious do-gooders who lead seemingly perfect lives" (Mattox, 1995, p. 40).

Identification Between the Familiar and Unfamiliar. Church-in-a-stadium is one way to describe Promise Keepers' mass rallies. The context brings together two traditions that seldom are blended so baldly: worship services and football. To many in a rally audience, the event meshes the familiarity of church activity with the unfamiliarity of a football stadium (unfamiliar in the sense that relatively few men generally ever visit a professional football stadium, much less worship in one). For others the opposite is true. Either way, identification is achieved by bringing men together in two known contexts they have never before integrated.

Also unique to the Promise Keepers rallies, and probably more potent in impact than the venue, is the singularity of gender in attendance. Songs of praise and kneeling for prayer are familiar activities to most in a rally audience, but not in a men-only crowd of 50,000 to 70,000. The context blends the familiar with something so starkly unfamiliar to produce an experience with which only participants in the rally will identify. It is reasonable to suggest that this identification adds to the potency and persuasiveness of the Promise Keepers message.

Identification Between Individual and Group. Much of the impact of the Promise Keepers message relies on transforming individual, personal issues into shared group issues. The movement holds to the philosophy that men must gather with other men, separately from their wives and other women, to be more open and forthcoming in talking and praying about the matters of life with which they struggle. The organization's leaders and speakers encourage men to carry on with the renewal they gain at the mass rallies by becoming involved in small accountability groups in their home churches or communities. One intent of these groups is to further develop the kind of openness about otherwise private issues that can only be dealt with and overcome if brought to the knowledge of other Christian men. Each individual's identification with a like-minded group is intended to produce a transformation from strict reliance on self-determination and independence to greater recognition of the need for accountability and responsibility to others. Consistent with the Promise Keepers message of Christ's centrality in life, abandonment of predominant self-determination in favor of accountability is meant to help each individual maintain his focus on Christ as his model.

Identification Between the Sacred and the Secular. Much of the Promise Keepers message relies on imagery drawn from sports. One of the few social scientific studies of Promise Keepers published to date (Beal, 1997; Chapter 11 in this volume) reveals three uses of sporting imagery in the movement's literature. First, sporting imagery is used to depict masculine styles of quality leadership and success. For example, a celebrity sports figure might be held up as an example of honesty and perseverence. Then, sports imagery is used to foster positive conceptions of Chrisitan masculinity. Men working together in the church, for example, may be likened to men attending a ballgame together. Too, sporting imagery evokes male roles of authority and superiority. For example, messages pertaining to father-and-son relationships or employee-and-employer relationships might be framed in a sporting image of coach-and-player.

Use of sports imagery in each of these ways forms for the Promise Keepers audience identification that tranforms the secular into the sacred. Sports become a metaphor for spiritual matters: there is "victory" in Jesus. Men should be able to dress for church just as they dress for a hockey game. Men's accountability groups are prayer "teams." One's pastor is his spiritual captain. And so on. The message of Christ's centrality in life is strengthened by calling on one of the most active and vivid contexts of men's lives—sports. In fact, speaking at the 1997 Dallas rally, Pastor Tony Evans constrasted his "*worship* of the Dallas Cowboys" with his true worship of Jesus Christ (Stewart, 1997), thus sanctifying men's interest in sport by tying it to their need for Jesus.

The forms of identification used by Promise Keepers to enhance men's receptivity to its message are critiqued by feminists and religious liberals as promoting male dominance and patriarchal hierarchy. It is okay to want to improve marriages and other relationships, but not at the expense of equality. Mass rallies exclude women, ostensibly because women will interfere with the men's openness to talk and pray about certain issues, especially sexual ones. Men's accountability groups are viewed as diminishing men's autonomy and self-determination, making them dependent not only on other men but on the Promise Keepers movement itself. Sports-related metaphors are believed by many feminists to reinforce an ideology of male dominance, and thus to unduly masculinize the Promise Keepers message. Comparing these criticisms to what Promise Keepers says and practices in order to identify with its followers reveals the clash of worldviews of which Hunter warns. An ideological impasse is revealed.

So, can the impasse be bridged? What would critics have Promise Keepers do? Perhaps the answer is that the message of Promise Keepers should be communicated in a form of invitational rhetoric rather than its apparently confrontational form.

IMPLICATIONS OF AN INVITATIONAL RHETORIC OF PROMISE KEEPERS

Invitational rhetoric is grounded in feminist principles of equality, immanent value, and self-determination, and has as its purpose the attainment of greater understanding given conditions of safety, value, and freedom (Foss & Griffin, 1995). Invitational rhetoric stands in contrast to a traditional rhetoric that imposes a patriarchal bias and attempts to achieve dominance and control by directly changing the audience's ways of thinking or acting. Rather than seeking direct change, invitational rhetoric asks the audience "to enter the rhetor's world and to see it as the rhetor [orator] does" (Foss & Griffin, 1995, p. 5). It involves more a sharing of perspectives than contrasting one perspective as superior to another.

Three feminist principles underlie an invitational rhetoric. The first is *equality*. Through invitation the rhetor strives for a relationship of equality with audience members. A speaker's perspective may be different from that of the audience, but no pretense is made that the speaker's is superior to the audience's. The speaker's work instead is to create, restore, or foster a shared perspective with the audience. The second principle is *immanent value*. The invitational speaker presents a message with recognition that all members of the audience have unique, inherent worth as human beings. As such, their perspectives also have value. Thus, the rhetor avoids requiring the audience to dismiss their own perspectives for that of the rhetor. The third feminist principle of invitational rhetoric is *self-determination*. Audience members are recognized as capable of making their own decisions. It is not for the speaker to impart to the audience a basis for decision-making that is superior to their own, but to give the audience an alternative perspective against which to weigh criteria for making decisions.

Just as the principles of invitational rhetoric are feminist rather than patriarchal, its methods also differ from those of a traditional rhetoric. One method is to *offer perspective*. Often embodied in narrative, invitational rhetoric expresses a perspective without seeking support. The narrative seeks understanding and is an end unto itself, in contrast to the traditional use of narrative as a means of supporting a move toward a speaker-desired change in the audience. The transformation sought through the offering of perspective is, again, simply a sharing of perspectives.

Another method of invitational rhetoric is to *create external conditions* of safety, value, and freedom. These conditions are required to ensure the proper environment for interaction wherein rhetor and audience may exchange perspectives while moving toward greater understanding. *Safety* enables audience members to find order in competing perspectives because the speaker "makes no attempt to hurt, degrade, or belittle audience members or their beliefs" (Foss & Griffin, 1995, pp. 10–11). *Value* is evident when the rhetor expresses thinking consistent with audience members' thinking, therein revealing the speaker's understanding of and respect for the audience. The audience's immanent worth is affirmed and upheld. Finally, *freedom* is an external condition of invitational rhetoric, wherein audience members retain their power to make decisions regarding the speaker's perspective. It is accomplished when audience members are allowed to make choices from among as many alternatives as they can envision.

How can invitational rhetoric be employed by Promise Keepers to profess its message that a relationship with Jesus Christ is essential to "what makes a man" (McCartney et al., 1992)? It must maintain or achieve equality. It must affirm immanent value in its listeners. It must recognize self-determination.

Promise Keepers and Equality. The most frequent and harshest criticism levied against Promise Keepers regards its adherence to the biblical principle of wifely submission to husbands. The principle flies in the face of efforts at affirming women's equality with men in leading their households. Exacerbating the criticism is the method by which this principle is presented—as a perspective that *must* be accepted and adhered to in order for men's marriages and families to be all they can be. The external condition of freedom is thus hindered. The invitational principle of equality would prescribe a different method—to share the perspective as one men may integrate into their own perspectives as they see fit.

Promise Keepers and Immanent Value. The crux of PK's message is that men are no good in and of themselves (Raab, 1996). Various speakers for the movement have suggested that, separate from Jesus Christ, men are likely to be failures in their families, friendships and careers. The perspectives most men bring with them to a Promise Keepers rally or to a reading of Promise Keepers literature are perceived as needing change, either by strengthening a weakened perspective that generally is in line with that of Promise Keepers, or by replacing a perspective that is out of line (e.g., the sort of machismo that subjugates a man's wife and prevents him from sharing open and honest concerns with other men). In terms of invitational rhetoric, such an approach to change is highly devaluing of the individual and violates the external condition of safety. Because safety precludes messages that hurt, degrade or belittle the perspectives of an audience, the Promise Keepers message would have to be presented in such a way as to allow for the audience members' perspectives. The aim will be less to "sell" the Promise Keepers message and more to show how it can benefit the perspectives already held by listeners.

Promise Keepers and Self-Determination. Some critics contend that the Promise Keepers message works to lessen its receivers' self-determination. In particular, some critics argue that the small accountability groups men are encouraged to join reduce their abilities to make decisions individually and independently. Carried further, such criticism suggests that the accountability groups overlook or even deny immanent value, at least in the feminist sense. Pointing to a need for accountability groups assumes men will "go astray" without the encouragement received from, and responsibility owed to, a small group of men with whom one can express one's strongest needs and seek appropriate direction. In contrast, the invitational principle of immanent value would maintain that Christian men are individually capable of discerning right from wrong and of "avoiding temptation." A perspective favoring accountability groups may thus be offered as something for a man to be aware of as potentially helpful to him, rather than offered as a method of spiritual growth that is required to be a better husband, father, and so on.

CONCLUSION

The ideological chasm between Promise Keepers and its critics is reflective of the larger culture war said to exist in this society. It is a war of differences in worldviews (Hunter, 1991). Whether actual or perceived, the war is important because worldviews, or ideologies, are what individuals rely upon to inform them of how things ought to be, what is "true," "good," and "right." When two groups who have opposing worldviews collide on the battlefield of ideas, generally no one wins because neither side will give in. Their ideologies are too firm and too vested to change. Applied to this case, it is arguable that Promise Keepers' detractors will exist and voice their opposition for as long as the movement exists. It is just as likely that Promise Keepers will maintain its stances on marital relationships, the spritual needs of men, and the supremacy of God's Word as the only true blueprint for how men should live their lives.

If the last statement holds true, then an important question is which rhetoric—traditional or invitational—will best enable Promise Keepers to bridge the gap in ideologies. Much of the message currently is delivered through a traditional rhetoric of identification and transformation. Critics seem to want the movement to use a softer, gentler rhetoric, and invitational rhetoric offers such an alternative. This chapter has attempted to show, in a general way, how an invitational rhetoric might be applied to the Promise Keepers message. But a pertinent question remains: Would an invitational rhetoric work for the avowed purposes of Promise Keepers?

A preliminary answer to the question is, not likely, for at least three reasons. One is the Promise Keepers' intended audience. For the most part, the audience as a whole already shares the Promise Keepers perspective. The movement's mission targets Christian men. It is not a message of conversion *per se* the movement delivers, but rather a message of admonition and encouragement. The aim is to strengthen an already extant perspective. A rhetoric of identification best serves this aim.

A second reason an invitational rhetoric is unlikely to work for Promise Keepers is the movement's message. As stated earlier, the message's crux is the centrality of Jesus Christ in being a man. An audience that is predominantly Christian to begin with shares the ideology behind the message. What most men in the audience need is a message that admonishes them to live by their ideology, rather than to change ideologies. The message goes beyond merely gaining understanding of the message while respecting personal perspectives. It means building on the ideology, sometimes with hard arguments that strike at the very person ("the sinner") in each audience member. In an Augustinian sense, "Ordinary men follow their feelings and habits, and for them to be taught the truth it is necessary not only to make use of logical reasoning, but to arouse their emotions" (Kennedy, 1980, p. 151). The need for such a message precludes the safety and self-determination of invitational rhetoric. In fact, acceptance of the message means acknowledging one's lack of full self-determination.

A third reason that invitational rhetoric is unlikely to work for Promise Keepers is the opposition itself. The movement's staunchest critics, while sharing PK's concern for stronger families, more stable marriages, a higher social integrity, and the like, adamantly oppose the conservatively Christian, biblically-literal basis for the movement's message. This opposition is rooted in an ideology so different from that of Promise Keepers that any sharing of perspectives as hoped for in an invitational rhetoric is improbable. Believers in the Bible as God's inerrant word will argue from a perspective not shared by nonbelievers. Any confrontation at that level will likely reflect and contribute to the ideological clash.

Hunter brings to a close his characterization of the culture war and its effects in society by outlining the most likely solution. It is, simply, "agreement within disagreement." He explains:

> No one is so naive to believe that under present circumstances the consensus pursued could be or even should be some form of consensus

of values and beliefs. The divisions, at this level, are firm and unyielding. If any consensus is achievable it could and should first be about *how* to contend over the moral differences that divide—a public agreement over *how* to publicly disagree. When consensus is realized at this plane, genuine disagreement becomes an accomplishment; authentic debate becomes a virtue [Hunter, 1994, p. 318].

Media coverage of the supportive and nonsupportive arguments pertaining to Promise Keepers makes them appear "firm and unyielding." Consensus between the supporters and nonsupporters seems unachievable. Even the more relative, other-perspective-taking approach of an invitational rhetoric is limited in bridging such a divide. Following Hunter's prescription, consensus in the form of "agreeing to disagree" will be the best medicine for treating the ills of ideological opposition. If a role exists for an invitational rhetoric in this matter, perhaps it is in building that consensus, for such an outcome will require discourse conditions of safety, value, and, to some extent, self-determination.

References

Beal, B. (1997). The Promise Keepers' use of sport in defining "Christlike" masculinity. *Journal of Sport and Social Issues 21*, 274–284.
Cooperman, J. (1997, October 6). For some, Promise Keepers is a threat. *ABCNews* [On-line]. Available: www.ABCNEWS.com.
Evans, T. (1994). Spiritual purity. In A. Janssen & L.K. Weeden (eds.), *Seven promises of a Promise Keeper*, pp. 73–81. Colorado Springs, CO: Focus on the Family.
Foss, S.K., & Griffin, C.L. (1995). Beyond persuasion: A proposal for an invitational rhetoric. *Communication Monographs 62*, 2–18.
McCartney, Bill, et al. (1992). *What makes a man? 12 promises that will change your life.* Colorado Springs, CO: Navpress.
Hunter, J.D. (1991). *Culture wars: The struggle to define America.* New York: BasicBooks.
Janssen, A., & Weeden, L.K. (eds.). (1994). *Seven promises of a Promise Keeper.* Colorado Springs, CO: Focus on the Family.
Kennedy, G. (1980). *Classical rhetoric and its Christian and secular tradition from ancient to modern times.* Chapel Hill, NC: The University of North Carolina Press.
Mattingly, T. (1997, October 8). The Promise Keepers' Catch 22. In *On Religion* [On-line]. Available: www.gospelcom.net/tmattingly/.
Mattox, W.J.Jr. (1995). Christianity goes to the playoffs. *The American Enterprise 6*(6), 39–42.
McDonald, M. (1997, October 6). My wife told me to go: Why Promise Keepers is thriving despite feminists' warnings. *U.S. News & World Report* [On-line]. Available: www.usnews.com/usnews/issue/971006/6prom.htm.

Palinkas, L.A. (1989). *Rhetoric and religious experience: The discourse of immigrant Chinese churches*. Fairfax, VA: George Mason University.
Raab, S. (1996, January). Triumph of his will. *GQ*, 110–117, 127–130.
Stewart, R.A. (1997, October 25). Personal observation of a speech given at Texas Stadium, Irving, TX.
Stodghill, R. II (1997, October 6). God of our fathers. *Time* [On-line]. Available: www.pathfinder.com/time/magazine/1997/dom/971006/cover1/html.
Wuthnow, R. (1988). Religious discourse as public rhetoric. *Communication Research 15*, 318–338.

CHAPTER 9

Promising to Be a Man: Promise Keepers and the Organizational Constitution of Masculinity

by Robert A. Cole

> Nay, faith, let me not play a woman; I have a beard coming. [William Shakespeare, *A Midsummer Night's Dream*].

The social activities of identity constitution and meaning infusion rely on manifold communicative actions to accomplish these tasks, just as language, for example, relies on metaphor (a vehicular trope) to infuse and bear linguistic meaning. Human beings' unique, situated identities are the polyvocal, heteroglossic process and product of communicative intersubjectivity (Bakhtin, 1935/1981 and 1929/1990). The process of "gendering" is a significant, inescapable feature of human subjectivity that is ontologically realized through this ongoing, ever-in-the-making conversation, and one site for both regulating and constituting gender identities is found within the rhetorical structures of various men's movements.

Organized men's movements not only serve to shape social and political policies, but they also stand as influential sources for their adherents' continual remaking of their own physical bodies and gendered modes of being. Participating in a contemporary men's movement, or any social movement for that matter, provides the discursive forum for articulating one's self as a subjective being. Embracing a movement's perspective on masculinity requires that a person at the very least "talk the talk" of that agenda, if not "walk the walk." Learning the party line, following the leaders, or evangelizing to others implies that one constitutes himself in the terms of that movement's discourse, at least for that moment. In short, a person both constitutes and has constituted a gender peculiar to the articulated discourse prevailing at that moment.

In this chapter I explore the Promise Keepers (PK) men's movement as a shared dialogic locus for gendered rhetoric. After a brief sketch of various men's movements, I outline the design of this phenomenological study of both the PK organization and its adherents. Then, I advance a critique of the rhetorical vision that PK promotes for constituting masculine subjectivity. Finally, I show how the individual men who constitute their gender under the auspices of PK's rhetorical artifacts differ from the vision the organization holds.

Promise Keepers As a Men's Movement

The oft-cited Stewart, Smith, and Denton (1994) define collective action and rhetoric as being a social movement if they conform to several characteristics. They argue that first, the social movement must have some minimal organization in which leaders and followers are clearly identifiable. Second, a social movement cannot be part of the established order of power that governs, legislates or adjudicates by virtue of its institutionalized powers to do so. Third, any social movement must have enough members, time, events, and geographic coverage to carry out its program for change. Fourth, a social movement must be committed to change in existing societal norms and values through innovation, resistance, or revivalism. Fifth, social movements must employ persuasion rather than coercion to bring about desired changes in their audiences. Sixth, a social movement finds itself in conflict with the established order as it attempts to carry out what it sees as correct moral actions, with a righteous sense of moral obligation, which is the seventh characteristic (pp. 5-16).

Several scholars examine the various men's movements (cf. Kimmel and Kaufman, 1994; Messner, 1997). Kenneth Clatterbaugh (1990, 1996) conveniently groups the collective beliefs of these movements under several headings, which may be condensed under five general orientations: the spiritual perspective, the men's rights perspective, the pro-feminist perspective, the group-specific perspective and the conservative perspective. Briefly, men who display a "spiritual perspective" employ mythology and pagan spirituality in a journey of self-actualization aimed at discovering their own deeply-masked masculinity; an example is mythopoetism. The "men's rightists" claim that men are victimized by social, economic, and political institutions that are manifest in traditional roles of masculinity. "Profeminists" maintain that traditional roles of both femininity and masculinity serve to oppress women and harm men by preserving patriarchal structures of privilege. The "group-specific" perspective, as labeled by Clatterbaugh, is made up of a potpourri of voices critical of a monolithic definition of masculinity that rests upon a white, middle class, heterosexual foundation. Lastly, men who take a "conservative perspective" want to maintain the traditional forms of masculinity based on either their belief in biological determinants for gender or their moral views on gender relations.

The moral conservative perspective springs from a fear that society and civilization are in decay. The traditional form of a family headed by a strong protector/provider is seen as rapidly dissolving and that dissolution is linked to the escalation of crime rates, drug use, teenage pregnancies, sexual promiscuity, sexually transmitted disease and a general climate of moral permissiveness. So, an evangelical zeal carries the conservative perspective to the masses of men and some women in this country to recover the roles of past (Clatterbaugh, 1996). Through the promotion of a return to Christian doctrine, gathering men under the auspices of the church, and with audiotapes, newsletters, videotapes and magazine publications, along with profiles in high visibility sacred and secular magazines and newspapers (Dart, 1995; Gilbreath, 1995; Hoffer & Smith, 1995; Johnson, 1995; Neill, 1995; Shapiro, 1995; Thompson, 1996; van Biema, 1995; Woodward, 1995), the conservative Promise Keepers organization is the most visible and fastest growing of all the men's perspectives.

PK draws strongly on the Christian evangelical tradition, seeking to return men to God and the teachings of Jesus as they relate to the family. The nuclear family is seen to be the core of American society, and this movement's persuasive efforts are directed at reviving values that champion and conserve the traditional family. Men are "lost," they claim, because the traditional family, considered the cornerstone of civilization and a moral society, is being destroyed as the roles of men as protectors and providers and women as child bearers, care givers, and nurturers come under attack.

When women are supported by moral conservative men it is usually because they are seen as an important moralizing force for tempering the male excesses of vice, temptation, and sin. Women's work to moralize the private sphere is sometimes seen as needed to enhance the public sphere. Therefore, some men promote women as agents for cleaning up the corrupt public realm of cities and the nation by, for example, supporting their efforts to hold minor appointed and elected positions in public office (Kimmel & Mosmiller, 1992).

PK enlists Christian clergy to conduct and moderate "Wake Up Calls" across the country. These local gatherings, of which some 300 were carried out in 1995, have a twofold purpose. They are designed to "stir men's hearts about needs within the community to encourage them to get together, pray, and form small groups" (Walker, 1995). More importantly, the "Wake Up Calls" are also intended to build interest and momentum for a series of national Promise Keepers Men's Conferences that in 1995 drew more than 750,000 men to a dozen sites, in 1996 more than 1 million men to 22 sites (Promise Keepers, 1996a), and in 1997 several hundred thousand to regional events and several hundred thousand more to Stand in the Gap. These conferences, held in sports stadiums (such as the Los Angeles Coliseum, Denver's Mile High Stadium, Chicago's Soldier Field, New York's Shea Stadium, New Orleans' Superdome, and Charlotte's Motor Speedway) seating tens of thousands, are an occasion for men to worship God, learn to improve their marriages and child rearing practices, to resist sexual temptation, to be accountable for their behavior and, foremost, to commit to PK's "Seven Promises."

The conferences were the engine resulting in PK growing to 500 staffers in 21 states with a budget of $115 million by 1996 (Promise Keepers, 1996a). Much of that income came from those hundreds of thousands of men paying $55 each in 1995, $60 each in 1996, and $70 in 1997, with countless more attending hundreds of local "Wake Up Calls" (Promise Keepers, 1996b). PK founder Bill McCartney and President Randy Phillips also built a hierarchical network of "Ambassadors" and "Key Men" by recruiting local church pastors to develop men's ministries.

Women are discouraged from attending conferences because coordinators say men's issues must be addressed within the emotional safety of an all-male setting. The organization is grateful, however, to women for their willingness to pray for their men, and values them for their behind-the-scenes work. These women are deemed "Promise Reapers" (Promise Keepers, 1996a) because, by supporting their men's efforts to recapture traditional definitions of masculinity, they will ultimately reap the benefits of a restored provider and protector.

Besides regional conferences, "Wake Up Calls," and local ministering, PK's rhetoric has been carried out through a monthly, widely available magazine, *New Man: For Men of Integrity*, whose contents were PK-approved until early 1998. PK merchandises a series of books and study guides expounding upon various themes concerning how men are to lead the way in a return to the church, the family, and the community, and the recovery of bygone values. Available by mail order or at the conferences, the books retail for from $5 to $15 each. PK also produces and distributes a line of audio and video cassettes that capture conferences' musical and discursive events. These sell for anywhere from $6 for an audio cassette to more than $100 for a seven-tape video library of a weekend's conference proceedings. In addition, apparel such as T-shirts, polo shirts, sweatshirts, wind breakers, and hats—all bearing the PK insignia or evangelical messages—may be bought for from $9 to $45. Finally, newsletters, men's ministry materials, and fund raiser mailings are sent periodically to a PK constituency mailing list.

Consistent with Stewart, Smith and Denton's (1994) definition of a social movement, PK's rhetorical hallmark is its commitment to moral action and a belief in the rightness of its moral obligation. The movement is at once revivalistic and resistant in its rhetoric for and against social change; persuasion, rather than coercion or bargaining, is PK's tactic. It is revivalistic in that it seeks a restoration of the traditional nuclear family values PK imagines to have been in place and well functioning as late as the 1960s (Boone, 1994), and its promotion of religious doctrine calls for a return to Christianity's earliest form. It is resistant in that it rejects sociopolitical and cultural changes that promote abortion, gay rights, women's liberation, and the excesses of freedom of speech manifest not only in pornography but in what it deems to be the moral corruption of secular television, radio, and newspapers.

As an organization, PK carries no institutionalized executive, legislative or judicial powers, because of its emphasis on maintaining the separation of church and state in this country. However, in October 1997, PK orchestrated the "million man" Stand in the Gap in the nation's capital. Defined as a prayer meeting, an estimated several hundred thousand attendees (Cose, 1997) gathered on the Mall to "unite with one another on behalf of our families, our churches, our communities and our nation, to share our hearts and seek repentance, that our nation may be transformed" (Promise Keepers, 1996a).

In sum, the Promise Keepers organization, bearing a moral conservative perspective on issues of gender, can be considered a social movement when measured by the criteria set forth by Stewart, Smith, and Denton (1994). As such, it serves as an organized constitutive locus for unfolding the concerted making of masculinity.

STUDY DESIGN

My goal was to explicate the PK phenomenon from both the "top down" and from the "bottom up"—sorting through the incidental and essential themes of constituting masculine subjectivity under the auspices of an organized men's movement. To gather data, I immersed myself in PK's rhetorical culture at both the local and national levels. Over six months, I attended three national two-day conferences during which thousands of men gathered in arenas and stadiums in a northwestern, a north central and a southern city. The first conference was primarily for orienting to the heretofore alien phenomenon, and that experience made the experience of the second conference richer and more fruitful in terms of where I focused my ethnographic gaze. The third conference provided an opportunity to revisit the phenomena from a more edified perspective, auguring in on still-elusive questions of meaning and structure.

Meanwhile, using two separate focus groups at the local level, I met with nine men from churches in a midwestern state who had participated in PK conferences and activities. These focus group interviews were audio-taped and transcribed for later analysis. I also attended twice-monthly meetings held by a church group where approximately 15 men met in a small-group effort focused on working through the *Promise Builders Study Series*. At these meetings, a Key Man typically broke the men into groups of five to study and discuss issues surrounding the Seven Promises. I was a participant/observer in these small groups, listening to the discussions and contributing my own views. Respectful of the naturalistic setting for these small-group meetings, I chose not to audio-tape or blatantly note on paper the proceedings. Instead, I later impressionistically reconstructed what went on during those sessions.

I also solicited open-ended, qualitative interviews with men from all parts of the country, which were audio-taped and transcribed. These men were contacted in a variety of ways to ask if they wished to share their PK-related experiences. For example, several World Wide Web sites and discussion groups have been formed on the Internet. I secured the permission of the Web Site operators to post a solicitation for research participants; this generated several contacts. One local interviewee was referred to me by a PK state office, and this person in turn referred me to another local interviewee. Other men were contacted through the two-day conferences, where I randomly passed out business-size cards.

Using a protocol generated from my experiences with PK rhetoric as an open-ended guide, I entered into dialogue with 14 men who were active in PK in an attempt to unfold their lived experiences with the phenomenon of constituting masculine subjectivity. The data from the dialogues, carried out through qualitative interviews, were combined with the focus group and small-group meeting data to serve as the source for phenomenological descriptions of men's lived experiences within PK. Subsequently, these phenomenological, existential descriptions served as a foundation from which to move among the analytic stages of phenomenological reduction, variation and warranted assertion.

Finally, I analyzed PK's rhetorical artifacts. In addition to participating in the two-day conferences, I studied video tapes, audio tapes, books and magazines that all are official material produced or approved by PK and sold to the public. Other documents such as financial statements, information and donation solicitation mailings, and product catalogues also were examined. Ultimately, I analyzed 14 individual interviews (45–65 minutes in length); 9 people in 2 focus groups (60–90 minutes in length); 6 small-group meetings/discussions (60–90 minutes in length); 9 hours of Promise Keepers video tapes (1996c-d; 1996g-l); 5 hours of Promise Keepers audio tapes (1996e-f); 4 Promise Keepers books; 2 issues of *New Man* magazine; and the miscellaneous PK documents and mailings.

CRITIQUE OF PROMISE KEEPERS' RHETORIC

Phenomenological analysis of the rhetorical construct of masculine subjectivity, as it is proffered by PK, is evidenced in four orienting clusters: (1) PK's creed and agenda; (2) assaults on manhood that PK perceives; (3) PK's belief in a Christlike husband the Redeemer; and (4) PK's directives for action.

For those committed to egalitarian perspectives on gender constitution, the most disquieting aspect of PK's rhetoric is the pervasive reinstanciation of a patriarchal hierarchy and privilege. That PK's vision and agenda are for men and exclude women is unmistakably evident in a mission statement that promotes the bonding and banding together of men in ministries to evangelize a specific, narrow interpretation of biblical scripture, the intent of which is to effect global cultural change. Throughout its rhetoric, PK privileges men in the material, earthly hierarchy of being. The only ones who stand above men are the Trinity of God, Jesus Christ and the Holy Spirit. Everyone and everything else is subordinated. The vision statement provides an image of men "on their knees in humility and on their feet in unity" (PK, 1996m, p. 8). This is to say that men are only humbled before the Trinity. Before women, children, animals, nature and the material world, men stand united as a common force. "We believe man was created in the image of God," they say (PK, 1996m, p. 24). This is the authority PK uses for confirmation that men are divine products crafted to evangelize the gospel of Jesus and reconcile the lost world to God's eternal salvation, and they open their conference with a prayer that announces to God that the army of men is assembled and awaits word of His plan.

To enlist the will of its all-male audience, PK establishes a dubious monolithic definition of what traits, behaviors, and roles men must possess if they are to be considered men according to their biblical interpretation: "Natural assertiveness flows through his blood. Even toddlers reflect it.... It is in our deepest nature as men to push forward, to step out, to take charge, to fight for higher ground. Pressure builds up inside a home where a man doesn't take an active role in family decision, doesn't put bread on the table, isn't the spiritual leader" (Smalley & Trent, 1992, pp. 40–41).

Next, PK congeals men *qua* men by demonstrating that while masculine traits remain stable, their behaviors and roles are unrealized because of assaults on their manhood and forced abdication of their proper role. Conditions conspire to prevent men from achieving their Christlike potential, according to the PK view. Despite men's hard work, performing and achieving so as to be valued, appreciated and loved, they still remain empty and unfulfilled. Instead of being appreciated, they come under attack from family, friends, and church leaders because they do not measure up. No matter the degree of men's efforts, it is never enough. Failure eventually results in inner conflict, emotional drain and a mechanical existence aimed only at trying to perform better. In the frenzy, spiritual peace and well-being give way to the escapism of food, alcohol and pornography, and propagate elitism, sectarianism and racism.

PK takes little notice of how men exploit and subjugate other men by setting their own standards of what passes as achievement, worth and masculinity. Conveniently, women and a nebulous, ill-defined "society" are pointed to as the culprits for men's angst and desperation.

Compounding the problem for men, PK says, are many women's attempts to feminize the world, making it over in their own image rather than in the godly image of men. PK points to the church as a cultural institution to illustrate its concern with feminization:

> [T]he church no matter what the denomination is essentially an institution that appeals more to women than to men.... I looked around and asked myself, Does anything here really attract men? Is anything here distinctly masculine? I noticed robes, flowers, and things being repeated that most men couldn't relate to. By contrast, one of the most memorable services I have ever experienced was held in the Australian outback.... After the service we roasted an entire lamb on the spit and shared it.... We must recapture the church for men, defeminize it... [Hicks, 1992b, pp. 154–155].

PK's alarm over societal feminization, and the general softening of men, is rooted in a misguided adherence to a standard wherein men are wild and untamed by nature, and women are a taming, civilizing force. This belief is a throwback to at least the last century, when it was especially popular to understand men that men were in need of temperance, purification and a moralizing force to channel them, but that too much civilization would weaken their constitution and interfere with the brute force required to master nature (Kimmel & Mosmiller, 1992).

Illogically, PK at once accuses women of softening men, that is, "sissifying" them, and then reluctantly taking over their vacated roles of manhood. However, if women do not want men's roles, and step in only because someone must uphold the structures of civility and, as a consequence, are emotionally and physically overloaded, it does not follow that women would intentionally conspire to bring about the condition in men that is supposed to make them abdicate their roles and thereby extract a high price—which is women's own suffering.

Still, in a sweeping generality, PK insists that men have indeed abdicated their positions of responsibility, and the result is a loss of conscience that their rhetoric sets about to restore. Although men have abdicated, PK offers them hope by telling them that "men who struggle with guilt, pride, or apathy are prodigal sons" (Gaultiere, 1992, p.31). The tacit argument advanced by PK is that the consciousness of men is to be understood as that of Christ the Redeemer. While Jesus is accepted as the Messiah sent by God to redeem the sins of humankind, men, by the authority of their likeness to God's son, are to redeem the secular earth and the doctrinally misguided.

In the material hierarchy posited by PK, men are stewards of the earth and the family, responsibilities first bestowed on Adam. PK draws on Genesis when it notes that men are to guide, guard and govern; direct, protect and correct; nourish, cherish, and admonish the family and the earth. Failing one's responsibilities leads to a world that is impaired, diseased and in peril of dying. In short, Promise Keepers clearly maintains that men are to provide and protect, as does a shepherd; in the home primarily, but also in the community.

Arguments buttressed by mind/body dichotomies are enlisted to sustain PK's narrow biblical hermeneutics of the man as household head. For example, official materials claim, "As the head it is your position to discern the needs of the wife. She represents the body, as it shows the body of Christ, and we show as the headship of Jesus Christ" (PK, 1996h). If woman is body, man is mind, runs the argument. Left unarticulated in this argument is that the body is presented by PK as subordinate to the mind. Invoking Jesus as body and mind is demonstrative of how a body hangs from the cross, but a mind (i.e., spirit) achieves transcendence by commanding the soul unto God. The head directs the body, mind is over matter and man is over women in this traditional, modernist line of thinking.

In other variations, women are further subordinated when their role is reduced to mere adornment as in the claim that "If the husband is the head, then the wife is the crown" (PK, 1996h). When granted incarnate status, man and woman are often dichotomous, women the "weaker vessel," "fragile," and "precious" compared to men's brutishness. Women are said to be circular in their reasoning, while men are straight; women are emotional, men are logical; women possess a feminine mystique, men are just plain men.

PK justifies its tilting the balance of power in the family by taking refuge in the New International Version's translation of Ephesians 5:22, which states, "Wives submit yourselves unto your own husbands as unto the Lord. For the husband is the head of the wife, even as Christ is head of the church; and he is savior of the body." They supplement this directive with myriad characterizations of women as "helpers" because Eve was a helpmate delivered by God from Adam's flesh. Such a literal interpretation is foreshadowed by PK's dependence on a Biblical translation whose preface emphasizes a "concern for clear and natural English," motivated by a Cartesian belief in the clarity, distinctiveness and transparency of God's Word.

When confronted with charges of misogyny, PK leaders insist that the organization respects, honors and treasures women. Their rhetoric suggests that they do in fact promote those three behaviors. But that is not the same as treating women as equals. Clearly, PK does not hold women on a par with men when they speak of cleaving through marriage and the woman becoming, for example, Mrs. John Smith. A woman's value, in their view, rests exclusively in the fact that she is a gift from God, and thus must be precious. What women might be, apart from one of the many godly creations inhabiting His earthly Kingdom and subjects of men's stewardship, is of little interest to PK.

Likewise, children are in need of protection and provision by fathers, PK believes. Why women cannot be surrogates for men, or why men are crucial for the provision and protection of families, is not made explicit, however. Instead, tenuous psychological assertions linking hatred, criminality, fascism, totalitarianism and megalomania to the absence of paternal influence are advanced as reasons why children must be reared in patriarchal family units. To wit:

> There were fifty-four great philosophers, from 600 B.C. to 1968 A.D., whose influence greatly impacted the peoples of this planet. Of those fifty-four, forty believed in God, fourteen did not. Of the fourteen who were atheists, eight were preacher's kids. Of the fourteen who were atheists, all fourteen hated their father. When a man hates his father, as did Darwin, Hegel, Freud and Nietzsche, when a man hates his father he has a tendency to fail in school because it's the one way to bring shame upon his father's name.
>
> It's the one way he has of taking revenge on the slight or the emotion of hatred or animosity towards his father.... There is another thing about those who hate their father. Not only do they fail in school, but they adopt a surrogate father. Both Hitler and Stalin hated their father. They were influenced by those four philosophers I mentioned, who also hated their father. Stalin danced in the street with his mother when his father died. Hitler as a boy stood at the door when his father entered and said, "Heil, father Hitler." And what he learned as a youth he practiced as an adult. After World War I, so few fathers came home that Germany became known as a fatherless nation. The disenfranchised, alienated youth adopted a surrogate father who called Germany the Fatherland, and gave them his face.... After World War II ... Russia became known as a fatherless nation. And they adopted a surrogate father and they erected statues to Marx and Lenin [PK, 1996c].

Sounding like strident alarmists, PK first claims that society has totally broken down, and then attributes the breakdown to the absence of the father in the family. Meanwhile, men's feminization is attributed to the absence of the fathers, coupled with pressures to achieve and perform. Together, these represent a paralyzing force that leads men to run away from their responsibilities.

The artifacts consisting of voices from PK-affirming women reveal them as co-conspirators in a hegemonic form of masculinity. They embrace a view in which men and women are essentially different in physical, cognitive and affective domains. PK-affirming women accept a biblical interpretation in which a woman's role is defined as a helper of man, though they maintain that this does not mean they are less than men—only different. These women take their value from carrying out what they see as a godly ordination to maternally nurture and support their husbands, emotionally and physically.

PK says, "[Christ] received and accepted the rejected. He loved the church with unconditional love. For while we are yet sinners, Christ died for us. We didn't deserve His love but He loves us anyhow. That is the kind of love we are called to demonstrate in our relationships with our wives.... It must reduplicate the love God has shown us in Jesus Christ" (PK, 1996h).

It seems that men are to become Christlike redeemers of their wives, their children and society. By analogy, PK establishes women and children as the undeserving and sinful to whom men shall give love and acceptance. Moreover, men must take on the sins of the world, since society would be redeemed were they to figuratively crucify their heretofore misguided ways and thus forego abdication for accession.

Arming men with Christlike credentials situates PK to order them into action. First, men must work with, rather than against, one another. They are to establish close relationships with a few other men to nurture, support, and encourage one another, while holding each other accountable for sinful behavior. Women cannot know what it is like to be men, nor can they validate men's experiences, PK says. Only another man "truly understands what it is like to be a man" (Hicks, 1992a, p. 137). They can find safety and growth with each other, thereby releasing themselves from their "deep-seated" emotional dependence on women. In addition, men are encouraged to revive the centuries-old, but now lost, practice of mentoring younger men. They are to initiate them into the ways of Christian manhood through involvement in men's ministries.

Problematic in all this is how PK elevates or, better said, reduces masculinity to an "old boys club." PK's club is a digital affair where one either stands with or against and, foremost, one is treated as either man or Other to establish a baseline from which everything else arises. Secondarily, one is a Christian man, understood in the evangelical, Biblical-infallibility sense, or one is an Other. In PK's version of masculinity, virtually no common ground is found between Christian men and the rest of the world. Presumably, for admittance to this club one shows evidence of a Christian phallus in lieu of a membership card or secret handshake, all the while winking at the shared belief that women are dependency-spawning, feminizing agents of societal destruction against whom the club must rally.

To rally men to action, PK warmongers with its own version of a religious jihad. The audience of men is mustered into an army whose commander is Jesus and whose leaders are the clergy. A war is to be waged in which these men wield divine power over the Satanic forces of evil. Says McCartney, "Men, you've been retreating. Men of God, we are calling you to war.... You are going to war tonight.... We contest anything that sets itself up against the truth, Jesus Christ" (PK, 1996g).

The war to be fought is for the leadership of families and communities, where strong male influence is to be reestablished. No hint of willingness to negotiate roles is found in one PK speaker's often-quoted mandate that a man say to his wife, "Honey, I've made a terrible mistake. I've given you my role. I gave up leading this family, and I forced you to take my place. Now I must reclaim that role" (Evans, 1994, p. 79).

By positioning its actions as a religious war, PK eliminates the chance for compromise or reasoned discourse. No point of entry or common agreement exists from which to counter a purported directive from Christ, the "Commander in Chief," for men to become "the salt and the light of the world," and to "return to the post of duty that God has assigned" (PK, 1996g). One either accepts men as God-given leaders, or is declared an antagonist.

Although it is difficult to rehabilitate the PK organization (and far beyond the intent of this chapter), it should be acknowledged that PK highlights an important issue when it notes the failure of some men to carry the financial and physical responsibilities attendant to creating children. PK also touches on an important concern when it addresses the need for racial reconciliation in this country, which was the theme of the 1996 conferences. Still, one cannot help but wonder if political expediency is not at work here. On the heels of the Million Man March in Washington, PK announced Stand in the Gap to unite men in Christian prayer in an attempt to transform what they characterized as a troubled nation.

VOICES OF THE PARTICIPANTS

In an attempt to resituate this phenomenological inquiry amidst the ontological condition of humans-in-the-lifeworld, my analysis and critique now turn to the experiences of some men who attend PK conferences and consume PK-sanctioned rhetorical artifacts. These men, whom I will refer to as interview subjects to distinguish them from PK speakers and administrators, comment on conflicting contemporary definitions of masculinity that problematize their heretofore stable and transparent gendered existences. In an effort to reestablish themselves, they search for answers that help them make sense of the competing definitions. Finally, relying to some degree on PK's rhetorical vision, these men remake their gendered selves in ways that differ from their original constitution, but that also differ from PK's hard line.

Analyzing the experience of men who constitute their masculine subjectivity under the auspices of this organized men's movement reveals four grounding conditions through which manifold themes emerge: (1) Conflict in the form of competing constitutive forces; (2) destabilization resulting in attendant crises of gendered identity; (3) arbitration, wherein the men seek counsel; and (4) remediation, whereby they reconstitute their gendered selves.

Interview subjects identified a conflict over definitions of masculinity. They acknowledged manhood's stereotypical images and appeared to discount traditional beliefs that men are tough, stoic, isolated, and unemotional. Meanwhile, they accounted for their own gendered being in terms of the influences and modeling by other men, to whom they were exposed from an early age. Becoming a man is understood as learning, predominantly from one's own father, how to carry oneself, in lessons either directly received or quietly observed. Later, male peers, male teachers, male coaches, male pastors and male authority figures influenced the continuous shaping of the interview subjects' masculinity: "My father was certainly my original role model. I mean that's where my jumping off point was. Everything I knew how to do I started with what I saw him do."

Some of these men are intent on maintaining a legacy of masculinity. They talk of the importance of acting in their own families the way their fathers did in theirs: "My father was the dominant role in the house and everything went through him before any decisions were made. In my own marriage we still hold to that to a certain extent."

Overall, these men can seem enlightened when speaking of masculinity as a learned condition. Unfortunately, they introduce an ambiguity when they insist on a natural and divinely-decreed order to gendered subjectivity. On the one hand, interview subjects understand gender to be a learned, conditioned, practiced set of behaviors and attitudes, while on the other hand they insist that men are born with essential characteristics that distinguish them from women, and that furthermore, God delineates what roles men and women shall assume. I will return to this ambiguity shortly.

While these men believe that they constitute their masculinity from the preferred stock of good models, they agonize over what they see as negative constitutive influences embraced by other men. To their minds, the media turn men into buffoons, dummies and objects of ridicule at the disrespectful hands of women: "It's almost as though the roles have reversed, especially I see it with the media, T.V. shows. We were watching a show the other night where the woman was the very dominant person and the male was kinda the tag-along type of person." The breakdown of the media family (which is no longer nuclear in its manifestation, nor is the male the head and leader) further undermines men.

Similarly, the interview subjects see further erosion of traditional masculinity in the larger secular society, where role distinctions have fused into a move toward gender homogeneity. A few men ascribe the change to aggressive women with feminist impulses to dominate the society. Others less vociferously suggest that a general move toward pluralism has diminished the leadership men once assumed.

These conflicting forces make the men feel undervalued since they are no longer needed for leadership, protection and provision. Everyone's roles have become interchangeable and no longer retain gender specificity. Interview subjects said that having their ideals of masculinity cast aside leaves them confused and insecure over their proper place in the home, work site and community. Internally, they thought they knew how to constitute manhood, but they are aware that their versions are now in external conflict with much of society: "I'm not internally conflicted about how to act. I think I'm pretty clear on what I need to do for me and my family. However, I do often find myself being a minority in talking to people who don't share my beliefs. Most of my conflict is external or personal, it's not very often internal."

To these men's minds, this conflict results in many men (though not they themselves) giving up the struggle and relinquishing control as they run from their responsibilities. Consequently, the world has fallen into moral decay, predicated on a disrespect for the spiritual, a redefinition of the family unit, the devaluation of men as leaders and men's own lack of accountability.

The interview subjects describe an emotional emptiness wrought by this conflict and instability, and they yearn for ways to restabilize themselves and the world. Some have tried to resist these new definitions of masculinity and others have given over to them, but all feel a desperate need to recapture an essence of importance and value as the leaders and models for the family and community.

It is difficult to fault these men for feeling confused once their assumptions about gender have become problematized. Previously, their constitutive activities had served them so well that they remained in the background of mundane, everyday practices. What seems unsatisfactory to me is these men's tendency to cling to their traditional understandings and to lash out, blaming others for turning them on their heads. The interview subjects fail to examine the possibility that their own and other men's formulas for patriarchal, heterosexist masculinity reached a critical mass of oppression that simply caused that masculinity to implode under its own density.

To their minds, most of the interview subjects have no common group with whom they can seek counsel. The handful of men who form support groups based on PK rhetoric are the rare exception. By their own testimony, few have close male friends in whom to confide their sense of inadequacy, anxiety, fears and confusion over a perceived assault on their gender roles: "I guess that's pride and feeling like that's not being a man, sharing your needs, your hurts or whatever with another man. Opening up and sharing your heart with other people, I personally have a problem with that."

The men are distrustful of other men, who are viewed as competitors before whom they cannot show weakness. However, they learn of PK as an organization that draws men together in a safe, if temporary, environment of relative anonymity, so the interview subjects turn to this synecdoche for Christian masculinity to arbitrate the gender conflict: "While there is some intimacy, there's quite a lot of anonymity. The guys all pretty much dress the same; everyone's in casual dress. There's no clergy, no blue collar worker, no professional people. There are just guys and everyone relates to each other on level ground. To some degree the power structure is no longer there; you don't have managers, supervisors and supervised employees, or anything like that."

PK conferences are carried out in venues that are familiar to the men. They have been to sports arenas full of cheering crowds, and they are comfortable shouting, whistling, and throwing beach balls. The interview subjects report an ethereal feeling moving them when they witness tens of thousands of men singing in unison. They say an exhilarating spirit is palpable when the thousands come together in prayer. Camaraderie, warmth, the dropping of pretensions and a desire to open up emotionally follow as the men begin to believe they are "partners in a grand movement rather than competitors."

Long after the conferences are over, the men identify their partners through shirts and hats bearing the PK logo and draw strength from knowing there are others who share their purpose. The "grand movement," as the interview subjects understand it, is an effort to confront men for failing in their responsibilities, and serves as a catalyst to assimilate and distribute PK's renewed vision of masculinity. They understand this vision of masculinity to be a corporeal manifestation of Christ by emulating Him through integrity, accountability and positively influencing the world. The men also rely on the prescriptive "Seven Promises" to resolve dilemmas about masculinity and appropriate behavior.

The interview subjects have no qualms about the conferences' occurring in all-male settings. Were it otherwise, they claim, they could not focus as fully on the events because women would prove to be a distraction or a source of competition among men. Nor could men respond honestly to the speakers' admonishments in front of women, they believe.

This line of reasoning is typical of the propensity of PK attendees to blame external forces for their own failings, inadequacies and inhibitions. Incidentally, that men break down and cry at the conferences, and do so with apparent impunity, is frequently highlighted by the interview subjects. The consistency with which the specter of crying men arises in their reporting of events is perhaps testimony to the absence of emotional displays in most of the other settings of these men's lives: "There, in that auditorium, you were allowed to be a male and to be human and to be frail, have emotions, to cry if you want…. Some men have said to me that they feel comfortable that they're able to cry in that environment and they don't know that they could do that if women were there."

But the interview subjects do not seem blindly to subscribe to PK dogma. While generally uncritical of PK's scriptural renditions, they are wary of the group's organizational aspects. The men have reservations about the financial aspects, equating the organization with an efficient big business when they consider the revenues generated from more than one million attendees, along with heavy sales of merchandise. Some of the men are also critical of PK for putting all its emphasis on a two-day, annual event, and then leaving them to their own devices at the local level until the following year. Despite their reservations about the organization, however, the interview subjects close ranks when confronted by detractors. They quickly become apologists for Promise Keepers when the organization is accused of promoting male supremacy or heterosexism.

After attending the conferences and consuming PK artifacts, the interview subjects begin to remediate their gender confusion by reconstituting themselves. Not surprisingly, they retain many foundational assumptions about gender promoted by PK: That men and women have biologically-based traits, instincts and natures that are different and complementary in the roles they fill. Like PK, the men believe that they must assume responsibility rather than run away, that they should be men who can be counted on to provide financially and spiritually, and that they should be role models and mentors for younger men, as were their fathers and grandfathers.

But when the talk turns to taking back their roles, the interview subjects exhibit a temperance missing from PK's rhetoric. While they speak of needing to act as stronger leaders in their families, churches and communities, no allusion is made to aggressively wresting control back from feminists, and they resist the hard-edged rhetoric of natural hierarchies. For the most part, the men seem to respect women as their friends and partners, and they often report the conference heightens their sensitivity of how they treat their wives and girlfriends: "Sometimes, we let our families down or our churches down, and it's time to ask for forgiveness from the past.... It is time for men to take note that, hey, we're letting it slide, and we need to pick some things back up and become a bigger part."

Neither do the men parrot PK's rigid religious war talk. Instead, they seem more willing to work toward negotiated settlements on roles and definitions of masculinity. This is not to say they do not have non-negotiable items, because they do: heterosexuality and Christianity are two.

Perhaps because these men are immersed in the day-to-day living of gender in ways that PK rhetoric is not, they seem more comfortable with softening the lines of responsibility and authority rather than invoking analogies between Christ and themselves. But then, this is a difference of the real from the ideal that is exactly the distinction between the conference attendees as members of a larger world and the PK organization isolated as though in a cloistered order.

PK conference attendees are not to be conflated with the Promise Keepers as an organization. The two stand as separate entities, guided by different exigencies. To be gendered as a male is a constitutive act arising from a situated context in which these interview subjects come into being in relation to an Other. These men are involved in the continuous living out of gender subjectivity and are not given the luxury of scholastic distance afforded the authors of PK rhetoric. They appear to do the best they can considering they are caught in the tension of an ambiguous commitment to both social constructionism on one hand, and biological and religious determinism on the other. It is difficult for the interview subjects to reconcile their acknowledgment that social forces shape and continue to temper their understandings of masculinity against their belief that God and biology destine them to fulfill predetermined roles.

The men not only constitute themselves in a multiplicity of masculinities, they remake themselves in a continuous hermeneutic spiral. That is, they may only rest for a short while with a remediated understanding of their masculinity and then reenter the stages of conflict, destabilization and arbitration, and arrive at a newly remediated understanding:

> I think [Promise Keepers] helps me recognize where I am in growth; it makes me more conscious of what I should be and what I should be doing. They encouraged me to say this is what I want to achieve, I want to better myself and achieve all these promises we talked about. And I think to myself, how can I facilitate that freedom in my life at a daily level?... I don't think [Promise Keepers] had grand illusions that they're going to be the end, that they're going to be a sustaining force in men's lives. I think they wanted to create an environment for men to be able to change, and I think they're doing that.

John Caputo (1987), in his book *Radical Hermeneutics*, explains why such a circular repetition might occur with issues of identity constitution. In writing about Søren Kierkegaard's coming to terms with the flux, Caputo says Kierkegaard does not deny it by embracing a metaphysics that subverts time and motion. Rather, Kierkegaard believes that through repetition one presses on in the flux. This opposes the Greek tradition of a Platonic moving backward toward where one has come, that is, recollection. Instead, in accord with Christian doctrine, one must move ahead in existential advance. This moving ahead occurs through repetition, from which something new is produced, writes Kierkegaard, who distinguishes this repetition from duplication, in which something is merely repeated. While recollection quiets the turmoil of flux, repetition "finds a way to maintain one's head in the midst of it" (Caputo, 1987, p. 17). Identity and actuality must be reestablished through repetition, and although flux threatens to disperse the self, says Kierkegaard, the power to forge oneself lies in repetition.

In sum, the lived experience of masculinity is not a neat, seven-step package of promises for these men. Rather, they muddle through, constituting and reconstituting their masculine subjectivity by seeking assurances from institutions, organizations, their spouses, their children, God and one another, and hoping to marshal an appearance of coherence. They have not the sanctimonious certitude of the Promise Keepers organization where performing gender is reduced to a zero-sum game of binary role fulfillment.

References

Bakhtin, M.M. (1935/1981) *The dialogic imagination: Four essays* (Holquist, M., ed.)(Emerson, C., & Holquist, M., trans.). Austin, TX: University of Texas Press.

Bakhtin, M.M. (1990). Marxism and the philosophy of language. In P. Bizzell, & B. Herzberg (eds.) (L. Matejka & I.R. Titunik, trans.), *The rhetorical tradition* (pp. 944–963). New York: Bedford Books of St. Martin's Press.

Bizzell, P., & Herzberg, B. (eds.) (L. Matejka & I.R. Titunik, trans.). *The rhetorical tradition*. New York: Bedford Books of St. Martin's Press.

Boone, W. (1994). Why men must pray. In A. Janssen & L.K. Weeden (ed.), *Seven promises of a Promise Keeper* (pp. 25–31). Colorado Springs, CO: Focus on the Family.

Brod, H., and Kaufman, M. (eds.) (1992). *Theorizing masculinities*. Thousand Oaks, CA: Sage Publications.

Caputo, J. (1987). *Radical hermeneutics*. Bloomington, IN: Indiana University Press.

Clatterbaugh, K. (1996). *Contemporary perspectives on masculinity: Men, women, and politics in modern society* (2nd ed.) Boulder, CO: Westview Press.

Clatterbaugh, K. (1990). *Contemporary perspectives on masculinity: Men, women, and politics in modern society*. Boulder, CO: Westview Press.

Cose, E. (1997, October 13). Promises ... Promises. *Newsweek 130*, 30–31.

Dart, J. (1995, May 6). Promise Keepers, a message to L.A. men. *The Los Angeles Times*, 4.

Evans, T. (1994). Spiritual purity. In A. Janssen & L.K. Weeden (eds.), *Seven promises of a Promise Keeper*, pp. 73–81. Colorado Springs, CO: Focus on the Family Publishing.

Gaultiere, W. (1992). Promises to God. In B. McCartney et al., *What makes a Man?*, pp. 30–31. Colorado Springs, CO: NavPress.

Gilbreath, E. (1995, February 6). Manhood's great awakening. *Christianity Today 39*, 20–26.

Hicks, R. (1992a). Why beer commercials make some men feel so good. In B. McCartney et al., *What makes a Man?*, pp. 136–137. Colorado Springs, CO: NavPress.

Hicks, R. (1992b). Why men feel so out of place at church. In B. McCartney et al., *What makes a Man?*, pp. 154–156. Colorado Springs, CO: NavPress.

Hoffer, R., & Smith, S. (1995, January 16). Putting his house in order (B. McCartney quits). *Sports Illustrated*, 28–32.

Janssen, A., & Weeden, L.K. (eds.) (1994). *Seven promises of a Promise Keeper*. Colorado Springs, CO: Focus on the Family Publishing.

Johnson, H. (1995). Broken Promise? *Church and State 48*(5), 9–12.

Kimmel, M., & Kaufman, M. (1994). Weekend warriors: The new men's movement. In H. Brod & M. Kaufman (eds.), *Theorizing masculinities* (pp. 259–288). Thousand Oaks, CA: Sage Publications.

Kimmel, M., and Mosmiller, T. (eds.) (1992). *Against the tide: Pro-feminist men in the U.S., 1776–1990: A documentary history.* Boston: Beacon Press.

Messner, M. (1997). *Politics of masculinities: Men in movements.* Thousand Oaks, CA: Sage.

Neill, M. (1995, July 31). Old ways, new men: B. McCartney, founder of Promise Keepers. *People Weekly*, 46–48.

New man: For men of integrity. Official magazine of the Promise Keepers. April, 1995; May, 1996; June, 1996; October, 1996.

Promise Keepers (1996a). Internet postings (including press releases) on its World Wide Web site, http://www.promisekeepers.org/.

Promise Keepers (1996b). Audited financial statements through December 31, 1995. Public Relations Department, Boulder, CO.

Promise Keepers conference session (1996c, May 11). Cole, Edwin. "Turning Your Heart to Your Children." Videotape, Detroit.

Promise Keepers conference session (1996d, May 10). Hybels, Bill. "Walking with God: Becoming a Man After God's Own Heart." Videotape, Detroit.

Promise Keepers conference session (1996e, June 8). Jackson, Larry. "Going All Out for Your Wife." Audiotape, Boise.

Promise Keepers conference session (1996f, June 8). Kimmel, Tim. "Turning Your Heart to Your Children." Audiotape, Boise.

Promise Keepers conference session (1996g, May 11). McCartney, Bill. "A Call to Intercession and Action." Videotape, Detroit.

Promise Keepers conference session (1996h. May 11). McKinney, George. "Going All Out for Your Wife." Videotape, Detroit.

Promise Keepers conference session (1996I, May 10). Ryle, James. "Meeting God: Reconciling with Your Heavenly Father." Videotape, Detroit.

Promise Keepers conference session (1996j, May 11). Wagner, Glenn. "The Highest Common Denominator." Videotape, Detroit.

Promise Keepers conference session (1996k, May 11). Washington, Raleigh. "Walking in Your Brother's Shoes." Videotape, Detroit.

Promise Keepers conference session (1996l, June 7). Whittinghill, Al. "Walking with God: Becoming a Man After God's Own Heart." Audiotape, Boise.

Promise Keepers conference program (1996m).

Promise Keepers Builders Series (1995). Boulder, CO: Promise Keepers.

Shapiro, J. P. (1995, October 2). Heavenly promises. *U.S. News & World Report 119*, 68–70.

Smalley, G. and Trent, J. (1992). The promises you make to yourself. In B. McCartney et al., *What makes a Man?*, pp. 39–47. Colorado Springs, CO: NavPress.

Stewart, C.J., Smith, E.A. & Denton, R.E., Jr. (1994). *Persuasion and social movements* (3rd ed.). Prospect Heights, IL: Waveland Press.

Thompson, K. (1996). The virtuous male. *Utne Reader 73*, 68–69.

Van Biema, D. (1995, November 6). Full of promise. *Time 146*, 62–63.
Wagenheim, J. (1996, January-February). Among the Promise Keepers. *Utne Reader 72*, 74–77.
Walker, K. (1995, March-April). 300 wake up calls planned for 1995. *New Man: For Men of Integrity*, 74–76.
Woodward, K.L. (1994, August 29). The gospel of guyhood. *Newsweek 124*, 60–61.

CHAPTER 10

Exodus and the Chosen Men of God: Promise Keepers and the Theology of Masculinity

by David S. Gutterman

In the United States today, the Exodus narrative and the prophetic jeremiads are once again being told with renewed vigor. In the tradition of past religious revivals, Promise Keepers is using the sacred story central to this nation's history and identity as a vehicle for generating its own organizational identity and its vision of prophetic politics. PK is emphatically a story-telling organization; it spreads its gospel of Christian brotherhood through an array of narratives of men ("just like you") struggling to lead "good Christian lives" in this land of sin and perfidy. These "mundane stories" of individuals take shape within the broader "sacred story" of corporate crisis and redemption—a story rooted in the Exodus narrative of promise, liberation, covenant and subsequent prophetic accounts of backsliding, crisis, punishment and the hope of renewal. Both the sacred and mundane stories employed by Promise Keepers offer accounts of a "chosen people"—the "mighty men of God"—who will lead a revival in the land and renew the covenant between God and his "newly chosen people." In this essay, I examine how PK employs these narratives and how these narratives shape the organization's identity and politics. My analysis will ultimately address how PK employs a theology of "chosen masculinity" and what the political implications of such an identity of chosen-ness might be in today's pluralist United States.

THE POWER OF NARRATIVES

In his PK-endorsed book, *The Coming Revival: America's Call to Fast, Pray, and "Seek God's Face,"* Bill Bright (1995, pp. 22–23), founder and President of the Campus Crusade for Christ, writes:

> When reading the many portions of the Scripture, including the major and minor prophets, we are reminded again and again that if we—as a nation and as individuals—obey God, He will bless us. But when we disobey Him, He disciplines us. Tragically, we as a nation have disobeyed and grieved God.... As a result, an avalanche of evil, crime, immorality, abortion, and drug addiction has devastated our country and broken the heart of our Lord. This disintegration of America is not news to you because, like ancient Israel, our nation has for the most part forgotten God and failed to obey his commands.

In this remarkable passage, Bright invokes the story of Exodus and the subsequent prophetic legacy to both describe and produce a state of crisis in the United States today. Bright defines the magnitude of the predicament (God's favor versus God's judgment), names the cause of God's displeasure, declares the social and political effects of this grievous sin of disobedience and concludes with the suggestion that redemption lies waiting if Americans—the modern "chosen people"—renew their covenant with God. I say "describe and produce" this crisis to indicate the power of narratives: while Bright is surely depicting what he conceives is the nature of the troubles facing the nation today, in telling this narrative, he is also generating a particular social, theological and political vision of crisis and solace. In analyzing this story, as with any historical, religious or political analysis, we ought to recall the oft-quoted assertion by Alasdair MacIntyre (1989, p. 216) that: "Man [sic] is in his actions and practice, as well as in his fictions, essentially a story-telling animal.... But the key question for men is not about their own authorship; I can only answer the question 'What am I to do?' if I can answer the prior question 'Of what story or stories do I find myself a part?'" Narratives, that is to say, do not just describe or reflect, but rather define and give meaning to, human existence. Analyzing the form and content of these stories, which we tell and of which we are a part, raises the question of politics. As Roland Barthes argues, "historical discourse," as is the case of all forms of storytelling, "is in its essence a form of ideological elaboration" (quoted in White, 1983, p. 13).

It is important to recognize, however, that not all narratives move and define us in quite the same way. Stephen Crites draws an important distinction between "sacred" and "mundane" narratives. While "mundane stories are set within the bounds of a particular context ... sacred stories" serve to define and establish that context. Crites (1989, pp. 70–71) explains:

> Sacred stories, and the symbolic worlds they project, are ... like dwelling-places. People live in them ... men's [sic] sense of self and world are created through them ... these are stories that orient the life of people through time.... [Sacred stories] form the very consciousness that projects a total world horizon, and therefore informs the

intentions by which actions are projected into that world ... every sacred story is a creation story: not merely that one may name creation of world and self as its theme but also that the story itself creates a world of consciousness and the self that is oriented to it.

In calling such stories "sacred," Crites does not mean to say that these stories are actually divinely authorized or inspired; rather, he suggests that certain stories are held "sacred" by a nation or people and thus serve as a foundational narrative invested with meaning *as if* it were divinely authorized—or at least "natural" to the community. Though in this essay I focus on one particular sacred story—the narrative in which Americans are a "chosen people"—I by no means want to suggest that this is the only sacred story in the United States or that this sacred story is above critical interrogation (addressing, for example, this story's implicit American triumphalism). The point, then, is not to posit the "truth" or legitimacy of this claim of chosenness, but rather to delve into the rhetorical and constitutive function of this trope in the United States. In this sense, the nation is both the subject of and (to borrow a phrase from Stanley Fish) the "interpretive community" amongst whom this sacred story holds a particular resonance.

The "sacred story" of crisis and solace told by Bright is in the spirit of what Sacvan Bercovitch has called the "American jeremiad" and is exemplary of the political sermons or prophetic narratives that have so indelibly shaped the identity and political sensibility of the nation. In the United States, the sacred stories of the American jeremiad set the context and the horizon of cultural understanding within which "mundane stories" help provide meaning and order for everyday existence. The sacred story reveals the identity and vision of the teller of the story (be it nation, community, organization or individual) and the mundane stories offer models of political practice often aimed at realizing the vision set forth by the sacred story. Sacred stories thus provide a sense of meaning and order that make particular mundane stories possible, and mundane stories, working within the context constituted by a particular sacred story, enable the process toward, if not the final attainment of, the vision set forth in the sacred story. Promise Keepers, I will illustrate, utilizes a version of the Exodus narrative that emphasizes the trope of "chosen-ness" as its "sacred story" and provides complementary "mundane" narratives to guide men in their lives amongst their envisioned "chosen brotherhood." To examine the politics that result from PK's combination of the sacred and mundane, I will begin by exploring the political themes of the foundational "sacred story" of Exodus and then address briefly how this narrative has functioned historically in the United States.

THE POLITICAL HISTORY OF EXODUS

The Exodus narrative that serves as the basis and inspiration for the prophetic jeremiad is fundamentally a political story: it is an ideological telling of a people's history—a story that, in its telling, not only engages in rhetoric in order to define and raise the political stakes, but also defines the identity of a people, the ancient Hebrews. The political themes of the Exodus story—"slavery and freedom, law and rebellion"—are manifested in myriad ways (Walzer, 1985, p. 12). Indeed, the tone of the narrative is established as political from the very outset of the biblical text. The book of Exodus begins with a new Pharaoh, "who did not know about Joseph" (Ex 1:8) coming to power in Egypt (all biblical citations are taken from Promise Keepers' *Men's Studies Bible* [*NIV*]). Joseph's brethren, who at the close of Genesis had achieved a comfortable and stable status in Egypt, were now cast into slavery, illustrating the theme of the contingency of the human condition and the fragility of politics. In his analysis of the Exodus story in *Moses: The Revelation and the Covenant*, Martin Buber (1965, p. 34) stresses the political and rhetorical quality of the narrative. For instance, Buber notes that the narrative of bondage in Egypt is not a chronicle but a "poesy" aimed at heightening and emphasizing the suffering and lowliness of the Hebrews in order figuratively to render their liberation—and their identity as a chosen and liberated people—that much more poignant.

The emphasis on the chosen-ness of the Hebrews raises political questions about exclusion—that is, who does and who does not belong to this chosen community and how are the boundaries established and maintained. It is not enough that the tribes of Israel are distinguished from the Egyptians (or, in other words, the oppressed distinguished from the oppressors). The true measure of inclusion and exclusion rests on the conditional covenant established at the foot of Mt. Sinai between all the people of Israel and the God of history. God's reminder of the historic act of carrying the people of Israel on "eagle's wings" out of Egypt initiates the covenant (Ex 19:4). That the people of Israel are supposed to know and worship their God as a force of history is stressed throughout the narrative, but perhaps most emphatically, as theologian Jurgen Moltmann reminds us, by the preamble to the Ten Commandments: "I am the Lord your God, who brought you out of Egypt, out of the land of slavery" (Ex 20:2; see Moltmann, 1975, p. 46ff). Much can and has been said about this part of the Exodus narrative, but here I want to focus on one feature of this story to help illuminate this point about chosen-ness and exclusion.

Recall that shortly after the covenant is established, Moses goes up Mt. Sinai to meet with God. The man who stood up to Pharaoh, demanded freedom for the slaves, led his people out of Egypt and through the Red Sea into freedom and, all the while, served as mediator between God and the people, providing a new order and sense of direction, now disappears. At precisely the time of what should have been Israel's greatest moment to date—life as God's newly-anointed and chosen people—their temporal leader departs and a crisis ensues. Without the guidance of Moses, doubt, disorder and instability quickly re-emerge and the Israelites, seeking security, convince Aaron to let them create and pray to a golden idol. Of course, rather than bringing them solace, this act serves to exacerbate the crisis. When he returns from the mountain and sees the people worshipping the idol, Moses, in a fury, throws down the tablets (which, presumably, would have brought some degree of stability to the Israelite social order) and a "civil war" occurs. Rallying those who are "for the Lord" (Ex 32:26), Moses leads a bloody purge of those so quick to break the covenant, excluding them forever from the community of the chosen.

This part of the Exodus narrative provides striking political lessons. Despite the assurances of divine sympathy and the mysterious promise of an idyllic future, the temporal needs and anxieties of life in the human realm of politics and history helps mark the difference between the sacred and the profane, or what Augustine would call the City of God and the City of Man. The distance between the sacred and the profane is, of course, dramatically illustrated by the contrast between the awesome new voice of Yahweh, which comes from on high, and the golden idol fabricated from jewelry around which the backsliding Israelites dance and pray. Even in the aftermath of displays of divine presence and power, backsliding will ensue and crisis will plague a chosen community. In times of crisis, endeavors to recreate order and stability may include a purge that lays low the sinner in order to re-purify the community of the chosen. However, as the ensuing biblical history of murmurings, backsliding and waywardness make clear, the stability of the obedience and order of the chosen community are never ensured and further purges are inevitable. Indeed, the prophetic writings take their impetus from the failure to establish fully and to maintain unchallenged the distinct identity of the ancient Hebrew people. For example, the prophet Isaiah proclaims: "See how the faithful city has become a harlot! She was once full of justice, righteousness used to dwell in her—but now murderers.... Therefore the Lord ... declares ... 'I will turn my hand against you; I will thoroughly purge away your dross and remove all your impurities'" (Is 1:21,25).

This pattern of seeking to re-configure the chosen community as a response to times of crisis was adopted by the inheritors of the jeremiadic tradition in America (see Note, p. 150) and continues to function as a sacred story in the United States today. As William McLoughlin illustrates in his analysis of the history of Great Awakenings in America, this trope of chosen-ness animates the theology of the revivals. Following the model of the biblical prophets, the preachers of the Great Awakenings have implored their wayward "chosen people" to renew their covenant with God before it is too late in order to avoid awful divine punishment. Historically, these Great Awakenings have occurred at periods of what McLoughlin has called "social distortion." McLoughlin (1978, p. 2) writes:

> Great Awakenings are the results ... of critical disjunctions in our self understanding.... Awakenings begin in periods of cultural distortion and grave personal stress, when we lose faith in the legitimacy of our norms, the viability of our institutions, and the authority of our leaders in church and state. They eventuate in basic restructurings of our institutions and redefinitions of our social goals.

The great sense of hopefulness that permeates the Exodus narrative—the solace of direction and order in times of crisis, confusion and suffering—resonates powerfully in such historical contexts. Indeed, John Barton (1990, p. 52) argues, this capacity to inspire a hope of order in a time of crisis was the

> genius of the classic prophets ... tak[ing] the highly recalcitrant facts of history, whose religious and moral implications were in fact extremely ambiguous, and [giving] an account of these facts which would convince people not only that the hand of God could be seen in them, but that the operations of the divine hand were entirely comprehensible in human moral categories.

Following the template of Exodus and the ancient prophets, the American "prophets" retell and reinvigorate these tropes of divine Providence and the ever-present possibility of the fulfillment of the Promise, if only the people obey their covenant. This sacred theme of a chosen people on a mission speaks to the anxiety and uncertainty always present in the human condition, and is especially acute in perceived times of crisis and cultural instability. These tropes offer an aura of a divine plan which—even if ultimately unknowable by humans—gives meaning and direction to the struggles and uncertainties of the human condition.

Moreover, the capacity of being able to measure the profane world of politics against the sacred realm of divine order, modeled by the ancient prophets, has served to animate provocative challenges to the polity. Indeed, as Perry Miller and Samuel Huntington (1981, p. 160) have illustrated, throughout the history of America, periods of religious revival have been followed by periods of profound political reform. "Religion was the source of the morality that required the saving of souls on the one hand and the regeneration of society on the other." Religious revivals raise the awareness of, and serve to define, the gap between "higher principles" and the lived experiences of individuals. In turn, these revivals raise similar political questions about the gap between the nation's higher ideals and its existing social institutions. Accordingly, Huntington (1981, p. 160) concludes, "The passion for reform is first directed to the conversion of the individual and then to the reformation of society." Indeed, as historian McLoughlin (1978, p. 11) asserts: "America's First Great Awakening led to the creation of the American republic, the Second Awakening led to the solidification of the Union and the rise of Jacksonian participatory democracy; our Third Awakening led to the rejection of unregulated capitalist exploitation and the beginning of the welfare state." PK is well aware of this legacy and explicitly seeks its place in the tradition of Great Awakenings. For example, in explaining the goals and philosophy behind the organization's 1997 Stand in the Gap event in Washington, DC, PK founder Bill McCartney (1997b) said:

> There are great precedents for such a gathering. Spiritual assemblies such as these played an important role in some of America's greatest spiritual awakenings—which always led both to transformed lives and to significant moral reform.... During the early 19th century, for example, tens of thousands of men and women converted to Christianity in revival campaigns that became known as the Second Great Awakening.... The flame of revival ... shaped the course of the great national debate on abolition.... We sense that America faces a cultural crisis as potentially destructive as that facing the nation in the era of slavery.

Adopting the story of Exodus and the politically forceful jeremiadic and revivalist tradition in America, PK is developing its own political theology. The resonant trope of chosen-ness employed by PK in its portrayal of, and response to, the "cultural crisis" in the United States has potentially profound political implications. To comprehend the political theology of PK, it is critical to explore how it articulates the crisis and in turn how the organization seeks to reconfigure the community of the chosen.

"THE MIGHTY MEN OF GOD" AND THE POLITICS OF CHOSEN-NESS

These Exodus tropes of chosen-ness and mission were pervasive at PK's Stand in the Gap event in Washington, DC. The "sacred assembly" opened with the blowing of the shofar by a group of Messianic Jews and a proclamation by the PK Chairman of the Board, Bishop Phillip Porter: "We are as Moses was, standing on holy ground." At the conclusion of the day, the men gathered by PK swore to a "DC Covenant" with God. This covenant of PK purposefully evokes the covenant made by the desolate ancient Hebrews at the foot of Mt. Sinai. Beginning with an admission of being "broken and humbled," the PK covenant included oaths to "serve no other Gods beside You," to "resist moral, ethical, and sexual temptations," to "honor all women" and to "intentionally love the brotherhood of believers" (Promise Keepers, 1997). This declaration to "love the brotherhood of believers" is somewhat surprising for a movement presumably devoted to following the inclusive ethic of Jesus; indeed, this jarringly exclusivist oath should recall for us the Exodus theme of the purging of the brotherhood of non-believers. Furthermore, the emphasis on separation and the reconfiguration of the chosen community is sharply evident in the prophetic passage from Ezekiel that PK used as the organizing theme of the Stand in the Gap event. Though PK used a part of this passage in its publicity only (the section I have italicized below), it is instructive to read it in context to illustrate the emphasis on chosen-ness and exclusion. In a time of crisis and social disorder, Ezekiel (22:23–26, 29–31) speaks to the people the "word of the Lord," proclaiming:

> Son of man, say to the land ... there is a conspiracy of her princes within her like a roaring lion tearing its prey; they devour people ... her priests do violence to my law and profane my holy things; they do not distinguish between the holy and the common; they teach there is no difference between the unclean and the clean; and they shut their eyes to the keeping of my Sabbaths, so that I am profaned among them.... The people of the land practice extortion and commit robbery; they oppress the poor and needy and mistreat the alien, denying them justice. *I looked for a man among them who would build up the wall and stand in the gap on behalf of the land so I would not have to destroy it but I found none.* So I will pour out my wrath on them and consume them with my fiery anger, bringing down on their own heads all they have done, declares the Sovereign Lord.

Ezekiel decries the pollution of that which is holy and warns that if the boundaries separating the sacred from the profane are not re-established, if the principles of social order and justice instituted at Mt. Sinai are not obeyed, God's wrath will come down on His wayward chosen people. In the United States today, PK asserts, a comparable "cultural distortion" is shaking the divinely ordained social order and thus it is necessary to reassert the boundaries between the clean and the unclean, to reconfigure the community of the chosen. As McCartney (1997b) states: "In Ezekiel's day the people of Israel had wandered far from God, their first love. The result for Israel was national disaster: military defeat from without, moral rot from within. Ezekiel despairs that no one is willing to come forward to climb the literal breach in Jerusalem's walls and act as a human rampart against the evils of his day.... We believe that God is again looking for a few good men who desire to honor Him in every area of their lives." Seeking to encourage those men to be holy enough to "stand in the gap" and "deliver the nation" (McCartney, 1997a) from God's wrath, PK proclaims that they should follow the example of Ezekiel. PK is calling out to men, asking them if they are willing to be the rare individuals—the "one in a hundred," as McCartney put it at the 1996 PK event at Shea Stadium—willing to stand tall in the face of disorder and follow the word of God. As McCartney said to those men gathered at Shea Stadium, "God is looking for obedient men who are not ashamed of the gospel of Jesus and who are willing to go to great extremes."

In responding to what it perceives as this current era of "cultural distortion," PK asserts that boundaries of identity and order must be reestablished; the holy must be separated from the corrupt, the chosen from the disobedient. This political and theological vision of separating the believers from the unbelievers is a recurrent theme in the books, resources and public sermons of PK. For example, in his video seminar series, *Personal Holiness in Times of Temptation*, Dr. Bruce Wilkerson (1997, pp. 9–12) asserts, "When God forgives you for your sins, He also separates you from the world and those who have rejected Him, and separates you to Himself. He adopts you as His son, and places you supernaturally within the Family of God. He transfers you from the Kingdom of Darkness to the Kingdom of Light. He saves you from eternal damnation and gives you eternal salvation." The stakes of this process of exclusion and separation are as high as imaginable. On the individual level it is the difference between heaven and hell; on the corporate level it is the very future of the nation and the fulfillment or the demise of God's promise to the "newly chosen people."

This emphasis on separation and exclusion may come as a surprise to those who have been moved by PK's emphatic call for racial and denominational reconciliation. PK has indeed made a central commitment to "racial reconciliation," seeking to "break down the walls" that divide men and stand in the way of "unity." McCartney (1994, p. 161) proclaims, "Racism is Satan's stronghold.... The unifying of Godly people of all colors in contrast to racism would be an undeniable witness of [God's] grace." It is crucial to recognize that the final goal of the racial reconciliation pursued by PK is not justice but "unity." This emphasis on unity is telling, for PK's approach to race is to attempt to transcend racial boundaries; that is, rather than focusing on historical racial difference, PK stresses the essential sameness of all men. As McCartney (1994, p. 164, italics in original) asserts, "we *are going to reconcile* with our Christian brothers of different races, cultures, and denominations. We're going to break down the walls that separate us ... [to] demonstrate the power of biblical unity based on what we have in common: our love for Jesus and our connectedness through Him."

However, this "inclusive" conception racial reconciliation among men—a conception of unity rooted in the essential sameness of all men—is made possible only through the exclusion of women. For all its talk about transcending those boundaries which divide men, PK is emphatic about re-inscribing these boundaries that divide men and women. To appreciate this complex relationship between inclusion and exclusion in the political vision of PK, it is crucial to explore more specifically how PK depicts the crisis in the United States.

What is striking about how PK portrays this "cultural distortion" is that the instability and moral decay are presented as a result of a "crisis in masculinity." Writing on the eve of the Stand in the Gap gathering in an article for *Policy Review*, McCartney (1997b) states:

> The absence of responsible men from the home is now widely regarded as the most important cause of America's social decline.... What America desperately needs today is men who take responsibility for their actions, who are faithful to their families, who keep their word, even when it is difficult or costly.

What is the essential cause of this crisis in masculinity that PK is so determined to resolve? As Ezekiel declared that the crisis of his era was the result of the confusing of categories, of the destabilizing of the boundaries providing order for the ancient Israelites, PK also is primarily concerned with the confusing of the "divinely ordained" categories of sex, sexuality and gender. PK is in large part responding to a world indelibly shaped by 30 years of feminist "gender trouble" in which the norms and boundaries of categories of sex and gender have been challenged, crossed and substantially destabilized. Central to PK's prophetic political vision is the belief that this confusion of categories is a fundamental deviation from the divinely ordained social order. Whereas in their approach to racial prejudice, PK emphasizes the sameness of men, in their delineation of the male gender crisis, PK stresses the essential differences between women and men, trying to repair or reassert the lines of identity that feminists have helped blur in their struggle for gender equality. For example, in his book *Locking Arms: God's Design for Masculine Friendship*, Stu Weber (1995, p. 50) states, "Feminists insist ... that men and women are the same, with no appreciable differences other than the obvious plumbing designs. Of course, nothing could be further from the truth." PK's approach to reasserting the boundaries between men and women takes many forms, but all share the same goal. Again, Stu Weber (1995, p. 44) confronts the issue bluntly, proclaiming:

> If we're going to be healthy again, men are going to have to become healthy men again (and women healthy women). It's time for men to stand up, get a grip on biblical manhood, and quit apologizing for being men. What this culture desperately needs are men who are confident in their God-given masculinity and His intentions for it.... Remember when men were men? And women women and the differences were obvious? Remember when you didn't have to wonder? And you weren't criticized for being a man?... But now, in a culture that wants to elevate a higher standard of so-called diversity, we're destroying diversity in its most beautiful and elemental form.

In this striking passage, Weber argues that both individual and social health are predicated on clearly defined categories of gender identity. The desire for separation along "God-given" lines of gender will be realized after those elements that pollute—or "infect" (to use a Weber metaphor of health)—those categories are abjected. Arresting this cultural distortion, which has led to the masculinization of women and the feminization of men, is central to both the identity of PK as the "mighty men of God," and to their political vision.

Pursuing the "proper masculinity" appropriate for "men of God" is predicated on excluding those forces that challenge or destabilize their vision of manhood. Principally, this means taking a stand against gay and bisexual men and against the challenges to "biblical" gender identity often at least implicitly attributed to feminists. As is well known, in 1992 McCartney was a member of Colorado for Family Values and served as a vocal proponent of the passage of Amendment 2, which attempted to prohibit the state from granting "special rights" to homosexuals. Although McCartney's efforts in support of this amendment were officially independent of PK, his political position on this issue is well known among members of PK. During his campaign to support the ballot measure, McCartney (Abraham, 1997, p. 25) proclaimed that homosexuality was "an abomination against Almighty God." PK's emphasis on challenging the political and social legitimacy of gay, bisexual and lesbian individuals is consistent with the sweeping political campaign of other conservative Christian organizations in their pursuit of a "traditional family values" platform (Rudy). The attendance of representatives of two anti-homosexual Christian organizations—one of which is "appropriately named" Exodus International—which are determined to "save" gay, bi and lesbian individuals from their "sinful lifestyle," is common at many PK events.

The most explicit component of PK's effort to re-assert clear definitions of "God-given" masculinity is its emphasis on the essential differences between men and women. Feminist critics of PK have often challenged the organization's assertions of divinely ordained gender identity. PK has responded to feminist critiques with the suggestion that they (and the media) should speak to the wives of PK men. One such woman is Holly Phillips, wife of Promise Keeper President Randy Phillips. Holly Phillips is one of the few women ever to speak at a Promise Keeper event and her 1995 speech is quite instructive regarding the demarcation of gender difference and the crisis in masculinity. She said the following to the "promise keeping men of God":

> On behalf of the women you men represent—sisters, moms, wives and daughters—I ask your forgiveness for not showing you the respect you deserve. I ask your forgiveness for the demeaning and belittling words we have uttered. I apologize for the ways we have coddled and smothered you with our protectiveness, thereby emasculating you. It has

been done in ignorance. Understand that "mothering" comes naturally to us. It is our God-designed makeup. We simply misappropriated our calling.

Women, therefore, are framed as responsible for the feminization of men and the corruption of the "God-given" categories of gender. Moreover, if women don't repent of their sins of emasculation and recognize their "calling," they might continue to interfere in the "promise keeping" of men. In each of these cases, then, not only are women at some level responsible for the "crisis in masculinity," but this crisis cannot be solved and men can not become "Godly men of integrity" unless clear lines of difference are "re-established" between men and women.

The capstone of PK's political vision of gender identity is its controversial concept of male headship. As McCartney (van Leeuwen, 1998) explained in an interview on National Public Radio shortly after the Stand in the Gap event: "Almighty God has mandated that the man take the spiritual lead in the home. Isaiah 38:19 says 'A father to the children shall make known the truth.'" So central is this notion of male headship, that it is even evident in PK's DC Covenant. To illustrate this point is it worthwhile to return the biblical model of the covenant and compare it to the covenant affirmed by PK participants. In the original biblical formulation of the covenant, the agreement between the ancient Israelites and God was individual and inclusive. Exodus reads, "The people all responded together..." (Ex 19:8), and when the narrative of the making of this first covenant is retold in Deuteronomy, the text is even more vivid: "All of you are standing in the presence of the Lord your God—your leaders and chief men, your elders and officials, and all the other men of Israel, together with your children and your wives, and the aliens living in your camps..." (Dt 29:10–11). Each member of the community makes an individual covenant with God. However, in the later reaffirmation of the covenant in the Book of Joshua, the commitment is made by each head of household on behalf of the entire household.

In its articulation of the covenant, PK follows the model of Joshua, proclaiming, "Today, each of us declares, 'As for me and my household, we will serve the Lord' (Josh 24:15)." Thus rather than employ the template of the inclusive covenant found in Exodus and Deuteronomy, in its covenant PK pointedly chooses to emphasize the fact of "headship." (In fact, this verse from Joshua is the basis of one of the most frequently sung songs at PK events.) PK's most well-known assertion of male headship is that framed by Tony Evans. In the central book of PK's political theology, *The Seven Promises of a Promise Keeper*, Evans (1994, pp. 79–80)—in his often-quoted direction—challenges the "sissified" men of America to

> sit down with your wife and say something like this: "Honey, I've made a terrible mistake. I've given you my role. I gave up leading this

family, and I forced you to take my place. Now I must reclaim that role."

Don't misunderstand what I'm saying here. I'm not suggesting that you *ask* for your role back, I'm urging you to *take it back*.... There can be no compromise here. If you're going to lead, you must lead. Be sensitive. Listen. Treat the lady gently and lovingly. But *lead*!

The political implications of this delineation of proper gender roles are profound. If men are divinely ordained as the "leaders" of the family, the question of power outside the household is, of course, closely related. PK has been careful to make public statements that this notion of male headship does not mean they are calling for women to give up the equality they have won in the public sphere. However, the sincerity of these public comments is belied by the sentiments expressed in their books. As Gary Smalley and John Trent (1994, p. 32) succinctly state in their book, *The Hidden Value of a Man: The Incredible Impact of a Man on His Family*: "There's no doubt that men, by God-given design, are leaders in science, industry, research and religion." Ultimately, the "chosen men of God" who—like Ezekiel—will strive to lead the nation back to "God's vision" of moral order by reasserting the boundaries between holy and corrupt, clean and unclean, will begin their "holy war" by re-establishing proper gender roles and the appropriate authority God has "given" to men.

THE WISDOM OF PROMISE KEEPERS

Thus far, I have focused on how PK generates its identity and political vision by utilizing the sacred stories of the exodus narrative and the jeremiadic tradition. Although both are essential to the success of PK and both illustrate PK's place within the American tradition of Great Awakenings, taken together they do not fully explain the PK's use of scriptural models. To gain a fuller appreciation of PK, we must also consider the "mundane stories" that lie within the context established by the "sacred narratives."

While some of the most striking elements of PK's canon comprise these jeremiads, the bulk of the books, resources and sermons of PK offer practical advice on how to strengthen marriages, achieve racial reconciliation, attain fiscal responsibility, avoid "sexual impurities" and redouble one's efforts as fathers, friends and members of the church community. These texts represent PK's "wisdom literature." In keeping with the inter-relationship of the two modes of biblical literature, PK uses the jeremiads to delineate the vision of the organization, and "mundane texts" to provide pragmatic recommendations on how to live in the contingent and troubled world of the human condition. The sense of crisis expressed in the prophetic narratives pervades in the "books of wisdom" as well, but rather than focus on the moment of salvation, PK's wisdom literature (as is the case of the books of Proverbs, Ecclesiastes, James, Lamentations and Job) offers considerations on how to live in the everyday world where there are still significant obstacles and fears blocking one's peaceful settlement in the promised land of "milk and honey." Much of PK's literature reflects the influence of the ever-expanding self-help movement in the United States (cf. Kaminer, 1992). In basing their "wisdom literature" on this new thrust in American culture, PK illustrates the dynamic and innovative potential enabled by "sacred stories." That is, it is short-sighted to think only of sacred stories as restricting imagination; indeed, as philosopher Paul Ricoeur (1995, p. 240) suggests, sacred stories generate a "flexible dialectics" of "sedimentation and innovation."

As I have already illustrated, the jeremiadic exhortations of PK are directed largely towards engendering an identity of "chosen men of God" and a political vision based on this exclusively drawn corporate identity. The wisdom literature is designed to give counsel to these same men, to enable them to triumph in the daily struggles to meet this standard of "holiness." As we should expect, given the stress placed on clear definitions of gender identity in their framing and employment of the sacred trope of chosen-ness, a central theme of PK's wisdom literature is advice on how to achieve and maintain a state of "proper Christian masculinity."

The most predominant feature of the "mundane stories" employed by PK are symbols and metaphors of athletics. The chosen people in the wisdom literature of PK are members of a team, specifically, as McCartney (1993) has said, "[God's] Dream Team." This athletic masculinity is, of course buttressed by the shirts, banners and other athletic accoutrements that define the ambience at PK's rallies in sports stadiums around the country. There is no more vivid symbol of the integration between the sacred stories of chosen Christian masculine identity and the mundane stories of athletic masculinity than the specially produced "Man of His Word" versions of the New Testament given to each Promise Keeper after he dedicates his life to Jesus. For an organization that stresses the importance of obedience to the literal and infallible word of God (Promise #2) as one of the fundamental markers of belonging to the chosen community of Christian brothers, it is a phenomenon of striking rhetorical significance that scattered among the canonical works of the New Testament are full-page color photos and biographies of prominent Christian athletes. (So, after Paul's letter to the Romans, one might find the Book of Reggie White or Michael Chang.) Perceiving these athletes and the other "promise keeping brothers" as fellow members of God's dream team is part of the "game plan" the PK's leadership has of creating a brotherhood of men who are willing to "act as bulwarks against [society's] ill-informed and destructive choices, like offensive linemen protecting the quarterback" (McCartney, 1997b).

Having built the implicit challenge of holy Christian masculinity ("Are you man enough to be a member of God's team?") into their valorization of the strength and toughness associated with normative athletic masculinity, PK books and other resources provide the men with models and practical advice about how to become a "mighty man of God." This "wisdom literature" utilizes a combination of two modes of expression: 1) narratives about men whose lives serve as models for the readers, and 2) clearly written "how-to" manuals with diagnostic devices, "discussion points" and didactic pieces of advice. For example, in *Strategies for a Successful Marriage* by E. Glenn Wagner and Dietrich Gruen (1994) and *We Stand Together: Reconciling Men of Different Color* by Rodney Cooper (1995), the authors offer personal testimony and lists of "do's and don'ts," guiding men towards PK's vision of divinely ordained families and racial unity. Rather than detail all of the specific strategies recommended by their wisdom literature, I will offer one example to illustrate how the political vision articulated by PK through the use of tropes derived from "sacred stories" is complemented by the advice on daily living offered in the organizations many books, tapes and resources.

Recall how central to PK's political theology is the importance of clearly demarcated boundaries of gender roles and identity and the pivotal tenet of male headship. Recognizing that establishing such a vision in one's daily life is more complex than simply reading Ephesians 5:23 to one's wife, in *The Hidden Value of a Man*, authors Gary Smalley and John Trent (1994) seek to provide clear models, lessons and recommendations for practicing what PK preaches. Beginning with an example of a man who struggles to learn how to properly (rather than selfishly) lead his family, Smalley and Trent (p. 44) proceed to explicate the call for headship they derive from Ephesians by comparing it to the type of military chain of command that enabled George Bush, General Powell, General Schwarzkopf and all the troops down to the individuals on the frontlines to "drive [Saddam Hussein] out of Kuwait":

> You didn't sense feelings of inferiority when pictures came in of General Schwarzkopf walking among his troops, shaking their hands, and praying with them before they went into battle. You sensed only loyalty, clarity of purpose and a mutual willingness to serve. And you sensed something else between he [sic] and his men—a genuine love. But someone still had to take the lead. They knew it. They needed it. And it brought them the quickest and most decisive victory in American military history.

What is the lesson to be derived from this model of masculine leadership and "family" unity? Smalley and Trent (p. 44) conclude it is, "Loving leadership and voluntary submission. The message of Ephesians 5 is that husbands and wives need to get their plans clearly established. What hill are you going to take with your family? What plateau do you want to reach with your children?"

The authors are aware that even this contemporary model of masculinity is not enough to provide a clear path to fulfilling the mandate for headship they derive from Ephesians. They (1994, p. 45) next offer a "mundane story" of how Smalley and his wife Norma personally created a "family constitution" with Smalley "taking the lead in accomplishing that goal, and Norma submitting to that plan and supporting me." But even this personal example is not enough to provide a clear path to the readers about how to follow and fulfill PK's vision of proper masculine headship. At the end of the book (just prior to the "Study Guide" appendix with chapter by chapter "fill-in-the-blank" questions to help the individual reader, as well as the small accountability group, process the lessons on practicing proper masculinity), Smalley and Trent provide specific models of "family constitutions." As is evident from this example, the "mundane stories" and didactic advice presented by PK in their wisdom literature serve as practical personal guidelines for meeting the political theology disseminated in the organization's jeremiads. The detailed political strategies contained in the organization's books and resources function as the necessary complement to PK's vision of prophetic politics.

THE NARRATIVE PROMISE OF "CHRISTIAN MASCULINITY"

When John Winthrop led his fellow Puritans to America, he told the community of God's "newly chosen people" that their holy status came with monumental responsibilities. In his sermon "A Modell of Christian Charity," he (quoted in Bercovitch, 1978, p. 3) proclaimed:

> If wee shall deale falsely with our god in this worke wee have undertaken and soe cause him to withdrawe his present help from us, wee shall be made a story and a by-word through the world, we shall open the mouths of enemies to speak evil of the wayes of god and all professours for Gods sake; wee shall shame the faces of many of gods worthy servants, and cause theire prayers to be turned into Curses upon us, till wee be consumed out of the good land whether wee are goeing.

Practicing a theology of exclusion, this chosen community sought to maintain their holy corporate identity and to stave off the crisis that would surely follow if they turned away from God. In the United States today, PK is breathing new life into this sacred American narrative. This brotherhood of

Christian men is preaching a political theology that holds the state of crisis in America is due to the fact that the leaders of God's social order have turned away from the Lord. As McCartney (1997d) said on *Meet the Press*, "The men of God in this nation have not stood in the gap for the gospel of Jesus Christ. We look just like society. We were never intended to do this. The guys that Almighty God has placed His spirit in should be living a life that offers an alternative to a world that is lost." Solving this "crisis" entails that the chosen community of God must be reconfigured; the men whom God has given the responsibility to serve as leaders in "His mission" in America must turn back to the Lord and rescue America—and God's church—from the very consequences feared by Winthrop. For PK, the crucial first step is recreating clearly defined boundaries of identity, so that the "chosen men of God" may understand and fulfill their responsibilities as the temporal "heads" of God's mission.

It is critical to recognize that the effort to respond to a sense of crisis by striving to re-secure masculinity through a process of abjection occurs on both corporate and individual levels. In its endeavors to resolve the "crisis in masculinity" and, with it, the broader moral crisis in America, PK engages in a process of exclusion that seeks to create a corporate brotherhood of "men of God" by abjecting those forces which they perceive as agents of corruption. PK encourages individual men, whose sense of stable masculinity has been troubled in part by dramatic changes in the politics of sex, gender and sexuality in America, to resecure their own sense of manhood by abjecting those doubts and fears about the traditional norms of diffused throughout our culture. PK gives that individual man license and authority to dismiss those challenges to stable masculinity by offering a divinely ordained and fixed vision of gender roles and identity. That is, on the corporate level, PK encourages the exclusion and abjection of those individuals who pollute this conception of the chosen community. On the individual level, PK invites men to reject those ideas that challenge their own efforts to realize normative conceptions of masculinity by framing those challenges as blasphemous and biblically unsound.

By popularizing a political theology, which responds to a "crisis in masculinity" with an exclusivist and absolute vision of "proper Christian masculinity," PK raises troubling political issues, three of which I want to raise here. First, because PK frames its vision as a moral absolute, this theology will likely make PK as an organization, and its individual members, less capable of and less interested in engaging in *political dialogue* about issues of religion, gender and sexuality—especially with those individuals and groups whose beliefs represent a form of "pollution." Second, the lessons of Exodus and of the prophets about backsliding (even in the face of divine presence) and the never complete success of the process of abjection in order to create either individual or corporate stability, should teach us to expect the exclusivist vision of

PK that has so often served as the basis for a divisive politics of purging. Given the historic relation between religious revival and periods of sweeping political reform, this could have profound consequences for the next millennium. Finally, in a political climate in the United States that has over the last 20 years been dominated by what Jim Wallis has called the "secular Left" and the "Religious Right," the success of the excluvisist political theology of masculinity disseminated by PK could further polarize the cultural discourse about the relation of religious and politics. What the rapid growth of an emphatically story-telling organization such as PK illustrates is the continuing resonance of the sacred story of Exodus in America. PK's interpretation of Exodus stresses the triumphal sense of chosen-ness and the divine legitimacy of the American "mission." But, emphatically, these are not the only resonant tropes we may derive from the exodus narrative and the legacy of the prophets. As I suggested earlier, the "sacred stories" provide a horizon within which meaning and identity may emerge—but even if the "sacred story" remains the same, different interpretations or conceptions of meaning and identity are always available to us. This type of innovation develops out of dialogue among citizens whose identities take shape; whose lives acquire meaning within the horizon of these "sacred stories." However, if the political theology of Promise Keepers exacerbates the current polarization of political discourse about religion, this type of valuable dialogue (within and) about the "sacred stories" in America will become even more remote.

Note

This is only one theme and interpretation of the exodus and prophetic narratives and, of course, it is not exhaustive of either the political lessons to be learned from this narrative nor, indeed, the only interpretation derived and employed by religious social movements in the United States. For example, there is the prophetic tradition rooted perhaps most dramatically in the Book of Amos, which stresses that God's "choosing" of the people of Israel did not accord them a special status amongst the world's peoples, but only a special responsibility to serve as a model of divine principles of justice—especially toward the lowly and oppressed. It is this element of the prophetic tradition which Martin Luther King, Jr., invoked during the Civil Rights movement, as illustrated by his most famous prophetic declaration: "Let justice roll on like a river, and righteousness like a mighty stream" (Amos, 5:24). The contrast between this prophetic watchword of the 1963 March on Washington and the passage from Ezekiel emphasizing purity, separation and exclusion chosen by PK as its featured prophetic passage for their 1997 Stand in the Gap gathering in Washington clearly illuminates the differences within the tradition of the prophetic jeremiad—and the political stakes at work.

References

Abraham, K. (1997). *Who are the Promise Keepers? Understanding the Christian men's movement*. New York: Doubleday.

Barton, J. (1990). History and rhetoric in the prophets. In M. Warner (ed.), *The Bible as rhetoric: Studies in biblical persuasion and credibility*. New York: Routledge.

Bercovitch, S. (1978). *The American jeremiad*. Madison, WI: University of Wisconsin Press.

Bright, B. (1995). *The coming revival: America's call to fast, pray, and "Seek God's face."* Orlando, FL: New Life Publications.

Buber, M. (1965). *Moses: The revelation and the covenant*. New York: Harper & Row, Publishers.

Cooper, R. (1995). *We stand together: Reconciling men of a different color*. Chicago: Moody Press.

Crites, S. (1989). The narrative quality of experience. In S. Hauerwas and L.G. Jones (eds.), *Why narrative? Readings in narrative theology*. Grand Rapids, MI: W.B. Eerdmans.

Evans, T. (1994). Spiritual purity. In A. Janssen & L.K. Weeden (eds.), *Seven promises of a Promise Keeper*. Colorado Springs, CO: Focus on the Family Publishing.

Fish, S. (1994). There's no such thing as free speech (and it's a good thing, too). In S. Fish (ed.), *There's no such thing as free speech: And it's a good thing, too*. Oxford: Oxford University Press, 1994.

Huntington, S.P. (1981). *American politics: The promise of disharmony*. Cambridge: The Belknap Press.

Kaminer, W. (1992). *I'm dysfunctional, you're dysfunctional: The recovery movement and other self-help fashions*. New York: Addison-Wesley Publishing Company, Inc.

MacIntyre, A. (1989). The virtues, the unity of a human life, and the concept of a tradition. In S. Hauerwas and L.G. Jones (eds.), *Why narrative? Readings in narrative theology*. Grand Rapids: W.B. Eerdmans.

McCartney, B. (1993, Winter). *Men of Action Newsletter*.

McCartney, B. (1994). A call to unity. In A. Janssen and L.K. Weeden, *Seven promises of a Promise Keeper*. Colorado Springs, CO: Focus on the Family Publishing.

McCartney, B. (1997a, January 20). Promise Keeper letter.

McCartney, B. (1997b, September-October). Promise makers. *Policy Review 85*, 14–19. Available online at www.policyreview.com/heritage/p_review/sept97/promise.html.

McCartney, B. (1997c, October 4). To save the nation. Interview in *The Washington Post*, C7.

McCartney, B. (1997d, October 5). Interview on *Meet the Press*, NBC.

McLoughlin, W.G. (1978). *Revivals, awakenings and reform: An essay on religion and social change in America, 1607–1977*. Chicago: The University of Chicago Press.

Men's Study Bible (New International Version). Grand Rapids, MI: Zondervan Publishing House.

Miller, P. (1956). *Errand into the wilderness*. Cambridge: The Belknap Press.
Miller, P. (1965). *The life of the mind in America: From the Revolution to the Civil War*. New York: Harcourt, Brace & World, Inc.
Moltmann, J., & Meeks, M.D. (ed. & trans.) (1975). *The experiment hope*. Philadelphia: Fortress Press.
Phillips, H. (1995). Costly promises. Published in *New Man*, available online at www.strang.com/nm/stories/nm296s.htm.
Promise Keepers (1997). DC Covenant. Available: ww2.promisekeepers.org/manual/sitg/covenant. html.
Ricoeur, P. (Wallace, M.I., ed.; Pellauer, D., trans.) (1995). *Figuring the sacred: Religion, narrative and imagination*. Minneapolis: Fortress Press.
Rudy, K. (1997). *Sex and the church: Gender, homosexuality and the transformation of Christian ethics*. Boston: Beacon Press.
Smalley, G., & Trent, J. (1994). *The hidden value of a man: The incredible impact of a man on his family*. Colorado Springs, CO: Focus on the Family Publishing.
van Leeuwen, M.S. (1998, January-February). Promise Keepers: Proof-text poker. *Sojourners 27*(1), 16.
Wagner, E.G., with Gruen, D. (1994). *Strategies for a successful marriage: A study guide for men*. Colorado Springs, CO: Navpress Publishing Group, 1994.
Wallis, J. (1995). *The soul of politics: Beyond "Religious Right" and "Secular Left."* New York: Harcourt Brace & Company.
Walzer, M. (1985). *Exodus and revolution*. New York: Basic Books.
Weber, S. (1995). *Locking arms: God's design for masculine friendship*. Sisters, OR: Multnomah Books.
White, H. (1983). The question of narrative in contemporary historical theory. *History and Theory 231*, 1–33.
Wilkerson, B.H. (1997). *Personal holiness in times of temptation* (Video and Course Workbook). Atlanta, GA: Walk Thru the Bible Ministries.

CHAPTER 11

The Promise Keepers' Use of Sport in Defining "Christlike" Masculinity

by Becky Beal

INTRODUCTION

The purpose of this chapter is to investigate how a fundamentalist Christian movement, the Promise Keepers, is using sport as one means of characterizing and promoting a specific style of masculinity and male leadership. This group has often employed sport examples and metaphors in its literature. A central theme of this male-only movement is that current social problems are caused by a lack of appropriate male leadership. The Promise Keepers is a calling for men to make a commitment to assume their "rightful" obligations as leaders in our society. A critical feminist analysis will be employed to examine how sport is used in the construction of the Promise Keepers' gender ideology.

EXAMINING THE CONNECTIONS AMONG THE PROMISE KEEPERS, SPORT, AND GENDER

Although I have been familiar with the Promise Keepers as a religious organization since 1990, I became interested in the Promise Keepers as a sport related phenomenon in 1994 when a Chicago suburban high school football coach used a controversial motivational technique that was highly publicized (the coach feigned being shot by a gun in front of his players). Through further investigations by journalists, other motivational techniques of this

Reprinted by permission of Sage Publications, Inc., from Journal of Sport & Social Issues 21(3), *pp. 274–284,* © 1997.

coach were reported including the use of a videotape of the 1993 Promise Keeper meetings. I wanted to know in what ways a men's evangelical movement could be linked to sport and sport participation. I talked with this coach over the phone several times, and face to face at his house where we spoke for more than two hours. After this interaction I inferred that the Promise Keepers were promoting an ideology similar to that associated with sport in the 19th-century British public schools, which emphasized "character-building" attributes such as loyalty, courage, leadership, and manliness. It was the use of sport as a means to link leadership and virtuous masculinity that caught my attention.

Methodology

In order to investigate whether the Promise Keepers were promoting these values, I contacted the organization and was given information and a booklist. I read two of their foundational books: *What Makes a Man* (WMAM) and *The Seven Promises of a Promise Keeper* (SP). These books are collections of writings by various authors. My initial investigation conducted with a colleague was to quantitatively document the use of sport and the definition of masculinity provided by these books (Beal & Gray, 1995). We found that a traditional definition of masculinity was promoted, one in which men and women's roles were segregated and men's roles were given more social status. The espoused qualities of masculine behavior included deference to authority, strength and assertiveness, and an acceptance of pain. We also found frequent references to sport, but there was more discussion around the general concept of competition especially in reference to the battle between good and evil.

This chapter specifically examines the connection between sport and gender. A critical feminist analysis will be used to interpret how the Promise Keepers literature uses sport to promote its gender ideology. To provide the necessary background information, a brief introduction to the Promise Keepers and their gender ideology will be given. Then an analysis of how sport is used in conjunction with that ideology will be presented.

The Promise Keepers and Their Gender Ideology

The Organization. The Promise Keepers is an organization whose main goal is to evangelize men. Bill McCartney, the former football coach of the University of Colorado, began this organization in 1990. The first revival meeting attracted approximately 70 people in Boulder, Colorado. By five years later, the Promise Keepers were holding meetings throughout the United States selling out stadiums. Hundreds of thousands of men have attended these events in the past two years. Beside the annual meetings, the Promise Keepers are able reach their audiences through various media. They have a booklist in which they promote their literature and an unofficial, previously official, monthly magazine called *New Man*. They also have video and audio tapes of their meetings for sale. These meetings and media are also used to promote small grassroots men's prayer groups.

The leadership of the Promise Keepers includes an impressive array of evangelical ministers. Main contributors to the Promise Keepers include Bill Bright, the founder of Campus Crusade; James Dobson, the founder of Focus on the Family; and Edwin Cole, the founder of the Christian Men's Network. The organization is growing and was economically very viable at least until early 1998. Not only have they built a permanent headquarters in Denver, CO, but, according to Diamond (1995), in 1995 the organization employed 250 full-time staff and had a $64 million budget. According to the *Rocky Mountain News*, the Promise Keepers planned to spend $115 million during 1996 (Weber, 1996).

Their Gender Ideology. The main purpose is to evangelize men. A Promise Keeper is defined as a man who lives in accordance with God's word and who makes a promise to live by those standards. As noted in the book *What Makes a Man*, "Our goal in sharing these (five standards of biblical manhood) is, again, to help us all develop into men who honor God and demonstrate the convictions, integrity, and actions of Christlike men—men who can keep a promise" (p. 39).

This evangelizing is done within a particular context that encourages an appropriate style of masculinity often referred to as "Christlike" masculinity. The elements of masculinity are stated in the book *What Makes a Man*, "If you could somehow freeze-frame biblical manhood or in some way boil it down into its component parts, you would see five elements that are always present" (p. 39). These are assertiveness, self-control, independence, self-confidence, and stability, which are noted as "an ever-present nature in all of us as men" (WMAM, p. 39).

Their message of revival is also given with a sense of urgency, an immediacy that is directed at the apparent ethical decay of our society. For example, a comment found on the jacket sleeve of the book *Seven Promises of a Promise Keeper* states: "Our nation is suffering from a severe shortage of integrity. It needs men able to stand strong in the midst of moral chaos."

Why Men? The Promise Keepers' message is aimed at men for one main reason. The Promise Keepers firmly espouse that the moral depravity in our society is due to the lack of appropriate male leadership. This lack of leadership has caused, most importantly, the breakdown of the traditional family. This assumed foundational problem has lead to "high school drop outs, a soaring crime rate, racism, divorce, homosexuality, and abortion." Even the women's movement is explained as a response to men not keeping their promises to a traditional family agreement (Stammer, July 8, 1994).

Many feminists are concerned with this emphasis on male leadership as a solution to social problems primarily because it dismisses the leadership women have taken and because it demotes the social position of women. As noted by several journalists (e.g., Diamond, 1995; Wagenheim, 1996) the standard retort given by the Promise Keepers is that they are not anti-woman nor do they promote the domination of women. In fact, they often note that men's leadership is not through domination but through service. Any insight that may be gained from this paradox seems to be lost through oversimplification, which is evidenced in some of the writings. In particular, the essays that illustrate this oversimplification reflect a noticeable masculine privilege. The following examples will serve to demonstrate this.

In the book *Seven Promises of a Promise Keeper*, one of the authors, Tony Evans, explains current social problems: "I am convinced that the primary cause of this national crisis is the feminization of the American male. When I say feminization, I am not talking about sexual preference. I'm trying to describe a misunderstanding of manhood that has produced a nation of sissified men who abdicate their role as spiritually pure leaders, thus forcing women to fill the vacuum" (p. 73). The use of feminization as a negative term and one that connotes ineptness is a blatant example of devaluing femininity and privileging masculinity.

In the same chapter as the above passage, under a subheading "Reclaiming your Manhood," Evans states that men need to tell their wives, "Honey, I've made a terrible mistake. I've given you my role. I gave up leading this family, and I forced you to take my place. Now I must reclaim that role." The author further explains to his audience, "Don't misunderstand what I'm saying here, I'm not suggesting that you ask for your role back. I'm urging you to take it back" (p. 79). He then provides advice for women, "Having said that, let me direct some carefully chosen words to you ladies who may be reading this: *Give it back!*" [italics in the original] (p. 80). Evans makes the claim that men and women have separate roles and that men's roles include leadership. An obvious privileging of men.

Not all the writings describe the separation of gender roles as conspicuously. Instead there are frequent references to the "natural" behaviors of men and women or to God's word that are used to justify these gender roles. The following is one of several examples used to demonstrate the apparent "naturalness" of traditional gender roles: "One mark of a man is his natural assertiveness that flows through his blood. Even toddlers reflect it. Instead of accepting the answer of ivory towered radicals who expound theories of androgyny and blur the distinction between the sexes, spend some time talking to a mother of a boy and a girl, their behavior patterns from the earliest ages show marked differences in natural aggression" (WMAM, p. 40). Leadership characteristics are also described as naturally male: "It is in our deepest nature as men to push forward, to step out, to take charge, to fight for higher ground" (WMAM, p. 40). Another frequent claim in the literature is that God intended men and women to have different innate behaviors and, thus, should be reflected in different social roles. One example of this claim is: "But God neither designed nor endorsed the kind of exaggerated imbalance we see today. In many cases women are forced to shoulder the leadership load alone and carry responsibilities God never intended them to bear" (SP, p.74). The following are two examples of the use of God's word to justify the Promise Keepers' claim of the rightful place of males as leaders: "How do we break the cycle? By getting men to assume their responsibilities and take back the reins of spiritually pure leadership that God intended us to hold" (SP, p. 75), and "If men forfeit their leadership in the church, they disregard the command of God" (SP, p. 142).

It is apparent through these and other examples that the Promise Keepers are advocating a gender ideology that privileges men and masculinity. Men are defined as having natural leadership qualities, particularly aggression, and God-given responsibilities to channel that aggression. On the other hand, women are described as providing essential and necessary support for men and their children. It is proclaimed that any disruption in this practice upsets our society causing social problems.

THE PROMISE KEEPERS AND MEN'S MOVEMENTS

The Promise Keepers movement is not an isolated incident. Several men's movements have appeared in response to the social and economic changes that have disrupted the underpinnings of patriarchal relations. Kimmel and Kaufman (1995) have noted that throughout the last century economic autonomy and security for men has eroded, and the movements of women and of gays and lesbians have challenged the essentialist notions of masculinity and men's position in society (pp. 16–18).

Messner (1997) has identified the organized responses to these challenges. He places the Promise Keepers and the mythopoetic men's movement in the same category, an "essentialist retreat." Each movement assumes that certain essential differences between men and women determine the best form of social relations: men in leadership positions. Messner (1997) claimed that these movements are a response to a perceived feminization of men, and they share the method of finding a segregated space for men to reclaim and reassert their masculinity: "Both groups see a need for men to retreat from women to create spiritually-based homosocial rituals through which they can collectively recapture a lost or strayed 'true manhood.' And both of these movements are asserting men's responsibility to re-take their natural positions of leadership in their communities" (p. 17). The following analysis will examine how the Promise Keepers invoke the ideologies of an historically predominant homosocial sphere: a sphere where masculinity is assumed to be essential and where patriarchy appears natural, and a sphere where young males learn what it means to be a man and learn their place in society—sport.

THEORETICAL FRAMEWORK

To analyze how sport is used by the Promise Keepers in supporting the ideology of male superiority, I employ a critical feminist analysis of the cultural meanings of sport in the United States. Many critical feminist scholars have documented the various ways in which sport has served to create and sustain ideologies of male supremacy (e.g., Bryson, 1987; Curry, 1991; Kidd, 1990; Messner, 1988; Whitson, 1990; Willis, 1994). These scholars have identified certain practices of mainstream sport as critical in promoting an ideology in which patriarchal gender relations are reproduced and celebrated. This ideology is founded on the assumption that males and females have innate and distinct characteristics. First, males are defined as naturally possessing superior physical and psychological capabilities such as aggression, strength, and mental toughness. These traits have often been assumed to be necessary for athletic excellence. On the other hand, women are defined as lacking these innate athletic characteristics, which is evidenced by their inability to successfully compete with men. Using this ideology, the domination of mainstream sport by males is explained "logically." In this manner, mainstream sport practices help promote a gender logic (e.g., Coakley, 1994) that can be used to explain and justify male domination in other competitive realms such as politics and business. It is also important to note that dominant forms of sport have been interpreted by feminist scholars as a public celebration of this gender logic, and are used as a means to unify and rally a variety of men under the conviction of male superiority (e.g., Kidd, 1990).

Using these insights from feminist theorists, I investigated whether sport was being used to perpetuate similar ideologies of male superiority within the Promise Keeper text. I have organized the use of sport in their literature into three categories: (a) sport as a demonstration of qualities of masculinity that are linked with superior leadership, (b) sport as a means to rally men around male superiority, and (c) sport images and metaphors which underlie and conjure mental images of male superiority. The categories are meant to describe an emphasis. However, the categories are not exclusive, and there is certainly overlap among them.

Use of Sport in the Promise Keepers Literature

Sport Used to Demonstrate the Qualities of Masculinity Linked with Superior Leadership. In the first chapter of the book *What Makes a Man*, authors Gary Smalley and John Trent set up the image of a Promise Keeper by giving three examples of those who kept their promises. They include Douglas MacArthur, Babe Ruth, and Jesus Christ. In this incident, a sport figure is held up as a model of a man who keeps his promises. The authors allude to Babe Ruth pointing his bat to the bleachers as a promise to hit a home run for his fans. It is only a narrow memory of this man, and the use of Babe Ruth as an image of a Promise Keeper is riddled with irony. If a Promise Keeper is supposed to conjure an image of moral, spiritual, and sexual purity, then Babe Ruth is not a good example because of his widely known drinking and womanizing. It appears that the use of Babe Ruth (and probably MacArthur) takes on a mythical dimension—one which involves great feats by men. In addition, these examples also invoke images of competitive settings that are male-dominated (i.e. mainstream sport and the military). The image of men as powerful is strongly conveyed by these examples.

The following illustrates the connection made among sport, masculinity, and success: "That day, as I sat for hours listening to Monte, three things stood out in our conversation. Actually, all three of them were steps he had taken to be a success in his sport, and now those same qualities would hold the key to a future full of potential" (WMAM, p. 226). Those three things were commitment, self-control, and a clear and significant challenge on which to focus his energy. Sport is often a significant setting in which virtuous masculinity is described: "We've now detailed three marks of masculinity: assertiveness, self-control, and independence. The next one is equally important as you look at keeping promises to your wife. Self confidence is what everyone else in the locker room looks like they have before you hit the field for the big game, or get ready to hit the golf ball off the first tee" (WMAM, p. 64). These examples illustrate how sport is used as a tool for depicting the style of masculinity that fosters quality leadership and success.

Sport as a Means to Rally Men. The following passage demonstrates an explicit use of sport as a means to rally men under the pretense of male superiority. In this call to men, the author highlights and celebrates masculine attributes, and he also ranks these masculine attributes as more powerful than the female attributes:

> How do we reclaim men for the Kingdom of God and get them into the doors of the church? I wish I knew the answer. But two images come to mind. One is the sterile, cold, formal, flowery image of the church with over half the audience women. The other image is the most recent Flyers hockey game I experienced, and I mean

experienced! I looked at the audience, by far more men than women. What were they wearing? Anything! Some were dressed for stock exchange; others for the Philly meat market. How did they behave? Were they passive, quiet, unemotional, refined gentlemen? Hardly. They were involved, vocal, upset, yelling, celebrating. I thought to myself, Here is a man's world, a place where he can let it all out, be himself, wear anything he desires, and they still let him in. And he actually pays to come. What about the church? No, there a man can't be himself; he has to watch what he says, act appropriately, and wear a neatly pressed and coordinated suit and tie. Then it hit me: We're all dressed the way our mommies wanted us to dress. We're all nice, clean little boys, sitting quietly so we won't get into trouble with our mothers [WMAM, pp. 155–156].

In the above passage, sport is used as a model for rallying men in a manner that reinforces strict gender roles and elevates the masculine role. The author's intent is to draw from the popularity of sport for men and apply that to the church. The description of the sport experience as compared with the present church services reveals a masculine bias. The church is described as feminine and the adjectives included being passive, quite, sterile, and cold. These connote detachment, and therefore, poor leadership skills. On the other hand, the description of the sport environment was "a man's world," one that epitomized masculine characteristics such as being vocal, upset, yelling, and celebrating. These characteristics connote an active engagement that is often associated with strong leadership.

The last sentence in the passage quoted above is indicative of what is feared if men try to appease women by living by feminine norms: men lose their masculinity, and their power. The logic of this passage could be read as: the recruitment of men involves creating a setting that celebrates and values masculinity over femininity. This is the same logic that feminists claim sport encourages.

Sport Images and Metaphors as Evoking Male Superiority. The two books that aid in expounding the Promise Keeper message (WMAM and SP) used sport metaphors and images more frequently than direct comparisons of sport to masculinity. Sport was often used as a context in which relationships were discussed. For example, there are numerous references to father-son interaction, or male-to-male friendships in a sport setting. Sport was also used metaphorically: "In the Official Scorer's Book of Life—the one that scores each of us daily as a husband, a father, a godly man—he went five for five and pitched a shut out game, when it came to using his personal power for good" (WMAM, p. 205). Other examples include: "Fourth down and a future to go" (WMAM, p. 226) and,

The mission of introducing one's children to the Christian faith can be likened to a three-man relay race. First, your father runs his lap around the track, carrying the baton, which represents the gospel of Jesus Christ. At the appropriate moment, he hands the baton to you, and you begin your journey around the track. Then, finally, the time will come when you must get the baton safely in the hands of your child. But as any track coach will testify, relay races are won or lost on the transfer of the baton (SP, p. 124).

I suggest that these metaphors, in conjunction with the overall message of the Promise Keepers, help reinforce their gender ideology by evoking images of male-dominated settings.

Use of Sport in Delivery Style. There are other uses of sport for the Promise Keepers, ones that I would also suggest add to the ambiance and provide support for an ideological underpinning of male superiority. Some of these include: Bill McCartney, the former University of Colorado football coach, as the founder of the group; the annual revival meetings that take place in football arenas, and the use of sport cheers during these meetings such as the wave, and the cheer in which fans challenge the fans of the opposing team: "We have spirit, yes we do. We have spirit, how 'bout you?" that becomes "We love Jesus, yes we do. We love Jesus how 'bout you?" (cited in Raab, 1996; Wagenheim, 1996). Further, the cover of the inaugural issue of the *New Man* magazine was an accomplished athlete (Dave Johnson). Sara Diamond (1995) stated that there is a regular column on Christian (male) athletes in this magazine, and the circulation is 500,000 copies.

CONCLUSION

Sport is one of the last social practices that is sex-segregated and dominated by men. It is a social practice that constructs and publicly displays the assumed essential differences of men and women and the resultant superiority of men. It is a powerful patriarchal symbol, and it is very popular. In her book *The Stronger Women Get, the More Men Love Football,* Nelson (1994) claimed that men make stronger links to this patriarchal symbol particularly at times in which women are gaining power. My investigation leads me to conclude that the Promise Keepers' sport examples, images, and metaphors are powerful cultural symbols that can rally men's support, under the assumption of the male's rightful place as leader in society. My interpretation is that this constitutes, in part, a backlash to real gains made by women and to challenging economic realities men face. In fact, the Promise Keepers are explicit about their concerns over men losing power, which they have referred to as the "sissification" or "feminization" of men.

This parallels similar concerns men faced during the turn of the century when the economy and gender norms were changing and undermining traditional forms of power. One response was to decry the fall of the American male and to re-establish leadership positions by displaying traditional manly traits such as aggressive, rugged individualism. During the first part of the century, sport was seen as one means of renewing hegemonic masculinity. As Messner (1988) stated: "Sport was a male-created homosocial sphere that provided men with psychological separation from the perceived feminization of society while also providing dramatic symbolic proof of the 'natural superiority' of men over women" (p. 68).

It is important to note that there can be a variety of interpretations of Promise Keepers literature and their movement. The purpose of this chapter was not to present the Promise Keepers and their participants as simply sexist, but to point out the more blatant uses of sexism in the literature and discuss how sport has been used in subtle, and not so subtle, ways to support an ideology of male superiority.

References

Beal, B., & Gray, J. (1995). *Bill McCartney and the Promise Keepers: Exploring the connections among sport, masculinity, and Christianity*. Paper presented at the annual convention for the American Alliance for Health, Physical Education, Recreation, and Dance. Portland, Oregon, March 28–April 1.

Bryson, L. (1987). Sport and maintenance of masculine hegemony. *Women's Studies International Forum 10*, 349–360.

Coakley, J. (1994). *Sport in society: Issues and controversies*. St. Louis: Mosby Press.

Curry, T. (1991). Fraternal bonding in the locker room: A profeminist analysis of talk about competition and women. *Sociology of Sport Journal 8*, 119–135.

Diamond, S. (1995, December). The New Man: Promise Keepers are on the road to stardom. *Z Magazine 8*(12), 16–18.

Janssen, A., & Weeden, L.K. (eds.) (1994). *Seven promises of a Promise Keeper*. Colorado Springs, CO: Focus on the Family Publishing.

Kidd, B. (1990). The men's cultural centre: Sports and the dynamic of women's oppression/men's repression. In M. Messner & D. Sabo (eds.), *Sport and the gender order: Critical feminist perspectives* (pp. 31–43). Champaign, IL: Human Kinetics Books.

Kimmel, M., & Kaufman, M. (1995). Weekend warriors: The new men's movement. In Michael Kimmel (ed.), *The politics of manhood: Profeminist men respond to the mythopoetic men's movement (and the mythopoetic leaders answer)* (pp. 15–43). Philadelphia: Temple University Press.

McCartney, B., et al. *What makes a man?* Colorado Springs, CO: Navpress.

Messner, M. (1988). Sports and male domination: The female athlete as contested ideological terrain. *Sociology of Sport Journal 5*, 197–211.

Messner, M. (1997). *The politics of masculinities: Men in movements*. Thousand Oaks, CA: Sage Publications.

Nelson, M.B. (1994). *The stronger women get, the more men love football: Sexism and the American culture of sports*. New York: Harcourt Brace & Company.

Raab, S. (1996, January). Triumph of his will. *Gentleman's Quarterly* 66(1), 110–117, 127–130.

Stammer, L. (1994, July 8). Promise Keepers: The aim: improving husbands and fathers. *Greeley (CO) Tribune*, A12.

Wagenheim, J. (1996, January/February). Among the Promise Keepers: An inside look at the evangelical men's movement. *Utne Reader 73*, 74–77. [Excerpted from *New Age Journal* (1995, March/April).]

Weber, B. (1996, June 20) Christian organization plans to spend $115 million in '96. *Rocky Mountain News*.

Whitson, D. (1990). Sport in the social construction of masculinity. In M. Messner & D. Sabo (eds.), *Sport, men, and the gender order: Critical feminist perspectives* (pp. 19–29). Champaign, IL: Human Kinetics.

Willis, P. (1994). Women in sport in ideology. In S. Birrell & C. Cole (eds.), *Women, sport, and culture* (pp. 31–45). Champaign, IL: Human Kinetics.

CHAPTER 12

Onward Broken Soldiers: A Rhetorical Analysis of the Atlanta Promise Keepers Clergy Conference

by John D. Suk

Between 13 and 15 February, 1995, about 38,000 pastors—what Promise Keepers preacher Tony Evans described as a tithe of all America's pastors—attended the Promise Keepers Clergy Conference for Men at the Georgia Dome in Atlanta. Over the course of three days, the gathered pastors lifted their hands to heaven, clapped them in tune to music, and folded them in prayer. The pastors sang majestically, waved hankies in the air and tossed beach balls from the galleries for fun. A few pastors even broke into dance or fell face down in response to some sermons.

Along the way, the 12 plenary preachers who addressed the Atlanta Conference presented their audience with a paradox. A promotional pamphlet advertised that the conference's purpose was to "refresh pastors and to renew their hope and courage, that they might lead His Church into full-scale revival." Similarly, in his opening sermon, PK founder Bill McCartney preached, "If each man here would truly commit to the blood covenant, we will set ablaze a wild fire that will sweep across our land. We'll revive it in the name of Jesus of Nazareth."

The paradox was created as most keynote preachers portrayed the gathered pastors not so much as leaders of revival but as broken, hurting men at serious risk of failing their churches, their families and God. Typically, Tony Evans argued, "We're in a slump. We keep missing the ball and wondering, 'So, do I belong here at all?'" This chapter's purpose is to explore both the rhetorical nature of this paradox and what the cumulative attempt to resolve it reveals about PK's religious world view.

The 12 sermons preached in Atlanta are examined here using a dramatic analogy. American rhetorician Kenneth Burke wrote that at least five questions may be asked of any drama and, by extension, of any rhetorical work. Each of these questions is related to what he calls the five dramatic "generating principles" (1969, p. xv): what was done? (what Burke calls the act); when or where was it done? (scene); who did it? (agent); how was it done? (agency); and why was it done? (purpose). When these five questions are asked of rhetorical works, the answers comprise a pentadic analysis. When these five questions are utilized in exploring the underlying drama of the Atlanta conference the following prototypical drama emerges: All across the polluted landscape of America (scene), hurting and broken pastors (agents) are invited to heal themselves (act) through Promise Keeping and related strategies (agency), to achieve a new era of national religious revival (purpose).

As PK leaders, the Atlanta preachers had similar goals for the conference, held some common theological commitments and participated in the same organizational, evangelical and American culture. These factors probably help account for the fact that their sermons displayed a remarkable degree of agreement as regards the core drama. The reader should understand, however, that this prototypical drama represents what one might call the majority view. While most preachers offered minor variations on this core drama, a few offered different dramas altogether. Furthermore, the prototypical drama represents a critical synthesis of the Atlanta sermons rather than a blueprint consciously followed by the preachers. What follows is an analysis of the rhetorical structure of the Atlanta conference that reveals the core drama and its relation to the paradox mentioned above. The chapter concludes with observations about what the core drama reveals about the Promise Keepers' world view.

POLLUTED SCENES
REQUIRE POLLUTED AGENTS

The dramatic scene in which PK sermons are most often set is America. Like the Puritans, the Atlanta preachers spoke of America as if it had a unique divine errand, much as did Old Testament Israel. This approach dissolves the borders between church and state so that PK preachers could move easily between describing the need for revival in America and the need for revival in the church. Typically, Atlanta preacher Wellington Boone equated church and state by substituting one for the other in parallel clauses. "He wants, God does, he wants that the church would be what it ought to be ... and it seems like he's not going to let God go until this nation is made of praise in the earth."

The 12 plenary sermons were unanimous and insistent in their assertion that America and all her associated institutions, including the church, are in deep trouble. First, for example, McCartney sets the tone for this position in his opening sermon by stating, "The truth of the matter is that this nation has been on a downward spiral, a decline morally since its very birth." Joseph Stowell describes the church as a place where he doesn't want to go. "Look at the people there. They're backbiting. The elders are callused, they're critical, they're hypocrites." Raleigh Washington illustrated his sermon on racism in America by telling the story of the rape, by a white man, of his wife's African-American grandmother when she was only 10.

The Atlanta preachers agreed nearly unanimously that their particular polluted American stage was populated by polluted American pastors. The registration packet included photocopied data taken from Wes Roberts' *Support Your Local Pastor*. Roberts stated that 90 percent of American clergy said they were not adequately trained to deal the demands of their ministry; 80 percent believed that their ministry was negatively affecting their families; 75 percent reported a significant stress crisis within the past five years; and 37 percent said they had been involved in an inappropriate sexual relationship with a parishioner.

Tony Evans underlined this theme by declaring, "Many of us have come here in a spiritual slump. We go through the motions of ministry, but the dynamic is gone, the life is not there, and we wonder whether we should be in it at all." Jesse Miranda said pastors were "contaged with the disease of the '80s and the '90s, of leadership. Emotional exhaustion. Compassion fatigue. Spiritual overload." Bill McCartney invited minority pastors to the altar, saying: "Every brother of color, come forward ... these guys have been wounded ... their souls have been damaged ... we love them and they need us."

Sometimes the Atlanta preachers offered an alternative, more heroic portrait of pastors to their audience. For example, in the opening speech, McCartney called the gathered pastors his "dream team," and added, "I've been in a lot of stadiums before, but never with this kind of talent." John Maxwell honored the retired pastors present who had well performed their responsibilities. These alternative descriptions of the gathered pastors were relatively few, and did little to undermine the pervasive portrait of pastors as broken and ineffective.

Kenneth Burke believes the conjunction of a poisoned scene and poisoned agents is almost unavoidable. He argues that the scene-agent relationship (Burke calls it a "ratio") is characterized by a "correlation between the quality of the country and the quality of its inhabitants." For example, he cites Swift's satire on philosophers and mathematicians, the Laputans, in the third book of *Gulliver's Travels*. "To suggest that the Laputans are, we might say, 'up in the air,' he portrays them as living on an island that floats in space."

A darker example of the scene-agent ratio may be found in Stephen Crane's *Maggie: A Girl of the Streets*. Burke (1969, p. 9) would explain sorry cases such as Maggie's by saying, "The logic of the scene-agent ratio has often served as an embarrassment to the naturalistic novelist" because a brutalized situation—a sweatshop, for example, or the Bowery in Maggie's case—requires brutalized characters as its dialectical counterpart. In a similar manner, the Atlanta PK preachers, having carefully and consistently described a polluted American scene, are dramatically constrained to populate it with similarly polluted heroes destined to live out some tragic end.

Thus the rhetorical paradox of the Atlanta conference. Somehow the 12 preachers must convince their audience that broken American pastors, mired in the polluted slough of America and her churches, will nevertheless be able to cleanse themselves sufficiently to lead an American revival. What follows is a brief summary of the two most important ways in which the Atlanta preachers tried to resolve the paradox.

THE DAVID AND GOLIATH REPRESENTATIVE ANECDOTE

The first strategy used by the speakers to address the problem of polluted pastors was the use of a representative anecdote, a paradigmatic symbol or analogy that sums up an underlying dramatic theme of the work in question. Burke (1969, p. 507) bases his idea of such representation on that of synecdoche, where the representative anecdote is to the entire work as "part for the whole, whole for the part, container for the contained, sign for the thing signified."

In six of the Atlanta sermons, the David and Goliath story functions as a representative anecdote. In the David and Goliath story, God uses the child David to defeat the giant Goliath. David defeated Goliath despite of his relative weakness because God worked through him. And in the rest of David's life, God continued to work through him even though David turned out to be a great sinner. Thus McCartney, for example, describes racism as "a giant that has never lost a battle—until today." And Max Lucado mentions the giant of denominationalism when he prays, "He scoffs your church, O God. And here we stand, O Lord, only five smooth stones in our hands."

Jack Hayford extends the David and Goliath anecdote, allowing for a dialectical reversal of the meaning of brokenness. Retelling the story of David dancing naked before the ark, Hayford claims, "Only as the alabaster box of our soul is broken open does the fragrance then begin to fill the house and the multiplying of divine life happen." Chuck Swindoll adds, "The word broken means, literally, shattered. The sacrifices of God, my sacrifice to God is a shattered spirit and literally a bruised heart. Is yours?" In effect, by regularly comparing the pastors to David, this representative anecdote offered the gathered pastors a *deux ex machina* solution to the problem of their pollution. They no longer had to overcome the scene's constraints on character because the anecdote suggested that God would use them as he used David. Ironically, this approach actually made a virtue of pastoral brokenness as the gathered pastors were supposed to find ways of healing themselves.

Featuring Agency

The prototypical drama suggests that Promise Keepers preachers are supposed to lead America to revival after healing themselves of their own brokenness. In Atlanta, the majority of sermons indicated that this healing would take place sometime in the future by means of several strategies they described. Thus, while the healing act is not very prominent in the sermons, the means by which such healing eventually may be accomplished played a very prominent role. Three of these means, or agencies, are described here.

Prescriptive Lists. Most of the sermons contained detailed prescriptions, which—if followed—would enable the audience to heal themselves. These sermonic prescriptions were analogous to the instructions for assembly one receives with a bicycle or model airplane. As such, they comprise enumerated lists of behaviors in which one must engage to accomplish a desired goal.

McCartney's sermon described the nine marks of a disciple and seven considerations on the blood covenant (although he got through only four of them). Jack Hayford explained the five principles of timeless worship. John Maxwell enumerated seven steps towards finishing well, including 10 commandments for avoiding sexual temptation. Wellington Boone went through the four stages of entering into a prayer relationship as well as the four steps of revival. Raleigh Washington and Glen Kehrein structured the second half of their speeches as four principles. In this context, Todd Yonkman (1995, p. 26) makes a significant observation when he writes:

> Promise Keepers has what I would call a "technical spirituality." Most articles use bullet points to clearly list spiritual techniques to be used to build a better marriage, combat sexual temptation, support the mission of the church, and the like. Almost every Promise Keepers speech that I have heard enumerates several steps that, if followed, will lead to a deeper relationship with Christ, financial security, or freedom from addiction.

These omnipresent lists add up to spiritual tool kits which, if properly used, will eventually help get pastors off the injured reserve lists and onto the churches' active duty rosters. They are the means by which pastors heal themselves, and in so doing, empower themselves to usher in revival.

Exemplarist Hermeneutic. Rather than wrestle with hermeneutic difficulties or shades of meaning, most of the Atlanta preachers cut through any and all exegetical difficulties by engaging in exemplaristic preaching. Exemplaristic preaching treats biblical characters as paradigms for living today. Such preaching focuses on agency by translating the ancient actions of biblical characters into road maps to guide contemporary audiences through the complexities of modern life. Thus, along with the prescriptive lists of instructions that will guide them in holding to a healing regimen, exemplaristic sermons offer biblical characters as models for how one should live.

In this manner, Tony Evans offers Moses as the model contemporary preachers ought to imitate if they want to be healed. By going to Mount Sinai, Moses returned to God's presence. "He met God where God hung out…. And when you hang out with ministry and don't hang out with God, ministry will drain you." Similarly, just as Moses took off his shoes at Mount Sinai, "If we're going to come close to God, then what I need to do, what you need to do is take off dirty shoes…. We gotta clean up our lives."

In addition to Moses, Evans suggested Jonah, John, Mark, Paul, Peter, Jacob, and finally even himself as models of how to practice ministry as a hale, whole, and healthy pastor. Besides Tony Evans, other notable examples of the exemplaristic method of commending antidotes to the gathered pastors included Chuck Swindoll's sermon on Isaiah. Swindoll used Isaiah as a model of pastoral brokenness: "He possessed a spiritual death that set him apart from his contemporaries." Swindoll notes that, according to the *Living Bible*, when God confronts Isaiah and tells him to go preach, Isaiah responds, "I'm a foul-mouthed sinner in the midst of a foul-mouthed race." Isaiah's example suggests to the gathered pastors that they should accept the role of weak, broken men of God. In this manner, Swindoll also reinforces the lesson of the David and Goliath anecdote.

The use of such preaching eschews thoughtful exegesis of the text by transforming it into a moralistic story full of characters who should be emulated if one desires healing and ministerial success. Traditional form, redactional, or even historical and grammatical exegesis is rendered unnecessary as the preacher collapses the horizon of the original text into the horizon of today's audience. Although such "literal" interpretation appears to pay close attention to the text, it usually takes biblical stories out of narrative context. They may then be selectively chosen to fit preconceived ideas about what the text should say.

Floor Exercises. Many of the Atlanta sermons concluded with short rituals that allowed the pastors to experience, proleptically and symbolically, the self-healing they were supposed to experience fully after following the instructions for healing in the sermons. Much as guided imagery may be used to calm people down or to exercise the imagination, these short, guided rituals were designed to suggest to the men that they were experiencing the beginning of inner spiritual healing.

Chuck Swindoll's ritual was typical and took so long that he had to ask the audience, part way through, not to leave. A few of his instructions, which account for fully a fifth of his sermon, are reproduced here:

Your hands. As you stare into the palms of your hands, you have thoughts of your own ... your greed, your envy, your gluttony ... close your hands ... keep your head bowed ... lift your hands and release [those sins] to him ... just leave your hands open ... stand quietly ... don't leave ... sing ... repent ... minister deeply ... leave the building without a word.

David Bryant led the audience in a concert of prayer. Such prayers are highly choreographed mass prayers where individuals are guided through a series of different kinds of private and shared prayer. For example, Bryant said: "Periodically, to get your attention, you'll hear ring very loudly a bell sound. It'll go bing, ding, ding, and when you hear that, whoever is praying at that moment, if you could just bring it to a close right then so I can give us instructions where to go next." The entire prayer consists of several paragraphs of such instructions, and lasts more than half an hour. Similarly, Jesse Miranda had the audience pray in unison, stand, raise hands, and make the sign of a crown. Jack Hayford asked musicians to play quietly while he instructed everyone how to come before the Lord, including instructions about how to breathe. In total, just over half the sermons concluded with this sort of rituals. Nearly all of them also involved holding hands or laying of hands on one's neighbor.

THE PARADOX REVISITED

The scene-agent conundrum amplifies the dramatic pollution problem the PK preachers need to resolve. Ideally, once the dramatic complication was well defined, the rest of the preachers could have devoted all their efforts to resolving the tension. The best reading of the convention's second day would suggest that this is, indeed, exactly what the speakers attempted. Agency was most clearly featured in day-two sermons by Hayford, Stowell, Maxwell, Swindoll and Bryant. Even though all the difficulties associated with the polluted scene-agent agency remained after the second day, the preachers had done as much as humanly possible to address those difficulties, using all the strategies described above. Whether these strategies would ultimately have been sufficient is questionable, but at least the preachers had made a start.

The beginning of day three offered a whole new perspective in that Henry Blackaby's sermon offered an alternative drama by equating the men in the audience with the scene where God works through his Spirit. To the degree that the audience was wondering how in the world they would be able to do everything they had been told to do on day two, Blackaby's speech must have come as a refreshing, encouraging breeze. Blackaby departed significantly from the prototypical drama by describing the gathered pastors as the scene of God's surprising, redemptive renewal. Blackaby's new drama had some potential for convincing the audience because it was not incompatible with the strategy outlined by the day-two pastors and because it built on one of the key elements of the David and Goliath representative anecdote, namely how God can accomplish great things through weak persons.

The next three pastors, however, returned to the themes of polluted pastor and polluted scene by describing at length the denominational and racial fractures in the church. Adding insult to injury, two of the speeches—those by Jesse Miranda and Raleigh Washington—were poorly conceived and delivered. Washington's speech was twice as long as any other delivered in Atlanta and was followed by what appeared to be an attempted patch up job on the theology of reconciliation by Tony Evans. The whole process lasted so long that the audience had to be encouraged to stay in their seats and not leave for supper. Whatever momentum had been building to a resolution of the core dramatic complication was dissipated. The small opportunity day three offered to drive home the theme of pastoral healing as a basis for national revival was lost.

If the purpose of the Atlanta conference was to send pastors home ready to deal with the pollution in which they were mired, the third-day preachers should have hammered home messages similar to Blackaby's. These messages would have announced God's transforming power and love as an additional, decisive resource for disheartened pastors. Ironically, such a turn was really the only plausible solution for a drama where broken agents are mired in a polluted scene. The traditional Christian answer to the problem of pollution is a *deux ex machina* resolution where the agents are miraculously forgiven their own individual sins. This resolution to the scene-agent conundrum would have been convincing to most in the audience because it matches the traditional Christian defining story. God, after all, so loved the broken world that he sent his only son, so that whoever believed in him would be saved from the world's pollution.

Conclusion: A Pragmatic Faith

In the Atlanta sermons the pastors tried to resolve their rhetorical paradox, in the main, by using rhetorical strategies that focused on questions of agency. More time and effort was spent explaining the means by which the gathered pastors might eventually heal themselves than on any of the other five dramatic questions. This is an important observation because, as Kenneth Burke (1969, p, 127) wrote, a different motivational source is suggested by each of the five pentadic questions:

> Dramatistically, the different philosophic schools are to be distinguished by the fact that each school features a different one of the five

terms, in developing a vocabulary designed to allow this one term full expression (as regards its resources and its temptations) with the other terms being comparatively slighted or being placed in the perspective of the featured term.

In other words, Burke believes that different philosophical outlooks, or world views, are associated with each of the five pentadic elements. In his theory, for example, idealistic theories of being are associated with an emphasis on agent, and its corollary, mind (Burke, p. 171), while realist theories of reality are associated with the featuring of act (Burke, p. 227). And in the case of Promise Keepers preaching in Atlanta, where agency is featured, Burke suggests that the rhetorical work will reveal that most American of world views, pragmatism. Pragmatism, Burke notes—quoting Baldwin's old dictionary of philosophy—is the prescription "of the means necessary to the attainment of happiness" (Burke, p. 275).

Indeed, the pendulum swing at the Atlanta conference was away from the traditional doctrinal concerns of Christianity toward practical concerns, away from a focus on truth to one on healing and therapy; and away from a theocentric emphasis on what God does and who God is to an individualistic emphasis on what each pastor should do to better himself. Pragmatism, says James, is like a hallway that gets you where you want to go. Down this hallway the Promise Keepers' sermons in Atlanta represented a faith moving away from first principles towards a faith focused on meeting personal needs. Along the way, Promise Keepers substitutes concern for personal pain and national pollution for old-fashioned sin, and offers prescriptive lists of things one must do—a sort of modern works-righteousness—for the traditional emphasis on Jesus' atonement for sin. This adds up to a significant secularization of traditional Christian language.

Another example of this secularization of language has to do with the Promise Keepers' fascination with numbers. Pragmatism, says James (1991, p. 26) in a phrase that he uses over and over again, and a phrase with which his critics have always hanged him, is concerned with the "cash value" of ideas, with their practical, measurable, numerical, therapeutic effects.

And if nothing else, Promise Keepers is religion by the numbers. In addition, the long, enumerated lists that nearly every sermon contained, the Atlanta audience was serenaded with accounts of how all of them were going to be given individual box lunches in less than 30 minutes. Promotional material for Atlanta promised that 80,000 would attend and, from there, the numbers went down. Miranda told us 50,000 were present, the next speaker lowered this to 43,000, and Tony Evans stated that we were a tithe of all the pastors in America because there were 40,000 of us, and this number in turn was lowered, finally, to 38,000—but only by way of an official press release that arrived in the press box after most of the press had left. Most Promise

Keepers literature rehearses the phenomenal growth of the movement, from an initial meeting of 25 to another with 70 present to the first conference with 4,200 to 22,000 to 50,000 to 700,000.

The numeric measure of Promise Keeper faith wouldn't surprise Kenneth Burke. He says the appeal to agency—to instrumentalism—derives its "prestige" from "the grammatical fact that it covers the area of applied science, the area of new power" (1969, p. 286). There is really nothing new here. Early in the 19th century, de Tocqueville (1873, II, p. 79) noted that the American democratic milieu was transforming American religion. In a passage wherein he describes the American fascination with commerce, he writes:

> The majority is more engaged in business than in study; in political and commercial interests, than in philosophical speculation or literary pursuits. Most of the words coined or adopted for its use will bear the mark of these habits; they will mainly serve to express the wants of business, the passions of party, or the details of the public administration. In these departments, the language will constantly grow, whilst it will gradually lose ground in metaphysics and theology.

Promise Keepers evangelicalism turns out to be an astonishingly American religion. However, its practitioners must ask themselves how much of historic faith and language they have—probably unwittingly—given up in order to make their faith fit with the American experience.

References

Blackaby, H. (Speaker). (1996). *The pastor and revival* [Cassette Recording]. Denver: Promise Keepers.
Boone, W. (1996). *The pastor and his character* [Cassette Recording]. Denver: Promise Keepers.
Bryant, D. (1996). *Season of prayer* [Cassette Recording]. Denver: Promise Keepers.
Burke, K. (1969). *A grammar of motives.* Berkeley: University of California Press. (Originally published 1949.)
Crane, S. (1995). *Maggie: A girl of the streets.* New York: Fawcett Books. (Originally published 1892.)
Evans, T. (1996). *The pastor and the call of God* [Cassette Recording]. Denver: Promise Keepers.
Hayford, J. *The pastor and his personal worship* [Cassette Recording]. Denver: Promise Keepers.
James, W. (1991/1907). *Pragmatism.* Buffalo: Prometheus Books.
Lucado, M. (1996). *The pastor and denominational harmony* [Cassette Recording]. Denver: Promise Keepers.
Maxwell, J. (1996). *The pastor and his accountability* [Cassette Recording]. Denver: Promise Keepers.

McCartney, B. (1996). *The vision: Why we are here* [Cassette Recording]. Denver: Promise Keepers.
Miranda, J. *The pastor and the kingdom* [Cassette Recording]. Denver: Promise Keepers.
Roberts, W. (1995). *Support your local pastor: Practical ways to encourage your minister.* Colorado Springs, CO: NavPress Publishing Group.
Schlafer, D. (1995). Letter to pastors in the registration pamphlet for the Fan Into Flame 1996 Clergy Conference for Men. Boulder: Promise Keepers.
Stowell, J. (1996). *The pastor and his family* [Cassette Recording]. Denver: Promise Keepers.
Swindoll, C. (1996). *The pastor and brokenness* [Cassette Recording]. Denver: Promise Keepers.
Tocqueville, A. de (1873). *Democracy in America* (Henry Reeve, Trans. 5th ed. 2 vols.). Boston: John Allyn.
Washington, R. (1996). *The pastor and racial harmony* [Cassette Recording]. Denver: Promise Keepers.
Yonkman, T. (1995). *Promise Keepers: Repentance, forgiveness, and male affirmation.* Unpublished manuscript.

CHAPTER 13

Ecumenical Promise Keepers: Oxymoron or Fidelity?
by J. Lynn Reynolds and Rodney A. Reynolds

Does the idea of secularity enable us to grasp the quicksilver soul of modernity, or does it mystify the enduring truths of culture [Douglas and Tipton, 1983, p. vii]?

It may be difficult for some observers to acknowledge and understand the growth of religion in America. This is because religion is no longer contained in its formal institutions; it has become diffused throughout the culture. Although the stained-glass windows and buildings of the inner-city churches often have been sold off as members have left for the suburbs, that does not mean that the ideals of Christian unity have been discarded. The "staid pew warmers" of the 1950s have donned their T-shirts and cut-offs and gone to stand in the mall.

But as the thousands of men flowed into the Washington, DC, mall area for Stand in the Gap, the national PK rally, C-SPAN continually flashed data along the bottom of the screen that might seem to contradict one Promise Keepers claim—that of their being ecumenical. Percentages displayed on the screen seemed to contradict the picture of the denominational diversity of people on stage. Is there a denominational dominance within PK event attendees, or can they be said to truly magnify the call of ecumenicalism? That is what this chapter set out to explore. In this essay the responses of constituents who responded to an on-line survey will speak about what unites them.

Those who choose not to see, may indeed fail to perceive that religion has firmly established itself within large subcultures in the United States. The observations of foreign visitors show that an "all-pervasive religion" has characterized American culture through the years (Lipset, 1963). Some observers point to the huge voluntarism movement in America and say that it is only the tip of the iceberg of the desire to connect with our fellow man in a spiritual way. It seems apparent that in the 1990s, when Americans no longer feel compelled to be religious, millions have freely chosen to be just that.

The Greek word for ecumenical basically means universal. The Promise Keepers as a social movement in the 1990s are trying to forge unity among men. As a group, they are trying to embrace the Christian ideal of the universal church and all that that implies. But cynical observers, often with the argumentative strategy of trying to reduce the movement to absurdity, continue to try to dismiss PK as just a part of that "anti–Disney" faction who always over-respond to everything. (It is surprising, even shocking, how favorable the media coverage of Promise Keepers has been, especially when compared with coverage of "televangelists" and other conservative Christian figures and organizations [see Allen, this volume; Claussen, 1996; Claussen, this volume; Waters, this volume]). But over the last 20 years we have seen what Professor Jacob Needleman of San Francisco State University felt to be true a long time ago: a new religious movement "can no longer be taken as a transitory cultural aberration but rather as a central feature of the profound change through which the American civilization is now passing" (Marx, 1977, p. 188). We cannot ignore these movements; instead, we must examine them.

Since 1959, and the election of Pope John XXIII, impressive moves in the United States have indicated progress in the area of interfaith relationships. Over the 40 years since this new openness, the wisdom and resources of thousands have attempted to make some contribution to ecumenical unity. Even though the "old-line" churches of Protestantism showed declines in membership through the 1970s and 1980s, a spiritual unity has been emerging that cannot be contained. Reformed Protestantism, with its focus on the Word of God and the intellectual explanations of doctrine, always has been big on ideas and how God's purposes are played out in the different avenues of life. But as John MacKay concluded, "ecumenical enthusiasm ... is in constant danger of overlooking the fact that ... the units that make up the church which is Christ's body are not denominations or organizations, but individuals' souls" (Jurji, 1959, p. 11).

But where is the proof of true ecumenicalism? What is it that the respondents to this idea of ecumenicalism are called to identify with or tolerate? Is it not, again to quote MacKay,

> that there exists a new, a hopeful people, united across all demarcation lines, because they know themselves to be the people gathered into one by God through his Son. [God] will always find new ways of bringing his scattered children together [Jurji, 1959, p. 34].

The ecumenical situation is often viewed differently from congregation to congregation. However, the goals must be received not only by church leaders but by the grass roots participants. It is important that all of the people of God have a connected consciousness, knowing that ecumenicalism's goal does not mean a loss of a specific continuity or local identity but instead means gaining both in far greater dimensions. The PK movement is the first ecumenical group truly to have sent this message. Men are encouraged to turn loose of neither their church membership nor their personal identity as participants in the movement but to join the integrity of Christ. What a novel idea.

Harvey Cox (1973), the Harvard theologian, spoke of four possible myths that could be believed by the cultural majority concerning new religious groups—that they (1) are subversive; (2) encourage sexual perversion; (3) refuse to tell the truth about themselves; and (4) employ means of duping followers. While subversive might be a word that the feminist movement has mentioned in connection with PK's attitudes and rhetoric, several items from the above list should be addressed here in light of the focus of this chapter, and the role of PK and Christian unity.

Does PK refuse to tell the truth about itself? Number six of its Seven Promises, published in all of its literature, states: "A Promise Keeper is committed to reach beyond any racial and denominational barriers to demonstrate the power of biblical unity." In another context, a quote from the *Promise Keepers Men's Study Bible* (1997) reads: "Reaching beyond racial, cultural, gender and ethnic barriers to demonstrate the power of Biblical unity is more than a nice idea. It is God's will and command. To miss this fact is to miss the message of [the story of God's love]."

Here, the stand for unity is clear, but do the facts about the movement support it? One group publication, *The Promise Keeper: Living a Life of Integrity* (1998), described PK participants as: Baptist, 31%; Non-Denominational 27%; Methodist, 9%; Assemblies of God, 6%; Lutheran, Presbyterian and Other, each 5%; and Evangelical Free, Nazarene and Roman Catholic, each 4%. If these data are accurate, then perhaps the movement is trying to tell the truth, and some Christian men really have found a niche where they can worship with other men as brothers. But such an ecumenical connection is so unusual that the culture will ultimately attempt to apply the other myths.

Cox's fourth myth is that new religious groups are trying "dupe" their followers. Multiple possibilities for being duped exist, and might be feared. Are new religious groups ecumenical or only pretending to be? Are they just about profit? Do they really think that society can be changed? They do believe society can be changed. Harold Brinkley, PK's national director of church relations, has claimed, "We're building men of integrity beginning at age eight" (*The Promise Keeper: Living a Life of Integrity*, 1998).

This is the part that is just too difficult for many in American culture to comprehend: PK is a foundation for teaching and otherwise preparing the next generation. (Eight attitudes have been incorporated into PK's sponsored Project Manhood Curriculum: I am teachable; I am determined; I am a gentleman; I am principled; I am loving; I am open-hearted and open-minded; I am a bridge builder; and I am a warrior [Nix, 1996]. With this approach to the bonding of fathers and sons, the promise of "breaking down barriers" and "having biblical unity" in the future sounds more obtainable.) But even if the next generation is believed to be more teachable, what about the ecumenical foundation that on which their fathers are standing today? Is it sound?

If the goal is to explore PK's success or even potential to reach an ecumenical ideal, then the first step is asking whether or not Promise Keepers themselves can agree on universal foundations of doctrinal issues. We composed a survey to highlight key ideas that traditionally have had potential for disunity among different Christian denominations. This process consisted of several brainstorming sessions with preachers and former preachers as well as lay people. An initial 38 items were reduced to 24 that we believed to be key. Doctrinal and traditional issues, as well as life issues, were included. Some of the following items were incorporated: speaking in tongues, the return of Jesus, the resurrection, the rapture, the infallibility of scripture, infant baptism, a literal creation account, the losing of one's salvation, the virgin birth, hell as an actual place, direct revelation, the incarnate Christ, the baptism of the Holy Spirit, tithing, participation in a local church, one's political position and women in leadership. The respondents were asked to score each question from one to five with one being "strongly disagree" and five being "strongly agree."

We distributed the survey on the World Wide Web to various religiously affiliated sites, and received 107 usable responses from males. Ages of responses were: 18–29 (10%); 30–39 (40%), 40–49 (36%), 50–50 (11%), and 60 and over (2%). One man refused to respond to the age question. Demographic questions included church background, which were very similar to the list above: Evangelicals (10%), Baptists (19%), Traditionalists (16%), Non-denominational (31%) and Other (24%). No Catholics responded. Respondents were clergy (4%), church lay leaders (39%), church members (40%), frequent attendees (8%), occasional attendees (3%), and 4% who marked other. No one marked "non-church attendee." Eighty-eight percent were married, 3% were no longer married, 8% had never been married. Seventy-nine percent had children, 18% had no children, and a few men did not respond to the question. By self-identified race, respondents were Asian Americans (4%), African Americans (1%), Hispanic (3%) and 88% Caucasians. The rest marked either "other" or gave no response. The vast majority (75%) had completed either a college degree or some graduate school work. They fell into conservative (72%), moderate (27%) and liberal (1%) groups on their self-report of religious beliefs. By political affiliation, they were Democrats (4%), Republicans (61%), Independents (22%) and Other (9%).

Using that list of beliefs deemed acceptable or not for another Christian to hold, a factor analysis was performed on the 24 items that defined various beliefs that different groups may or may not hold. (A factor analysis is used when an author has measured subjects on a large number of variables.

This statistical analysis shows which variables are correlated or related with one another and now with other variables. Each group of variables is called a factor. A factor loading shows the relative connection that each variable has to the others; coefficients for those factor loadings range from -1 to +1, with +1 being a perfect positive correlation. This factor analysis involved an oblique rotation).

The following factors were supportable as forming three groups. The "Biblical Basics" group had a reliability of .89; the "Conservative Doctrine" group had a reliability of .86; and the "Spiritual Gifts" group had a reliability of .76. The specific loadings are listed below.

Factor Analysis Table

Biblical Basics

Item number and Item	Loading
63. Mary was not a virgin.	(.89)
54. Jesus did not rise from the dead.	(.90)
70. Jesus was not divine.	(.86)
64. Hell is a metaphor.	(.74)
66. God does not act directly now.	(.73)

Conservative Doctrine

Item number and Item	Loading
55. The rapture will occur before the tribulation.	(.80)
59. The strict biblical account of creation is true.	(.76)
57. Infant baptism is against the Bible.	(.75)
72. The rapture will, in fact, occur.	(.71)
56. Scripture is never in error.	(.68)
53. One's political position should be consistent with one's Christian beliefs.	(.67)
52. Jesus will return within the next few years.	(.64)
58. Women leaders in the church goes against the Bible.	(.64)

Spiritual Gifts

Item number and Item	Loading
51. Speaking in tongues is a gift.	(.81)
68. God speaks directly to people.	(.74)
73. Baptism in the Holy Spirit occurs.	(.73)
60. Lose salvation.	(.56)

After the items above were grouped, they were considered with regard to the demographic data gathered. Older men were more positively correlated toward all three groups. Education level was positively related only to the Biblical Basics group. This would be consistent with the enlightenment movement, because a great deal of pride is placed on the ability to reason to a particular intellectual position.

But the most important result to report here is that no significant differences were found among denominations. The statistical means for each group were: (1) Biblical Basics, 7.25, with scores ranging from 5 to 45 and a standard deviation of 4.6; (2) Conservative Doctrine, 30.62, with scores ranging from 8 to 72 and a standard deviation of 7.2; and (3) Spiritual Gifts, 14.21, with scores ranging from 4 to 36 and a standard deviation of 4.1. The higher the score, the more it was acceptable for people to believe differently from another group.

A significant number of respondents—in fact, a plurality—marked "strongly disagree" or "5" on the Biblical Basics group. Thus, these items are considered core issues on which there should be no disagreement.

The means for the Conservative Doctrine and Spiritual Gifts factors were slightly above neutral. Again, no statistically significant differences were found across denominations on Conservative Doctrine or Biblical Basics. In other words, respondents were saying, "I may not endorse it but I do not deny that it may be acceptable for others."

But a statistically significant difference ($F = 4.519$, $df = 4/101$, $p = .002$) did exist between what the Baptists saw and what the traditionalists and others believed about being tolerant of others' beliefs about Spiritual Gifts. Baptists ($M = 11.65$, $sd = 3.6$) were significantly less willing to accept belief in Spiritual Gifts than were traditionalists ($M = 15.18$, $sd = 2.6$) and others ($M = 15.56$, $sd = 3.2$). Nevertheless, all groups were generally neutral to the acceptance of belief in Spiritual Gifts.

In conclusion, then, survey results showed a true spirit of ecumenicalism within the PK constituents. Survey items clearly placed the responses into the three categories named above: Biblical Basics, Conservative Doctrine and Spiritual Gifts, and the responses of the three groups do not indicate any strong opposition to another group. Respondents generally were not shutting out either Conservative Doctrine or Spiritual Gift beliefs but neither were they saying that others must subscribe to all of these ideas. They supported, by the way they scored their responses, the ability of others in the different groups to differ in their opinions.

Since the late 1950s, ecumenicists have called for an appreciation of the Pentecostal and other spirit-oriented and Bible-believing groups because of the need to understand all groups that are at work in the cause of Christ. PK men responding to the survey seem to realize their need for tolerance and their need not to judge their fellow Christians. They appear, in this survey, to be united across what might seem to be seen as lines of demarcation. Since the responses were anonymous and respondents were urged to "answer as honestly and truthfully as you can," no reason exists to believe that these men would have any motive to manage an impression other than the one represented here.

Max Lucado, minister of the Church of Christ in San Antonio, TX, spoke on ecumenical issues at Stand in the Gap. He called for attendees to repent of sectarianism, repent of their pride in particular denominations, repent of boasting about the name of a particular church, repent when jealousy has arisen, and to repent about time spent focused upon controversies. These are admirable goals, and the results above indicate that PK men have built within themselves a broad tolerance for their brothers' beliefs beneath the larger umbrella of what it means to them to be Christians.

Lucado also mentioned that "harmony is not the result of persuasion." Our on-line survey did not have a motivationally-written scenario that attempted to manipulate particular responses. It asked, "We want to know if you think [the following item] is acceptable for another Christian to believe." Again, referencing Lucado, "No man has the wisdom to disentangle" the mess denominations have created, but it appears that the PK is trying to lead by example and demonstrating this by its members accepting one another.

References

Claussen, D.S. (1996). *United States print mass media coverage of two men's movements: Robert Bly, Iron John, and the mythopoets, and Bill McCartney and the Promise Keepers.* Unpublished master's thesis, Kansas State University, Manhattan.

Cox, H. (1973). *The seduction of the spirit: The use and misuse of people's religion.* New York: Simon and Schuster.

Jurji, E.J. (ed.) (1959). *The ecumenical era in church and society: A symposium in honor of John A. MacKay.* New York: The Macmillan Co.

Lipset, S.M. (1963). *The first new nation: The United States in historical and comparative perspective.* New York: Basic Books.

Marty, M. E. (1983). Religion in America since mid-century. In Douglas, M., & Tipton, S. M. (eds.), *Religion and America: spirituality in a secular age.* New York: Simon and Schuster.

Marx, H.L. (1977). *Religions in America.* New York: H.W. Wilson Co.

Nix, S.D. (1996). *I am an African-American man of God.* Woodbury, NJ: Renaissance Productions.

The Promise Keeper: Living a life of integrity. (1998, January/February). Denver, CO: Promise Keepers.

CHAPTER 14

Reading a Promise Keepers Event: The Intersection of Race and Religion

by Billy Hawkins

In the United States, the ecclesiastical community presented the earliest examples of racial segregation (Franklin, 1988). Today, a demonstration of the progress of race relations in this country still may be found in churches on Sunday morning. The intensity of racial segregation among individuals supposedly worshipping the same God is easy to demonstrate. But contradictory as this may seem, few religious organizations or denominations have addressed the racial divide.

The only time racial division becomes an issue is when some tragedy draws public attention, locally or nationally. For example, it was not until black churches throughout the South began suffering arson attacks that Christian Coalition leader Ralph Reed proclaimed, "We are saying loud and clear that we are one in Christ and that we are not going to allow the racial divisions that parted us in the past to do so ever again" (Crouch, 1996). While Reed has many times pointed out the relatively poor record on race issues of conservative Christians as a group, Pastor Kenneth Hagin, Jr., of the Kenneth Hagin Ministries of Tulsa, OK, recently startled many of those who heard about it when he preached a sermon (biblically referenced) against interracial dating and marriage (Harris, 1998). Rather than apologize, or intentionally perpetuate racial divisions, others have dismissed the racial division of Christian churches as simply differences between white Christians and black Christians as regards styles of worship or expressions of belief.

Promise Keepers, however, finally has decided to address the issue of the racial divide among American Christians, and to affect an apologetic stance as well. For Bill McCartney, the issue of race and religion is greater than a difference in styles of worship. To him, the issue is a heavy burden, especially after Promise Keepers' first stadium conference consisted of a predominantly white male audience (McCartney, 1997).

Promise Keepers' religious message admonishing men to take back their rightful position in this country as leaders and godly men has packed stadiums and arenas around the country, making PK one of the major religious movements or revivals of recent times. But with a predominantly white male audience in attendance, these events have drawn criticism in part because of this message, and made it seem to some like a white male-centered movement not based on Christian principles. Some have criticized PK as embodying merely a backlash to the small gains women and ethnic and other minority groups achieved through affirmative action, and that gays and lesbians have accomplished through a combination of legislation, court rulings, demonstrations and comings out—since federal affirmative action programs never have included them. Finally, PK events have been critiqued for promoting an essentialist ideology of masculinity (e.g., Kimmel & Kaufman, 1995; Messner, 1997).

One of the main questions guiding me has been whether Promise Keepers can have an impact on breaking down racial barriers or, as the theme of these events suggests: "Breaking Down the Walls"? I offer here a critical reading of my attendance of a Promise Keepers Racial Reconciliation Breakfast and discussion, and a Promise Keepers event held at Soldier Field in Chicago, IL. I have attempted to examine the intersection of race and religion and, I hope, to identify Promise Keepers' realistic potential to affect race relations in America.

The assumption of the "Breaking Down the Walls" theme suggests that despite the removal of legal forms of racial segregation (e.g., Jim Crowism), various forms of racial segregation still exist in this country. From the neighborhoods in which they live to the churches they attend, an apparent degree of racial and denominational segregation became problematic to those behind Promise Keepers. While PK conferences were efforts to address this issue at the national level, Promise Keepers members in local areas organized a racial reconciliation breakfast to discuss race and denominational segregation at the community level.

THEORETICAL CONSIDERATIONS

Race and religion (specifically within the European and American versions of Christianity—i.e. religious doctrine interpreted by people of European descent) have shared a long and controversial history. Numerous researchers (Baird, 1844; Boles, 1988; Elkins, 1963; Franklin & Moss, 1988; Genovese, 1974; Jordan, 1968, 1974; Lincoln, 1984; Tocqueville, 1994; Stampp, 1956; and Wood, 1990) have addressed how Europeans' versions of Christianity were used by whites to justify the colonization and slavery of African people, and European Christianity's overall function in the relationship between "masters and slaves" and ultimately race relations in the U.S.

Several of these researchers also have documented how many African Americans transformed this religious doctrine to cope with and liberate themselves from forms of white supremacy (Stampp, 1956). For example, the biblical account of the children of Israel held in slavery by an Egyptian nation and eventually freed by an Almighty God became evidence for them to hope and call upon the God of Israel. They identified with the Israelites and coped with their oppression by waiting for their deliverer to appear.

When it came to whites' use of religion to justify slavery and colonization, this effort was supported by the enduring beliefs in the Curse of Ham ideology (i.e., where Noah cursed the descendants of his dark-skinned son, Ham, consigning them to serve his lighter-skinned sons). It served as a framework to justify the mistreatment of dark-skinned people throughout the world, including slavery in the United States. Wood (1990, p. 84) writes:

> [Ham] had watched his father sleeping naked and had shown disrespect by telling his brothers Shem and Japheth about it. Not sharing Ham's taste in humor, the brothers covered their father with a robe, all the while respecting his privacy by looking the other way. When Noah awakened and learned what had happened, he punished Ham by placing a curse on Canaan, the youngest of Ham's four sons, making him a "servant of servants"—that is a slave—to Shem and Japheth.

Many Europeans during the 15th, 16th, and 17th centuries used this passage to justify slavery and to explain the complexion of Negroes, since Ham connotes hot or dark (Wood, 1990; Jordan, 1968). Therefore, not only was Canaan cursed to be a servant, but he was supposedly cursed to be African and then, by history, African-American.

Another tenet of European Christianity, also associated with the curse of Canaan, was the "Chain of Being." It started out as a characterization of beings; later, in the 1730s, Carolus Linnaeus transformed this characterization into a science (Jordan, 1968). Initially, Linnaeus, one of the 18th century's great naturalists and called the father of taxonomy, did not classify variant kinds of men but, instead, arranged and classified all living creatures (Jordan, 1968). However, during the 17th and 18th centuries, the notion of the "Chain of Being" emerged and became a dominant mode of thinking among European intellectuals. Jordan (1974, p. 100) explains:

> The Chain of Being, as usually conceived, commenced with inanimate things and ranged upwards through the lowliest forms of life, through the more intelligent animals until it reached man himself; from man it continued upward through the myriad ranks of heavenly creatures until it reached its pinnacle in God.

Apes were considered the first link in the evolution of man; Negroes in this Chain of Being were considered two links above the apes, one link above orangutans, and several links below Europeans, the European being the link below heavenly creatures. In this Chain of Being, Africans and, later, African Americans were considered spiritually and intellectually inferior to whites. Jordan (1974, p. 105) also suggests that this "Chain of Being"

> led to a mode of thinking about the basest members of society as primarily and merely physical creatures. It was especially the day-to-day business of commercial slavery which placed a premium on the Negro's purely physical qualities. New slaves off the ships were described as "well-fleshed," "strong-limbed," "lusty," "sickly," "robust," "healthy," "scrawny," "unblemished."...The everyday buying and selling and deeding of slaves underscored the fact that Negroes, just like horses, were walking pieces of property.

This mode of thinking justified the mistreatment of African Americans, their denial of equality as humans, and their need to be evangelized.

Both Wood (1990) and Tocqueville (1994) suggest that Christianity of America (this term will be used from this point on) has been the cornerstone for slavery and racism in this country. Douglass (1845, p. 117) refers to the Christianity of this country and its relationship with the African American in slavery, as a

> climax of misnomers, the boldest of frauds, and the grossest of all libels. Never was there a clearer case of stealing the livery of the court of heaven to serve the devil in.

American history has demonstrated some of the shortcomings of religion, and the misunderstandings and mishandling of race in this country. Most significantly, Christianity of America has made its contributions towards defining race, establishing race relations, and supporting racial segregation here. Thus, Promise Keepers did not emerge out of the Christianity of America untouched by historical principles or fundamental biblical beliefs: Undoubtedly, Christianity of America's racial ideology affects members of this religious organization. The question then is: can this religious movement be used to tear down the walls of racial segregation?

For the purposes of this discussion, it should be mentioned that I assume that both race and religion are social constructions or social formations. Basically, as social constructions, race and religion are socially defined and constructed: therefore, overlapping themes and ideologies may occur. Race and religion, as social constructions, are formed along distinct biological (for race) and denominational or doctrinal (for religion) lines, supported by ideological and cultural customs and, undoubtedly, beneficial to the power-elite (see

Omi & Winant, 1986, Miles, 1984, for examples of race as a social formation and Higgs, 1995, for an example of the socio-cultural construction of religion). This approach also can evaluate the possibilities or inabilities of religion functioning as a means to remove barriers of racial segregation.

THE ORGANIZATION AND DEMOGRAPHICS OF EACH EVENT

Although, initially, PK's activities were concentrated in stadiums and arenas, they have expanded to include educational conferences and workshops, small group meetings for Bible study and personal accountability for men in their communities, and community service resources and projects.

I attended a racial reconciliation breakfast and discussion hosted by members of a local PK group, and the Soldier Field PK event as an observer hoping to obtain an informed perspective on their attempts to break down walls of racial segregation. The racial reconciliation breakfast and discussion session were held at a predominantly white, community church in a small Midwestern city outside Chicago. This city has a population of 46,000 with 54 local churches, and hosts a major university (student population of 24,000), several factories, and many businesses and farms. Attending were 47 men (13 African-American and 34 white between the ages of 20 and 60) from various area churches. The event consisted of an informal breakfast and a discussion group that followed. The focus of the discussion group was how racial barriers developed and why they still exist in our lives.

The Soldier Field event, held over two days, attracted 68,972 men (PK NET, 1996) and included speakers from several religious denominations, singing, prayer groups and dialogue with other men participants. Of the seven speakers, two were African-American, one was Asian-American, and four were white. The program was structured in a way that provided attendees with a specific message about breaking down the walls of racism, denominationalism, sexism, and classism, and a time to reflect and pray individually or with a group of men. Singing was incorporated as a means of maintaining the momentum from one speaker to the next.

DISCUSSION

Racial Reconciliation Breakfast. As men entered into the cafeteria of this church, an obvious "gravitation towards the familiar" occurred, in which African Americans grouped and communicated with African Americans; whites with whites. This segregation was nothing less than ironic because of both the Breaking Down the Walls theme and the breakfast's specific goal:

dialoguing to begin the process of racial reconciliation. I do not think this racial segregation was necessarily the result of conscious decision but, rather, behavior grounded in years of legislation and the social conditioning enforcing it. In other words, we were simply acting "normal." Finally, we were asked by the breakfast organizers to move and sit into different groups. Being asked to sit in racially mixed groups, in fact, illustrated our initial reluctance to step outside our racial comfort zones.

These mixed race groups brought stares of suspicion and discomfort. One of the white men broke this tense atmosphere with the statement, "You gotta like those [Chicago] Bulls." This relieved tension in the group, and the common interest in sports these men shared sparked various intra-group conversations. Eavesdropping after that point, I noticed that the discussions had moved from sport to family- and job-related issues.

Although the topic of sports helped ease the tension within the group, I attributed the initial hesitancy to communicate with one another to the fact that some men generally have difficulty communicating about sensitive issues. During the breakfast and within the group I observed, the issue of race was not discussed. Surprisingly, sports appeared to be of more common interest than shared religious beliefs. In fact, our beliefs did little to dismantle the tension, suspicion and misunderstandings surrounding race. This resistance to communicate cross-racially suggests that our profession of common faith and our common spiritual heritage does not necessarily reduce tensions hindering communication.

The breakfast groups moved into the main sanctuary, where a discussion began that focused on individuals' perception of how racial barriers had developed in their lives. The floor was open to allow each participant to address voluntarily this question with his own testimony. Initially, several men, both white and African-American, used this time to make apologies for past behaviors, and several of the white men apologized for the behavior of their ancestors regarding the mistreatment of our (African-American) ancestors.

Finally, a few participants began to share the reasons they had erected and maintained racial barriers in their lives. The most prominent explanation centered on the ways in which the men had been socialized by family, friends, churches and other institutions. For example, one white man, who was not American-born, attributed the development of his own racial barriers to segregation patterns and the mistreatment of blacks he had noticed as a young child growing up in this country. He said that his community (i.e., home, school, church, etc.) displayed patterns of segregation that often mistreated African Americans (e.g., African Americans were not welcomed in certain places and they were denied equal treatment), and that he simply cooperated with these patterns of segregation. He admitted that he had thought it was the norm for African Americans to be treated as second-class citizens. For him, it was "the way things were." In short, he had submitted to America's social order instead of being an antagonist to it.

Two other white men gave personal testimonies citing fear of African Americans generally and African-American men, specifically, along with the socialization they had experienced through family, friends and other social institutions. It was "the physical size and color" that produced fear and thus encouraged him to segregate himself from African Americans, said one of the men. Another white man explained that his fear stemmed from childhood, when his parents told him that the "bogeyman" (an evil, beastly figure often depicted as being African-American and often an African-American male) would "get" kids when they acted up.

These two accounts illustrate two historic notions—African Americans are evil and physical brutes—that have contributed to the mistreatment of African Americans. Though these accounts are few, they speak volumes about African-American men's perennial role as prime suspects. The Rodney King version of black men as suspects is only one of a multitude of effects of perpetuating a racial ideology that identifies African-American men as frightening, evil brutes. Both men concluded that they had never had close contact with African Americans and, especially, African-American men, because childhood folklore and stereotypes had created images of African Americans that supported segregation.

The African-American men who gave testimonies said that mistreatment by an unjust system, into which they had been born, left them no alternative but to protect themselves by developing their own racial barriers. One man explained how codes of "maintaining your place" were passed down to him from his father and how he was passing them on to his sons in hopes of ensuring their safety in this racially hostile country. These codes or mores (e.g., places not to go to ensure safety, appropriate mannerisms, etc.) were passed on so that African-American men might reduce the chances of physical, psychological or emotional harm.

I gather from these explanations, from both the white and African-American men, that U.S. society has prescribed the need for racial barriers and the construction of these barriers out of a sense of necessity: white men had a need to maintain the status quo and safety from the socially-constructed fear they have of African Americans; and African-American men had a need for racial barriers because of their greater requirements for protection and safety.

The Promise Keepers Event at Soldier Field Stadium. Segregation such as was evidenced at the racial reconciliation breakfast was also evidenced in the seating at Soldier Field. Unlike a church (building), however, a stadium would seem to embody a less threatening environment. Since sports in the U.S. still generally comprise a masculine domain, the stadium represents a place of convocation, enjoyment and refuge for many men.

The program included music, prayer and speakers. Each speaker addressed the issue of and the need for breaking down the walls of racial and denominational segregation. Strategic plans couched in some of these messages encouraged each participant to increase cultural diversity within the scope of his daily social interactions. We also were encouraged to break out of our immediate, racially segregated groups and to introduce ourselves to men of different races—to embrace them in brotherly love.

This permitted us to enter uncharted racial spaces, not to mention uncharted masculine spaces. For some men, this was a passionate moment that seemed to uncover deep-seated emotions of fear, guilt, anger and hurt, emotions occasionally expressed by crying. Overall, it was unusual and intriguing to witness a brief disarmament of masculine and racial shields as African-American and white men hugged and cried. Our—men's—efforts typically are endless and sometimes tediously annoying when we try to maintain our masculine and racial identities at all times and at all costs. As we all know, embracing another man—especially one of another race—and men crying among men are generally not culturally acceptable acts in the U.S., except in certain settings (e.g., religious and sports settings often afford men excusable opportunities to cry and hug without the fear of being labeled unmanly).

I was approached several times by white men with tears in their eyes who apologized for their previous racial attitudes and behaviors. Other men stated that their social surroundings had not required them to change—their predominantly white neighborhoods and all-white churches were comfortable settings in which they largely avoided race issues.

One participant explained to me the awkwardness he experienced attending worship services at a predominantly black church. He said he was more accustomed to a conservative worship style, and admitted that he was not comfortable with the free physical and verbal expression of worship he experienced at this particular church. Both liberal and conservative styles of worship (these often vary culturally and denominationally) were evident at this conference and were accommodated to minimize any discomforts; there were times during the program available for free physical expression (raising and waving of hands, clapping, etc.) and times requiring more conservative forms of worship.

Each speaker addressed the responsibilities Christian men have for tearing down racial and denominational walls. They expressed needs for racial and denominational unity in combating the country's social problems. Attendees, in a tremendous emotional outpouring throughout the stadium, cheered and applauded these mandates from the speakers. Commitments were made orally by participants after speakers asked them to do their part in tearing down racial and denominational barriers after returning to their communities.

Conclusion

Promise Keepers events are in many ways complex, and will continue to evoke questions and critiques as they evolve. Highlighted in this chapter is the fact that PK events represent intersections—by design—of race and religion, which are both social constructions. In this reading I have tried simply to answer some of the questions I had before attending them. The racial reconciliation breakfast provided insight about how racial barriers had been created in the lives of men who attended. The men's explanations for their racism illustrated the power of socialization and how racial ideology is perpetuated and grounded in this country.

This event and breakfast provided white men and men of color an opportunity to tap into deep-seated beliefs, fears and other emotional responses—mostly hidden deep in our psyches—related to race, masculinity and other PK issues. Both events provided participants opportunities to think and dialogue about the racial assumptions they took for granted. Opportunities also were afforded for participants to try to minimize their thoughts and feelings about racial differences and to highlight their common beliefs in Christianity.

But as I walked out of the stadium and towards downtown Chicago, among all those white faces, I could not help wondering what exists outside the stadium to keep these deep-seated beliefs and emotions from settling back into their original hiding places. What is there to prevent us from returning to business as usual? What pressing need is there for men of color and white men to break down the walls? One of the men had even admitted he had no compelling need to move beyond his racial comfort zone.

The racial segregation that historically has prevailed in this country, first legally and even now at an ideological level, has confined us within racial enclaves that we seldom feel the need to exit, unless tragic circumstances make it necessary, or it is economically desirable. It appears to be the unwritten goal of Promise Keepers' organizers that men who attend these events be spiritually touched and inspired enough to dismantle the walls of racial segregation in their lives.

I concluded that these events, though well intentioned, mainly tapped into the emotional side of the complex issue of breaking down racial barriers. For many men this is a significant start, but it appears that yet other men do not even wanted to get out on a road to racial reconciliation. McCartney (1997, pp. 180–181), though professing optimism about race relations overall, noted that

> of the 1996 conference participants who had a complaint, nearly 40 percent reacted negatively to the reconciliation theme. I personally believe it was a major factor in the significant fall-off in P.K.'s 1997

attendance—it is simply a hard teaching for many. But many in Jesus' day also turned back from His "hard teaching" and followed Him no more (John 6:66). In all actuality, I suspect that much of the criticism leveled at Promise Keepers from within the Christian community—typically cloaked in assorted, usually untested claims that we're an ecumenical movement, or that we preach a gospel palatable to Mormons or fringe cults—has as its true root a deep-seated cultural resistance to the message on reconciliation. It simply tells me we're on the right track.

So tapping into emotions is not enough; social structures (e.g., political, economic, educational, etc.) must be transformed in order truly to address the breaking down of racial barriers. In fact, for PK to function as an avenue for racial reconciliation, religious ideology and its fundamental beliefs about race (especially concerning African Americans) must be deconstructed.

Tapping into emotions and informing one of his Christian responsibilities are noteworthy acts, but changing fundamental beliefs and reshaping the ideological structure are the much-needed requirements for improving U.S. race relations. These requirements are far beyond the scope of weekend PK events, because they will involve a denunciation of former ways and a resocialization into what Douglass (1845) classifies as the Christianity of Christ, i.e., the pure, peaceable and impartial Christianity that Christ exemplified throughout His life here on earth.

Finally, white men were and are the majority of participants at PK events. They also are in the majority among PK administrators and leaders. This limits PK's potential to sufficiently (beyond an emotional exercise) affect racial and denominational issues in our society. The privileged positions of "whiteness" and "maleness" provide a limited frame of reference, not the larger one necessary for deconstructing racial ideologies that exist in the institution of religion and thus in society at large. One reason for this limitation is that both "whiteness" and "maleness" must be deconstructed. In other words, PK's efforts to achieve racial and denominational reconciliation could and should start with an observance of, and strict adherence to, the Apostle Paul's instructions in Galatians 3:28: "There is neither Jew nor Greek, slave nor free, male nor female, for you are all one in Christ Jesus" (New International Version, 1978). Many biblical scriptures have been interpreted to establish racial segregation. But why are those that de-emphasize the significance of race in the seeking of common good, and those that provide instructions for racial harmony both ignored, when themes are developed for theological seminaries, doctrinal beliefs, and religious conferences?

Fortunately, many of the challenges regarding race relations this country faced during its early history have been modified significantly. Through legislation, racial morality has been altered, but not enough for the demands of our increasingly multicultural society. Further changes in ideological structure are needed to advance race relations to meet the increasing global social demands. Thus, the institution of religion will require the efforts of Promise Keepers and other religious movements to aid in these structural changes.

With the expansion of Promise Keepers into Mexico, South America and other parts of the world, future research is needed to see what impact the organization has, if any, in reducing international racial and cultural rifts. At the national level, future research might address whether the emotionalism and sense of Christian responsibility generated at these events carries over to the local level to in fact facilitate racial reconciliation—after the weekend events are over. I would like to know if men who return to their communities isolate themselves racially and denominationally less than before, seek to diversify culturally their social circles, and encourage interdenominational fellowship with local churches.

References

Baird, R. (1844). *Religion in the United States of America, or an account of the origin, progress, relation to the state, and present condition of the evangelical churches in the United States. With notices of unevangelical denominations.* New York: Harper.

Boles, J. B. (1988). *Masters & slaves in the house of the Lord: Race and religion in the American South 1740–1870.* Lexington, KY: The University Press of Kentucky.

Crouch, S. (1996). *Black in America.* New York: The New Yorker.

Douglass, F. (1845). *Narrative of the life of Frederick Douglass: An American slave.* New York: Anchor Press/Doubleday.

Elkins, S.M. (1959). *Slavery: A problem in American institutional & intellectual life.* New York: The University Library.

Franklin, J. H., & Moss, A. A. (1988). *From slavery to freedom: A history of Negro Americans* (6th ed.). New York: Alfred A. Knopf.

Genovese, E. D. (1976). *Roll, Jordon, roll: The world the slaves made.* New York: Vintage Books.

Harris, T. (1998, May-June). Accountability & Christian leadership. *Gospel Today* [on-line]. Available: www.gospeltoday.com/1998/MayJn98_feat.htm.

Higgs, R. J. (1995). *God in the stadium: Sports and religion in America.* Lexington, KY: The University of Kentucky Press.

Jordan, W. D. (1968). *White over African American: American attitudes toward the Negro, 1550–1812.* New York: W.W. Norton & Company.

Jordan, W. D. (1974). *The white man's burden: Historical origins of racism in the United States.* New York: Oxford University Press.

Kimmel, M., & Kaufman, M. (1995). Weekend warriors: The new men's movement. In M. Kimmel (ed.), *The politics of manhood: Profeminist men respond to the mythopoetic men's movement (and the mythopoetic leaders answer)* (pp. 15–43). Philadelphia: Temple University Press.

Lincoln, C. E. (1984). *Race, religion, and the continuing American dilemma.* New York, NY: Hill and Wang.

McCartney, B. (1997). *Sold out: Becoming man enough to make a difference.* Nashville, TN: Word Books.

Messner, M. (1997). *The politics of masculinities: Men in movements.* Thousand Oaks, CA: Sage.

Miles, R. (1984). Marxism versus the sociology of "race relations"? *Ethnic and Racial Studies* 7(2), pp. 217–237.

Omi, M., & Winant, H. (1986). *Racial formation in the United States.* New York, NY: Routledge & Kegan Paul.

PK NET (1996). *Official PK Website: Chicago Men's Conference.* Available: http://www.promisekeepers.org/222e.htm.

Stampp, K. M. (1956). *The peculiar institution: Slavery in the ante-bellum South.* New York, NY: Vintage Books.

Tocqueville, A. de (1994). *Democracy in America.* New York, NY: Alfred A. Knopf.

Wood, F. (1990). *The arrogance of faith: Christianity and race in America from the colonial era to the twentieth century.* New York, NY: Alfred A. Knopf.

CHAPTER 15

Keep the Faith and Go the Distance: Promise Keepers, Feminism, and the World of Sports

by Randy Balmer

Throughout church history, dating back to the New Testament, Christians have used two metaphors for spirituality: militarism and athleticism. St. Paul admonished the early Christians to run the race and to put on the full armor of God in their battle against the wiles of the devil. These metaphors have been played out in various ways across the centures. The monks were spiritual athletes of a sort, training in godliness and implicitly competing with one another in the quest for holiness. The Crusades provided a religious legitimacy—and absolution—for military conquest, and the Society of Jesus was mobilized explicitly as the pope's army.

In American history the military metaphor dominated the 19th and early 20th-century piety. It took various organizational forms—the Salvation Army, the Knights of Columbus, Awana Clubs, the Christian Service Brigade, and the Campus Crusade for Christ—but it also pervaded evangelical hymnody, as suggested by "Onward Christian Soldiers," "We're Marching to Zion," and "Rise Up, O Men of God."

Both the military and the sporting metaphors were especially appealing to men and were appropriated shamelessly by the muscular Christianity movement, which combined seduction and taunting in roughly equal parts. At the turn of the 20th century, Billy Sunday, formerly a baseball player for the Chicago White Stockings, cajoled the men in his audiences to "hit the sawdust trail" and give their lives to Jesus. "Many think a Christian has to be sort of a dishrag proposition, a wishy-washy, sissified sort of galoot that lets everybody make a doormat out of him," Sunday intoned. "Let me tell you the manifest man is the man who will acknowledge Jesus Christ" (quoted in Frank, 1986, p. 193). A few years later, at about the same time that Charles

Sheldon's novel, *In His Steps*, portrayed Jesus as an astute businessman, an organization called the Men and Religion Forward Movement summoned men back to the churches with the slogan, "More Men for Religion, More Religion for Men." The campaign held rallies in places such as Carnegie Hall, rented billboards on Times Square and placed display ads in the sports sections of newspapers (Smith, 1987; Bederman, 1989).

Immediately after World War II, muscular Christianity drew more heavily on the militarism metaphor, but the athletic ideal was never entirely absent. James C. Hefly published edifying biographical sketches of professional athletes who professed to be Christians: Bobby Richardson, Dave Wickersham, Bill Glass, Al Worthington, among many others. The movement encompassed such organizations as Athletes in Action (a subsidiary of the Campus Crusade for Christ, thereby combining the motifs of militarism and athleticism), the Fellowship of Christian Athletes, and the Power Team for Christ, a weightlifting troupe that travels to various venues and intersperses evangelistic testimonies with spectacular feats of strength.

In more recent years, athletics has gradually eclipsed militarism as the predominant metaphor for evangelical spirituality. The Vietnam War dimmed somewhat our collective enthusiasm for the military. Even Ralph Reed, executive director of the Christian Coalition, claims to have eschewed militaristic rhetoric. "Early in the 1990s, I occasionally used military metaphors for effect," he wrote, but Reed (1996, p. 120) recognized the perils of such language and "sent out a memorandum to our grassroots leaders urging them to avoid military rhetoric and to use sports metaphors instead." It should come as no surprise, then, that the muscular Christianity of the 1990s should be hung about with the accoutrements of athleticism. Promise Keepers founder Bill McCartney was a highly successful football coach who led the University of Colorado Buffaloes from obscurity to national rankings and, in 1990, the Associated Press National Championship. (McCartney retired after the 1994 season "to spend more time with his family and to pursue a closer personal relationship with God.") Promise Keepers rallies and publications often feature athletes, and the gatherings themselves take place in sports arenas.

By now the media have become inured to the specter of large stadiums filled with men praying, chanting and singing at the top of their lungs, many with their arms outstretched in that familiar pentecostal gesture of openness to the Holy Spirit. Promise Keepers, the latest avatars of the muscular Christianity impulse in American history, traces its origins to an automobile trip between Boulder and Pueblo, Colorado. On March 20, 1990, McCartney, then the head football coach at Colorado, and his friend, Dave Wardell, were traveling to a meeting of the Fellowship of Christian Athletes in Pueblo, and in the course of their conversation, they came upon the idea of filling Colorado's Folsom Stadium with men dedicated to the notion of Christian discipleship.

More than 4,000 men showed up for the first gathering, and by July 1993, McCartney's original vision had been fulfilled: Fifty thousand men piled into Folsom Stadium for singing, hugging and exhortations to be good and faithful husbands, fathers and churchgoers. In 1996, more than a million men attended 22 rallies at stadiums across the country. PK is unabashedly an evangelical organization; witness its purpose statement and statement of faith (see p. 4).

The venue is significant. The sports arena in particular and sports in general are manifestations of a subculture no less than the subculture of American evangelicalism, the most important social, religious and cultural movement in American history. The evangelical subculture was constructed in earnest during the half century between the Scopes trial and Jimmy Carter's campaign for the presidency. It provided a place of refuge for beleaguered Protestants who felt alienated from the larger culture. Evangelicals, disturbed by the social and intellectual currents in the broader world, constructed their own universe of congregations, denominations, Bible camps, Bible institutes, colleges, seminaries, publishing houses and mission societies.

The evangelical subculture was marked by a bunker mentality, and in many ways it was more than a subculture; it was a counterculture, in that it defined itself against the prevailing norms of the larger culture. It had its own rules and customs and standards. Whereas the broader culture was enamored of "modernist" ideas in science, theology and culture, evangelicals stubbornly clung to "orthodox" understandings of Protestant Christianity, including the virgin birth, the inerrancy of the Bible and the authenticity of miracles. When flappers were all the rage in the 1920s, evangelicals placed all manner of behavioral and sartorial standards—including proscriptions on the use of jewelry and cosmetics—on their wives and daughters in order to shield them from the corrosive influences of "the world" (see Rice, 1941; Bendroth, 1993).

One element of the larger culture especially did not sit well with evangelists: feminism. It is no secret that, despite evangelicalism's noble heritage of activism on women's concerns in the 19th century, feminist sensibilities have not flourished within 20th-century American evangelicalism (Dayton, 1976). The women's movement and the concomitant sexual revolution threatened evangelical mores, and evangelical leaders (an overwhelmingly male cohort) responded with determined attempts to reassert the mythical ideal of feminine spirituality and domesticity (DeBerg, 1990). Evangelicals have blamed feminism for abortion, the rising divorce rate, the proliferation of sexually transmitted diseases, low test scores and a general moral decline in the country. A number of evangelical organizations were formed, notably Focus on the Family and Concerned Women for America, to counteract and to reverse the tide of feminism in the United States.

Here, on the issue of feminism—or, more precisely, in opposition to feminism—the subculture of sports and the evangelical subculture, as manifest in the Promise Keepers movement, intersect like circles on a Venn diagram. The passion for organized sports in recent years has surged at the same time as growing political discontent, especially within the middle class. This so-called "white rage" fueled the political ambitions of Ross Perot in 1992 and has helped to sustain Pat Buchanan's endless campaign for the presidency. The contours of this discontent, rehearsed endlessly on talk radio—Liddy, Limbaugh, Michaelson, North, Reagan—have been amply documented, but Thomas L. Friedman's column on the op-ed page of *The New York Times* during the 1996 presidential primaries provides a useful summary. "If the economy is doing so well," Friedman (1995, p. 9) asks rhetorically on behalf of his readers, "why have I just been downsized out of a job and why do I feel like my community is eroding?" Friedman and others refer to this as the politics of resentment, and its symptoms are that "our schools no longer teach right from wrong, that our nation can't control its borders and that patriotism is giving way to multiculturalism."

The world, in short, is out of control. (Bendroth [1993, chapter 2] argues that much of the appeal of dispensational premillennialism—and its concomitant success in defining limited roles for women—derived from a quest for order among evangelicals late in the 19th century.) This politics of resentment, when articulated by other oracles, has exposed different demons. In the past, it has fingered communism and the United Nations; more recent targets include the North American Free Trade Agreement (NAFTA), foreign aid, welfare, affirmative action, Hillary Rodham Clinton and, more generally, feminism.

Feminism. The biggest social revolution in American history began in 1963 with the publication of *The Feminine Mystique*, by Betty Friedan. The women's movement brought radical changes in gender roles, economic expectations, sexual behavior, the composition of families and language. In 1945, the number of American women in the labor force stood at 29 percent; by 1970 that number had risen to 38 percent and, in 1995, to 46 percent (Samuelson, 1996). Women have not been content to stay at home and, despite the well-publicized glass ceiling, they have entered every arena of American life, from the military to the Supreme Court, from the picket lines to the corporate boardroom.

Every arena of American life, save one: the sports arena. Despite Title IX provisions, women's athletics still lags behind men's, and in the realm of professional sports, women are virtually nonexistent, aside from golf and tennis and now a fledgling basketball league. Even though the San Diego Clippers drafted Iowa basketball whiz Denise Long some years ago, and every so often you read of a female referee or umpire aspiring to make it into the major leagues, women have not been able to break into the male preserve of professional team sports.

The venue chosen for Promise Keepers rallies underscores the sympathies between sports and masculinity. The world of athletics offers an alternative universe, a subculture that provides a refuge from the larger world. In contrast to that larger world, the world of sports is an orderly universe. Of course, this is not a new observation. In every major sport, the ball represents the world; when the ball stops, play itself stops. In football, which is essentially a military game concerned with the capture and defense of territory, the movement of the ball signals the beginning of play. Basketball, an urban game invented by a YMCA secretary in Springfield, MA, mimics the urban landscape in that it demands that players maneuver within very narrow confines, similar to the constraints of the urban world itself. Baseball, the only game in which the defense controls the ball, is a game developed and played by immigrants, and it perfectly mirrored their own world. In baseball, the batter is outnumbered nine to one in his attempt to disrupt the defense's control of the "world." The defense is malevolently successful most of the time, and anyone who is successful three times out of 10 will probably find a place someday in the Hall of Fame. For the batter, as for the immigrant, the greatest—and most elusive—triumph is to return home, but it is a journey fraught with perils and very few islands of safety along the way.

McCartney's affinity for football, as opposed to baseball or other sports, merely underscores the sense of beleaguerment claimed by evangelical males. From its earliest origins in the Northeast's bastions of privilege, football was unabashedly militaristic. One early enthusiast (quoted in Fimrite, 1996, p. 8) equated the brutality of warfare with the violence of football. "War," according to John Prentiss, Jr., a fullback, "is the greatest game on earth." Whereas baseball, the game of immigrants engaged in the overwhelming struggle against stiff odds, represented a view of America from the bottom up, football, a game of brute force and relentless domination, offered an elitist vision. The big three football powerhouses at the turn of the century—Yale, Princeton, and Harvard—imposed their will on opponents, sometimes racking up scores in the triple digits (Murrin, 1996).

What all major sports have had in common since the age of industrialization are clear boundaries and precise delineations. The rules may be complex, but they too are precise, with every situation and contingency provided for. Something is either in bounds or out of bounds, safe or out, fair or foul. The only thing that can disrupt this orderly universe is a misjudgment. Nothing enrages a sports devote more than a bad call from an official, whose job it is to act as an impartial judge and benign authority figure. The official has no prerogative to be a judicial activist. He cannot hear mitigating arguments before rendering his judgment. A batter thrown out by a step at first base, for example, cannot argue that he should be called safe because, had he not injured his ankle back in spring training, he would almost certainly have beaten the throw from the shortstop and that to call him out on that play betrayed the umpire's bias against players who are in some way disabled. The wide receiver who failed to plant both feet in bounds before falling out of the end zone cannot argue that he simply forgot to do so and that such negligence should not be held against him and that, furthermore, any adverse ruling would unfairly punish the entire team for the inadvertant lapse of one of its players. No, the officials must render simple, impartial judgments lest they violate the orderly universe that is the world of sports.

If the domain of sports provides an alternative, male-dominated universe where the voices of women rarely intrude, the same may be said of Promise Keepers. Women are not allowed at Promise Keepers rallies because, the organization says rather vaguely, "the conferences are designed for specific men's issues in the context of an all-male setting." Women, they add, serve in a supportive capacity: "There are many women volunteers praying and working behind the scenes to ensure that these events go smoothly. One of the primary goals of the conference is to deepen the commitment of men to respect and honor women" (PK web site, 1997).

Indeed, Promise Keepers, which has won a ringing endorsement from Beverly LaHaye, president of Concerned Women for America, has a great deal to say about men and their relationships with women (PK web site, 1997). For example, LaHaye proclaims, "Often, when a man goes to a Promise Keepers meeting, he gets his life turned around, and becomes totally committed to those promises. Then you've got a stronger family unit. I will do all I can to encourage Promise Keepers." Promise number four (of seven) reads: "A Promise Keeper is committed to building strong marriages and families through love, protection and biblical values." It would be difficult to gainsay the importance of such a sentiment, and if the Promise Keepers movement succeeds in encouraging men to be more attentive to their wives, to visit museums with their sons and to take their daughters fly-fishing, it will have served a useful purpose. Part of the appeal of Promise Keepers is that it reassigns men to the private sphere in addition to the public sphere. But the ideology surrounding Promise Keepers, with its paradoxical pairing of the soft-breasted male with their reassertion of patriarchalism, refuses to acknowledge the corollary—that women can find their niche in the workplace as well as in the home. Women, who since the emergence of the cult of domesticity in the 19th century have, evangelicals believe, been the spiritual guardians of the home, are not to engage in the male-dominated public sphere. The essentialist ideal of femininity, so desparately nurtured by the leaders of evangelicalism in the 20th century, demands that women stay home and remain submissive to their husbands.

In *Seven Promises of a Promise Keeper*, for example, the manifesto of the movement, Gary Smalley (1994, p. 105) cites the case of the Brawner family, who live in a small town in Missouri. They have a son, described as "a national swimming champion and freshman in college," a "17-year-old who's an outstanding three-sport athlete in high school," and Jill, "their beautiful and talented 13-year-old." That description is itself revealing: the sons are athletes—successful athletes—and daughters are "beautiful and talented." Smalley goes on to describe the return of the eldest son from college and the potential for family tension because of an earring in one ear, part of his initiation to the college swim team. Mom, who is clearly a stay-at-home mother, meets him at the door and, after a brief exchange, they wonder how Dad will greet this new development when he returns from work. (After a brief suspense Dad, it turns out—newly attuned to the demands of family life—manages to keep his temper.)

What is the role of men in the domestic sphere? After decrying "the feminization of the American male," which has "produced a nation of 'sissified' men who abdicate their role as spiritually pure leaders," Tony Evans, an African-American preacher who also serves as chaplain to the Dallas Cowboys, makes it clear that it is "proper—in fact, essential—for children to be nurtured, guided, and cared for by women." But the man must, in Evans' words, reclaim his manhood and take charge of the household. "The first thing you do," he writes, "is to sit down with your wife and say something like this: 'Honey, I've made a terrible mistake. I've given you my role. I gave up leading this family, and I forced you to take my place. Now I must reclaim that role.'" Evans (1994, pp. 73,79) insists that this is not a matter for negotiation. "Don't misunderstand what I'm saying here," he writes. "I'm not suggesting that you *ask* for your role back, I'm urging you to take it back."

There can be little question that masculinity is a protean notion in the latter decades of the 20th century. Promise Keepers represents an intriguing response to that malleability, an impulse to impose order on a world widely perceived as chaotic and to provide identity, direction and solidarity for a cohort of white, evangelical, middle-class men. Much has been made of the male bonding that takes place at Promise Keepers rallies, but even that might be understood in the context of militarism and athleticism.

For the older generation of American males in the 1990s, military service in World War II and the Korean War provided the venue for bonding with other men. Strong ties of friendship and camaraderie were forged in bunkers, in air squadrons, or on board destroyers. The baby boom generation, now come of age in the '90s, sought to avoid the draft, so they have no regimental reunions to show for their friendships; they do not gather in VFW halls to swap war stories and renew ties with their war buddies.

The stories of this younger generation are stories of athletic prowess: the improbable touchdown pass, the no-hitter, Michael Jordan's latest violation of the laws of gravity. Sports provide a common vocabulary for male interaction and bonding, so it is no accident that McCartney would choose sports arenas for his gatherings or that he would pepper them with sports personalities and athletic analogies. He is simply speaking the language of the disaffected male.

Many men feel confused and angry about the women's movement—shifting gender roles, changing sexual politics and morphing expectations, from the workplace to the bedroom. For many American males, feminism has been disruptive. A letter by Edward Abbey, written from "Winkelman (pop. 225 incl. dogs.), Arizona," to the editors of "Mizz Magazine," merits extensive quotation as an admittedly extreme—and risible—expression of this sentiment (1979, p. xvi):

> Are old wimmin is trouble enuf to manage as is without you goldam New Yorkers sneaking a lot of downright *sub-versive* ideas into their hard heads. Out here a womin's place is in the kitchen, the barnyard and the bedroom in that exackt order and we don't need no changes. We got a place for men and we got a place for wimmin and there aint no call to get them mixed up. Like my neighbor Marvin Bundy says, he says, "I seen men, I seen wimmin, I haint *never* seen one of them there *persons*. Least not in Pinal County." Thems my sentiments too. You ladies best stick to tatting doilies. Much obliged for your kind consideration, I am
> Yrs truly,
> Cactus Ed

The irrepressible and inimitable Abbey captures, albeit in caricature, the sentiments of many American men bewildered by the vagaries and the implications of feminism.

The responses have been manifold, ranging from the primal yearnings of Robert Bly and his *Iron John* to unabashed chauvinism and spousal abuse. But just as the interest in sports and sports memorabilia connotes a nostalgia for the simpler days of childhood and the quest for an orderly world, so too recent evangelical preachments about gender roles and so-called family values seek to impose an order on what they perceive as the chaos created by feminism. What the world of sports and the evangelically inspired Promise Keepers movement have in common goes beyond the mere fixation on athleticism, where the criterion for superiority is usually physical strength and where men, therefore, can still dominate women. Promise Keepers, wittingly or not, taps into a symbolic world that resonates with American males late in the 20th century. Both the athletic and the military metaphors, moreover, point to dualistic views of the world; on the athletic field as on the battlefield, with rare exceptions, there are winners and losers, and the evangelicals' penchant for dualism in the 20th century has been amply documented (see, for example, Hunter, 1991). McCartney, drawing on male—specifically, white male—anxieties, has marshalled the traditional Christian metaphors of militarism and athleticism to combat feminism, all in the guise of a benevolent patriarchalism.

Both Promise Keepers and the world of sports provide the shelter of a subculture, a contrived universe with its own standards, rules and values. In both cases—and in contrast to the larger culture—the rules are clear and vigorously enforced. In a world perceived as disordered, these subcultures provide an illusion of safety, a common language, shared assumptions and the assurance of camaraderie.

References

Abbey, E. (1979). *Abbey's road.* New York: Penguin Books.
Bederman, G. (1989). "The women have had charge of the church work long enough": The Men and Religion Forward Movement of 1911–1912 and the masculinization of middle-class Protestantism. *American Quarterly 41*, 432–465.
Bendroth, M.L. (1993). *Fundamentalism and gender: 1875 to the present.* New Haven, CT: Yale University Press.
Dayton, D.W. (1976). *Discovering an evangelical heritage.* Peabody, MA: Hendrickson.
DeBerg, B.A. (1990). *Ungodly women: Gender and the first wave of American fundamentalism.* Minneapolis, MN: Fortress Press.
Evans, T. (1994). Spiritual purity. In A. Janssen & L.K. Weeden (eds.), *Seven promises of a Promise Keeper.* Colorado Springs, CO: Focus on the Family Publishing.
Fimrite, R. (1996, October 14). Once powerful, still proud. *Sports Illustrated 85*, 8.
Frank, D. (1986). *Less than conquerors: How evangelicals entered the twentieth century.* Grand Rapids, MI: William B. Eerdmans Publishing Co.
Friedman, T.L. (1995, December 24). Buchanan for President. *The New York Times*, 9.
Hunter, J.D. (1991). *Culture wars: The struggle to define America.* New York: Basic Books.
Murrin, J.M. (1996, October 10). *Rites of domination: Princeton, the Big Three, and the rise of intercollegiate athletics.* Paper delivered at Princeton University.
Promise Keepers (1997). Web site. Available: http://204.120.228.146/PK/pressrel/950528e.html
Reed, R. (1996). *Active faith: How Christians are changing the soul of American politics.* New York: Free Press.
Religious extremism, Religious truth (1995, December 20–27). *Christian Century 112*, 1235–1237.
Rice, J.R. (1941). *Bobbed hair, bossy wives and women preachers: Significant questions for honest Christian women settled by the word of God.* Wheaton, IL: Sword of the Lord Publishers.
Samuelson, R.J. (1996, Janury 8). Great expectations. *Newsweek 127*, 24–33.

Smalley, G. (1994). Five secrets of a happy marriage. In A. Janssen & L.K. Weeden (eds.), *Seven promises of a Promise Keeper*. Colorado Springs, CO: Focus on the Family Publishing.

Smith, G.S. (1987). The Men and Religion Forward Movement of 1911–1912: New perspectives on evangelical social concern and the relationship between Christianity and Progressivism. *Westminster Theological Journal 49*, 91–118.

CHAPTER 16

Building a Social Evangelical Organization: The Lincoln Bedroom or Oval Office Model?

by Bryan W. Brickner

Let us begin by suggesting two metaphors: the Lincoln Bedroom for traditional evangelicals, such as Billy Graham, who may one day influence the social order to the degree that they are invited to the White House, and may sleep in that famous room; and the Oval Office for new evangelicals, such as Pat Robertson, who also may be invited to sleep in the Lincoln Bedroom, but who harbor aspirations for presidential power.

These metaphors frame an important question that has been left unaddressed by much of the discussion of the Promise Keepers. What kind of evangelicals are these? Are they "traditional" evangelicals, modeled after the likes of Billy Graham, or are they "new" evangelicals, similar to Jerry Falwell and, more recently, Pat Robertson? And, more importantly from a political perspective, are the men involved in leading Promise Keepers part of a new "crypto–Religious Right" movement, as they have been depicted (Clarkson, 1996, 1997; Conason, Ross, Cokorinos, 1996; Kimmel, 1996), part of the traditional anti-political strain of evangelicalism, or, rather, are the Promise Keepers the product of a new form of evangelicalism?

Promise Keepers claims to be an apolitical organization. Many social and political commentators have questioned the integrity of this position and have preferred to characterize the Promise Keepers as the Trojan Horse of the Religious Right. Such commentators are both correct and incorrect. As I have argued in other research (Brickner, 1997), the men who are involved in PK at the local level and attend the stadium conferences are generally antipolitical; that is, they are akin to traditional evangelicals but, for reasons discussed below, part of a different generation. The men leading Promise Keepers (founder, president, board members, conference speakers and boosters) are clearly a mix of traditional and new evangelicals. The mixture of traditional and new evangelicals among the leadership of PK is not a simple division where one side does not affect the other. Rather, the mixture, made possible by Bill McCartney's focus on the team, produces a new form of evangelicalism—social evangelicalism.

In many ways, ostensibly beginning with Jimmy Carter's election in 1976 and his declaration that he was a born-again Christian, evangelicalism has played an influential role in contemporary American politics and culture. Historically, evangelicals shunned the political realm. Politics was viewed as an encounter with sin, a realm of human frailty that God intended individuals to eschew. But, with Carter's election, the rise of Jerry Falwell's Moral Majority during the 1980s and Pat Robertson's 1988 presidential campaign, the relation of an evangelical to politics was transformed (Wilcox, 1992; Zwier, 1982).

Evangelicals are a diverse category of Christians who commonly accept three basic tenets, but who vary on the tactical implementation of one tenet. The three basic tenets that define an evangelical are conversion, biblicism and activism (Bebbington, 1994; see also Fackre, 1993; Fowler, 1995). Conversion, being born-again, and biblicism, a respectful and literal interpretation of the Bible (Bebbington, 1994; Fowler, 1995), foster little debate among evangelicals. It is the interpretation of the third defining characteristic, activism, that often differentiates what I refer to as "traditional" and "new" evangelicals.

Traditional evangelicals, epitomized by Billy Graham, "emphasize personal conversion and mass evangelism" (Fackre, 1993, p. 22). New evangelicals, epitomized in the 1970s by Jerry Falwell and recently by Pat Robertson, also emphasize personal conversion and mass evangelism, but stress the political import of faith. Within the two categories there are other important characteristics, such as the degree of fundamentalism (how strictly one interprets the Bible), charismatic worship (glossolalia, healing, contemporary music, intense group experiences) and ecumenism. While all three aspects are important to an understanding of evangelicalism in general, none affects the potential political mobilization of evangelicals as much as the way in which they relate to the tenet of activism.

Typically, but with varying degrees of fervor, evangelicals portray secular (liberal) society as chaotic, while also calling for a return to a more traditional, that is, biblical, moral order. Traditional evangelicals focus their activism primarily on the individual experience of regeneration and little, if at all, on the negative implications of a liberal social order. New evangelicals, however, advocate involvement in the political system to combat the influence of secular humanism. Both traditional and new evangelicals are committed to the great commission (Matthew 28: 19-20), to spread the good news (evangelism), but they differ regarding tactical implementation. So traditional and new evangelicals focus on all three tenets, but only new evangelicals attempt to use activism to affect the political process. Thus, traditional evangelicals might one day be invited to spend the night in the Lincoln Bedroom; new evangelicals work towards one day occupying the Oval Office.

The Promise Keepers' ideology broadens traditional evangelicalism and limits new evangelicalism to form what I refer to as "social evangelicalism." Social evangelicalism maintains the importance of personal faith but is not inclined to political action. Social evangelicalism focuses on social relationships. As Bill McCartney states in his first autobiography, *From Ashes to Glory* (1995), Promise Keepers is a ministry of reconciliation between men and their God and men and others. Promise Keepers intends to help men heal the broken relationships in their lives.

The Promise Keepers organization is modeled after a team, and every team has goals. Goals organize and focus a team's efforts and will. PK goals are summarized and outlined in its Seven Promises. All the promises together are, and a fundamental goal of Promise Keepers is, an attempt to promote reconciliation. Reconciliation is how one comes to terms with an object, be it God, Christ, sin, marriage or a brother. A Promise Keeper is called to reconcile his lived perspective to the experienced world as God's will, described in 2 Cor. 5:18–20 (New International Version). His happiness and melancholy, joy and sorrow, his feelings of sacred and profane things, are all part of his walk with Christ and can be reconciled to God's will.

This reconciliation distinguishes PK from either traditional or new evangelicalism. A list of individuals one potentially may need to work towards reconciliation with was distributed at a PK Key Men leadership training session. The list included wife, son, daughter, mother, father, brother, sister, neighbor, pastor, former friend, white person, black person, Hispanic person, Native-American person, Asian person, difficult person. This list involves more than reconciliation between an individual and God; it involves more than traditional evangelicalism. The list is different from a call to transform the political order to something reflecting God's Kingdom on earth; it is less than new evangelicalism.

PK's third kind of evangelicalism, social evangelicalism, binds one's life to a relationship with an other. Whereas traditional evangelicals (as well as PK) foster reconciliation between an individual and God, and new evangelicals promote the reconciliation of politics to God's way, Promise Keepers, as social evangelicals, promote reconciliation of a man's relationship with God, the man's wife, children, family, friends and co-workers.

The Team as Community

As co-founder/CEO of PK and former University of Colorado football coach, McCartney's *From Ashes to Glory* (1995) combines his growth as a coach with the development of his spiritual relationship with Jesus Christ. The book interweaves one of McCartney's passions, football, with his lifelong walk (search) for Christ-likeness, defined as spiritual growth and maturity in the image of Christ.

McCartney views life, football and spiritual growth as a confrontation with potentially destructive forces which, if survived, can be used to build one's character. And, as the successful coach of a team sport, McCartney knows the value of enduring life's battles with the support of teammates; thus the significance of Pro. 27:17, a commonly cited scripture in the Promise Keepers organization: "As iron sharpens iron, so one man sharpens another."

Coach McCartney, the man who rebuilt the University of Colorado football program and led it to a national championship, is not unlike Promise Keeper McCartney. The evangelizing McCartney encourages men to commit to Jesus Christ instead of the University of Colorado's football team but, in both cases, it is in order to lead the group to a championship season.

In *From Ashes to Glory* (1995), McCartney details how he and others (staff, players, boosters and University officials) rebuilt the Colorado football program. McCartney readily acknowledges that winning football programs are not built through the efforts of one man. He stresses the premises that, in a team sport, championships are never won alone and champions are never made in isolation. McCartney believes that every organization needs leadership and goals; a group needs to understand what it is working towards and how it is going to get there.

McCartney said that when he arrived in Boulder, the football program lacked direction. It lacked talent, organization, motivation and, most important, team goals. McCartney gave the program direction. He brought focus to an unorganized team and instilled a standard of excellence. Part of the standard of excellence was built upon the image of the Nebraska football team, the team the Buffaloes most wanted to defeat. The game against Nebraska became the touchstone for measuring success. The Nebraska football team provided Colorado two things: a program to be modeled on and an enemy to be defeated.

But coaching football used to be McCartney's passion; bringing men into a relationship with Christ is McCartney's new passion. The two are not altogether different. The same leadership principles, organizational skills, strategic thinking, relationship building (i.e., recruiting and teaching) and competitive attitude that made him a successful coach also have contributed to the amazing growth of the Promise Keepers organization.

Researching McCartney as coach, a role he describes as being a "motivator, manager, and defender" (McCartney, 1995, p. 219), also gives one insight into the language he uses. Football coaches often use the language of combat in order to motivate players; "the line of scrimmage," "in the trenches," "it's war out there!" McCartney (1994, p. 207) wrote (to other Promise Keepers), "We're in a war, men, whether we acknowledge it or not. The enemy is real and he doesn't like to see men of God take a stand for Jesus Christ and contest his lies" (McCartney, 1994, p. 207). He is the football coach turned pulpit layman, the coach as motivator.

As motivator and defender, McCartney has called Promise Keepers to rally together in order to battle a common foe and to help their fellow man (teammate). In a 1992 article, McCartney details the team element of social evangelicalism when he calls men to recapture the spiritual climate in their homes and cultivate Christian love for other men (McCartney, 1992, p. 11). His message is clear: men cannot worry about their own salvation alone, but must strive to help others in their lives, beginning with their own families, but extending to encompass the greater community. This community encompasses their neighbors, other families, co-workers, Christians and not-yet-believers. It is a form of activism not usually exhibited in other forms of evangelicalism. It is a social form of evangelicalism that attempts to strengthen the structures within a particular community.

Promise Keeper McCartney sees a civil society led astray by false values, a typical evangelical perspective, and a situation similar to that of the misguided team he found in Boulder upon his arrival in 1982. McCartney believes good players will compete if given the proper conditioning, training and coaching. Reading Bill McCartney as the motivator, manager and defender of the Promise Keepers team is a way to understand the social evangelicalism inherent in PK and the difference between traditional and new forms of evangelicalism.

THE COACHES

The men who lead the Promise Keepers team bring to the movement diverse background experience, success in founding and leading other Christian evangelical organizations, and an unyielding belief in ecumenism. I focus on the leadership for the remainder of the chapter because distinctions should be made regarding various men and organizations supporting Promise Keepers. This does not mean that research on the men involved in PK at the local level is less important. That is hardly the case. Rather, my research has shown these men to be almost wholly social evangelicals (Brickner, 1997). They are adamantly concerned with their own salvation (traditional) but understand they must help and support the men in their community in order to foster their own growth as Christians (social). They firmly believe in the second promise of a Promise Keeper: "A Promise Keeper is committed to pursuing vital relationships with a few other men, understanding that he needs brothers to help him keep his promises."

It must be understood that within PK are traditional and new evangelicals. Both sides have their influence, but what comes out of this combination is not an emphasis on traditional personal salvation or some form of political activism. Rather, in the combination of the two, Promise Keepers comes to embody social evangelicalism.

The majority of Promise Keepers may be categorized as traditional evangelicals, although often they are more charismatic than most evangelicals. Two prominent traditional evangelicals with social emphasis are Dr. Ed Cole and Dr. Jack Hayford. Cole, founder and president of the Christian Men's Network, is a PK conference speaker who has devoted his ministry to organizing Christian men. Dr. Jack Hayford is a PK conference speaker and the senior pastor of Church on the Way, Van Nuys, CA. Hayford serves on the board of directors of the National Religious Broadcasters and World Impact, a church-planting ministry for America's inner cities.

Other notable traditional evangelical board members and speakers include: Ronald Blue, founder of a financial planning firm in Atlanta, GA; Dr. Jesse Miranda, PK conference speaker and an associate dean of Urban and Multi-Cultural Affairs, Haggard School of Theology, Azusa Pacific University, Azusa, CA; Dr. David Bryant, founder and president of Concerts of Prayer International, Wheaton, IL; Dr. Tony Evans, founder and president of The Urban Alternative; The Reverend Franklin Graham, president of Samaritan's Purse, a non-profit Christian relief and evangelism organization; Pastor Bill Hybels, senior pastor of the Willow Creek mega-church in South Barrington, IL; Dr. Crawford Loritts, Jr., national director of Legacy Ministries and the director of the 1997 National Congress on the Urban Family; Gary Smalley, president of Today's Family and a popular speaker on family relationships; Dr. Joseph M. Stowell, president of the Moody Bible Institute.

An example of a new evangelical is Charles W. Colson, founder and chairman of the board of Prison Fellowship Ministries. A PK conference speaker and contributor to the PK book *Go the Distance* (1996), he is the host of the daily radio commentary "Breakpoint," which attempts to foster a political discussion of morality and individual responsibility. Colson, special counsel to President Nixon, was convicted for his involvement in Watergate, and uses himself as an example of one who did not place matters in God's hands, and concludes that personal integrity has great importance to the nation.

Other new evangelical boosters usually placed in the "right-wing" of Christian politics include James Dobson and Pat Robertson. Dobson's Focus on the Family provided early financial support through a donation to PK as it was beginning its ministry (Raab, 1996, p. 128). Focus on the Family also provides broadcast support and publishes many of the PK study guides and books, including *The Power of a Promise Kept* (1995) and *Go the Distance* (1996). It also maintains a presence at PK stadium conferences with a booth in the ministry section, providing pamphlets and selling books and videos.

Pat Robertson's 700 Club also has provided promotional segments at PK events and conferences. The organization produced six segments promoting various aspects of Stand in the Gap, including Bill McCartney's discussion of the goals for the assembly on September 30, 1997, immediately prior to the gathering.

Another new evangelical involved with Promise Keepers is Dr. Bill Bright, author of *The Coming Revival: America's Call to Fast, Pray and "Seek God's Face"* (1995). Bright is the founder and president of the Campus Crusade for Christ International and a PK conference speaker. Bright's activism also includes involvement with the Coalition on Revival (COR), recently renamed The Alliance for Revival & Reformation (hereafter COR unless the new name is appropriate). In 1988, Bright was the "Plenary Speaker at COR's ratification of the 42 Articles" (Tarkowski, 1996, p. 1). COR is a restorationist evangelical organization of Christian leaders. On July 4, 1986, it declared its foundational theology in the organization's *Declaration and Convenant*, which advocates a restoration of biblical principles in public life. Included in the document is a list of "Social Evils to Oppose" and the affirmation that "all Bible-believing Christians must take a non-neutral stance in opposing, praying against, and speaking against social moral evils" (1986). The list of evils includes common Christian moral issues, such as the unjust treatment of the poor and disadvantaged, abortion on demand, pornography, and euthanasia, but it also includes several political and economic positions that place the group firmly within the pale of the Christian Right. Examples of social evils to oppose include:

1. State usurpation of parental rights and God-given liberties.
2. Statist-collectivist theft from citizens through devaluation of their money and redistribution of their wealth.
3. Atheism, moral relativism, and evolutionism taught as a monopoly viewpoint in public schools.
4. Communism/Marxism, fascism, Nazism and the one world government of the New Age Movement.

The document, affirmed in 1986 and listed on The Alliance for Revival & Reformation web site in 1998 (repent.org.manifesto), outlines the organization's new evangelical, ecumenical and restorationist (dominionism) principles. Formed and directed by an executive committee of four (Jay Grimstead, Pierre Bynum, Pat Mahoney and Harry Valentine) and a 37-member steering committee, COR is a counter to the theology of dispensationalism. Dispensationalism emphasizes "the futility of trying to change the world in the current age, maintaining that Christ has the authority to reign but has chosen not to exercise it until he returns" (Frame, 1990a, p. 42). COR argues otherwise, that "Christ is now reigning, and his followers with him" (Frame, 1990a, p. 42) and that the church must fulfill the Great Commission

(Tarkowski, 1996). The distinction fundamentally affects how one views activism. With Christ on their side, COR members advocate an evangelical activism that "proposes Christian takeovers in virtually all aspects of human endeavor: education, the arts, politics, and even the military" (Frame, 1990b, p. 57).

PK and COR share many similarities, at least concerning language and intentions. In 1996, the Alliance for Revival & Reformation held a "National Solemn Assembly" of church leaders in Washington, DC, to "repent, to seek God, and to pray for our beloved nation"(this is also when the group renamed itself The Alliance for Revival & Reformation). In 1997, PK's Stand in the Gap was held with the purpose of calling men to "repent before Almighty, Holy God" and to "seek His face and pray so that He might pour out His Holy Spirit to heal our land" (PK NET, 1997). Both groups emphasize 2 Chron. 7:14 as a call to pray for the nation. Both groups plan on "going global" with their ministries after the year 2000; PK already has expanded to a few other countries. The Alliance for Revival & Reformation also listed its only national Steering Committee Meeting for October 2, 1997, arranged as an opportunity "to piggyback Promise Keepers' Stand in the Gap Gathering in Washington, DC" (repent.org, 1997).

Several PK leaders have been associated with COR. PK's Bishop Wellington Boone is founder and president of Wellington Boone Ministries, Atlanta, GA, and also a board member for March for Jesus. He is the author of *Breaking Through: Taking the Kingdom into the Culture by Out-Serving Others* (1996). Boone, a prominent speaker at PK conferences, offers a traditional evangelical message of "genuine humility" to be used in serving others. His ministry encourages men and women to reach beyond race barriers to form multi-racial prayer groups.

But Boone's involvement with COR seems extensive. Conason et al. (1996) reported in *The Nation* that Boone was a member of COR's executive committee, editor and columnist for its theoretical journal *Crosswinds*, and the head of COR's black mobilization seminar project (1996, p. 14; see also Goeringer, 1997).

Conason et al. (1996) report that other PK leaders were involved in COR, including Joseph Garlington, E.V. Hill and John Perkins. Garlington is a PK speaker and the Senior Pastor at Covenant Church of Pittsburgh, a non-denominational, multi-racial ministry. Hill serves as vice president of the National Baptist Convention, USA, and board member for both the Billy Graham Evangelistic Association and the National Institute on Biblical Inerrancy (PK NET, 1997). Perkins, founder and president of the John Perkins Foundation for biblical and economic justice, is the publisher of the *Urban Family Magazine*.

All four men are black, causing concern among some commentators that the Christian Right is recruiting within the black congregations (Clarkson,

1996; Kimmel, 1996). Conason et al. (1996) report that all the men are part of COR's steering committee. Recent correspondence with COR, under the new name of The Alliance for Revival & Reformation, did not list any of the men as serving on either its executive or steering committees. Their relationships, in the capacity reported by Conason et al., have been discontinued, at least publicly.

With their previous official association with COR, these four Promise Keepers appear to be involved in what I have been referring to as new evangelicalism. The similarities between COR and Promise Keepers' semantics and assembly is important to note, but it is less than clear how this "relationship" would affect PK ministry (particularly in its less than COR-like demands) or how it might affect the men involved in Promise Keepers at a local level.

That leaves McCartney himself. McCartney has a long history of political involvement, including speaking engagements at Operation Rescue events and his advisory position on the board of Colorado for Family Values, which sponsored Colorado's Amendment 2. This amendment (struck down by the U.S. Supreme Court after narrowly winning voter approval) forbade government from enacting legislation that would give homosexuals protected status or the right to claim discrimination.

But, as described above, McCartney has another side: the coach who fosters an environment where men can help and support other men. In a recent article in The Heritage Foundation's *Policy Review* (1997), McCartney states, "Social problems are moral problems, which ultimately have a spiritual cause." Could there be a political impact from social evangelicalism? Of course. History tells us that social movements, by nature, have political implications. But is Promise Keepers' message grounded in new evangelicalism and political activism? It does not appear to be.

Even though Promise Keepers is a mix of traditional and new at the leadership level, that does not explain the essential nature of PK, which is of a social, rather than personal or political, quality. Social evangelicalism is based on social relationships rather than personal salvation alone or the addition of political activism. It is an evangelical ministry based on the reconciliation of a man to his relationship with God, his wife, children, family, friends, and co-workers.

How Promise Keepers develops in the future will depend on how much influence the new evangelicals have in developing and shaping Promise Keepers ministry. The counsel in a 1994 editorial in *Christianity Today* summarizes the dilemma. It argues that one challenge confronting Promise Keepers is how "to be socially and morally engaged in society without succumbing to a narrow political agenda" (Snyder, 1994, pp. 21-22). The dilemma may be resolved in PK's emphasis on social evangelicalism. As long as traditional evangelicals are influencing PK, and it maintains its focus on reconciliation and relationship building (social evangelicalism), the movement may socially and morally engage society without succumbing to a political agenda. When one begins discussing new evangelicals—the Oval Office model of influence—one is in the realm of a rather narrow political agenda.

References

Bebbington, D. W. (1994). Evangelicalism in its settings: The British and American movements since 1940. In M. A. Noll, D.W. Bebbington & G. A. Rawlyk (eds.), *Evangelicalism: Comparative studies of popular Protestantism in North America, British Isles, and beyond, 1700–1990* (pp. 221–251). Oxford: Oxford University Press.

Brickner, B.W. (1997). *The promise keepers: Politics and promises.* Unpublished doctoral dissertation, Purdue University, West Lafayette, IN.

Bright, B. (1995). *The coming revival: America's call to fast, pray and "seek God's face."* Orlando, FL: New Life Publications.

Clarkson, F. (1996, August 5). Righteous brothers. *In These Times.*

Clarkson, F. (1997). PK's promise—A Christian nation? *Promise Keepers watch: Monitoring the Promise Keepers movement.* Available on-line at web site www.cdsresearch.org

Colson, C. W. (1996). A man and his integrity. In J. Trent (ed.), *Go the distance.* Colorado Springs, CO: Focus on the Family Publishing.

Conason, J., Ross, A., & Cokorinos, L. (1996, October 7). The promise keepers are coming: The third wave of the religious right. *The Nation 263*, 11–19.

Declaration and covenant (1986). Alliance for Revival & Reformation. Available on-line at www.repent.org.manifesto.html.

Fackre, G. (1993). *Ecumenical faith in evangelical perspective.* Grand Rapids, MI: William B. Eerdmans Publishing.

Fowler, R. B., & Hertzke, A. D. (1995). *Religion and politics in America: Faith, culture, and strategic choices.* Boulder, CO: Westview Press.

Frame, R. (1990a, March 5). Is Christ or Satan ruler of this world? *Christianity Today 34*, 42–44.

Frame, R. (1990b, November 19). Plan calls for doing away with public schools, IRS. *Christianity Today 34*, 57–58.

Goeringer, C. F. (1997, Spring). Godly men with a Dominionist agenda. *American Atheist 35.* Available on-line at www.americanatheist.org.

Kimmel, M. (1996). Promise keepers: Patriarchy's second coming as masculine renewal. *Tikkun 12*, pp. 46–50.

McCartney, B. (1992). It's time for men to take a stand. In B. McCartney et al., *What makes a man?* (pp. 9–13). Colorado Springs, CO: NavPress Publishing Group.

McCartney, B. (1994). Seeking God's favor. In A. Janssen & L.K. Weeden (eds.), *Seven promises of a Promise Keeper* (pp. 205–207). Colorado Springs, CO: Focus on the Family Publishing.

McCartney, B. (with Diles, D.)(1995). *From ashes to glory* (Rev. ed.). Nashville, TN: Thomas Nelson Publishers.

McCartney, B. (1997, September-October). Promise makers. *Policy Review 85*, 1–8. Available on-line at www.policyreview.com.
Raab, S. (1996, January). Triumph of His will. *Gentlemen's Quarterly 66*, 110–130.
Synder, H. A. (1994, November 14). Will Promise Keepers keep their promises? *Christianity Today 38* , 20–21.
Tarkowski, E. (1996). *Part two: Foundations for apostasy: 1986–1996* [On-line]. Available on-line at www.ncinter.net/~ejt/founda2.htm.
Wilcox, C. (1992). *God's warriors: The Christian right in twentieth-century America*. Baltimore, MD: The Johns Hopkins University Press.
Zweir, R. (1982). *Born-again politics: The new Christian right in America*. Downers Grove, IL: InterVarsity Press.

CHAPTER 17

The Irresolvable Tension: *Agape* and Masculinity in the Promise Keepers Movement

by Kevin Healey

As a religious movement, Promise Keepers aspires to achieve certain spiritual goals. Dr. Bill Bright, a contributor to the PK text *Seven Promises of a Promise Keeper*, says that the central spiritual goal is the achievement of a state of unconditional, universal love, or *agape*. Bright defines *agape* as a type of love "given because of the character of the person loving rather than because of the worthiness of the object of that love" (Janssen, 1994, p. 186). This love, he says, "is for us to claim, to grow on, to spread to others, and thus to reach hundreds and thousands of others for Christ" (p. 190). As a movement that claims to be interracial, non-denominational and non-political, it seems that PK may indeed be capable of transforming the lives of many men and women from a wide range of backgrounds.

But PK also is a men's movement. In its speeches, rallies, articles, books and small-group meetings, PK attempts to construct a unified, ideal model of gender and sexuality. All constructions of gender and sexuality contain symbolic systems as well as prescriptions for social structures—systems of roles, statuses, values and norms that "add order and predictability to our private lives" (Newman, 1997, p. 280). As a Christian men's movement, PK asserts that the symbolic systems and social structures contained in its construction of gender and sexuality are compatible with the realization of *agape*.

In this chapter, I claim, on the contrary, that the symbolic systems and social structures prescribed by PK's model of masculinity are inconsistent with the realization of *agape*. PK ultimately succeeds in constructing a new model of masculinity that is satisfying and rewarding only to a limited range of social actors; the goal of *agape* is often cited but impossible to achieve within the scope of the movement's ideology. Thus, the movement is incapable of achieving both its own spiritual goals and the larger social transformations that it seeks for modern culture.

Theoretical Framework

Agape and Non-Violence

Many political activists and theologians have stressed the relationship between *agape* and non-violence. Dr. Martin Luther King, Jr., is perhaps the most well known of such figures. Although *agape* is more commonly discussed in a theological context, it may in fact be understood as an advanced stage of cognitive development. Dennis Krebs and Frank Van Hesteren, for example, use the term to describe what they consider to be the "final stages of personal and social development" (Krebs and Van Hesteren, 1992, p. 158). Here, in this psychological context, *agape* and non-violence are interrelated: the final stage's goal in Krebs and Van Hesteren's cognitive-developmental model is "to mesh with an ultimately transformed and unified *non-violent* world" (p. 158, italics added). The symbolic systems and social structures prescribed by PK must therefore be fundamentally non-violent in order for the movement to succeed in facilitating the achievement of *agape* among members.

Symbolic and Structural Violence

Violence, after all, does not merely exist in physically observable forms (Galtung, 1968). It need not even consist of harsh words or gestures. At the most basic level, violence consists of a decision about the quality of the interaction that one actor is willing to have with another. *Agape* involves an engagement with the voice of another, a belief that the voice of another is worth hearing. Violence, on the other hand, begins with the decision that the voice of another is not worth hearing: that, for whatever reason, it must not be heard. It is the "cause of the difference between the potential and the actual" in an actor's ability to express him or herself (Galtung, 1968, pp. 5–6).

The ideology of a social movement is violent if it prescribes symbolic systems or social structures that maintain or increase this difference. Symbolic violence may involve the use of "loaded words" that "destroy the basis for communication"—words such as "pig," "racist," or "capitalist" (Bruyn, 1979, p. 45). Structural violence, on the other hand, involves a larger system of statuses and roles that precludes the survival of certain voices, whether in particular contexts or in all contexts (Galtung, 1968). Structural violence may include, for example, the imposition of outside decision-making on individuals in a community or the strict control of the context and content of communication with those individuals (Bruyn, 1979).

If PK exhibits any of these types of violence in its construction of masculinity, then the possibility of achieving *agape* is effectively nullified. In other words, PK's construction of gender and sexuality may be an obstacle to the achievement of its own spiritual goals.

METHODOLOGY

In designing an appropriate methodology, I wanted to find data that described not only the movement's "official" ideology but also how the individual members interpret this ideology in their daily lives. I chose to couple a content analysis of the movement's literature with an ethnographic account of a PK community.

The first of my methodological tools for this study was a qualitative content analysis of the Promise Keepers' primary text, *Seven Promises of a Promise Keeper*. The text contains articles written by 18 authors, including James Dobson, president of the conservative group Focus on the Family; PK founder Bill McCartney; and PK President Randy Phillips. The book purports to explain the movement's ideology and goals, while offering worksheets and discussion topics for small, male peer groups.

The second method I employed was an ethnography of an electronic community that PK men have created with an "unofficial" PK "list server." List servers are generally established with a certain subject in mind, with the intention that list members will communicate with one another and share their thoughts about a shared interest. The "Promise Keepers List Server," which accommodates about 450 subscribers, primarily in the United States, operates on a more personal level than simply as an arena for dispersing information about upcoming PK events. It creates, electronically, an intentional community of men who wish to discuss important issues, to share personal stories and problems, and to hold one another accountable for their thoughts and actions.

My participation in the list server lasted from September to December of 1995. I observed the messages posted to the list server for two weeks before posting any messages myself. I did this to get a feel for how useful it would be to me and to become accustomed to the community's general atmosphere before entering it visibly. One of the conversations I took note of in the course of my initial two-week observation period was a discussion about why a certain member had been removed from the list. The man in charge of list membership (the "server") sent a message to the list explaining that this man had been removed because he was not conducting himself in a way appropriate to the list community. For fear I might lose a potentially rich source of data, I decided that I should adopt a strategy of gradual disclosure rather than immediately announce my status as a researcher.

While I observed many conversations initiated by list members, the most important data I collected were responses to messages that I myself posted. All personal stories I related to the list members were true; I chose only to change characteristics of certain persons to ensure their anonymity. For the same reason I also have here changed the names of the men on the list server.

"We're in a War, Men": War Terminology in PK Literature

One of the most striking themes that recurs throughout *Seven Promises of a Promise Keeper* is the use of war imagery and terminology. In the first chapter, Phillips suggests that the book itself is intended to serve as a "trumpet call" for a "spiritual war" already underway in America. "This book," he says, "gives us our marching orders!" (p. 9).

The book includes numerous references to "the enemy," which term does not necessarily refer to specific individuals or groups. Phillips describes "the enemy" more abstractly as a malignant force against which readers must take swift action. "While we have been asleep in our routines," he says, "the enemy has attacked relentlessly, cutting away the spiritual heritage of America. If we don't respond now, time could run out!" (p. 9). McCartney also is rather ambiguous in his descriptions; the reader knows only that "the enemy" is skillfully deceptive. "The enemy is real," he writes, "and he doesn't like to see men of God take a stand for Jesus Christ and contest his lies" (p. 207).

Although the authors are clear that a war is raging, they imply that PK and other Christians are not responsible for its occurrence, nor are they interested in participating in it with hostility. McCartney tells his readers, "We're in a war, men, whether we like it or not" (p. 207). During a rally in 1993, McCartney told his listeners, "We have been *in* a war but not *at* war" (p. 9, italics original). The reader is left with the impression that unfortunately, "the enemy" has started a war and PK has no choice but to play its proper part in the war's resolution.

Another theme that recurs throughout *Seven Promises* is the use of good-versus-evil imagery and terminology. "Satan," "sin" and "evil" are as present as "God" and "Jesus." "Satan" is the epitome of these types of images, as he is the embodiment of "sin" and "evil."

In his chapter, "Your Word is Your Bond," Edwin Louis Cole portrays Satan as the ultimate enemy in PK's quest for virtue, positing him as God's moral nemesis: "God is a maximizer of men; Satan is a usurper. Christ is truth; Satan is the father of lies…" (p. 38). He suggests, in fact, that PK participants are always the potential victims of a "satanic conspiracy" meant to "steal their words, kill their influence, and destroy their success and relationships" (p. 39).

References to "enemies" in the PK "war" are thus ambiguous because although they may take the form of specific individuals or groups, these are manifestations of a much more essential tension between absolute forces of good and evil.

"LOVING THE SINNER": LIST MEMBERS DEAL WITH HOMOSEXUALITY

In the first message I posted, I described a friend of mine who is gay. I mentioned, among other facts, that he considers himself a Christian, attends a Unitarian Universalist church, teaches elementary school and often has vivid dreams with spiritual content. "I know that many Christians disagree with his lifestyle and believe that it is sinful," I said. "But I know few people who are as spiritually wise as he is. I often wonder how this person could be such a threat to Christian values?" I asked the members on the list to offer their advice.

The first response, from an active list member I will call Mike, was clearly hostile. In it, he quoted several parts of my message and inserted rather curt and disapproving comments after each. He ended his message with a question: "Suppose Adolf Hitler had dreams of Jesus and was good with children?" he asked. "Would he be less of a madman than he was?" Fearing that a consensus of hostility toward me would threaten my status on the list (and leave me with no data), I quickly apologized and attempted to establish an "acceptable incompetent" persona. In other words, I wanted to be perceived as someone who was not a full-fledged community member, but who was sincerely interested and simply did not yet understand the organization's nature. "I am just beginning to understand the Promise Keepers," I said, and "I appreciate your patience and your helpfulness." Subsequent messages from the list members were quite supportive, addressing my concerns respectfully and seriously.

In reference to my friend, some list members suggested that in fact "spirituality" and "sin" often co-exist. This is a "paradox," David explained, which "gets greater when you see someone who has large amounts of both." An important distinction exists, however, between being "spiritual" and being a "Christian," he said. "Being spiritual," Arnold said, "does not equate to being Christian." Indeed, Howard explained, "All Christians do sin.... But a true Christian cannot do what he knows to be a sin and not feel the Holy Spirit tug at his conscience."

Other respondents pointed out problems that they have with the Unitarian Universalist church. Many agreed that the church is actually a cult. "Not to be judgmental," Arnold said, "but from my understanding the Unitarian Universalist church is a cult, not a church of Jesus Christ." He then listed a number of reasons for his position and even suggested some literature on cults. Dale agreed and stressed that the church "is *not* Christian" and in fact is "homosexually biased."

The discussion soon turned to offering more specific advice for my friend and me. Although the list members believed that I should continue our friendship, they coupled this belief with a strong suggestion that I get my friend out of the Unitarian Universalist church and into a support group or another church in which his lifestyle is regarded as sinful. "Kevin," Gary advised, "in the most loving way I know how, I would encourage you to get your friend into a Bible-believing, Spirit-filled church that proclaims the Gospel without apology." Andy suggested I find my friend a support group that condemns homosexuality: "My prayer is that he can get into a support group where the mission is for repentance and change; not where the Sin is endorsed or encouraged."

The basic strategy as defined by several respondents is to "love the sinner but hate the sin." Several respondents lamented that too often Christians emphasize the hate rather than the love. Nevertheless, "loving the sinner" became the dominant theme in many messages, and a number of messages were posted in which list members essentially engaged in a collective round of "virtual backslapping" for the degree of sensitivity they felt they were exhibiting. "One of the things that I love about this list," someone wrote, "are the frequent insightful, compassionate posts." Even Mike, who posted the first response to my message in a hostile tone, apologized for using such "harsh and strong language":

> Publicly, I wish to apologize on behalf of any Christian who with sincere "self-righteous indignation" has bashed any homosexual brother.... So often in Christian circles we ream homosexuals as if God has a special (and very hot) place in hell for them. But, that is not true, adulterers, gluttons, drunkards, embezzlers, those that cheat on their taxes, lie—we *are all under sin*. Let those without sin be the first to cast the first stone! And for us to single out a specific sin is very unloving [emphasis original].

He concluded with a plea: "Brothers, let's speak the truth, but let's do it in love."

Perhaps the most ironic development I observed on the list was the continued presence of an admittedly homosexual Promise Keeper and the lack of response he received to his messages. Philip was a homosexual man who described his situation as a process of ongoing reform. He posted a long message in reply to mine in which he explained how he came to "know Christ," and he offered his advice for how I should deal with my friend:

> What I would suggest to you is to be a friend without placing conditions on him.... Make him a regular part of your life; invite him to your home once a week for supper and socializing. Take him out to sports events once in awhile. Take an active interest in him as a person; invite him to special church events. Basically, show him that you care for him and that you're not ashamed to be around him just because he's gay.
>
> My sister sang a song in church today with the words: Don't tell

them (any unsaved person) Jesus loves them unless you're willing to love them too. Too many times in the past I heard how Christians loved the sinner but hated the sin. Unfortunately the message that came out the loudest was how much they hated the sin; not much love was ever shown.

Philip's postings were particularly thoughtful and gentle in tone, but as long as I was on the list no one responded to him directly nor did anyone mention his name in their messages.

"TAKING BACK THE REINS": HOW MEMBERS UNDERSTAND MALE LEADERSHIP

The authors of *Seven Promises of a Promise Keeper* often claim regretfully that in the last several decades men have become emotionally distant and uninvolved in the lives of their families, churches and communities. They suggest that one PK goal is to bring men back—to help men become more intimately connected to their families and to take responsibility where they have been absent.

Dr. Tony Evans refers to this historical process of decreasing male involvement as "the feminization of the American male." This process has "produced a nation of 'sissified' men who abdicate their role as spiritually pure leaders, thus forcing women to fill the vacuum" (p. 73). The solution, he suggests, involves "getting men to assume their responsibilities and take back the reins of spiritually pure leadership God intended us to hold" (p. 75). He recommends that his male readers have a serious talk with their wives in which they acknowledge the "mistake" they have made and inform them that they must "reclaim [their] role" (p. 79). "I'm not suggesting that you *ask* for your role back," he clarifies, "I'm urging you to *take it back*" (p. 79, italics original). His advice for wives is also clear:

> *Give it back!* For the sake of your family and the survival of our culture, let your man be a man if he's willing. Protect yourself, if you must, by handing the reins back slowly; take it one step at a time. But if your husband tells you he wants to reclaim his role, let him! God never meant for you to bear the load you're carrying [p. 80, italics in original].

I thought this passage was particularly controversial, probably even in the eyes of many Promise Keepers, so I posted a message in which I quoted the passage and asked the list members for their interpretation of Dr. Evans' remarks.

A number of respondents affirmed the role of the man as "head" or "leader" in the family in strong and unapologetic terms. Norman used his military background to illustrate his position:

> [I]n His wisdom, [God] appointed the man to have the leadership role—the ultimate decision maker.... When I was a squadron commander I had the authority and responsibility to make the decisions for my squadron.... I sought out [the advice of my junior officers] but when the decision had to be made, I had to make it and take the responsibility for the decision.... The same thing happens in the family and the church.

Other respondents, such as David, also stressed the husband's role as decision-maker, explaining that the wife should submit herself to her husband as her husband submits himself to Christ:

> The husband should be the teacher, preacher, and decision-maker in the home.... The wife is to submit herself to the husband as he submits himself to Christ.

Mike agreed that "the man has the right to delegate his responsibility to his wife—he is entirely free to do so," but stressed, however, that PK encourages men to take on more responsibility rather than delegate it to others. Tim lamented that negotiating the decision-maker's role is often difficult: "I am currently praying for better wisdom on when to lead (or, more precisely, to make a forceful decision) and when to back off for the sake of peace! That is a very difficult distinction for me."

While many list-server members asserted man's role as household "head" or "leader," many qualified their position by claiming that "leadership" actually means service or submission. "[I]f the husband is to be a head of the wife as Christ was the head of the church," Peter explained, "this is a role of servanthood and sacrifice." Yet others stressed, in fact, that the Bible prescribes that men and women submit to *each other*, and that although the man should assume the primary leadership role in the family, that leadership is part of a reciprocally submissive relationship. David, however, was not pleased with these qualifications:

> [M]ost of the E-mail I have read about the man's role in this life is a watered down version of the Bible. Men seem to be afraid to just say "I am the head of the family" without some qualifying "but" statement at the end.

In response, Stuart suggested a reason for such qualifications:

> For myself, I frequently will use some kind of qualifier ... because we live in a society that doesn't understand what is meant by being head

of the family. To the world (not to mention a fair amount of the Body), if I say that I am the head of my family and my wife is to submit to me, this means that I sit in my chair watching TV while my wife waits on me hand and foot. The use of these terms gives a lot of people the image of a totalitarian dictator rather than a benevolent monarch.

"What Is Your Agenda?": How I Was Thrown Off the PK List Server

Although I phrased my initial message in what I considered to be a diplomatic tone, the first response was, as I mentioned earlier, quite hostile. But after I established a persona as an "acceptable incompetent," I gradually began to express my own opinions more clearly and I revealed more and more about my status as a researcher with background in Women's Studies.

When I had become comfortable expressing my own opinions in my messages, I phrased one in the form of a survey rather than in my usual conversational tone. Phrasing my questions in this manner drew considerable hostility from the "server." He warned me that "Doing 'research' in the net, especially e-mail, is a poor substitute for going to a library or making a few phone calls to the Promise Keepers organization for their position, or literature."

Mike—the man who posted the first response to my messages and with whom I had developed a strong rapport—also responded with suspicion, asking me whether I had an "agenda" and if so, what it was.

In the next few days I noticed that I had not received any new messages from the list. I sent a direct e-mail to Mike asking him if he knew what was happening. He said that the "server" had removed me from the list as "a temporary thing ... to get your attention," and that he would soon contact me directly. I never did receive a message from the "server" and, unable to send or receive messages to and from the list, I was forced to declare my data collection complete.

The Symbolic Foundations of Violence

PK's use of war terminology and good-versus-evil imagery as exemplified in *Seven Promises* lays a symbolic foundation for the structural violence in the PK ideology. The image of Satan as the ultimate enemy suggests that the war that is supposedly taking place is merely a historically specific manifestation of deeper, more permanent cosmological tension. This symbolic system thus not only prepares PK participants to encounter the voices of *specific* groups and individuals in a spirit of suspicion and hostility; it suggests that this attitude is a fundamental and necessary attribute of a virtuous masculine identity. The numerous disclaimers from movement leaders such as McCartney ("We're *in* a war but not *at* war") are an attempt to obscure the constructedness of this symbolic system, thereby eliminating any need for individual members to acknowledge their responsibility in its constant maintenance.

STRUCTURAL VIOLENCE AND HOMOSEXUAL VOICES

The use of distinctions such as that between "spirituality" and "Christianity," as well as the identification of certain churches as "cults," creates conceptual and symbolic boundaries around PK men's sexual identity. While the ideal of "loving the sinner" ostensibly involves a spirit of dialogue and engagement with homosexual voices, it is virtually indistinguishable from the strategy of introducing homosexuals into churches where their lifestyle is regarded as "sinful." This social structure thus allows PK men to engage homosexual voices only on the condition that gatekeepers in ideologically sanctioned churches or support groups are escorting them into the bounds of the movement's sexual identity. As the clear lack of response to messages from "Philip" indicates, even this condition may not be sufficient to solicit an active engagement from the movement's members.

STRUCTURAL VIOLENCE AND WOMEN'S VOICES

While the Promise Keepers movement may succeed to a great degree in generating intimacy between men and their families, the structure of men's prescribed leadership role precludes women's equal involvement in defining the precise nature and quality of familial reality. Again, movement members disclaim the inequity of this structure by, for example, defining leadership as "submission." Nevertheless, the operational definition of male leadership in the family is the husband's authority to make the final decision in times of crisis or disagreement. Thus, while the metaphorical "conch shell" may seem to pass freely from one hand to another, as long as the husband has the authority to reclaim it at any time the potential for men to silence women's voices is ever present in the relationship.

Conclusion: Social Comfort and the Illusion of Agape

I imagine that many Promise Keepers participants and their supporters will object to my use of the term "violence" in reference to the movement's attitudes toward women and homosexuals. Most Promise Keepers, I would agree, are peaceful men, and many women are pleased with the difference the movement has made in their families' lives. I would suggest, however, that the feelings of love and peace experienced in Promise Keepers families indicate not the presence of *agape* but rather a profound sense of comfort within the safe boundaries of a rigidly maintained system of identity. As illustrated by my experience on the Promise Keepers list server, the social networks of the movement's members are exclusive, so unpleasant interaction with outsiders is unnecessary. Once these boundaries are broached, however, responses may be quite hostile. Furthermore, I have demonstrated that even within the confines of such comfortable social spaces, violence is nevertheless present, both symbolically and structurally. As long as this is the case, Promise Keepers will fail to achieve its avowed spiritual goal of *agape*.

References

Bruyn, S.T., G. Rayman, P.M. (eds.)(1979). *Nonviolent action and social change.* New York : Irvington Publishers.

Galtung, J. (1968). *Sociological theory and social development.* Kampala, Uganda: Transition Books.

Janssen, A., & L.K. Weeden (eds.) (1994). *Seven promises of a Promise Keeper.* Colorado Springs, CO: Focus on the Family Publishing.

Krebs, D.L., & Van Hesteren, F. (1992). The development of altruistic personality. In Oliner, P.M., Oliner, S.P., Baron, L., Blum, L.A., Krebs, D.L., & Smolenska, M.Z. (eds.), *Embracing the other: Philosophical, psychological, and historical perspectives on altruism.* New York: New York University Press.

Newman, D.M. (1997). *Sociology: Exploring the architecture of everyday life.* Thousand Oaks, CA: Pine Forge Press.

CHAPTER 18

Silencing the Voice of God: Rhetorical Responses to the Promise Keepers

by Colleen E. Kelley

> All scripture is given by inspiration of God, and is profitable for doctrine, for reproof, for correction, for instruction in righteousness. [2 Tim. 3:16]

Burke (1970, p. v) argues that "the religious always ground their exhortations (to themselves and others) in statements of the widest and deepest possible scope, concerning the authorships of men's motives." Theological doctrine is about "words about God" and a search for a term so "ultimate" or "radical" (p. vi) that it is virtually impossible to counter that term with any other known word. This chapter is an examination of rhetorical strategies of the Promise Keepers that have empowered them to occupy a "rhetorical high ground" when encountering criticism of their movement. It begins with a brief review of rhetoric and rhetorical criticism followed by an introduction to ideographic analysis. Next is an examination of the competing rhetorical visions of the Promise Keepers and the National Organization for Women (NOW), a group Pollitt (1997) argues has essentially stood alone in taking a stand against Promise Keepers.

RHETORIC AND "GOD TERMS"

Rhetoric originated with the ancient Greeks as the practice of public persuasion and, in Burke's view (1969, p. 43), comprises the use of language as a symbolic means of "inducing cooperation in beings that by nature respond to symbols." This cooperation (or persuasion) occurs when one person is able to "identify" with another through "talking his language by speech, gesture, tonality, order, image, attitude, idea" (p. 5). Burke (1970, p. 274) illustrates the distinction between the thing (non-symbolic) and the word (symbolic) by asking, "What hungry belly could be quieted by a poem in praise of food?"

More important, language adds a new dimension to nature in that words "transcend" nonverbal nature. As Burke (1970, p. 305) writes, "The fall of all the trees in the world will not bring down the meaning of the word 'tree.'"

While a rhetorical perspective assumes symbols present a source's view of reality (Cooper, 1989), a rhetorical analysis examines how these symbols are put together to achieve identification between a source and a receiver. Identification in turn produces an ideology, a coherent world view that allows interpretation of events, justifies power and guides action. This "common sense" ideology, rhetorically created, provides its participants with criteria for determining "good," "bad," "right" and "wrong." Such an ideology also provides a discursive defense for the beliefs, values and myths accepted by members of the rhetorical community sharing this vision. Those not identifying with the vision may find fault with it, but those immersed in the ideology will likely accept it "as an accurate representation of the way the world works" (Cooper, 1989, p. 164).

The ideologies at work within competing arguments—such as those of PK and NOW—may be revealed by identifying "god terms" ("which symbolize the ideals of a culture" [Weaver, 1970, pp. 88–89]) or "ultimate terms" ("that express the universality of a perspective" [Burke, 1969, pp. 188–190]). McGee (1980) suggests locating "ideographs," one-term or phrase sums of a perspective or world view. Such terms serve as a guiding idea or "unitary principle" for an ideology. Further, the "rhetorical strength" of a particular ideograph is dependent on its position in a hierarchy of ultimate terms (Burke, 1969, pp. 188–190). Such terms provide a symbolic means for members of a rhetorical culture to identify with one another, and furnish the symbolic means for condemning those who reject that culture. Cooper (1989) details three characteristics of ideographs. First, such terms express and reinforce a group's ideals, uniting and dividing people into communities. Second, ideographs produce a symbolic reality or make concrete or visible concepts that are not concrete or visible. Third, ideographs "command an alliegiance" that makes them "impervious to logical investigation" (pp. 164–165). In Burke's view (1970, p. vi), "words-about-God" are "as far-reaching as words can be" because even one who does not believe in the supernatural must acknowledge that languages provide ideographs for the supernatural. Such words for "God" may only be used analytically, as in the physical analogy of God's "powerful arm" or the socio-political analogy of God as "lord" or "father" or the linguistic analogy of God as the "Word" (p. 15).

An Ideographic Analysis of Promise Keepers

Nimmo and Combs (1990, p. 186) refer to the most recent incarnation of American evangelical Christianity as an elaborate fundamentalist rhetorical vision that simplifies confusing social and political changes for the benefit of the faithful. Boone (1989, p. 10–12) believes that fundamentalism is a "tendency" or "habit of mind" rather than a discrete movement, whose distinguishing feature is a verbal system or body of discourse arising from the belief in the sole authority of an inerrant Bible. While literal readings may reveal textual discrepancies, an inerrant reading allows fundamentalists to move arbitrarily between literal and nonliteral biblical translations because the Bible must be shown to be without error (Hawley and Proudfoot, 1997, pp. 14–15). Rhetors—orating ministers and lay people—play a major role in fundamentalism by making The Word accessible to the "plain man," depending on Bible text as the sole sanction for the truth of their rhetoric (Boone, 1989, p. 15).

Once the Bible has been established as a God-given text, free of error and plain in message, that very fundamentalism perpetuates itself in the minds of believers, binding them to their belief solely because the Bible tells them so (p. 7).

Hawley and Proudfoot (1997, p. 4) argue that the most powerful message of fundamentalists may be social rather than scriptual inerrancy. As their predecessors did in the 1920s and 1950s, contemporary American fundamentalists often define themselves against a "threatening backdrop" of social and economic problems of the "modern" age. Theirs is a moral drama, a holy war against Satan and his agents, which may include liberals, homosexuals and feminists (Nimmo and Combs, 1990, p. 195). Often evidenced is a desire to return to an earlier, albeit mythical, way of life in order to reclaim an ideal of culture and femininity that they believe has been abandoned. Fundamentalism and gender are thus connected by a kind of "religious machismo" (Hawley and Proudfoot, 1997, p. 27) resulting in religiously sanctioned control of women (Brown, 1994). Balmer (1994) believes women serve as a kind of "bellwether" for fundamentalist culture at large: if women abandon their "God-given" responsibilities in the home, America is in trouble. If, however, women embrace Bible-based notions of submission, nurture and domesticity, America's future is secure (p. 59), according to fundamentalists.

Balmer (1994) suggests fundamentalists have found changing views of women in recent times "utterly disconcerting," so that what is especially striking about fundamentalists' influence in American culture is the extent to which the issue of gender has shaped their political agenda (pp. 54–60). Therefore, PK participants are "fundamentalists" not because of what churches they belong to, but because of what they have to say and their justification for saying it.

That Promise Keepers are fundamentalists, with a rhetorical vision grounded in ideographs taken from an inerrant text, is revealed in their Statement of Faith (The Ministry, 1997, p. 2), the doctrinal foundation for the organization:

> We believe that the Bible is God's written revelation to man and that it is verbally inspired, authoritative, and without error in the original manuscripts.

In fact, PK's Seven Promises are all ideographic compositions drawn from scripture. A Promise Keeper (The Seven Promises, 1998; Bohan, 1996, p. 37) is committed

> to honoring Jesus Christ through ... obedience to God's Word ... [to] spiritual, moral, ethical, sexual purity ... [to] building strong marriages and families through love, protection, and biblical values ... [to] supporting his church [and] pastor ... [to] demonstrate the power of biblical unity ... [to] being obedient to the Great Commandment [Matthew 28:19–20—to love God above all else and to love your neighbor as yourself] and the Great Commission [Matthew 28:19–20—to spread the gospel of Jesus Christ].

God-linked or Bible-based ideographs permeate PK's rhetorical vision. Participants are "godly men on their knees in humility" (Promise Keepers, 1997, p. 1), to be "godly influences" (Bohan, 1996, p. 38), to "lead godly lives" (The Ministry, p. 3) and become promise keepers in their relationships "with God, their wives, their children, and each other" (Fact Sheet, p. 1). Promise Keepers "inspire, encourage and equip" others; are "men of integrity," believe in "serving and sacrificing for others" (McCartney, 1997a, p. 7) and are "trustworthy" (The Ministry, 1997, p. 1). They strive for "Christlikeness," realizing that only the "strength of the Holy Spirit" and a "personal relationship with Almighty God" and "allegiance to Jesus Christ" (McCartney, 1997a, p. 2) will allow them to become more like Jesus Christ, who is their "supreme model for manhood" (McCartney, 1997a, p. 8). Promise Keepers must "pursue godliness" that they might "grow as Christians" (What is the Role, 1997). They are identified with "mentoring" by "receiving Godly teaching and guidance"; "brokenness" because "men's hearts are being broken for sin ... including neglect of wives and families" and "being convicted in their hearts for having abdicated their leadership roles and placing undue responsiblities and pressures on spouses whose shoulders could not bear them alone"; "camaraderie" as men "no longer isolated and alone"; "vision" with a "yearning for spiritual maturity," and "reconciliation in the church"—so all Promise Keeper men "become the best leaders, best husbands, best fathers, and best of friends" (Phillips, 1998).

PK founder and CEO Bill McCartney exemplifies the fundamentalist rhetor whose message both legitimizes and is legitimized by its biblical grounding. Quoting Isaiah 38:19, McCartney argues, "God almighty has proclaimed husbands to be the spiritual leaders of their families" (quoted in van Leeuwen, 1997, p. 933). Promise Keepers "deepen men's commitment" while "honoring women" (Why Is Promise Keepers, PK web site) and admonishes men to "love and serve our wives and children"; "honor their word to their wives" (McCartney, 1997a, p. 5) and "give them first priority in our prayers and schedules" (McCartney, 1997b, p. 1). The PK family is a patriarchal "man, wife and children" unit undergirded by Ephesians 5:22-23: "Wives, submit yourselves unto your own husbands, as unto the Lord. For the husband is the head of the wife, even as Christ is the head of the Church." And their rhetorical response to "feminists" as a group is illustrated by Evans' (1996) description of feminists as "frustrated women unable to find the proper male leadership" (p. 185).

Sports metaphors ideographically produce identification with a "muscular Christianity" (Kimmel, 1997, p. 47) through stereotypic appeals to "real" or "true" men, much "as a coach can get the toughest jocks to huddle for prayer" (Ostling, 1997, p. 1). "Coach" McCartney, often from a sports stadium platform, asserts (1997a, p. 4):

> as a former coach, I know it's not enough simply to get men worked up in the locker room about winning a ball game. They need a game plan.

He relies on "some of my experiences as a football coach in learning how to bring men together" (1997b, p. 1); speaks of Promise Keepers as "the people of God" protecting the "ill-informed ... like offensive linemen protecting the quarterback" (1997a, p. 4) and recalls (p. 2) how

> in the game of football, if your team is getting trounced, you'd better have a serious talk with the men at halftime and identify the problem.

ARGUING WITH GOD: THE VISION OF THE NATIONAL ORGANIZATION FOR WOMEN

Boone (1989) warns of the potential for abuse in a discourse that argues it is the word and will of God. Ideologies generated by such discourses are difficult to counter since "hidden authorities" are virtually impossible to challenge, particularly those "parading in the guise of holy scripture" (p. 11). This is one of the constraints facing PK critics, particularly NOW.

Alleged connections with the Religious Right and sexist attitudes toward women are two of the major criticisms of PK. The organization has been called the "third wave" of the Religious Right (Conason et al., 1996), and a "recruiting arm for the Christian Right" (Clarkson, 1997, p. 190).

Kimmel (1997, p. 48) believes that PK promotes a "soft patriarchy" whose rhetoric is one of a "male surpremacy with a beatific smile," while Hetherly (1997) argues that PK wants an authoritative nation segregated along gender lines. Others argue the Promise Keepers have created a safe public space that is a "jock-friendly venue with a cock-friendly theology," and that this links patriarchy and theocracy (Stoltenberg, 1995, pp. 4–5) intent on "carving God's masculine face back onto the spiritual tableau" (Lawton, 1997, p. 1). In this view, PK has tapped into a general insecurity in society and induced a kind of "gender panic" (Clarkson, 1997, p. 192) by rhetorically targeting men's anxieties (Kimmel, 1997, p. 48) and communicating at a "gut level" with men "reeling from a radical feminist tidal wave" (Stoltenberg, 1995, p. 3).

NOW has provided the single loudest criticism of PK's discursive vision with a basic argument that Promise Keepers "promote homophobia, patriarchy and misogyny" (Recer, 1995). This is not to suggest that others are not resisting or countering PK's message. However, the most publicly well-known and so publicly heard opposition, whose voice is "always solicited by the media" (Sobran, 1997, p. 2), belongs to NOW. While an in-depth discussion of NOW and Promise Keepers media coverage is beyond the scope of this chapter, a brief examination of Hahn's (1998) perspective may be useful. In this view (pp. 36–37), the commercial media, like any business, do what they must to make money:

> Political ideologues who assume media personnel are in the business of "selling" political positions misunderstand the business in which media owners and practitioners are engaged. What media really do is sell their readers and viewers to their advertisers. The more readers or viewers they have, the more they can charge for an ad. That means they have to keep the public happy.... Their commerical nature favors whatever will make money and leads to at least two deleterious efffects that have political consequences—trivialization and a conflict orientation.

Media tend to both simplify and sensationalize reports, replacing extensive coverage of issues with more trivial entertainment-oriented images, simultaneously choosing to create polarized messages for an audience eager to "watch a fight" rather than become informed. Further, since business-oriented media executives believe American audiences are turned off by incremental or long-term coverage of news stories (Hahn, 1998, p. 38), contemporary media coverage tends to present these "simplified extremes," via "photo-ops" and sound-bites rather than the more realistic but often less entertaining "complex middle" (p. 37).

As consumer-targeted businesses, the media must maintain a viable profit margin, which mandates that "news" be presented in a way that American audiences will most likely "buy" it. Hence, American media tend toward a "sound-bite and headline" format as opposed to in-depth, detailed and extensive reporting of issues. One unfortunate outcome of this for-profit news climate may be a media emphasis on the apparent but not necessarily polarized rhetoric of "opposing" viewpoints. In other words, even if a middle ground exists for discussion by the "two sides" or if yet other, less audible or recognizable voices might contribute to the dialogue, chances are that only the media's "edited" version reaches the American public.

Audiences also are targeted with information that rises primarily from what they "know best" or with which they are most familiar. Therefore, even though PK has other critics, ranging from ultra-conservatives who fear PK's "liberalism," to mainstream Protestant denominations with more moderate concerns, it should not be surprising that NOW has taken center stage as the media's enactment of a polar opposite of Promise Keepers.

Remember also that the media often leave out as much information as they "edit" into a story. Certainly this applies to the news capsules presented to the American public by the media as representations of NOW's rhetorical position regarding the PK. NOW is serious about its call for solidifying oppositional support, as evidenced by the launching of a national campaign to counter the Promise Keepers (NOW, 1997a). This campaign seems to have become as high a priority of NOW as its other priority agenda items, which include reproductive rights (Restraining Order, 1998); women's health (Toledo, 1998); economic and education equity (Amendments Threaten, 1998), and fighting sexual harassment (Keen, 1998).

Ultimately, NOW's relatively high profile, combined with the lack of an organized coalition of Promise Keeper opponents, resulted in the "anointing" of NOW, for the mass mediated realities of the American public at this point, as "the" critic of the Promise Keepers.

NOW's message through the media has been voiced primarily by NOW president Patricia Ireland, who created a rhetorical composite of defensive, sarcastic and accusatory ideographs to counter PK. Ireland speaks of NOW's "no surrender" campaign (quoted in NOW Issues, 1997); attacks McCartney's "male-supremacist agenda" and association with "right-wing extremists"; and argues "the true voice of tolerance and acceptance" belongs to NOW (Ireland, 1997a). Promise Keepers "check their wives and daughters at the door like coats" (quoted in Christian Men, 1997, p.4); want to "take control" rather than responsiblity by way of an "authoritarian, theocratic society" with an ultimate goal of "the submission of women to male authority (quoted in National Organization for Women, 1997b). PK, the "hottest religious-right marketing tool since televangelism," wants women to "take a back seat in this and every other area of our lives," is composed of "political extremists" who appeal to the "biblically correct," are linked to the "firebombed clinic," and "fanaticism and intolerance." Ultimately, PK is only "one large self-help group" pitching a "feel-good form of male supremacy" rather than preaching godly male bonding (Ireland, 1997a).

CHRIST OR CHAOS? COMPETING RHETORICAL VISIONS

Kerston (1997) says that NOW may object to PK's reforms program, but asks "can [NOW] offer an alternative vision capable of inspiring men to change their ways?" (p. 17), while PK President Randy Phillips answers NOW's concerns with the biblically-based conviction that "no woman should feel threatened" by his group "because the ground is level at the foot of the cross" (quoted in Christian Men, 1997, p. 4). These comments represent two major reasons for Promise Keepers' rhetorical superiority over the National Organization for Women: failure to provide a comparable counter-vision and inablility to ideographically trump words from The Word.

PK's vision is generally pro-active, describing its participants' goal of becoming godly men and representing their scripturally-derived knowledge of God's truth. NOW's vision is essentially re-active, arguing that PK is not about men becoming more godly and criticizing what NOW conceptualizes as an inerrant and misinterpreted dogma. It becomes difficult if not impossible for NOW to discursively compete with PK because it is difficult if not impossible to rhetorically surpass a vision derived almost entirely from "god terms" or ideographs, which themselves originate in The Highest Authority and the ultimate source of His Word: the Bible. Boone (1989, p. 2) suggests a text's authority is constituted in part by those who interpret that text. And Promise Keepers has been successful in sustaining their vision because leaders such as McCartney say they are only relating the Word of God, directly from His Book; it is difficult to dispute that authority, as it seems to originate in the word of God itself.

Boone (1989, p. 11) believes those who do not embrace the fundamentalist message often fail to appreciate the "binding power" of that message for Bible believers. PK's rhetorical strategy of maintaining a Bible-based discourse also may account for the strength of their vision even for secularists. The belief in the Bible as a "True Book" is not necessarily a particularly religious belief at all. People want to believe that "somewhere some one book" is "absolutely true and correct" and, in American society, that book is likely to be the Bible (Barr, 1977, p. 139). A vision will be almost impossible to deconstruct if it derives from an almost universally recognized source of "good words." The Bible in a sense functions for most Americans as an ultimate ideograph, comprising ideographic terms. This might account in part for what some argue has been generally superficial and non-critical media examination of PK (Claussen, 1996; Claussen, this volume; Waters, this volume) as well as the failure of many "supposedly liberal and gender-enlightened mainline denominations" to participate in NOW's vision of the Promise Keepers (Stoltenberg, 1995; Clarkson, 1997; Hetherly, 1997; and Pollitt, 1997).

Some may argue that the National Organization for Women's message, as framed by the media, has provided extremist and even "silly" rather than credible criticism of Promise Keepers. For example, NOW says the Promise Keepers are bad for women, while Promise Keeper wives say the organization is good for them (Doughney and Kneisly, 1997). However, from a discursive perspective, NOW's response to Promise Keepers was not "silly" or radical or "out-of-touch" with its audience. It simply was not rhetorically smart.

Lifton (1961) believes that the control of human communication—all that is seen, heard, read, written, experienced and expressed—is the basic feature of thought reform, and Bosmajian (1983, p. 1) argues "the importance, significance, and ramifications of naming and defining cannot be over-emphasized." He (p. 4) continues:

> The power which comes from names and naming is related directly to the power to define others—individuals, races, sexes, ethnic groups. Our identities, who and what we are, how others see us are greatly affected by the names we are called, and the words with which we are labelled. Through definition we restrict, we set boundaries, we name.

Hahn (1998, p. 51) addresses the power and centrality of language in the human experience by arguing that through definitions, language can persuade people to admire a person or idea, or hold them up to contempt. NOW's response fails not because its message is frivolous or emotional or extreme or even groundless. On the contrary, NOW's serious and complex—albeit presented in abbreviated fashion by the media—message fails to rhetorically counter that of the Promise Keepers because it is not framed in biblically-based, "God-term" ideographs. This lack of rhetorical sophistication ultimately meant that the National Organization for Women would not have its definition of Promise Keepers-related issues adopted into the American societal dialogue (Hahn, 1998, p. 53).

Unless the National Organization for Women's counter arguments are grounded in the same biblical authority as PK's arguments, NOW's rhetorical efforts will almost certainly continue to fail. NOW has been left in a state of rhetorical paralysis, aware of what it believes are the dangers of Promise Keepers, yet powerless to criticize PK members who, in Boone's (1989, p. 109) view, are "only obeying the rules of a discourse for which they are not the masters, of which no one is the master."

CONCLUSION: THEIR LAST WORDS

In his epilogue to *The Rhetoric of Religion*, Kenneth Burke (1970, p. 304) imagines a conversation between The Lord and Satan during which both discuss The Lord's creation of humans as Word-Using Animals. The dialogue explores the connection between the form of words and the form of The Word, and ultimately examines "the way in which the idea of a supernatural God is built out of human components," the foremost of which is language. Satan and The Lord both unhappily conclude that when the "Word People" are gone, so too will the "life of words" be gone and with them, "we, too" will be gone (p. 315).

Within this perspective, all knowledge is rhetorically constructed and all ideologies are discourse driven. The strength of any belief system, supernatural or not, is therefore directly proportional to the strength of the words used by believers of a particular system. Powerful words produce powerful visions and empower ideologies to resist critique, particularly from less vigorous rhetorical communities.

Promise Keepers are immersed in a scripture-based fundamentalist ideology. They have managed to occupy the rhetorical high ground when challenged by the National Organization for Women because NOW has failed to ground its vision in discourse that originates from a source whose authority is comparable to the Bible's. As long as Promise Keepers' rhetoric is so credentialed, it does not matter very much who speaks against them because, so far, no word has emerged that is able to surpass The Word.

References

Amendments threaten access to education. (1998, April 29). [On-line]. National Organization for Women Home Page. Available: http://www.now.org/issues/affirm/alerts/04-29-98.html.
Balmer, R. (1994). American fundamentalism: the ideal of femininity. In J.S. Hawley (ed.), *Fundamentalism and gender*, pp. 47–66. London: Oxford.
Barr, J. (1977). *Fundamentalism*. Philadelphia: Westminister.
Bohan, D.H. (1996, November 25). A look at Promise Keepers. *New American* 12(24), 37–39.
Boone, K. (1989). *The Bible tells them so: The discourse of Protestant fundamentalism*. Albany: State University of New York Press.
Bosmajian, H. (1983). *The language of oppression*. Lanham, MD: University Press of America.
Brown, K.M. (1994). Fundamentalism and the control of women, in J.S. Hawley (ed.), *Fundamentalism and Gender*, pp. 175–201. London: Oxford.
Burke, K. (1969). *A rhetoric of motives*. Berkeley, CA: University of California Press.
Burke, K. (1970). *The rhetoric of religion*. Berkeley, CA: University of California Press.
Christian men share joy, pain. (1997, October 4). *USA Today*. [On-line]. Available: http://www.usatoday.com/
Clarkson, F. (1997). *Eternal hostility: The struggle between theocracy and democracy*. Monroe, ME: Common Courage Press.
Conason, J., Ross, A., & Cokorinos, L. (1996, October 7). The Promise Keepers are coming: The third wave of the religious right. *The Nation 263*, p. 11–19.
Cooper, M. (1989). *Analyzing public discourse*. Prospect Heights, IL: Waveland.

Doughney, M., & Kneisly, L. (1997, December). Promise Keepers, compulsory pregnancy advocates, and the "biblical America" movement. Biblical American Resistance Front Official Web Site. [On-line]. Available: http://www.barf.org/articles/bp9712.html. 10 pp.

Evans, T. (1996). *No more excuses*. Wheaton, IL: Crossway Books.

Fact Sheet. (1998). Promise Keepers Official Web Site. 2 pp. Available: http://www2.promisekeepers.org/21ca.html.

Hahn, D. (1998). *Political communication: Rhetoric, government and citizens*. State College, PA: Strata.

Hawley, J.S., & Proudfoot, W. (1997). Introduction. In J.S. Hawley (ed.), *Fundamentalism and gender*, pp. 3–44. London: Oxford.

Hetherly, M. (1997, September). PK publicity and production: Between the lines and behind the scenes. *The Humanist 57*(5), 14–18.

Ireland, P. (1997a, August 15). Open letter to activists. National Organization for Women Home Page. [On-line]. 1 p. Available: http://www.now.org/issues/right/promise/letter.html#background.

Ireland, P. (1997b, September 7). Beware of "feel-good" male supremacy. *The Washington Post*, C3.

Keen, J. (1998, April 221). NOW considers filing court brief on behalf of Paula Jones. *USA Today*, 4A.

Kersten, K. (1997, November). Male models. *American Enterprise 8*(6), 16–17.

Kimmel, M.S. (1997, March). Promise Keepers: Patriarchy's second coming as masculine renewal. *Tikkun 12*(2), 46–50.

Lifton, R. (1961/1989). *Thought reform and the psychology of totalism*. Chapel Hill, NC: University of North Carolina Press.

McCartney, B. (1997a, September-October). Promise makers. *Policy Review: The Journal of American Citizenship 85*, 14–19.

McCartney, B. (1997b, October 4). Stand in the Gap press briefing. Official Promise Keepers Web Site. [On-line]. Available: http://www.promisekeepers.org/media/Oct4.html. 2 pp.

McGee, M. (1980). The "ideograph": A link between rhetoric and ideology. *Quarterly Journal of Speech 66*, 1–16.

The ministry of Promise Keepers. (1997). Promise Keepers Official Web Site. [On-line]. Available: http://www2.promisekeepers.org/2a0e.html. 5 pp.

National Organization for Women. (1997a, August 22). To mark women's equality day feminists launch national "no surrender" campaign to counter upcoming Promise Keepers' march. News Release.

National Organization for Women. (1997b, October 2). "Promise us equality!" is women's leaders challenge to Promise Keepers. News Release.

Nimmo, D., & Combs, J. (1990). *Mediated political realities* (2nd ed.). White Plains, NY: Longman.

NOW issues attack on Promise Keepers. (1997, September 10–17). *Christian Century 114*(25), 785.

Ostling, R. (1997, October 6). God, football and the game of his life. *Time 150*(14), 38–39.

Phillips, H. (1998). Costly promises. *New Man* magazine. [On-line]. 3 pp. Available: http://www.strang.com/nm/stories/nm296hp.html.
Pollitt, K. (1997, October 27). The promised land. *The Nation 265*(13), 10.
Promise Keepers. (1997, Sept. 11). No political speeches, no protests, no fireworks. Press Release. 3 pp.
Recer, J. (1995, August). Whose promise are they keeping? *National NOW Times*, 1.
Restraining order on Wisconsin abortion ban denied. (1998, May 26). National Organization for Women Home Page. [On-line]. 1p. Available: http://www.now.org/issues/abortion/alerts/05-26-98.html.
The seven promises of a Promise Keeper. (1998). Official Promise Keepers Web Site. [On-line]. 1 p. Available: http://www2.promisekeepers.org/hp html.
Sobran, J. (1997, October 7). Smirking at virtue. Universal Press Syndicate: Opinion. [On-line]. 3 pp. Available: http://www.uexpress.com/ups/opinion/column/js/archive/js971007.html.
Stodghill, R. II (1997, October 6). God of our fathers. *Time 150*(14), 34–40.
Stoltenberg, J. (1995). Male virgins, blood covenants and family values. *On the Issues*. [On-line]. 8 pp. Available: http://mosaic.echonyc.com/~onissues/male.html.
Toledo, E. (1998, May 16). Cashing in on insecurity. *The Washington Post*, A13.
van Leeuwen, M.S. (1997, October 22). Mixed messages on the mall. *Christian Century 114*(20), 932–934.
Weaver, R. (Johannesen, R.L., Strickland, R., & Eubanks, R.T., eds.) (1970). *Language is sermonic*. Baton Rouge, LA: Louisiana State University Press.
What is the role of the seven promises in the life of a Christian? (1997). Promise Keepers Official Web Site. [On-line]. 1 p. Available: http://www.promise keepers.org/29b6.html.
Why is Promise Keepers a ministry for men? (1998). Promise Keepers Official Web Site. [On-line]. 1p. Available: http://www2.promisekeepers.org/2a8a.html.

CHAPTER 19

Liberated Through Submission? The Gender Politics of Evangelical Women's Groups Modeled on the Promise Keepers

by Tanya Erzen

In August 1997, 16,000 women gathered at the Civic Arena Stadium in Pittsburgh to create a forum for spiritual guidance and inspiration, and to listen to speakers' testimonials about healing and reaching out to other women during tough times. At first glance, the event bore a resemblance to a massive consciousness-raising session replete with calls for sisterhood and solidarity. However, this was neither a feminist organization nor political rally, but rather part of the national Joyful Journey conference series sponsored by Women of Faith, a Christian women's organization modeled on Promise Keepers that brings women together to equip them to become vital parts of their churches and communities. Joyful Journey is hardly unique, as the past four or five years have witnessed the emergence of a burgeoning Christian women's movement spurred on by PK's initial organizational successes, and by the personal changes women have observed in the men in their lives as a result of attending PK events. While most of these women's organizations support and emulate the structure of PK in some way, they maintain few organizational links with one another and eschew coordinating joint events. The message of these groups is twofold: they appeal to women's need for spiritual renewal while emphasizing the centrality of women's submission to God and a biblically mandated male-headed household as the key to fulfillment and happiness.

This essay analyzes Women of Faith and Chosen Women: Daughters of the King, two of the numerous evangelical Christian women's groups, focusing on their adherence to a doctrine of submission as the foundation for their conferences, stadium events and small group meetings. Women join these organizations out of fervent religious beliefs and a desire to build community and empowerment. As part of their participation, women in these groups conceptualize their identities as part of the discourse of submission and acquiesce to rigid conceptions of proper masculine and feminine gender roles. In an unusual variation on women's liberation, the leadership and participants in both organizations have re-appropriated the term submission to represent what author P.B. Wilson terms "liberation through submission." Women involved in the leadership and conference attendees interpret submission in relationship to traditional notions of masculine and feminine roles and identity, and popular cultural ideas about therapy and healing. While these organizations remain complicit with the PK agenda of biblically-mandated male leadership in families, women interpret and incorporate submission into their daily lives in multifarious ways. Women bring various meanings and interpretations to the biblical conception of submission and, at times, create a more flexible discourse in which spaces are available for alternative family and gender configurations.

Similar to the PK model, the organizations mainly grow and develop through women's participation in stadium conferences. Although women have returned to their communities and formed small groups based on the models of Women of Faith and Chosen Women, the stadium conferences are the galvanizing event that produces a collective experience and temporary group identification for many of the women who attend. Spectacular and highly emotional, the evangelical conference event is a means through which communities are constructed as women network with other women, hear anecdotal testimonials about their lives and even re-dedicate themselves to Jesus. Loosely structured on the religious revival model, the conferences have five speakers who give long testimonials punctuated by singing, praying and small group testimonies. The speakers urge women to experience life to the fullest while also relating grueling experiences of poverty, death and marital discord that can only be overcome by faith and submission to God. By understanding how the speakers' testimonials invoke the concept of submission and how women interpret the meanings of submission, it is possible to analyze the cultural logic by which women organize their lives and activism on deeply emotional and affective levels. This is central in addressing how the members of Chosen Women and Women of Faith view themselves in terms of cultural and political change and in relation to feminist movements and secular women's organizations.

The Chosen and the Faithful

Despite the overwhelming support for Promise Keepers expressed by women involved in Women of Faith and Chosen Women, both organizations are firm in distancing their events and agenda from PK. The overall sentiment at Chosen Women's Rosebowl event was that this was a women's "fishing trip," not to be construed as solely a female version of a PK event. In Pittsburgh, Connie McCoy, the public relations director of Women of Faith, stated:

> women come from different nationalities, backgrounds, and age groups and share common emotions. We know that the powerful overruling thing is faith in God and that God will see us through. Our approach is different than Promise Keepers, and we're not tied in to Promise Keepers. Different needs are addressed in terms of different gender type things. A woman can only be a mother just as a man can only be a father [McCoy, 1998].

Unlike other groups such as Praise Keepers and Suitable Helpers, these organizations are not directly supporting PK, but using the PK model to build spiritual communities of women that are distinct from yet supportive of men involved in PK. Stephen Arterburn, Women of Faith's founder, emphasized, "Men go to Promise Keepers and cry. Women come to this and they laugh. There is a need for men to get together in order to commit and repent and to tell ourselves we will do better. But women have been talking to each other, staying true to their commitments and trying harder for a long time" (Lindelof, 1997).

Chosen Women: Daughters of the King was formed in 1994 by Pat Clary and Susan Kimes out of a decade-old organization called the Network of Evangelical Women in Ministry, which provided support for women clergy leaders. Chosen Women literature states that its goal is creating an organization dedicated to striving for reconciliation between races and religious denominations (Chosen Women, 1997). Chosen Women sponsored a massive conference at the Rosebowl in Los Angeles on May 16, 1997, with 40,000 women in attendance. The organizers said that the conference would be a one-time event rather than the kernel of a more far-reaching Christian women's movement. However, Susan Kimes, founder of Chosen Women, sponsored an even more ambitious conference in May 1998 and has plans for future stadium gatherings. Chosen Women collaborates closely with Calvary Chapel, the Billy Graham Crusade, and James Dobson's right-wing Focus on the Family. In preparation for its stadium event in May 1998, Chosen Women attended a 1996 Pasadena PK event to gain experience with the logistical aspects of organizing a large stadium event.

Women of Faith, the Joyful Journey was initiated by Stephen Arterburn, chief executive officer of the Laguna Beach, CA, Minirth Meier New Life Clinics. New Life Clinics is a Christian mental health care provider and psychological counseling center headquartered in Richardson, TX. In 1996, more than 150,000 women attended 10 "Joyful Journey" conferences sponsored by the New Life Clinics throughout the U.S. (Women of Faith, 1997). Arterburn is quoted in a Women of Faith press release as saying that, "Our desire is for women across this nation to have their lives transformed and their spiritual passion restored" (Women of Faith, 1997). Bill Bright, head of the Campus Crusade for Christ and a longtime right wing political activist, is a partner in Women of Faith's outreach program, lending financial support for conferences and meetings.

Women of Faith has recently created partnerships with *Christian Woman* magazine, a publication of Christianity Today, Inc.; Women Today International, a ministry of Campus Crusade for Christ; and World Vision, a program which raises funds for women living in poverty around the world (Women of Faith, 1998). The organization planned to hold stadium events similar to the one in Pittsburgh in 30 cities in 1998.

Unlike Chosen Women and Women of Faith, other women's organizations such as Suitable Helpers, Promise Reapers and Heritage Keepers have formed, as their names suggest, to specifically support Promise Keepers. These ministries emulate PK and hold conferences for women where they are "empowered" to fulfill their roles as support for men.

Suitable Helpers, established in October 1993 by Cheri Bright, has a national office in Colorado and regional offices in Indiana, Kansas, Michigan and Virginia Beach. Bright said 5,000 women's names are on their mailing list and about 200 to 700 women attend their conferences. Suitable Helpers is a non-denominational organization that expands through local community prayer core groups whose ostensible purpose is to pray effectively for their husbands. The organization's flyers state that Suitable Helpers exists "to teach women to be a servant unto the Lord and then a helpmate to whomever He may bring into their lives. Our charge is to be in prayerful support of the army of men that God is raising up."

Promise Reapers was founded in 1994 by Mary Ann Bridgewater, and claims to have more than 1,000 women on its mailing list. The organization exists to support PK through the creation of prayer guides, organized prayer in churches in cities where PK holds events, and often to be on site at the conferences to pray for the men.

Founded in December 1995 by Lori Beckler, the Heritage Keepers had its first conference in August 1996, with 2,000 women attending, in Wichita. It is a non-denominational group that exists alongside PK to encourage and affirm men involved. Beckler, however, has expressed that Heritage Keepers is not only for PK wives, and the organization actively encourages young women and elderly women to attend its events. One of the organization's stated purposes is to build fellowship among Christian women, create an environment in which God can heal the hurts of women and encourage women to make an impact within their home, church and community. "We are hoping that women leave these conferences with a stronger relationship with their lord and savior," said Beckler (1997).

Despite the groups' gestures to the contrary, Suitable Helpers, Promise Reapers, and Heritage Keepers exist fundamentally as PK auxiliaries, whereas Chosen Women and Women of Faith openly refute the notion that they are female Promise Keepers. In 1997 Cheri Bright wrote in the Suitable Helpers newsletter about the formation of the group:

> And I was praying that night for the men, all of a sudden my prayers changed. The prayer went, "Lord, help the women to receive these men with love and open hearts when they come home. Don't let them blow those fires out that you have lit in their lives this night." And the lord said, "Yes, the women Cheri. I'm building a mighty army out there and now I'm calling upon the women to know how to receive that army when they come home."

At conferences, speakers discuss prayer, marriage and their relationship to God, but PK seems to dominate testimonials, outreach and even prayer. Although the groups do not work together to coordinate events, many of the conference speakers, such as Barbara Johnson, rotate between women's conferences. Wellington Boone and Kathryn Boone have spoken frequently at Heritage Keeper conferences. PK's prominence was evident at the April 1996 Suitable Helpers New Beginnings conference in Abilene, KS. Conference attendee Karen Kurth wrote in the Suitable Helpers newsletter:

> Saturday afternoon several testimonies were heard and then the Promise Keepers who were present were invited to come to the podium. They got two standing ovations and many shouts. (They were present to help out in any way they could and were praying over the many prayer requests that we put into a small basket in the front of the church.) They were asked to kneel and some of the women in the audience went up and placed their hands on the men's shoulders while prayers were said for them. Then they stood and were hugged by several women. Prayers were said for the PK conference to be held in Kansas City on April 27.

Chosen Women and Women of Faith vie for the same constituencies, and have significant crossover in terms of purpose and overall structure, yet proclaim ignorance of all but the most basic facts about each other. Women of Faith's stated purpose is to "help women experience a deeper encounter with God and with each other .... to become vital parts of their churches and communities" (Women of Faith, 1998). Chosen Women's stated purpose is for women "to reevaluate their relationships and participate in a form of spiritual renewal for women to be transformed" (Herdrich, 1997). The publicly stated purpose of both organizations is to build a non-denominational ministry for Christian women from all nationalities, age groups and backgrounds who also are involved in their own churches. As in PK, the spring and summer are allocated for stadium conferences while the rest of the year is spent planning and fundraising. Women of Faith views the conferences as opportunities for women to address disparate concerns such as how to be mutually supportive of one another, how to pray, how to control weight, how to avoid having affairs and how to assist women in their own spiritual growth. Other participants interviewed in Pittsburgh utilized the event as a rare opportunity to "get a break from the kids," "get rejuvenated," "be with other Christian women" and "jump-start our walk with the Lord" (Grave, 1997). Minus the overriding religious aspect, these rationales and motivations resonate with the initial consciousness-raising purpose of feminism in the 1970s.

The leadership and spokeswomen for Chosen Women and Women of Faith are careful to distance the organizations from political issues and a wider political agenda. Connie McCoy said that Women of Faith employs a "testimonial rather than topical approach," and that "the issues look political but are really spiritual and emotional" (McCoy, 1997). However, it is apparent that politics lurks just below the surface in the organizations' financial connections and speakers' choice of topics. Chosen Women's director, Susan Kimes, has been active in anti-abortion counseling, and added in her speech at the Rosebowl that abortion was contributing to the nation's moral decay. Barbara Johnson, a Women of Faith speaker, is a founder of Exodus International, the main organization in the "ex-gay" movement seeking to change gay men and lesbians. In addition, the fact that the organizations receive funding from Focus on the Family and the Campus Crusade for Christ links them to a wider right-wing agenda. Speakers at the Rosebowl and Civic Arena events focused on the issues of submission, gender roles and homosexuality, using personal experience to intervene in wider political and cultural debates.

The political and cultural impact of both organizations will become more evident as their plans to open ministries in Thailand and Latin America begin to materialize. The international expansion of evangelical women's groups will require the economic support of religious organizations already extant in those countries as well as possible financial leverage from global corporations that are in line with their agendas. The previous models of missionary groups will no longer be relevant as these women's organizations have begun to conflate ideas about therapy and self help with evangelical religious precepts such as submission. This model of "therapeutic" healing, based on the success of groups on the United States such as Alcoholics Anonymous, may not function as effectively in countries that are overwhelmingly Catholic. The expansion of Chosen Women and Women of Faith will confront the cultural and political agendas of liberal and leftist women's organizations already functioning in Thailand and Latin America that may view submission quite differently. They also must contend with entrenched ideas about the legitimacy of women gathering together to publicize concerns that traditionally have been relegated to the private realm. It seems apparent that the imminent globalization of Chosen Women and Women of Faith will alter the organizations profoundly, and force the leadership to evaluate how ideas about gender roles and submission translate into other cultural, religious and economic contexts.

"I Surrender All": The Discourse of Submission

The organizations voluntarily embrace the concept of male authority and female submission grounded in evangelical interpretations of submission in the Bible at the leadership and participant levels. According to the biblical principle of submission, a wife submitting to her husband is submitting to Jesus and thus, "a woman does so with love and trust, knowing that the husband must love his wife as his own body and as Jesus loves us" (Kimes, 1997). A woman at the Pittsburgh Women of Faith conference was nonplussed in her assertion that, "I submit out of love not out of a power struggle" (Schneider, 1997). The religious belief system surrounding submission functions as a way to regulate social behavior such as gender roles and sexuality. Therefore, while gender roles are considered essential and divinely ordained, the manner in which women and men enact them varies according to how the discourse of submission is negotiated at the local level and in secular contexts.

The groups' leadership and literature describe the cultural narratives of submission and enforced heterosexuality as Christian norms to which women involved in the groups should ascribe. However, individual women interact with these discourses differently depending on their own circumstances. Local interpretations of submission illustrate how the discourses of submission and heterosexuality circulate differently in a conference as opposed to the domestic sphere. One woman said, "A lot of things are going to change in my house when I get home. I'm struggling to listen to my husband because I know that's what God wants me to do" (Lezynski, 1997). P.B. Wilson, a Chosen Women speaker and author of *Liberated Through Submission: The Amazing Paradox*, told women never to accept physical abuse, yet stated that some women have waited for God to work in their lives and the abuse has ended. Others advocated submission to the will of God, but not necessarily to their husbands. Wilson's anecdotes illustrate that the meanings of submission change in a variety of contexts. This was evident in Wilson's anecdote about a woman whose husband stopped having extramarital affairs after 15 years because she had submitted, prayed and been patient. Even in the case of battering, Wilson (1990) writes that a woman should never "desert a difficult marriage

... she needs to challenge her spouse to get help through Christian counseling." A Pittsburgh conference participant put it succinctly when she said, "The man is head of the household with God leading him, and it's wonderful to surrender to God. What's the big deal if he has to submit to God as well?" (Tippincott, 1997).

The most formidable task Chosen Women and Women of Faith have is to recast a traditionally Christian doctrine of female submission to male authority into formulations that are appealing to women. In order to translate a religious principle into a secular context, speakers and organizational literature invoke the currently dominant therapeutic ideas about healing and transformation. Intersections of religious and secular interpretations of submission are at the crux of these organization's arguments. To demonstrate the appeal of submission, Women of Faith and Chosen Women stress that submission is a form of religious liberation. P. B. Wilson (1990), who spoke at the Rosebowl conference, wrote,

> submission ... means to yield—yield to people, precepts and principles that have been placed in our lives as authorities.... Submission without faith is slavery. Submission with faith is power! It takes faith to believe that God is correcting a relationship, situation or circumstance when all outward signs show the opposite.

As Wilson explained, God is not the only arbiter of submission; it is within the realm of gender roles in a universally heterosexual world that the doctrine of submission will have the most impact.

The transmission and re-articulation of submission into the worldly or secular context of marriage, dating and even single status comprises the bulk of Wilson's book and the content of both the Rosebowl and Pittsburgh conferences. Wilson and other leaders of these groups believe in the "God-given right" of male authority. Fundamentally, submission translates into relegating all decisions and leadership to the authority figure in a woman's life: boss, pastor, boyfriend or husband. A Pittsburgh conference attendee explained the decision making process as "if together we're trying to make a decision and if in the end we still differ, he makes the decision. It may not be the right decision and we should have done it my way, but I'm blessed by the Lord for submitting to my husband" (Schneider, 1990). Biblical precepts are transfigured for a secular context as when Wilson (1990) writes,

> Woman was created to be man's helpmate. That means she should be an integral part of her husband's life, enabling him to fully develop into the kind of man God wants him to be.... However, without some very specific guidelines—husbands lead, wives submit—our sinful natures will cause us to make adjustments to God's sovereign plan.

How else to describe the concept of submission except as blatantly bolstering male authority and dominance within traditional configurations of the heterosexual family? But Wilson and other Chosen Women members view submission as inherently liberating. The ultimate paradox of liberation through submission releases women from "rebellion, defensiveness, contempt and frustration" through faith in God's power to guide the worldly relationships between men and women (Wilson, 1990). With God directing gender roles and heterosexuality firmly entrenched, masculine and feminine identities are clearly delineated and life is generally less conflict-ridden. A woman who refuses to submit not only forfeits the possibilities of her own adherence to God's will, she emasculates and undermines a natural and divinely-mandated masculine identity. Wilson (1990) writes, "When a woman takes over the role or otherwise finds herself being head of the house, she usually adopts certain attitudes toward her husband: one is disdain, the other is disrespect."

The anxiety around submission and proper masculine and feminine identities revolves around the inability of the groups to conceptualize other gender configurations besides heterosexuality. Heteronormativity enables the concept of submission to work as long as it is continually posited as the norm against which other deviant sexual identities are defined. The highlight of the Pittsburgh Women of Faith conference was the presentation by Barbara Johnson, a speaker whose wryly humorous take take on the ordeals of her life characterizes her book *Where Does a Mother Go to Resign?* Johnson's two-hour testimonial detailed the death of two sons, and the metaphorical death of the third when he admitted his homosexuality to her. The speech functioned as a narrative of personal regeneration that moved from Johnson as "victim" of a homosexual son, to a rebirth that culminated in the founding of Exodus International and Spatula Ministries—a ministry for fundamentalist Christians who suffer when their children come out of the closet. Throughout her narrative of redemption, Johnson emphasized the trauma of her experience because of the incompatibility of homosexuality with her evangelical Christian beliefs. "I believed there was nothing God and mothers couldn't fix," she said (Johnson, 1997). After her son left home for 15 years, it was only his subsequent decision to come out of what she calls "the gay lifestyle" that could placate and comfort her. Although she believes in a Christian concept of unconditional love, she clings to the concept of loving the sinner and hating the sin. Johnson adamantly differentiates her ministry from something like PFLAG (Parents and Friends of Lesbians and Gays), emphasizing that she would never march in a parade or carry a banner in support of gay people.

Johnson also would never advocate submission as a way of dealing with her son's sexuality. Submission, say Wilson and Johnson, is only applicable when it reinforces male authority in a heterosexual context. Within a discourse of submission and heteronormativity it is imperative for Women of

Faith and Chosen Women to position homosexuality as a lifestyle choice that perverts the normal masculine or feminine identity. Without this rigid notion of masculine and feminine identity, the identities of the women in these groups are thrown into disarray. The organization's concept of submission and sexuality renders it virtually impossible for the groups to even consider women's experiences in non-heterosexual contexts.

Submission is not a static concept, but one that has a long history in evangelical culture. Similarly, as has been shown, the scripts of submission available to women in Chosen Women and Women of Faith vary among individuals, speakers and even events. Bunny Wilson and Susan Kimes argue that submission leads to freedom and transformation because it becomes a means of asserting power over negative circumstances and accepting that God eventually eases pain and heals survivors. They situate submission as a question of semantics, consisting of dependency and compliance rather than helplessness or grim resignation. From my interviews, it was apparent that submission was a concept to which women bring a wide variety of interpretations in their local applications. Some adamantly refused to adhere to submission in any guise; others stated that it was an ongoing process; some stated that they utilized submission as a manipulative strategy to get what they needed from their husbands; and some women were unabashed in stating that they enjoyed being free from having to make stressful decisions.

Despite the potential for reinterpretation, the highly-gendered language of submission clearly places the power of decision making and control with a man. The meanings informing male authority and female submission are intimately attached to the ideals of home and family as the authentic and natural set of interlocking roles and identities. Many women interviewed stated that through acting out submission, they were actually able to negotiate more power for themselves in their relationships. How these negotiations play out on the local level of the domestic sphere would require further ethnographic research. It seems possible, however, that women can operate within a rigid gender model and still gain power and leverage for themselves in their relationships. Marie Griffith (1997) writes that this is "power in vulnerability or the willed effacement to a gentle omnipotence which, far from 'complementing' masculinism, acts as its undoing." It remains to be seen how this subversion of submission would function in a non-domestic sphere such as the workplace, in which other types of power are constantly negotiated.

EVANGELICAL THERAPY

Evangelicalism is a tradition saturated with narratives of personal experience, and the speakers utilize a vocabulary of healing, transformation, liberation and deliverance when they give their testimonies. The conferences serve most tangibly as support groups in which participants are encouraged to feel safe about speaking about traumatic as well as humorous life experiences. Women of Faith speaker Patsy Clairmont, author of *Normal is Just a Setting on Your Dryer*, asked women if they had brought their emotions with them and then held up a tangled bundle of rope to represent how she was feeling that day (Clairmont, 1997). As Bunny Wilson spoke on stage at the Rosebowl, she directed women to gather in groups of three to testify to their own hardships and difficulties in submitting. This set up a dynamic of female bonding in the stadium that many women posited as their impetus for attending the event. One participant in the Rosebowl event said, "The speakers are living proof that the Lord sustains what he ordains" (Tippincott, 1997). These life stories as both spoken and written texts are flexible vignettes and anecdotes with specific ends: the lesson of God's constant guidance and the storytellers' need to surrender to God's and men's loving will transform them into different and better women.

The structure and rhetoric of the groups borrows from the therapeutic small group movement with its narratives of healing, transformation and sharing as a model for personal and political change. Women of Faith sponsors small group "intensives" with titles such as "Friends Through Thick and Thin" and "Change Your Life." Booths at Woman of Faith sell speakers' books; including such titles as *Let Prayer Change Your Life* by Becky Tirabassi; *Pack up the Gloomies in a Great Big Box Then Sit on the Lid and Laugh* and *Somewhere Between Estrogen and Death* by Barbara Johnson; *Bumblebees Fly Anyway—Defying the Odds at Work and Home* by Thelma Wells; and *Holding Onto Heaven with Hell on Your Back* by Shelia Walsh. Each narrative contains a traumatic event, a feeling of victimization, the realization of God's guidance once a woman is willing to submit and final redemption and renewed insight as the just reward. Shelia Walsh, former co-host of the 700 Club, discussed her battle with depression—a depression that happened, she said, because she had always tried, for God, to do everything perfectly. Eventually Walsh realized she didn't have to be perfect, and "learned the companionship of brokenness. People who love God but don't understand everything" (Reeves, 1997). Speakers have appeared in media venues such as talk shows and Christian television programs in order to bring their messages to a wider audience. In Chosen Women and Women of Faith, Christian piety and popular culture are reconfigured to work in religious and secular contexts. As a result, the structure of the texts and speeches at conferences involve humor, anecdotes, and sense of camaraderie along with the assumption that the listener is a devoted Christian or soon will be.

The testimonials also act as a strategy through which what have been considered private concerns (family, female roles and religion) are brought into a public realm. By situating the testimonies as the central organizing factor of the conferences, Chosen Women and Women of Faith complicate the rigid separation between public and private issues. Testimonies are imbued with communal experience rather than remaining consigned to the realm of the personal. Therefore, the testimonies circulate beyond the site of the conference just as the ideas the groups draw upon also are borrowed from the therapeutic and self-help popular cultural ideas of the wider culture. The testimonies' therapeutic role enable the women's private concerns to be shared publicly and reconfigured. For example, at the Rosebowl, thousands of women poured down to the stage to sing "I Surrender All" in order to demonstrate their commitment to a submission doctrine. This performative emotional event epitomized the dramatic and community-building aspect of the conferences. The conference is a semi-public space where private evangelical women's concerns enter into a wider public realm. However, even as these groups make inroads into wider publics through the use of the media and self-help rhetoric, the audience for the books and conference events remains fairly homogenous and limited to evangelical Christian women.

As part of the drive to broaden the organizations' constituency, both organizations are striving to increase racial sensitivity and promote multiculturalism. P. B. Wilson and other speakers urged each woman to make a concerted effort to talk to a woman of another race during the conference breaks or small group testimonies. She reiterated that this personal communication was "the most important step in bringing down the walls of racism" (Wilson, 1997). This type of racial sensitivity is one of the ways that evangelical organizations have appropriated the discourses of liberal multiculturalism without addressing the structural or economic issues of racism. At the Pittsburgh conference, Thelma Wells discussed the discrimination she had experienced in the job market and schools as well as her family's economic struggles. "We moved up to the projects," she said (Wells, 1997). However, her message emphasized that these obstacles are only overcome by faith, and it seems that for Women of Faith and Chosen Women, racism, sexism and poverty are erased by trust in God. In addition, P. B. Wilson's (1997) speakers' perfunctory answers to questions about gays and lesbians—"God did not want anyone to be homosexual"—make it obvious that an evangelical Christian version of liberal multiculturalism extends only to race and not sexuality. While Chosen Women and Women of Faith stress that their agendas are non-denominational and multicultural, all the women interviewed were part of evangelical rather than mainline Protestant churches, and the overwhelming majority of the attendees were white. Racial diversity is a way that both groups are attempting to attract a wider constituency that would include conservative evangelical women of color. Conference speakers continually stressed that the discourse of submission functions as a universalizing doctrine that crosses national, racial and class lines.

Chosen Women, Women of Faith and Feminism

The shifting debates on gender and sexual equality in the law, politics, economics and family have inevitably influenced evangelical discourses on submission. It is not coincidental that, as more support develops in religious circles for women in ministry and other occupations, groups such as Chosen Women and Women of Faith continue to emphasize traditional and god-ordained roles for women as wives and mothers. Bunny Wilson and Barbara Johnson advocate women's submission to authority figures while, at the same time, they have expanded their roles from mothers and wives into conference speakers and leaders. These shifting notions of female occupation and power are implicated in changing social patterns such as the increased visibility of single motherhood and non-traditional nuclear families. Both groups acknowledge these differences in women's lives but rarely address the implications these circumstances might have on ideas about submission. The leaders of Chosen Women and Women of Faith support the idea that women should bring private concerns, such as marital problems and infidelity, to wider secular and religious publics. This is considered to be the crucial role that "God has called them to play in the making of history" (Wilson, 1997). When evangelical women begin organizing conferences and events, it demonstrates how strict interpretations of submission have given way to more fluent and flexible interpretations in which women take on different roles and responsibilities.

Although the submission doctrine and its concomitant ideals of womanhood and heterosexuality are said to be divinely sanctioned, it also is apparent that the roles women take on as part of this discourse are culturally constructed in response to wider cultural movements such as the rise of feminism. As one of its initial tasks, the feminist movement attempted to focus on women ignored or marginalized in history, politics and the world of social relations. Since the advent of feminism both as a political movement and a set of influential cultural meanings, debates over whom feminism can claim to speak for have perpetually tested the limits of feminist solidarity and inclusion. Many of the women involved in Women of Faith and Chosen Women explicitly position themselves as non-feminists. A woman at the Pittsburgh conference said, "Years ago I joined NOW (The National Organization for Women), and I believe all that stuff about women having rights in the working world, but NOW seems like men-haters—that there is something wrong with men gathering together. I'm not a feminist" (Lezynski, 1997). Women involved in Women of Faith and Chosen Women often articulate the difficulties of incorporating their Christian identities into a feminist organization, and that women with traditional Christian beliefs are often marginalized. Chris Fitzgibbons, a mother and homemaker, expressed these sentiments at a Women of Faith Conference: "Sometimes in the world, as a Christian, you feel very much like the minority. Here you realize there's a majority of us and I guess there's a strength in that" (Berg, 1997). While many women may feel this isolation, it is also a strategy of both organizations to position themselves—white, heterosexual and family oriented—as an embattled minority. Cindy Patton (1993) writes that this New Right strategy in general fuels long simmering anxieties in fundamentalist and evangelical circles about what the New Right claims is the gradual cultural dominance of gay men and lesbians, feminists and racialized groups. This majority-as-embattled-minority stance erases the fact that white, heterosexual and Christian women rarely experience the economic and structural effects of discrimination in the same way as racial groups and gay people.

Another strategy the groups use to argue against feminism is asserting that the 20th-century version of feminism is rampantly materialist and imitative of men. Susan Kimes stated in her Rosebowl speech that feminists judge gender equality in purely commercial terms—promoting women's equal right to money and status and thus pushing them to join the economic scramble of the market (Kimes, 1997). This critique of feminism as capitalist juggernaut reduces the widely contested and multivalent history of feminism and the feminist movement to a monolithic narrative. It also disparages crucial ongoing battles over wages, work and economic justice within the women's movement. Within the context of submission, these groups' participants situate themselves as dissidents who are opposed to the elitism, materialism, apathy and greed of the wider culture that includes feminists. PK also has drawn upon the idea that feminism frees men from their responsibilities to support and protect their families. The assertion that feminism is anti-family positions the blame for wayward husbands or boyfriends upon feminist women rather than on the men themselves. It also assumes that the ideal experience of gender and sexuality centers around the procreative heterosexual family. Single working mothers or single women are accepted as part of the conference events, but the rhetoric of submission is aimed at women in heterosexual relationships. Divorce and the problems single women or mothers face are completely ignored in the conferences because they threaten to undermine the organizing principle of submission. This willful choice or inability to conceptualize other identities beyond a family-centered heterosexual discourse allows the blame for social problems to be attributed to women's inability to submit rather than the economic and political factors that lead to poverty, single motherhood, divorce or abusive relationships.

Despite the vast gaps between feminism and evangelical women's organizing, the ways in which evangelical women communicate their stories to one another and feel transformed by this sharing are not dissimilar to some feminist versions of sisterhood and consciousness raising. "A lot of us have secret tragedies, like a child given up for adoption or memories of sexual abuse," said Mari Hedron, a Women of Faith attendee. "Here, we're sharing those things for the first time with women who can relate and won't condemn us" (Berg, 1997). A more useful way of analyzing the relationship between the two would be to look at overlapping female cultures: what is considered feminism on one hand and evangelical women's groups on the other. A cultural analysis of these opposed constituencies would not be utilized as forms of consensus and continuity, but as tools for understanding the processes by which particular identities are constructed.

CONCLUSION

Chosen Women and Women of Faith have capitalized on the success of PK by tailoring the stadium events and overall structure of PK for women. Unlike the chastisement and vows to become better husbands at PK events, Chosen Women and Women of Faith represent the gentle side of Christian motivation; women find empathy for their troubles and encouragement as long as they're heterosexual, Christian and willing to incorporate submission into their lives. Both groups represent new forms of political and cultural organizing that publicize issues previously deemed highly personal and religious. These organizations' politics are claiming to be constructing female community and spiritual renewal, while also stressing the primary importance of women's submission to God and biblically-mandated male leadership. The appropriation of self-help therapeutic models for religious beliefs has ignited a movement that mobilizes already existing cultural ideas about gender and sexuality in order to further an agenda advocating divine and worldly submission.

Chosen Women and Women of Faith would not be motivational movements without a commercial component. Both organizations state that they subsist on the sale of their books, tapes, calendars, journals, fees for the events, as well as the generosity of the Lord. However, as the early 1998 economic fiasco at PK demonstrates, outside funding is crucial, and the support of organizations such as the Campus Crusade for Christ and Focus on the Family is a necessary economic and political component of both organizations. When questioned, both groups claim they aren't interested in building a larger Christian women's movement, but the Women of Faith press release (1997) states, "What started as a simple idea, has since evolved into one of the most significant and powerful women's movements of this decade." The wider political and cultural impact of these groups will be measured when or if the groups mobilize their members into voter campaigns, local elections or organizations that address specific issues such as abortion or school curricula. Until then, the impact on gender roles and women's leadership is less quantifiable.

The manner in which discourses of submission reinstate male authority and traditional gender roles is one strategy to counter the organization's claims that submission leads to liberation. However, this type of critique cannot ignore that many women claim to experience an improvement in their domestic situations as a result of their adherence to submission. Many interviewees said that when they don't submit, women create marital discord and contribute to the emasculation of the men in their lives. Their local experiences and negotiations of submission are one of the sites where women's identities are reshaped and the rhetoric of submission is negotiated. Because the submission discourse has been appropriated by a fairly homogenous and culturally specific group of women, it will have to be malleable enough to function in disparate cultural contexts as the constituency of the organizations change. This will be crucial as both organizations complete their plans to open ministries in Thailand, Australia and Latin America. How the evangelical discourse of submission is negotiated in local and global cultural contexts is important because, despite where it travels, it nonetheless hinges on fundamentally conservative notions of gender and sexual identity.

References

Beckler, L. (1997, February 18). Personal phone interview.
Berg, T. (1997, September 14). Christian women unite. *The Orange County Register*, A6.
Bright, C. (1997, February 16). Personal telephone interview.
Clairmont, P. (1997, August 11). Recorded speech.
Grave, L. (1997, August 11). Personal interview.
Griffith, M. (1997). *God's daughters: Evangelical women and the power of submission*. Berkeley. CA: University of California Press.
Herdrich, J. (1997). Chosen Women: Daughters of the King information packet.
Herdrich, J. (1997, May 15). Personal interview.
Johnson, B. (1994). *Where does a mother go to resign?* Minneapolis, MN: Bethany House Publishers.
Johnson, B. (1997, August 11). Recorded speech.
Kimes, S. (1997, May 15). Recorded speech.
Lezynski, J. (1997, August 11). Personal interview.
Lindelof, B. (1997, June 27). Christian women to take joyful journey. *The Sacramento Bee*, C3.
McCoy, C. (1997, August 2). Personal interview.
McCoy, C. (1998). Women of Faith press release.
Patton, C. (1993). Tremble, Hetero swine! In Michael Warner (ed.), *Fear of a queer planet: Queer politics and social theory* (143–177). Minneapolis, MN: University of Minnesota Press.
Reeves, B. (1997, November 8). Faith, joy mark women's conference. *Lincoln Journal Star*, B4.
Schneider, L. (1997, August 11). Personal interview.

Tippincott, S. (1997, August 11). Personal interview.
Wells, T. (1997, August 11). Recorded speech.
Wilson, P.B. (1990). *Liberated through submission: The ultimate paradox*. Eugene, OR: Harvest House Publishers.
Wilson, P.B. (1997, May 15). Recorded speech.

CHAPTER 20

Who Are These Guys? The Promise Keepers' Media Relations Strategy for "Stand in the Gap"

by Ken Waters

> *Many motives drove people to travel sometimes long distances to attend camp meetings. Along with religion, they sought camaraderie, diversion from routine, and relaxation from labor. The gratification and the pleasure were not even disguised. People looked forward to revivals in the same way they looked forward to a "mammoth picnic"; campsites came complete with concession stands selling gingerbread, lemonade, and, in the days before temperance took over, liquor"* [Moore, 1994, p. 45].

On October 4, 1997, Promise Keepers held one of the largest camp meetings in history, a six-hour gathering of prayer and fellowship the group called "Stand in the Gap: A Sacred Assembly of Men." Nearly a million men jammed the Mall in Washington, DC, and enjoyed camaraderie, diversion from the routine and a relaxation from labor. As with camp meetings on the American frontier, the religious faithful prayed, praised and listened to a plethora of speakers dispensing words of encouragement and exhortation.

Journalists worldwide covered Stand in the Gap, presenting an image of a religious gathering that was both old-fashioned in its call for repentance, and high tech in its use of massive video screens to bring the activities on the stage to the assembled masses. Comparisons with other large rallies and marches—for Civil Rights, against the Vietnam War and for African-American male solidarity—also dominated the principal frame through which the story was told. While the "historic march" frame dominated news discourse about PK, a second frame highlighted the desired news value of conflict. The conflict came from the persistent and shrill opposition voiced by the National Organization for Women and other feminist groups.

Students of religion and culture might note that the favorable media coverage of Stand in the Gap seems at odds with the traditional viewpoint that secular media are biased against, and don't understand or appreciate, evangelical Christians (Claussen, 1996; Dart & Allen, 1995). But a well-executed strategy by PK and its public relations counsel influenced a reporting agenda focused on the sacred assembly of faithful pilgrims undergoing continual harassment at the hands of a marginalized feminist minority. Ultimately, PK answered its critics without engaging them in a potentially damaging debate, and—to use classical marketing terminology—let its satisfied customers speak about the efficacy of its product. A thorough reading of several hundred print and broadcast news stories found that media reported that the PK pilgrims did exactly what they said they would do— they came to Washington to pray and repent—nothing more, nothing less.

THE NATURE OF FRAMING AND AGENDA SETTING

Two theoretical concepts are important to an understanding of how the media covered Stand in the Gap. Framing is a construct that helps explain why and how certain facts and impressions of a news event become prioritized as a story is written. Gitlin defines framing as "persistent patterns of cognition, interpretation, and presentation, of selection, emphasis, and exclusion, by which symbol-handlers routinely organize discourse, whether verbal or visual" (Gitlin, 1980, p. 7). Frames guide our attention and help us determine what is relevant. Additionally, they serve as "tuning mechanisms by directing our exploration and attention; they lead us to selectively attend to information" (Yows, 1996, p. 15). Framing is a social process, conditioned by the personal beliefs of the journalists and the organizational and professional constraints imposed upon them (Tuchman, 1978). Creating a news story, then, is a value-laden process that advocates to audiences a certain way of understanding an issue or event. Finally, once the associations and symbols have been created and communicated through a news piece, that story's influence throughout future discourse is assured (Entman, 1991; Gamson and Modigliani, 1989).

Agenda setting is a concept often discussed in parallel with framing (Shaw and McCombs, 1972). Agenda-setting theory states that when editors choose and display news, they play an important part in shaping the political and social reality of news consumers. Through the placement of a story, or the words and images used to describe the event and its characters, media people in essence tell their audience: "Here is something to think about now." Cohen noted that the media "may not be successful much of the time in telling people what to think, but it is stunningly successful in telling its readers what to think about" (Hanson & Maxcy, 1996, p. 82).

While framing particular events into a news story (and thus setting the agenda for what we ought to think about) is the task of the journalist, suggestions for how the story should be framed or "spun" increasingly originate with communication experts employed by companies or organizations. These public relations practitioners exert strong influence over the news gathering agenda of any given day. Many newspaper and most television news operations are shrinking; the exponential increase in events to write about and issues to explore means news gathering is at best a haphazard art or craft rather than a science. Public relations practitioners are thus in a strong position to provide journalists with information and access to sources. Through this control, PR people influence both the availability and the shaping of information, and thus influence the creation of the frame the journalist uses to communicate an event or issue to his or her audience.

CREATING A NATIONAL MEDIA STRATEGY

PK attracted ever-increasing media attention in America during the early 1990s, as evangelical men flocked to stadiums for weekend rallies. But the organization had shied away from any formal public relations program, and had answered media inquiries only as they arose. In October of 1996, PK retained the Russ Reid Agency, a pioneer in direct mail and direct response fundraising for nonprofit agencies (Waters, 1998). The organization also contracted with the DeMoss Group to provide media services such as logistics and the issuance of press credentials for Stand in the Gap. Both of these agencies have extensive ties to conservative Christian issues and causes. Reid's first client in the 1970s was World Vision, now one of the world's largest relief and development agencies. Reid's marketing expertise helped that agency grow exponentially through the 1970s and 1980s, and the agency also assists St. Jude's Hospital, Habitat for Humanity and other cause-related organizations. Bill McCartney may have been "only" a football coach, but the networks that he and his vice presidents had established were linked deeply into a core of evangelical Christianity that holds Christians can remain outside the negative cultural pull of society while working to redeem it through their influence. Evangelicals such as Billy Graham, Pat Robertson, Dr. Jim Dobson and Reid contend that "communication technologies are potent forces that will transform evil into good" (Schultze, 1987). These evangelicals have readily embraced the latest technology and media expertise to communicate their conservative religious beliefs to mass audiences. Thus when PK began looking for help in promoting Stand in the Gap, Reid presented a natural blend of communication expertise and philosophical compatibility.

Reid proposed to PK a PR strategy aimed at piquing media curiosity to the point that reporters would ask: "Who are these guys?" Along with supplying historical information about PK, the Reid agency suggested stressing to the media the uniqueness of an event on the Washington Mall devoted solely to prayer and confession, not to protest. "We wanted to leave the American people with the image of a man praying on bended knee, not gesturing with a clenched fist," said the Reid agency's Mark McIntyre (1998). PK leadership also decided not to talk about how many men might attend, because they believed such speculation could backfire, as it apparently had for organizers of the Million Man March. "Promise Keepers leadership genuinely felt that the number of men coming was not as important as the fact that those who did come knew why they were there" (McIntyre, 1998).

The first PR effort of the newly formed PK/Reid team was to quietly "leak" information to selected columnists and religion editors, and feed the media's built-in perception that given past attendance at stadium rallies, a national PK event could be massive. Reid media relations specialist Peter Arnold spoke in early December with Laurie Goodstein, a religion writer with *The Washington Post*. Although the date for Stand in the Gap had not been confirmed, and the conversation was more a "heads-up" than a pitch for an article, Goodstein (1996) wrote the next day that PK planned to muster "a massive spiritual revival on the Mall." The article also noted that the intent was "evangelical, not political," while giving readers a seven-paragraph background on the movement—the first of many "Who are these guys?" articles that would be published in months to come.

The first official announcement of Stand in the Gap took place in Washington, DC, in February 1997. PK communication director Steve Ruppe (1997) described the assembled media as "skeptical" of Stand in the Gap. Still, the leads of both *The Washington Post* (Loose, 1997) and *Newsday* (Keeler, 1997) articles referred to the upcoming gathering as "massive" and "mammoth," respectively, and both invoked comparisons to the Million Man March of October 1995. In concert with the announcement, PK unveiled an extensive web site devoted to Stand in the Gap. In addition to providing general information regarding the event, the web site also served to provide answers to frequently asked questions so that men who might be interviewed by local media would have the benefit of knowing how PK's leadership would answer those questions. This facilitated a strategic need for as many PK adherents as possible to "speak with one voice" when interviewed by the news media.

A succinct summary of Promise Keepers' central messages is contained in an August 1 news release posted on the web site. First, the release claimed the Mall would be "the site of a massive gathering unlike any in history," noting that PK had since 1992 drawn 2.6 million men to 58 stadium conferences. The second message emphasized that momentum for the event was snowballing. Evoking that imagery of eager pilgrims, the release informed media that trains, planes and buses were being chartered by the hundreds and that most local hotels were booked solid. The third theme reiterated the purpose of Stand in the Gap. McCartney was quoted as saying the event would "gather a diverse multitude of men to confess personal and collective sin.... We believe God wants men to accept responsibility for the well-being of their families." The fourth theme stressed the need to gather in Washington, DC. President Randy Phillips explained that the Mall was chosen because it was "the emotional heart of America, set apart as a piece of land for all people, not owned by any one state."

NOW's COUNTERATTACK

Even before PK announced its intention to gather on the Mall, national women's groups had expressed their concern. The National Organization for Women (NOW) began speaking out against PK in 1996 as NOW leaders became increasingly alarmed by large numbers of men assembling in stadiums espousing conservative biblical interpretations on gender issues. In 1997, NOW launched a "No Surrender" campaign, using news releases, speeches, staged news events and a comprehensive web site to launch "a nationwide campaign to expose the Promise Keepers' hidden agenda" and to counter the organization's desire to create "an ultra-conservative nation with men at the helm of all political and religious institutions" (NOW web site). NOW president Patricia Ireland said in a press alert, "The Promise Keepers have created a false veneer of men taking responsibility, when they really mean men taking charge. Their targets are women, lesbians and gay men, and anyone who supports abortion rights or opposes an authoritarian, religiously-based government" (NOW web site).

One month later, marking her re-election as president of NOW, Ireland vowed to continue to expose PK and other ultra-conservative groups "who hide behind a cloak of religion." A few days later, a *New York Times* columnist blistered NOW for its campaign (Ingraham, 1997). Laura Ingraham, also a conservative news analyst for CBS, accused NOW of adopting an anti-Christian agenda, rather than a feminist agenda. "By crusading against a group working to help me be more virtuous, NOW reveals just how out of step it has become with ordinary women," Ingraham charged. Ruppe (1998a) says NOW's attacks on PK caused several female columnists and women's groups to vocalize support for PK. "One of our public relations objectives from the beginning was to defer the discussion about gender issues in society to women. We didn't see that as our issue; we tried to remain fixed on our goal of encouraging as many men as possible to come to Washington to pray." To ensure that women's issues were discussed by women, PK's strategy called for its leaders to avoid direct confrontation with women's groups, referring media inquiries to the wives of PK leaders.

That strategy was tested in the wake of a *Washington Post* op-ed piece

(September 7, 1997) Ireland penned in September. She charged that PK was the "hottest-religious-right marketing tool since televangelism." She said that in adhering to conservative biblical interpretations of the role of women, PK encouraged men to take control of their families, to exert leadership in the home and, thus, to undermine the equal status of women. Second, Ireland said, PK was a tool of right wing conservatism, the so-called Third Wave of the Religious Right following Jerry Falwell and Pat Robertson. She charged, but produced no evidence, that PK was funded by Falwell, Robertson and other religious conservatives, and that PK founder McCartney was instrumental in helping pass Colorado's Amendment 2, the anti-homosexuality law later overturned by the U.S. Supreme Court. Ireland also expressed fear at McCartney's past assertions that PK men must contend for their values through the political process. "There is no way this group can restrict itself when it comes to public policy," McCartney is said to have told a packed stadium in 1993.

In addition to urging the media to capitalize on the resources of its web site, NOW also sent e-mail messages to journalists suggesting questions PK leadership should be asked to answer. PK communication director Ruppe said that when NOW singled out PK as a threat to women's equality, "We were surprised to be so dangerous" (Ruppe, 1998a). He added that once NOW's web site was in place, "it seemed like every journalist we talked to had their questions written for them by NOW." From a media standpoint, NOW's diatribes fulfilled an important journalistic role, that of the addition of conflict to the story. NOW became the anointed opposition to the PK movement, the perfect antagonist for a meta-narrative on gender and culture wars. McIntyre (1998) said that NOW's attacks vis-à-vis PK succeeded in getting the organization mentioned in a number of journals that would not normally write about PK. "Patricia Ireland really helped us," he noted.

WHO ARE THESE GUYS?

Newspaper and Magazine Coverage. Most news stories during September and early October focused on the NOW controversy, although others sought perspective by interviewing the wives of PK adherents (Greene, 1997). Typical were leads such as this (Jones, 1997): "When as many as a million Promise Keepers march on Washington on Oct. 4 for a 'Stand in the Gap' prayer rally in front of the nation's Capitol, a powerful national feminist group will protest it." A mid–September article in the *Christian Science Monitor* (Tyson, 1997) began: "Promise Keepers, the fast-growing Christian revival group that has packed stadiums nationwide, plans to rally a million men in Washington next month for what it calls a day of 'personal repentance and prayer.' Yet swirling around this ostensibly inward-looking, spiritual gathering is a mounting controversy over how the evangelical men's group addresses such hot-button issues as gender, race, and religion in America." As the day of the rally drew near, Philip Terzian (1997), associate editor of the Providence (RI) *Journal-Bulletin*, speculated that despite its numbers, PK would get the "yes, but" treatment in the press. He claimed that reporters would focus more on the naysayers, in this case NOW, than on the overwhelming numbers of well-meaning men assembled in Washington. Expressing surprise at NOW's virulent attacks on PK, Terzian added: "A religious movement that is devoted to rehabilitating the traditional family structure in American life must seem ominous indeed to an extreme political organization that has nothing but contempt for the nuclear family."

The *Washington Post* provided PK the most extensive coverage—58 articles and opinion pieces during 1997 alone. The questions posed by NOW were evident in an interview PK founder McCartney conducted with *The Washington Post* just days after Ireland's opinion piece was published in that paper. In that interview (Escobar & Murphy, 1997a), McCartney reaffirmed that PK would avoid politics at the rally, and would focus instead on its spiritual purpose. In addition, McCartney was quoted as saying that PK's admonition to men to reassert leadership in their families "had been misinterpreted." He agreed with *Post* editors that the statement could lead to skepticism among women's groups, but reiterated PK's contention that a man who is leading does so through servanthood.

One of the first major articles growing out of McCartney's visit with *Post* editors was a 2,400-word story by reporter Caryle Murphy (1997)—an extensive "Who are these guys?" piece. The article highlighted the testimony of dozens of men who planned to attend Stand in the Gap, followed by an analysis of the group's history and appeal using noted theologians and religious commentators as sources, rather than spokespeople from NOW or other feminist groups. A week later, *Post* reporter Gabriel Escobar (1997) traveled to Denver to profile the organization and its leadership. Ruppe (1998b) said Escobar "put us through our paces looking for the hidden agendas" that NOW had promised reporters they would find. The following day the *Post* took a close look at PK's financial arrangements and accounting, noting that the organization "seems as much about big business as about religion" (Torry, 1997). Neither article provided proof that PK was a front for the Religious Right, nor that it had an agenda to suppress women. Ruppe said in dealing with all media, his staff pursued an open policy of providing all financial data and diligently answering media questions, which he believes helped PK establish trust and credibility with *Post* reporters. The newspaper did not uncover a political plot, or financial malfeasance, or Neanderthal attitudes about women, as NOW claimed they would.

Other publications such as *Time* magazine (Stodghill, 1997) also failed to find the nefarious side of PK so feared by NOW. Two other noteworthy articles painted generally favorable impressions of PK, employing both the frames of the great gathering and of the controversy with NOW. Gustav Niebuhr (1997) of *The New York Times* profiled PK in a 1,831-word front-page article the day before Stand in the Gap. Niebuhr's piece looked not only at the movement, but talked to "friendly critics" of PK—women theologians who supported the aims of the group, but not all of its theological justifications. Putting the organization in a context largely ignored by other media, Niebuhr noted that the fact that a coach had built such a large religious movement was evidence that Christianity's energy was coming from "outside traditional institutions ... by men and women skilled at mass communications, entertainment and organization, who possess a keen understanding of the public's hopes and fears."

Columnist David Gergen came to PK's defense just days before Stand in the Gap. Gergen was among a handful of influential columnists visited by Russ Reid public relations specialists intent on helping media better understand the goals of Stand in the Gap. In his *U.S. News & World* report column, Gergen (1997) put the PK event into a perspective of past Great Awakenings in American history. He concluded, "We've had enough stone-throwing. With tens of thousands of men coming to Washington to kneel in prayer, this should be a moment for respect and reconciliation."

Television Coverage. The influence of key print media no doubt influenced television coverage of Stand in the Gap. That news coverage did not begin until the week before the event, focusing on the potential crowd, while answering the question, "Who are these guys?" An *NBC Nightly News* story on September 30 featured PK detractors such as Ireland; but most of the time was spent interviewing PK men who told their story as video footage showed thousands of them singing and praying at past stadium events. Correspondent Jim Avila then interviewed Donna Minkowitz, a freelance reporter who had secretly attended a PK rally in Tampa for *Ms.* magazine. The Minkowitz clip was short, but in it she expressed surprise that the event moved her so deeply. Later in that same news program, anchor Tom Brokaw introduced Holly Phillips, whom he identified as "the wife of one of the original Promise Keepers." More accurately, Holly Phillips is the wife of PK president Randy Phillips, a fact Brokaw should have shared with his viewers. In the Phillips piece—called "In Her Own Words"—Holly Phillips said she had "no problem yielding" to her husband when important decisions needed to be made. "That is not offensive to me and I'm not a doormat; I'm not easily walked upon." Later she added, "People out there are having a problem with personal choices," a not-so-subtle hint to NOW to let women decide for themselves what type of marriage relationship they prefer. Holly Phillips' voice floated over video bites of her husband Randy tossing the dinner salad, and of the happy family settling down for the evening meal.

CNN's October 3 evening news piece on PK ran two minutes, with only 15 seconds devoted to a sound bite from Ireland. The remainder focused on pilgrims arriving by plane, bus and motorcycle and then fanning out to help rebuild Washington, DC. The piece noted that Stand in the Gap would be a Woodstock for Christian men, the largest religious gathering ever held in the United States.

That same evening on its national news show, ABC devoted five and a half minutes to PK. Again the overriding imagery was of men arriving in town, praying in huddled groups and cleaning schools. Religion reporter Peggy Wehmeyer's background piece frames the PK story as a gathering of men to redefine masculinity: openly weeping, praying and forging new bonds of friendship. Ireland's comments were relegated to a five-second sound bite, followed by a rebuttal from a PK leader.

The most interesting pre-event television confrontation that could have happened, didn't. Citing his commitment to be in prayer with the platform speakers the evening before Stand in the Gap, McCartney turned down a request to appear live on *Nightline*. Instead, he taped a segment earlier in the day in which he responded to questions from host Ted Koppel. The news/analysis introduction to the *Nightline* issue stressed the controversy and the possibility that McCartney was another Elmer Gantry. Detractors such as Ireland and the Rev. Barry Lynn were featured at the top of the news report. Once those initial objections were raised, however, the bulk of the program stressed PK's positive contributions with interviews from pastors, PK men and their wives. Koppel asked McCartney the questions posed by NOW, but the tone was even-keeled and respectful, lacking in the cutting follow-up demeanor for which Koppel is known. Koppel questioned McCartney about homosexuality and female submission, allowing the PK founder to quote scripture unchallenged by alternative interpretations of these key biblical passages.

The interview ended with McCartney telling Koppel why he has no political ambitions, saying, "We don't believe that's where the solutions are. We know that man thinks that's where they are, but the Bible says trust in the Lord with all your heart and lean not onto thine own understanding."

MEDIA COVERAGE OF STAND IN THE GAP: WHO'S NOW?

To assist the electronic media in covering the Saturday events of Stand in the Gap, Peter Arnold (1998) of the Russ Reid Company met with CBS officials during the summer of 1997. "We discussed what the networks must have, would like to have, and could live without." By providing a well-built platform for cameras near the stage, easy access and egress through the crowd, and risers for commentator stand-ups at other locations, the job of reporting on the massive event was made easier. "I'd like to think that by working with television to ensure they did their job well, we were able to impact the coverage" (Arnold, 1998).

Perhaps the creation of a more comfortable reporting environment did influence coverage, but it was the massive numbers of men prostrate in prayer, or crying with upraised arms, or embracing men of other ethnic groups that made for a first-rate visual spectacle. CNN reporter Jonathan Karl, standing amidst the assembled men during the rally's final hour, told a live TV audience that the sight was "remarkable; it's something else." Reporter Chip Hale of NBC narrated aerial footage of "a sea of men a mile-and-a-half long." PK men spoke of their commitment to Jesus, to their male friends and family and to spiritual—not political—values. Ireland and feminist protesters received a few seconds of coverage about three minutes into the five-minute NBC story; other protesters, including—among others—topless members of the Lesbian Avengers, were ignored.

Print coverage also waxed eloquent. The *Washington Post* front-page story the following morning said PK converted "Washington's most symbolic open space into a massive revival tent," adding later that that the scene was "often profoundly moving and symbolic" (Escobar & Murphy, 1997b, p. 1). A 660-word story on page 16 (Thompson, 1997, October 5) profiled those who came to protest, but their voices were drowned out by other articles on a father and his son attending Stand in the Gap (Nakamura, 1997, October 5), the views of other women in Washington, D.C., that day (Moreno, 1997, October 5), and an op-ed piece in which PK president Phillips stated again, "We have come to display our spiritual poverty that Almighty God might influence us" (Phillips, p. A20).

Articles in other newspapers around the nation focused on the experiences of hometown pilgrims who had traveled to Washington (Beltrame, 1997; Otto & Kuhnhenn, 1997; Hughes, 1997). A few dozen regional newspaper articles mentioned NOW (Jackson, 1997; Milling, 1997; Rivera & Folkenflik, 1997; Romano, 1997) in their more global stories, but the controversy was buried by descriptions of the massive gathering and comments from those who traveled great distances to attend.

Because no political statements were made by speakers during the conference, NOW's ability to set the agenda for how the rally should be interpreted all but disappeared. The lead in Britain's *Daily Telegraph* (Gordon, p. 12) noted, "Detractors had labeled it a 'festival of anti-feminist and anti-homosexual bigotry.' But it was they who became the butt of criticism yesterday after President Clinton joined those applauding a religious revival that saw up to a million Christian men attending a weekend rally on Washington's Mall."

THE AFTERMATH

Most post-event stories also praised PK for doing what its leaders said it would do, and for cleaning up after themselves. Several columnists and writers cited a *Washington Post* poll (1997, October 11) as substantiating claims made by PK that its followers were not politically motivated; further, the poll reported, most men shared decision-making in the home with their wives, and that their understanding of the biblical idea of submission did not mean oppression. These findings, coupled with the dearth of political statements from the rostrum, were often cited in Monday morning quarterbacking by columnists, especially those who had been cultivated by Reid's McIntyre and Arnold. Conservative columnist Cal Thomas (1997, October 7), among others, praised the non-political bent of Stand in the Gap. He noted that political leaders in Washington were "flummoxed," unable to explain how a million men could come to the capital to "petition a much Higher Authority for a remission of personal and national sins. The gathering could not be explained and those in the big media who tried were mediocre at best."

As Thomas suggests, the secular news media may have been lax at delving into PK's theological and social complexities, and the deeper gender issues raised by Stand in the Gap (cf. Groothuis, R.M., & Groothuis, D., 1997; Stouffer, 1997). Reporters often have been criticized for their inability to properly cover religious movements and the religious motivations of average citizens. Thus the news frame used by most journalists to explain "Stand in the Gap" was that of the largest gathering ever held on the Washington Mall. "Part of the reason we perceive the Promise Keepers rally and the Million Man March as seminal events ... is because numbers matter to the media.... The incantation of 1 million, a magic number, was important" (Head, 1997).

That this mass assembly came not to petition but to pray fit well within a corollary frame of faithful pilgrims assembling for religious instruction and fellowship, just as they had in our romantic conception of American frontier life. NOW added a necessary news ingredient to the Promise Keepers story—that of conflict between the sexes, an irresistible news angle. But when reporters began to ask other American women what they thought, a favorable or neutral impression of the organization emerged. When reporters investigated charges that PK comprises a front for the Religious Right, they could find no smoking gun. At the rally itself, the political polemic PK detractors said would emerge, did not emerge. Thus most of the vocal opposition was marginalized and the focus increasingly shifted to statements from the masses of faithful pilgrims—the "satisfied customers" who came to Washington to stand up for spiritual values with an attitude of humility and solemnity. The pilgrims dripped with credibility; these average Americans spoke with conviction, a conviction that backed up statements from PK leaders.

The central media frame for understanding Stand in the Gap would have been the massive influx of pilgrims regardless of PK's public relations strategy. But by creating a strategy even before announcing Stand in the Gap, and by constantly monitoring that strategy in the face of NOW's onslaught, the organization was able effectively to respond to media investigations and questions, and to engender credibility with key columnists and television executives. Nor should the political savvy of media relations specialists in the Washington office of Russ Reid be overlooked. East Coast–based reporters might have had difficulty taking seriously the claims of a religious men's group with headquarters in the Rocky Mountains. It helped that this group's chief publicists were well-known and well-connected in Washington. Thus the lasting visual and written impression of Stand in the Gap conveyed through the American media closely mirrored the focus PK leaders hoped for when they planned their strategy. The only way the secular media could answer the question, "Who are these guys?" was by invoking the metaphor of faithful pilgrims gathering in record numbers, and by painting a picture of sincere believers with harmless intentions praying for the spiritual survival of their families and their nation.

References

Arnold, P. (1998, May 4). Personal communication.

Avila, J. (1997, September 30). Untitled news story about Promise Keepers. *NBC Nightly News with Tom Brokaw*.

Beltrame, J. (1997, October 5). Promise Keepers pack D.C.: Rally draws up to a million as well as the ire of women. *Montreal Gazette*, A1.

CNN (1997, October 3). Untitled news story about Promise Keepers.

Claussen, D.S. (1996). *United States print mass media coverage of two men's movements: Robert Bly, Iron John and the mythopoets, and Bill McCartney and the Promise Keepers*. Unpublished master's thesis, Kansas State University, Manhattan.

Dart, J., & Allen, J. (1995). *Bridging the gap: Religion and the news media*. Nashville, TN: Freedom Forum First Amendment Center.

Entman, R. (1991). Framing U.S. Coverage of international news: Contrasts in narratives of KAL and Iran Air incidents. *Journal of Communication 41*, 6–27.

Escobar, G. (1997, September 28). He's the coach for the faithful—Or the far right? *The Washington Post*, A1.

Escobar, G., & Murphy, C. (1997a, September 12). Promising a spiritual, apolitical day in D.C. *The Washington Post*, B1.

Escobar G., & Murphy, C. (1997b, October 5). Promise Keepers answer the call: Thousands of men flock to mall for rally both massive and moving. *The Washington Post*, A1.

Gamson, W.A., & Modigilani, A. (1989). Media discourse and public opinion on nuclear power: A constructionist approach. *American Journal of Sociology 95*, 1–37.

Gergen, D. (1997, September 29). Promises worth keeping. *U.S. News & World Report 123*, 78.

Gitlin, T. (1980). *The whole world is watching: Mass media in the making & unmaking of the New Left*. Berkeley, CA: University of California Press.

Goodstein, L. (1996, December 10). Promise Keepers planning massive rally in D.C. *The Washington Post*, A11.

Gordon, H. (1997, October 6). Million Christians confound critics, call for male spiritual leadership. *The Daily Telegraph*, 12.

Greene, M.S. (1997, September 27). Promise Keepers evoke strong emotions. *The Washington Post*, A1.

Groothuis, R.M., & Groothuis, D. (1997, Spring). Women keep promises, too! *Priscilla Papers 11*, 1–9.

Hale, C. (1997, October 4). Untitled coverage of Stand in the Gap. *NBC News*.

Hanson, J., & Maxcy, D. J. (1996). *Sources: Notable Selections in Mass Media*. Guilford, CT: Dushkin Publishing Group.

Head, J. (1997, October 12). Do two marches make a movement? *The Atlanta Journal and Constitution*, 1P.

Hughes, J. (1997, October 5). O.C. group drinks in the promise of the movement. *Orange County Register*, A1.

Ingraham, L. (1997, July 10). Men who can do nothing right. *New York Times*, 1/23.

Ireland, P. (1997, September 7). Beware of "feel-good male supremacy." *The Washington Post*, C3.

Jackson, D. (1997). Promise Keepers' spirit fills DC rally, Christian men vow to be better husbands, dads. *The Dallas Morning News*, 1A.

Jones, J. (1997, September 20). Feminists to protest Promise Keepers. *The Houston Chronicle*, p. 3.

Karl, J. (1997, October 4). Untitled coverage of "Stand in the Gap." *CNN*.

Keeler, B. (1997, February 5). It's a guy thing: Men's rally set for D.C. mall. *Newsday*, A33.

Koppel, T. (1997, October 3). *Nightline*.

Loose, C. (1997, February 5). Promise keepers headed for the mall; Men's Christian group plans Oct. 4 rally. *The Washington Post*, B3

McCombs, M., & Shaw, D.L. (1972). The agenda setting function of mass media. *Public Opinion Quarterly 36*, 176–187.

McIntyre, M. (1998, May 4). Personal communication.

Milling, T.J. (1997, October 5). Prayerful men pack capital's Mall in quest for spiritual renewal. *Houston Chronicle*, p. A1.

Moore, L.R. (1994). *Selling God: American religion in the marketplace of culture*. New York: Oxford Press.

Moreno, S. (1997, October 5). Choosing a place in the crowd: Women's opinions reflect a wide gap. *The Washington Post*, A17.

Murphy, C. (1997, September 21). Seeking God, man to man. *The Washington Post*, B1.

Nakamura, D. (1997, October 5). A father and son stand in the generation gap. *The Washington Post*, A17.

National Organization for Women website (1998). Available: http: www.now.org.
Niebuhr, G. (1997, October 3). Religious rally in capital is a test of faith. *New York Times*, p. A1.
Otto, M., & Kuhnhenn, J. (1997, October 5) They prayed; they pledged: Promise Keepers rally draws thousands of men to Mall in D.C. *The Kansas City Star*, A1.
Promise Keepers website (1998). Available: http: www.promisekeepers.org.
Rivera, J., & Folkenflik, D. (1997, October 5). Multitude fills Mall for revival. *Baltimore Sun*, 1A.
Romano, M. (1997, October 5). Promise Keepers keep faith in huge D.C. rally. *Rocky Mountain News*, 3A.
Ruppe, S. (1997, April 29). Personal communication.
Ruppe, S. (1998a, March 10). Personal communication.
Ruppe, S. (1998b, April 19). Personal communication.
Schultze, Q. (1987). The mythos of the electronic church. *Critical Studies in Mass Communication 4*, 258.
Stodghill, R. II (1997, October 6). God of our fathers. *Time 150*, 34.
Stouffer, A.H. (1997, Spring). Promise Keepers and the third wall. *Priscilla Papers 11*, 10–12.
Terzian, P. (1997, September 6). How will Promise Keepers fare? *The Providence Journal-Bulletin*, 13.
Thompson, C.W. (1997, October 5). Voices of protest raised on the mall: Feminists and atheists are suspicious of prayer rally's agenda. *The Washington Post*, A16.
To save the nation. (1997, October 4). *The Washington Post*, C7.
Promise Keepers poll. (1997, October 11). *The Washington Post*, C7.
Thomas, C. (1997, October 7). Something is stirring in the land. *Buffalo News*, 3-B.
Torry, S. (1997, September 29). Promise Keepers' success also measured in dollars. *The Washington Post*, A1.
Tuchman, G. (1978). *Making news: A study in the construction of reality*. New York: The Free Press.
Tyson, A.S. (1997, September 12). A new stir surrounds men's role. *The Christian Science Monitor*, 1.
Waters, K. (1998). *From obscurity to prominence: The evolution of World Vision's television fundraising programs, 1972–1982*. Manuscript submitted for publication.
Wehmeyer, P. (1997, October 3). Untitled news story about Promise Keepers. *ABC World News Tonight*.
Yows, S.R. (1996, August). *Towards developing a coherent theory of framing: Understanding the relationship between news framing and audience framing*. Paper presented at the meeting of the Association for Education in Journalism and Mass Communication, Anaheim, CA.

Chapter 21

They Just Don't Get It! Promise Keepers' Responses to Media Coverage

by L. Dean Allen II

Several scholars have shown that Promise Keepers (PK), contrary to almost all previous research on coverage of religion—particularly the coverage of conservative Christianity—has received almost wholly uncritical and often clearly positive coverage from the American mass media (Claussen, 1996; Claussen, this volume; Waters, this volume). When critics or opponents are quoted at all, particularly in newspapers and magazines, typically they are represented by a single critic or opponent, often quoted only once in the story, and that single quote is buried anywhere from one-third to three-quarters of the way into the article. Usually, one feminist, one gay rights activist or one liberal theologian essentially is used to represent not only all critics with the same identifying label, but to stand—willingly or not, knowingly or not—for all of PK's critics. And PK critics range from fundamentalists to the right, to liberals to the left, to people interested in upholding the constitutional principle of separation of church and state.

One would not think that PK was receiving overwhelmingly favorable coverage based on the few public statements by PK leaders on their media coverage. PK president Randy Phillips, for instance, was quoted in October 1994 as saying, "When we started out, the media coverage wasn't always so friendly" (Shiflett, 1994). In his autobiography, PK founder and CEO Bill McCartney (McCartney & Diles, p. 292) wrote, "Editors have attacked me every step of the way, and cartoonists have had a great time with their caricatures." But the only specific media coverage McCartney mentioned was a very atypical 1989 article in *Westword* (Denver's alternative newsweekly) headlined, "CU football players score! But Coach Bill McCartney is the loser." Calling the article "terrible and scathing" (p. 53–54), McCartney claimed, "The only accuracies in the entire article were the descriptions of my priorities and goals for the team; my public stand on my relationship with Jesus

Christ and the balanced comments from players who both favored my religious posture and those who thought it cornball at best and destructive at worst." In his book *Sold Out: Becoming Man Enough to Make a Difference*, McCartney discussed media criticism following his 1994 resignation as football coach at the University of Colorado. He (McCartney & Halbrook, pp. 258–260) said that initial reports were positive as they focused on accomplishments at CU during his tenure but, "as expected," media coverage turned negative as reporters began to criticize his decision to leave coaching because it was "definitely not 'politically correct.'" McCartney mentioned specifically a story in *Sports Illustrated* (Hoffer & Smith, 1995) that asserted, "There is a word for this behavior. 'Un-American.'" McCartney claimed that the article was based on "deeply flawed assumptions about [his] resignation" and that it "mocked [his] reasons for leaving CU." McCartney further said the article sought to "portray [him] as a hand-wringing, Bible-thumping eccentric." Reflecting on the article three years after it was published, McCartney said, "In hindsight, I was naïve to allow a *secular* publication to cross-examine my motives. God makes it clear that 'the message of the cross [of Jesus Christ] is foolishness to those who are perishing,'" (emphasis added). McCartney concluded his discussion of the article by emphasizing that some people resist "the gospel of Jesus Christ" because "their hearts have been hardened." Obviously numbering members of the media among the hard of heart, McCartney said, "In this light, when directed at me, personal attacks from the media are like spitwads bouncing off an aircraft carrier."

Like McCartney, participants in PK complain about mass media coverage. In fact, one easily forms the impression that even a single negative fact or negative quote in a published or broadcast story about PK may color the entire story as negative or critical for PK men. This reactivity is reminiscent of former presidential candidate Bob Dole's assertion in 1998 that conservative Christian groups seem never to be satisfied with a politician's voting record that agrees with their views any less than 100 percent. And it overlooks issues such as whether PK has been receiving coverage more favorable than other evangelical groups, now or in the past, or what PK as an organization was or was not doing that would affect its coverage. A 1996 *Christianity Today* article (Rabey, 1996) contained this line, "PK did not respond to numerous requests to be interviewed for this story," and it was not the only story about PK that included no official comment even when one was or probably was sought.

For two years I conducted participant-observation research among men involved in PK and found out, first-hand, what they think about the mass media. I learned that they have an antagonistic attitude to the media in general and are frustrated with the media's coverage of PK in particular. They believe that they are not understood adequately by members of the mass media and, as a result, are portrayed unfairly in media reports. Such frustration is present at all levels of the organization: among men involved in local groups, among speakers at PK conferences, and in books published and marketed by PK. In this chapter, I explore this antagonistic attitude to the mass media as held by PK men, presenting examples that help analyze the roots of their frustration.

Briefly, the antagonistic attitude to the mass media among PK men is rooted in their world view, which emphasizes spiritualized dichotomies such as good and evil, right and wrong, God and Satan. From this world view springs a proclivity to view reality in strictly dualistic terms, with little room for gray areas of indecision, doubt or questioning. Because of this thinking, PK men tend to view people who do not wholeheartedly support the organization as outsiders and enemies. PK participants often view the media as composed of liberal people who do not support their cause and are opposed to their activities. Most of the men involved in PK are theologically and socially conservative, and they see the media workers as liberals who stand in opposition to their deepest-held beliefs.

CULTURE WARS

The sociologist James Davison Hunter (1991) describes tensions in the United States between conservatives and liberals in terms that also describe the strained attitudes toward the mass media I encountered among PK men. In his book, *Culture Wars: The Struggle to Define America*, Hunter argues that the United States is in the midst of a cultural conflict over how we will order our lives. The conflict stems from competing sources of moral authority and differing world views and is waged by people who generally can be characterized by two main tendencies (Hunter, 1991, pp. 42–43). The first tendency, cultural orthodoxy, derives moral authority from an external and transcendent source that provides a degree of consistency and an absolute character to values (p. 44). The second tendency, cultural progressivism, derives moral authority from rationalism and subjectivism. Rather than a moral authority that descends from above and beyond and is the same for all times and places, moral authority for cultural progressives is understood to change, develop and unfold over time. The first group generally comprises cultural conservatives such as PK participants, and the second group generally includes cultural liberals, including most mass media workers (pp. 44–46, 227). Hunter writes that the conflict is carried out in the arena of public culture where vying parties attempt to gain dominion over the symbols that define the life of the nation (pp. 53–54). The main protagonists in the culture war, Hunter argues, are cultural elites such as public policy specialists, lobbyists, writers and community leaders and activists (p. 60). These people work to create "elaborate systems of meaning" based on "fundamentally opposing visions of the meaning of America" (pp. 53, 63).

The mass media comprise one important battleground for the culture war. Hunter argues that those on the orthodox and conservative side are convinced that the overwhelming majority of mass media workers are cultural progressives and liberals who are prejudiced against them and intolerant of the values they cherish (Hunter, 1991, pp. 226, 245). Because of this perceived prejudice, those on the orthodox and conservative side believe that the mass media do not present their positions fairly. Battles over the media result in mutual misunderstanding and hostility along the cultural divide of orthodox and progressives.

I relate Hunter's culture war thesis to PK in three ways. First, I examine the reactions of PK men to the organization's media coverage. During my research among local PK groups, I joined men at early-morning prayer breakfasts and small group meetings in local churches. I also attended PK training sessions for volunteers, seminars conducted by PK staff for laypeople, clergy conferences led by PK staff, large stadium rallies and Washington's Stand in the Gap. I learned that PK men are adequately described by Hunter's category of cultural orthodoxy because they believe in a transcendent source of moral authority rooted in their Christian beliefs. I also heard them express an antagonistic attitude toward the mass media in general and frustration with the media's coverage of PK in particular. Second, I focus on PK men's world view to understand the source of their antagonistic attitudes toward the mass media. Hunter (1991) argues that the cultural conflict is the result of differences rooted in divergent sources of moral authority and the world views that grow from that moral authority. Because the cultural conflict is related to sources of moral authority—that is, with the commitments that people hold most strongly—the conflict extends beyond mere differences of opinion over specific public policy issues. To understand the conflict, therefore, one must examine participants' world view. Third, I extend Hunter's thesis beyond the domain of cultural elites to the level of the ordinary "man in the street" in PK (Hunter, 1983, p. 10). Hunter focuses his attention on cultural elites and, as one would expect, the books, training materials and speeches produced by PK leaders reflect the tensions he describes. But I argue that the types of conflict described by Hunter among cultural elites also are found among typical PK participants.

They Just Don't Get It

During the June 1996 PK conference in Charlotte, NC, former Nixon administration official and Prison Fellowship Ministries founder Charles Colson began his address to the thousands of men gathered by referring to Supreme Court Justice Antonin Scalia's speech at a prayer breakfast two months earlier. In that speech, Scalia referred to First Corinthians 4:10 and said that Christians are "fools for Christ's sake." Scalia discussed the scorn encountered by Christians who profess their belief in miracles such as the virgin birth and the bodily resurrection of Jesus. In his address to the PK rally, Colson complained about the media's response to the speech, noting, "Justice Scalia said he believed in the resurrection, and he was ridiculed in the press and media" (Allen, 1997, p. 12). Later in his speech, Colson described an interview he had completed recently with reporters. During the interview, one reporter asked Colson, "Are you one of those Bible-believing Christians?" Colson replied, "I didn't know there was any other kind." Then, drawing a strict boundary between PK men and supposed outsiders in the media, Colson said to the assembled crowd of thousands, "They just don't get it!"

An attitude antagonistic to the mass media similar to the one displayed by Colson on a PK stadium rally platform also is found in small groups of men involved in PK at the local level. While attending an early morning prayer breakfast at a neighborhood restaurant, I heard men discuss their frustration with news media. The morning's first topic of conversation was the professional football playoffs and the big game their local team had won two days earlier. In the local newspaper, one player was quoted as saying that his team won because God was on their side. The player also said that his team had been "on a mission" after Billy Graham held an event in their home stadium. The player further suggested that his team received divine help in the victory because a lot of Christians live in the city. The men reflected lightheartedly on his comments and cautioned against being too optimistic about the upcoming game because, they said, a lot of Christians also live in the city of their next opponent.

After these jovial comments, however, the men's conversation became much more serious. They discussed a picture that accompanied the victory stories in the newspaper, which showed several football players gathered for prayer after the game. The men were upset because, although the picture was printed in the newspaper, no mention was made of the group of players praying. One man's voice was filled with frustration when he said, "They showed it [the picture of players praying]. Of course, they didn't mention it [the players praying]." Another man replied sarcastically, "It would be against the law to mention it."

The frustration with the media expressed by PK members at the prayer breakfast seems typical. They genuinely believe, as Hunter (1991, pp. 226–227) describes, that the media are controlled by liberals who, at best, do not understand Christianity and its impact in their lives or who, at worst, are openly hostile to Christians and refuse to publish positive stories about the role of religious faith in the lives of Christians.

I learned about the participants' frustration with media coverage of PK when I traveled with a large group of men to attend Stand in the Gap. On our way to Washington, I sat with a group of men who were discussing the

October 6, 1997, issue of *Time*, which featured PK as its cover story. The article's writer said that PK's "patriarchal fervor has already set off political alarms" (Stodghill, 1997, p. 36) and that "Promise Keepers declares it has no political agenda. Nevertheless, it makes no attempt to hide its allies on the Religious Right" (p. 37). When one man read these statements aloud, another man quickly responded, "Oh, I don't have a political agenda." A friend challenged him by saying, "When people get together like we are going to do, there is great potential for political action," to which the first man replied, "But, we aren't going to demonstrate against Congress or something like that." When yet another friend asked, "Don't you have a political agenda?" he said, "Not with this [trip to Washington and involvement in PK]." Then, referring to the media and its coverage of PK, he said, "They just don't get it!"

I also heard men involved in local PK groups express their frustration with media coverage of the organization. As one group assembled to travel to a stadium rally, several men discussed local media reports of controversy surrounding the PK meeting. One man, obviously expressing a great deal of frustration, said, "Well, you know we are all just a bunch of radicals who beat our wives. That's what it says in all the newspapers." Another man echoed this, responding, "The problem I have with the coverage of Promise Keepers is that the reporters don't know anything about it. If someone covers a baseball game, at least he has attended a ball game before, and he knows something about baseball." Clearly, these men believed they were misunderstood, maligned and attacked. As I would find out subsequently, the dichotomous mentality of "us versus them" they exhibited in their discussion of PK's media coverage forms a large part of their world view—and not only with respect to the news media.

Dichotomous Thinking

Hunter (1991, p. 42) explains that the conflict between cultural orthodoxy and cultural progressivism over specific public policy issues is rooted in a much deeper conflict emerging from different world views. To understand why PK men hold such antagonistic attitudes toward the media, attention must be focused on their world view.

After attending small group meetings and larger conferences, and reading materials published by PK, I am convinced that PK men's antagonistic attitude toward the group's media coverage is shaped by a world view grounded in spiritualized dichotomies. Throughout my contact with PK participants, I heard numerous references to realities that exist in polarities such as good and evil, God and Satan, right and wrong, and believers and unbelievers. In *Seven Promises of a Promise Keeper*, for example, Cole (1994, p. 38) says, "God is a maximizer of men; Satan is a usurper. Christ is truth; Satan is the father of lies." Another example of spiritualized dichotomies is found in a PK study guide in which the authors describe temptations Satan brings to followers of Jesus. They say, "Let the Word of God abide in your heart and you will have great power over the enemy ... the Word of God is our greatest power against the temptations of Satan" (Horner, Ralston & Sunde, 1996, p. 25).

The dualistic view of reality also is found in sermons delivered by platform speakers at PK rallies. Throughout 1996, many platform speakers explained the church burnings across the country and the bombing of Atlanta's Olympic Park by describing a dualistic contest between God and Satan. At one rally, the pastor of an African-American church destroyed by fire described the church burnings as the result of Satan's influence. He said, "What the enemy is doing [by burning churches], he meant for evil. But God used it for good." At another rally, a PK staff member said, "Satan has a book of matches, and he seeks to destroy the church. But God has a firehouse. Go ahead, Satan, light your fire. God used for good what Satan intended for evil."

At another PK stadium rally, a platform speaker described the Centennial Olympic Park bombing as Satan's attempt to destroy the "spiritual impetus" that brought the games to Atlanta. To solve the problems caused by the Olympic Park bombing, one PK preacher referred to Second Chronicles 7:14: "If my people who are called by my name humble themselves, pray, seek my face, and turn from their wicked ways, then I will hear from heaven, and will forgive their sin and heal their land." The preacher then said, "*My people*, not politicians. *My people*, not unbelievers. But, *my people*" (emphasis added). The preacher used dichotomous categories to differentiate between people he believes are Christians and people he does not believe are Christians.

In addition to PK publications and speakers, men involved in PK locally also display a dualistic world view. For example, during the Saturday lunch break at one PK stadium rally, Liberals United—a group protesting the rally – was discussed in dichotomous terms. One man said, "If outsiders protest, you must be doing something right." Another man used a believers-unbelievers dichotomy, saying, "They just don't get it. Unbelievers cannot really understand what we are all about."

Strict dichotomies such as God and Satan, right and wrong, and believers and unbelievers contribute to the antagonistic attitude toward the media coverage of PK events. Because members of PK believe that the media are composed of outsiders who either do not understand PK or who are opposed to the organization's message and activities, they view them with suspicion. PK men are quick to point out examples of stories that make them believe the media portrays PK negatively and unfairly. Thus, their world view, which is characterized by dualistic thinking, fosters an antagonistic attitude to the mass media.

One may find many examples of PK supporters' antagonistic attitude to the mass media in letters they have written to newspaper editors. In general, supporters complain about media coverage because it is either too scarce or too biased against PK. One writer (Moen, 1995, p. 4A) charged that Louis Farrakhan's Million Man March received a great deal of coverage because it focused on racial strife while PK stadium rallies were "barely reported" because their "common peaceful goal" grew out of a desire "to praise and glorify Jesus Christ" and, thus, was "not very politically correct." Another writer (Tucker, 1997, p. A14) complained that the media covered Stand in the Gap only because "protesters and Christian-bashers" drew their attention to PK. "Without opposition from liberals," the writer contended, "media coverage would have been scant." Another writer (Clay, 1997, p. 9A), the wife of a man in PK, charged that the media were biased against PK. She said that "media coverage" was "confined to angry women's groups," ignoring "thousands of wives" who support PK and urge their husbands to participate. One PK supporter (Priester, 1997, p. A10) charged that comics, television and radio "make fun of the participants" in PK and that "they are told to be silent and mind their own business" because their views are not "politically correct." He then said, "It seems that Christians aren't full-fledged citizens anymore. Their opinions don't matter. Their votes don't count. The Constitution doesn't extend to them. They're not up with the times, according to many 'progressive' voices." When expressing frustration with media coverage of PK, one writer (Oliveto, 1997, p. 8) used dichotomous categories of "spiritual" versus "intellectual" to explain why media interpretations of PK's message "do not match" PK's "actual message." The writer claimed it is futile to attempt to understand "spiritual principles in purely natural or intellectual terms" as the media try to do.

GOD IS ACTIVE IN THE WORLD

A conviction that God is actively engaged in world affairs is another component of PK men's world view. Even the creation of Promise Keepers is viewed as a result of God's active leadership. When McCartney describes the conversation during which he and a friend first dreamed of an organization like PK, he says, "We both felt that God had put these visions in our hearts, and that we should work to keep them alive" (McCartney, 1995, p. 286). PK president Randy Phillips says that PK came into being because God answered the prayers of many Christian women who asked God to raise up godly men (Phillips, 1994, p. 4). At stadium rallies, platform speakers describe God's action bringing PK into existence. At one conference, for example, a preacher said, "Promise Keepers ... is the beginning of a mighty move of God. You can't let it die."

PK men in small groups believe that God also is involved in the events of their own lives. For example, one man described an automobile accident involving his wife and daughter. They both escaped without injury because, he said, God protected them. Then, he described the way in which God intervened to work out details for their new car. He said, "God really worked in the situation. We needed a bigger car, but when we went to the car dealership, the car we wanted wasn't available. So we drove to another car dealer [in a nearby town], and the exact car we wanted had been delivered the night before. So, you know God was in it." At another meeting, one man described how strongly he believes that God is in control of the events of his life. After 16 years as a successful officer in the military, he was passed over for a promotion. He said that he was deeply hurt by the experience, but he now believes it was the result of God's action. He said, "God had other plans for my life. God put a roadblock in my path along the way. And He wanted me follow the path He prepared for me." PK men are convinced that their lives are a part of God's plan because they believe God is actively involved in the affairs of this world.

SPIRITUALIZED DICHOTOMIES

The combination of dichotomous thinking and a belief that God is actively involved in world affairs creates spiritualized dichotomies often expressed by PK men as a battle between God and Satan. They often believe that conflicts in life are the result of spiritual battles being waged between God and Satan, and they demonstrate a strong conviction that they—as followers of God—also are engaged in a battle with the forces of Satan and evil. In *Seven Promises of a Promise Keeper,* McCartney (1994b, p. 207) writes,

> We're in a war, men, whether we acknowledge it or not. The enemy is real, and he doesn't like to see men of God take a stand for Jesus Christ and contest his lies (see 2 Corinthians 10:3-5). But Almighty God is for us, and we know that if we walk the narrow road that leads to life, we have an extremely capable leader in Jesus, the King of kings and Lord of lords. And He is faithful to provide the grace and strength we need along the way.

This tendency for PK men to spiritualize dichotomies, especially as a battle between God and Satan, is seen in the way PK leaders discuss two of the organization's main emphases—the family and anti-racism. In a PK study guide, Glenn Wagner (1994, p. 104) describes Satan's attacks on Christian families, saying, "We live in a ... kingdom of darkness.... Christian marriages are under attack as never before, and we must wage war against sin and the spiritual forces of evil." Frequent PK speaker Steve Farrar (1990, pp. 20–21) says, "War has been declared on the biblical family ... [by] Satan." When PK leaders discuss racism in the United States, they tend to focus on its spiritual causes. For example, McCartney (1994a, p. 161) says, "Racism is Satan's stronghold ... one of his best tools for breeding hatred and undermining the work of the church." He (1997a, p. 5) adds later, "Men, we are at war! Satan has used race and sectarianism to divide and alienate us to keep us from being the bride of Christ." McCartney (1995, p. 292) also believes that opposition to PK's initiatives to combat racism is the result of Satan's influence: "Satan has worked tirelessly to thwart our efforts."

Spiritualizing dichotomies also is prevalent among men in local PK groups. At one meeting of PK lay volunteers, a PK staffer explained that he was "in the foxhole" with PK men active in churches. He then prayed, asking God to help men "on the ground facing the enemy as they storm the gates of hell." After his prayer, the PK staff member asked PK men if they were ready for war and declared that the forces of evil get stronger every day because we are getting closer to Jesus' return to earth. He concluded by reminding the men that Satan will hurl more fiery darts at them as they follow God more closely. Men throughout the audience nodded their heads in agreement as he described the spiritual warfare faced by people who are faithful followers of God.

I heard similar discussions of spiritual warfare at a prayer meeting to help men prepare for Stand in the Gap. One man said that the enemy would be in Washington, DC, before PK's assembly, and he encouraged men in local churches to respond by praying actively for the assembly. But he warned the men that they would face counterattacks from Satan as soon as they began praying. He said that their names would be placed on Satan's bulletin board for special attacks because they would become a threat to Satan the moment they began praying for God's blessings on the assembly. In response, the participants agreed to increase their prayer efforts to fend off Satan's attacks.

After Stand in the Gap, McCartney emphasized spiritualized dichotomies when he described PK's motivation for holding the assembly. McCartney (McCartney & Halbrook, p. 318) said that sacred assemblies in the past were "catalyst[s] for change" in which God's people "set themselves apart from pagan people and unclean practices." McCartney included the media in his description as a key part of the cultural crisis against which PK was acting. He (McCartney & Halbrook, p. 318) said, "God is calling us out ... His church, His people, to separate themselves from a culture of sacrilege and debauchery. On a practical level, He is calling us to turn off the TV; to stop being seduced by Hollywood and an increasingly vulgar, hedonistic media."

Conclusion

As Hunter (1991, p. 42) argues, the cultural conflict between cultural orthodoxy and cultural progressivism results from deep differences in sources of moral authority and differing world views. Certainly, this is true for men involved in PK. Their animosity toward the mass media is grounded in their world view of spiritualized dichotomies—strict contrasts such as right and wrong. As one author says in *Seven Promises of a Promise Keeper*, men in PK must practice "black-and-white living in a gray world" (Oliver, 1994, p. 83). Further, because they believe God participates actively in the world, they are convinced that a cosmic struggle is raging between the forces of God and the forces of Satan. As obedient followers of God, they believe they are participating in the battle. This belief strengthens their commitment to PK and injects fervor into their opposition to people they consider outsiders.

Out of a tendency to think in spiritualized dichotomies grows their conviction that members of the mass media are outsiders who are used by the forces of evil in the spiritual battle against the forces of God. They believe that mass media workers do not understand them and are opposed to the convictions they hold dear. Consequently, any criticism of PK by the mass media—which seems to include simply publishing or broadcasting any negative opinion or fact about PK—is immediately viewed as an attack. Thus, the media are easily seen as enemies, and the intractable nature of the attitudes of men involved in PK toward the mass media results in an uncompromising stance.

The contentious attitudes of PK participants toward the media demonstrate the accuracy of Hunter's thesis that public life in the United States is characterized by a culture war. The deep roots of the antagonistic attitude toward the media also demonstrate the accuracy of Hunter's thesis that the culture war is grounded in a commitment to different sources of moral authority and divergent world views. Finally, the attitudes of men active at the local level toward the mass media show that the cultural conflict extends beyond the level of elites and is raging at the level of ordinary men involved in Promise Keepers.

References

Allen, L.D. II (1997, January). Breaking down the wall? An inside observer says the "Godly men" of Promise Keepers may be ready to remove the barrier between religion and government. *Church and State 50*(1), 10–13.

Claussen, D.S. (1996). *United States print mass media coverage of two men's movements: Robert Bly, Iron John and the mythopoets, and Bill McCartney and the Promise Keepers*. Unpublished master's thesis, Kansas State University, Manhattan.

Clay, A. (1997, October 6). Lot of supporters. *The Atlanta Journal-Constitution*, 9A.

Cole, E.L. (1994). Your word is your bond. In A. Janssen & L.K. Weeden (eds.), *Seven promises of a Promise Keeper* (pp. 33–40). Colorado Springs, CO: Focus on the Family Publishing.

Farrar, S. (1990). *Point man: How a man can lead his family*. Sisters, OR: Multnomah Books.

Hoffer, R., & Smith, S. (1995, January 16). Putting his house in order. *Sports Illustrated 82*, 27–32.

Horner, B., Ralston, R., & Sunde, D. (1996). *Applying the seven promises.* Colorado Springs, CO: Focus on the Family Publishing.

Hunter, J.D. (1983). *American evangelicalism: Conservative religion and the quandary of modernity.* New Brunswick, NJ: Rutgers University Press.

Hunter, J.D. (1991). *Culture wars: The struggle to define America.* New York: Basic Books.

McCartney, B. (1994a). A call to unity. In A. Janssen & L.K. Weeden (eds.), *Seven promises of a Promise Keeper* (pp. 157–168). Colorado Springs, CO: Focus on the Family Publishing.

McCartney, B. (1994b). Seeking God's favor. In A. Janssen & L.K. Weeden (eds.), *Seven promises of a Promise Keeper* (pp. 205–207). Colorado Springs, CO: Focus on the Family Publishing.

McCartney, B., & Diles, D. (1995). *From ashes to glory (2d Ed.).* Nashville, TN: Thomas Nelson Publishers.

McCartney, B. (1997). Foreword. In Washington, R., & Kehrein, G., *Break down the walls: Experiencing Biblical reconciliation and unity in the body of Christ* (p. 5). Chicago: Moody Press.

McCartney, B., & Halbrook, B. (1997). *Sold Out: Becoming man enough to make a difference.* Nashville, TN: Word Publishing.

Moen, S. (1995, October 31). Breath of fresh air. *The Bismarck Times*, 4A.

Oliver, G. (1994). Black-and-white living in a gray world. In A. Janssen & L.K. Weeden (eds.), *Seven promises of a Promise Keeper* (pp. 83–90). Colorado Springs, CO: Focus on the Family Publishing.

Oliveto, F. (1997, October 14). Spirituality hard to grasp. *The Tampa Tribune*, 8.

Phillips, R. (1994). Seize the moment. In A. Janssen & L.K. Weeden (eds.), *Seven promises of a Promise Keeper* (pp. 1–10). Colorado Springs, CO: Focus on the Family Publishing.

Priester, D. (1997, October 9). Society benefits when promises are kept. *The Detroit News*, A10.

Rabey, S. (1996, April 29). Where is the Christian men's movement headed? Burgeoning Promise Keepers inspires lookalikes. *Christianity Today 40*, 46–49, 60.

Shiflett, D. (1994, October 12). Dads vs. the devil. *The Wall Street Journal*, p. A1.

Stodghill, R. II (1997, October 6). God of our fathers: The Promise Keepers are bringing their manly crusade to Washington. Are they men behaving nobly? Or a threat to freedom? *Time 150*, pp. 34–40.

Tucker, D. (1997, October 24). Views about promise keepers. *The Austin American-Statesman*, A14.

Wagner, E.G., & Gruen, D. (1996). *Strategies for a successful marriage: A study guide for men.* Colorado Springs, CO: NavPress Publishing Group.

CHAPTER 22

"So Far, News Coverage of Promise Keepers Has Been More Like Advertising": The Strange Case of Christian Men and the Print Mass Media

by Dane S. Claussen

Scholarly analysis of the media coverage of Promise Keepers (or of the Million Man March, or mythopoetism, for that matter) is as fraught with difficulty as covering PK for the media—without prior knowledge of other men's groups or of evangelical Christianity: the scholar and journalist both have little to go on that is relevant.

Almost all previous scholarly research on media coverage of evangelical Christianity in the United States would have predicted that PK would receive coverage that was negative or faulty in just about every way: minimal, late, biased, shallow, inaccurate, incomplete, and negative (Claussen, 1996). All previous scholarly research on media coverage of the country's previous gender-related movement, feminism, concluded that the feminist movement was covered in at least three distinctive phases: black-out, in which the movement received little to no coverage; ridicule, in which the movement was portrayed as bizarre, small and most probably temporary; and mainstreaming, in which the movement, once it was realized feminism wasn't just going away, was portrayed as non-threatening, on most Americans' sociopolitical agenda, etc. (Robinson, 1978; Lieb, 1991). But if men's movements in the United States have experienced this tripartite progression, it has been over a very long period of time—the blacking out of the profeminist and men's rights groups, followed by the ridiculing of the mythopoets, followed by the mainstreaming of Promise Keepers. Such a scenario would assume that media group all of these phenomena together as a long-term, broad-based "men's movement" and that media as individuals and groups of workers have elephantine institutional memories. Given the lack of subject-matter expertise of so many reporters, the turnover on reporting staffs, and the orientation of media towards the present tense, it hardly seams likely that either of these conditions—let alone both—would obtain.

Academic journal literature on other news coverage of men, men's movements and masculinity, particularly in print, also is extremely limited. This may be because so much attention is devoted to media coverage of women and minority groups. Or it may be because media content largely is controlled by, and is about, men (Butler and Paisley, 1980), the resulting rhetorical question logically being: so what do men have to complain about? And other possible explanations may exist. In any case, as Craig (1992) explained, "[M]en's studies has only begun to have an impact on media research, and so far, only a few scholars have published work that focuses on the media and their relationship to men as men" (p. 1). Clearly the reverse — that mass communications research has only begun, if that, to have an effect on men's studies—also is true. Fejes (1992) complained that only five mass communications studies in the previous decade had "focused primarily on men and masculinity" (Cantor, 1990; Gray, 1986; Meyers, 1980; Postman, Nystrom, Strate and Weingarter, 1987; Skelly and Lundstrom, 1981), all five addressing fictional entertainment shows or advertisements, not news content. For example, Postman et al. (1987) found a strong relationship between drinking and stereotypical views of masculinity after studying 40 beer commercials. Interestingly, McCartney's anthology (McCartney et al., 1992) includes a chapter entitled, "Why Beer Commercials Make Some Men Feel So Good," noting that beer commercials show close friendships while, unfortunately, most real U.S. men have few or none. Strate (1992) explained that "in the world of beer commercials, demonstrating one's masculinity requires an audience to judge one's performance and confirm one's status" (p. 88). Some observers might argue that this is not unlike the relationship between PK's stadium rallies and local accountability groups.

Relatively few studies present evidence of how men are portrayed in news or other non-fiction settings, and Fejes (1992) claimed that none were solely or even primarily studying masculinity or men as men. One exception (Jolliffe, 1989, 1996) found that media coverage of men in 1885 occasionally referred to their family lives, personalities and appearances. But a century later, in 1985, media coverage all but ignored these aspects of men's lives. In fact, Jolliffe found, while men were pictured in the *New York Times* up to 20 times as often as women, they dominated photos of only those activities outside the home. News stories studied referred to men by their job titles alone 50 percent of the time (versus 1 percent for women). Jolliffe also found that news photos generally depicted men (and only their heads a third of the time) as violent, criminals, loners, emotionless, anonymous and/or as workers. Not surprisingly, she concluded that "news photographs present a skewed view of men's reality" and therefore of reality in general (1996, p. 102).

Claussen (1996) showed that print mass media coverage of both the mythopoetic men's movement and Promise Keepers had been favorable overall, that the tone of the coverage did not become more or less positive over time, that both movements were covered primarily in feature stories rather than news stories (although PK coverage was becoming more news-oriented by the second half of 1995), and that national elite print media did not clearly set the agenda for coverage of these men's movements by regional and local print media. He also showed that Promise Keepers' coverage overall was obviously more favorable than had been the coverage of mythopoetism.

Other media-oriented studies have shown that men receive longer obituaries, except when adjusted for occupational content (Spilka, Lacey and Gelb, 1979); men's sports made up 95 percent of all sports coverage (Coakley, 1986); newspaper sports editors disproportionately publish photographs of women athletes in "emotional and helpless states" and disproportionately reject similar photos of men athletes (Wanta and Leggett, 1989); over a 3½-year period, men accounted for 90 percent of the guests on ABC's Nightline program (Hoynes and Croteau, 1989); male athletes in sports coverage are shown as active, female as reactive (Duncan, Messner and Williams, 1990); men who don't like sports, chafe at sports-oriented culture, or want to change sports almost never appear in media (Connell, 1990); men are portrayed more often than women in newspaper photographs in every section except the lifestyle pages (Luebke, 1989); and "battered husbands" has not become a public issue because the news media have not made it one (Lucal, 1995). Apparently no academic articles in mass communication journals have addressed the Men's Movements, and only a few Men's Movements–oriented articles have focused on mass media—and then almost entirely on film (Seyfarth, 1992; Shor, 1993; Tompkins, 1994).

MEDIA COVERAGE OF PROMISE KEEPERS

If the rather thin record of academic studies of men and masculinity in the media predicts anything, then, it is that men tend to receive more news coverage just because of their sex and that men engaged in stereotypically male activities receive favorable, if often superficial, coverage. Thus, PK should have received negative media coverage—superficial or not—because it is an organization of men not acting in stereotypical ways; because they have been advocating a message not stereotypically male (Christian teachings), expressed in nontypical ways (not through politics, business or sports); because they have questioned the status quo in criticizing U.S. culture for being unethical, immoral, racist, materialistic, and unfriendly, among other things; because PK has been yet another conservative (some media say evangelical, others have called PK fundamentalist) Christian organization in the public sphere; and for other reasons. Previous research also has concluded that the American mass media generally are incompetent at covering religion news, unfriendly to conservative Christian groups and, at least initially, apathetic or hostile to new social movements (Claussen, 1996). The fact that PK has been receiving extensive media coverage since only about mid–1994 makes it perhaps premature to make conclusions about "phases" or trends in PK's coverage over the long run. But as of mid–1998, the most significant aspects of media coverage of Promise Keepers were that: 1) American media had given PK almost entirely favorable coverage (the quote in this chapter's title is from Solomon, 1996); 2) American media generally had not considered PK within any sort of larger religious, historical, cultural, political, or economic context, as was evident in both the stories that were published and broadcast and, in particular, the choice of which stories not to pursue; and 3) PK members and leaders complained about PK's media coverage anyway—not because of that lack of context, but because the coverage was considered still not favorable enough. (PK must also be one of the few organizations that have looked better, not worse, to objective observers due to the mass media's errata, such as a 1997 *Richmond Times Dispatch* editorial's claim that PK "literature does not criticize liberalism.") This chapter provides evidence and explanation for these first and second conclusions; Dean Allen (this volume) has addressed the third.

Overwhelmingly, PK has received neutral to positive media coverage (for example, see Wolf, 1995), most articles being straight news accounts (Claussen, 1996) of PK stadium rallies, clergy conferences, Stand in the Gap, and other event- or announcement-oriented journalism. In fact, most coverage is rather unremarkable simply because PK has so often been covered like most other news: factual descriptions of events, plenty of quotes from "official" sources, and an occasional pithy comment from a vocal—and sometimes the most extreme—critic, with moderate critics quoted rarely and the entire spectrum of critics never introduced.

Christianity Today (1992) said it was "enthusiastic" about PK because it was "good news" and "needed," and later added that PK is an "evangelical movement in the best sense," and "a much needed asset to the kingdom if it keeps the promise expressed in its seven key commitments, and settles for nothing less" (Snyder, 1994). *The Wall Street Journal*, in addition to providing favorable coverage of its own, called *Newsweek*'s PK coverage "angelic" (Shiflett, 1994). *The Los Angeles Times*, publishing a Religion News Service (1996a) article, reported, "'They're doing better than an awful lot of evangelical ministries,' said Mary Stewart van Leeuwen, a gender specialist at Eastern College in St. Davids, Pa. 'They are really bending over backwards.' At a time when churches are often segregated, she said, McCartney is challenging Christians to change their ways." And a minister, "simultaneously critical and deeply moved" by PK's Atlanta clergy conference, concluded (DeCelle, 1996) that, "Curiously, *Christianity Today* and *Christian Century* were equally bland and cautious about the movement." *Ms.* magazine (Minkowitz, 1995) surprised with this:

> Some feminists may scoff at the Promise Keepers' emphasis on men's personal healing and self-growth. But I don't see how society can change in the ways we want it to if men have no support to start acting less like "men" and more like caring, loving, ethical, and nondominating human beings.
>
> The process by which men grow into cultural manhood is so repressive that enabling them to leave this state requires active healing—not just women's understandably impatient suggestion that they cease their misdeeds. But, apart from a few lonely male activists like John Stoltenberg, progressives have never been able to mobilize men for this sort of healing and change. The Promise Keepers have stepped into this vacuum.
>
> Our best response may not be to attack PK's members as dupes or unmitigated reactionaries, but to understand the contradictory impulses that have brought them swarming to the stadiums. And to tap into the very needs Bill McCartney and his friends have mobilized.

Even less positive coverage tended to criticize or ridicule only McCartney while praising his organization, as the *Newsweek* coverage showed (Woodward, 1994):

> The hit of the weekend was coach McCartney. Welcomed by wild cheers, he mounted the platform, surrounded by members of his football team. Suddenly the coach called for his wife, Lyndi, in order to "show 'em how the Black and Gold [his team's colors] do it." The crowd roared as he bent his wife over backward in a long kiss.
>
> McCartney then launched into a rambling, Hemingway-esque speech about death, risk-taking, winning and racial harmony—all flavored with anecdotes from the Bible and sports. "We are the brotherhood," McCartney shouted. "We're connected. We're going to look out for each other." A chant filled the stadium, echoing his words. An African-American in the stands began to weep and was hugged by a tattooed white man with no shirt. Nor were they the only pair to embrace.
>
> "One guy confessed his addictions to drugs and sex to me," said Larry Dong, 35, a real-estate broker from Phoenix, Ariz. "If my wife were here, I wouldn't have been able to talk about things like sexual impurity." From the podium, McCartney looked out and saw that it was good. "It doesn't get any better than this," he said.

GQ (Raab, 1996) was unusually nasty (so much so that their writer may have undermined his opportunity to present reasoned, credible criticisms of PK):

> McCartney, 55, looks like a junior high shop teacher, with a low forehead, meaty arms and thick, black-rimmed glasses. His air of fogged sincerity is underlined by a perceptible goofiness that only begins with his semi-crossed eyes. It's plain why Promise Keepers makes sure his only contact with the press comes during the stadium conferences and is limited to a few minutes: He's a raving lunatic....
>
> This is the visible essence of Promise Keepers' primal appeal to the anxious American male: Life is a football game. The opposing team is scary as hell, and pissed off to boot, but we've got a humdinger of a coach and God's own playbook. Be a man, stick together, and we're gonna kick ass. Exactly as a coach would, Promise Keepers' literature and speakers whipsaw men between accusations of being "feminized" and "sissified" and the insistence that they subsume themselves completely in the cause of victory....
>
> The Saturday-night program is devoted to the preaching of racial and denominational reconciliation, the feel-good goals that set Promise Keepers apart from most previous evangelical movements and assure them of relatively hands-off press....
>
> There's nothing new, much less revolutionary, in what Promise Keepers is pushing, which is not really about Jesus Christ at all, but about Satan. After listening to all the speeches and the prayers, after reading their books and magazines, it's abundantly clear that these guys see the Archenemy everywhere, but especially in the mirror. What PK offers men finally is protection—from themselves.

One article in *Christian Century* (Spalding, 1996) was similar both in the tone and rarity of its vitriol:

> After a brief account of the resistance he's encountered trying to sell his message about racism at Promise Keepers events (angry letters, eerily silent responses from largely white audiences), McCartney's talk suddenly becomes a breathless, nearly incomprehensible rant that prompts the guy next to me to observe that he's "never seen anyone so filled with the spirit as Coach Mac." ...
>
> Neck bulging, arms flailing, spit flying, McCartney builds to his point. "What Almighty God is doin' is waitin' for the church to come together in harmony! He's got a whole backload of things up there he wants to do. He's got so much on his heart he's wanted to do for so long but the church is divided...."

But *Christian Century* and *Christianity Today* have relatively small circulations, and although *GQ*, The *Wall Street Journal*, and even The *Los Angeles*

Times reach more readers, they aren't read by a broad cross-section of the general public. Most Americans have received almost all of the information and analysis available to them about Promise Keepers from either local daily newspapers, local television stations or the national television networks. And PK has fared especially well in those venues (Claussen, 1996; Daniels, 1998). For example, the *Fort Worth Star-Telegram*, the *Tampa Tribune*, and other newspapers published in late December 1996 Suzanne Fields's column (distributed by the Los Angeles Times Syndicate) that read, "What's fascinating to me about the Promise Keepers is the way they express God-given moral issues from the gut. It's unfair to call them anti-feminist because they don't bash women or women's issues but, like the Million Man Marchers, insist on meeting without women." She added that "it's easy to scoff at Promise Keepers or to satirize them." But she offered no evidence that PK was being scoffed at or satirized. In fact, the latter treatment has been extremely rare, certainly dramatically less common than satirizations of the mythopoetic movement (which included two books, *Fire in the John* and *Iron Joe Bob*). In fact, cartoonist Tom Tomorrow, whose work often is brutally cutting, said (Conniff, 1997) about PK, "I don't want to just make fun of them." At about the same time, Diaz (1996) was announcing that because of PK, Athletes in Action and other Christian organizations, "religion and sports, much like Elizabeth Taylor and husbands, were [no longer] an uneasy mix."

One characteristic of many PK articles was particularly noteworthy with regard to reporters' professional norms and practices: every story read neutral or positive until about two-thirds or three-quarters of the way through; then there would be one or two negative paragraphs, followed by a favorable conclusion. (Examples of this pattern appeared in the Aug. 5, 1995, *Orlando* [FL] *Sentinel*, the Oct. 14, 1995, *Portland* [ME] *Press Herald* and, most notably, in Laurie Goodstein's *New York Times* article about Stand in the Gap, an example spotted by Eastland [1997].) Other articles mentioned criticism and opposition only in the middle (Sept. 16, 1995, *Asbury Park* [NJ] *Press*) or one-third of the way through the article and again two-thirds of the way through the article (Nov. 5, 1995, *Santa Fe* [NM] *New Mexican*); in any case, the pattern of a positive beginning, positive ending and generally positive coverage overall persisted. Apparently reporters believe that skepticism toward, or opposition to, PK can't be ignored but, for whatever reason, they don't want to give skeptics or opponents much attention and certainly not the more visible attention they would obtain from more prominent placement. It should be noted that skeptics and opponents to PK have not been limited to isolated individuals or extreme groups; they have included mainstream Protestant clergy and seminary professors as well as authorized representatives of major feminist, gay rights and other national organizations.

COVERAGE OF STAND IN THE GAP AND PK'S RESTRUCTURING

Perhaps the major test cases of how media would cover the maturing PK were the Stand in the Gap rally in Washington, on Oct. 4, 1997, and, it seems to me, PK's decisions to fire and then rehire its staff in early 1998. As Daniels (1998) has shown, media coverage of the Stand in the Gap rally was overwhelmingly positive; of 110 articles in the *New York Times, The Washington Post* and four Georgia dailies he analyzed, 67 were judged "extrinsic" (little to no negative information or opinion in the story), 29 were judged "critical" (negative information or opinions balance other content to at least some extent), and only 14 were judged "negative." In fact, media coverage was essentially completely favorable other than attention given to the National Organization for Women. Large newspapers, such as *The Los Angeles Times*, produced entire packages of articles—the article the day before the rally making it sound like a glorious, even patriotic crusade (Stammer and Granberry, 1997), and nearly breathless news reports the day after (Fulwood, 1997; Parsons, 1997; Risen, 1997; Wilgoren, 1997). Eastland (1997) asserted that *The Washington Post* assigned to the rally 23 reporters who wrote eight bylined articles. Protesters other than NOW were all but totally ignored, with perhaps the most information about one such group, the Lesbian Avengers, found in *Flagpole*—the alternative newsweekly in Athens, GA (Swanson, 1997).

NOW itself, intentionally or not, was represented by a series of soundbites that seemed generally uninformed and reactionary, even to many liberals (Swanson, 1997). And as Eastland (1997) points out, "[T]he NOW storyline did not dominate. Remarkably, the more common journalism was sympathetic to the [PK] organization and rally, and some pieces—such as in *U.S. News & World Report*—explicitly rejected NOW's take. A story the *Post* published the day before the rally noted that PK opponents who had flocked to Washington to spread 'their own message' were now admitting that their message had been 'drowned out by the generally favorable coverage the [PK] group has received.'" *Time* magazine (Winners & Losers, 1997) commented, "Patricia Ireland disses Promise Keepers. NOW more irrelevant than ever." And, indirectly, Pollitt (1997) made PK look pretty good by pointing out who did not protest:

> Where was the A.C.L.U.? People for the American Way? The new, female friendly A.F.L.-C.I.O.? Missing too were the supposedly liberal and gender-enlightened mainline denominations—the Episcopalians, Presbyterians, Methodists, Unitarians, Reform Jews and so on. Indeed, the United Methodists displayed a huge banner welcoming the Promise Keepers at their Washington headquarters. And what about the supposed "left wing" of the Democratic Party, the progressive caucus, the women's caucus, Jesse Jackson?

Eastland (1997) added, "There can be no question that the frame of the story would have been sharply changed had McCartney or any other of the many speakers at the rally declaimed on abortion rights or vouchers—or if religious-Right figures like James Dobson or Gary Bauer or Ralph Reed had spoken."

Rosin (1997), writing in *The New Republic*, called PK "undoubtedly the most benign group of men I'd ever met," and added:

> They represent the mass culmination of an embarrassing phenomenon: the feminization of the American right.
> By the standards of Christian warriors, the Promise Keepers are a disappointment....
> The Promise Keepers ... fill their fists full of Kleenex. They describe their rebirth with schoolgirl giddiness, using words like "awesome" and "neat."

Sandy Banks (1997) waxed philosophical about women-only gatherings and expressed confidence in men-only gatherings:

> I hope the Promise Keepers and Million Man Marchers can learn to look to other men for more than just conversation about sports, the weather and the stock market's ups and downs.
> Too few men, it seems, have male friends with whom they can talk about their problems, confess their insecurities, explore how to make their way in this hostile and demanding world.

The liberal *Nation* published an article quite critical of PK (Conason, Ross, et al., 1997), but at least took notice of PK; it even included PK claims such as the assertion by Dale Schlafer, PK's vice president for church relations, that PK's February 1997 clergy conference "was a turning point in the church of Jesus Christ, and a turning point in the history of the United States of America." *The New York Times*' Steinfels, using Stand in the Gap as his "news peg," asserted, "The familiar charge that the news media ignore religion looks a little unconvincing right now." One of the few negative articles on the event also was in the *Times*, where television critic Walter Goodman—though having little doubt that the event was captivating for those present—called the event "a no-show for the home viewer" and "a television washout," and noted that CNN did not cover it more because its executives "could not afford to put people to sleep."

After Stand in the Gap and the McCartneys' book tour, mass media attention to PK waned dramatically, but not for long. On February 18, 1998, PK told its more than 300 full-time staff members that they wouldn't be paid after March 31 and, the next day, at a regional PK clergy conference in St. Petersburg, FL, McCartney told the 3,000 attendees that, "What I'm going to say right now is hard, but I believe it's what God had given me to say. I believe that every church that names the name of Jesus is supposed to give Promise Keepers $1,000." A *Denver Post* headline screamed, "Promise Keepers to Halt Payroll," while the *Detroit Free Press* reported, "Promise Keepers Layoff Workforce" (quoted by Gilbreath, 1998).

Media treated the layoff as a straight news story (Promise Keepers 1998), but it is apparent that reporters didn't know quite how to handle the story. Was PK dying? They dutifully reported PK's plans to hold 19 stadium conferences during 1998, with an all-volunteer staff if necessary. However, in two months, word spread that those 300+ office staff members would be reinstated, with only one paycheck out of pocket. Was this all a public relations ploy to raise money, and thus an indication of how the overwhelmingly positive coverage of this movement had perhaps gone too far? Were journalists gullible, falling for the tactics televangelists had used just a decade earlier?

On Friday, June 19, 1998, less then nine months after Stand in the Gap, and only about two months after PK rehired its staff, subscribers to the NBC NewsChannel wire were sent this: "Thousands of men turned out for the Promise Keepers rally in Columbia, Missouri this afternoon. The rally was held at the football stadium at the University of Missouri. Rallies have been held across the country to help men change their lives to become better husbands, fathers and sons. Organizers of today's rally were expecting more than 30-thousand" (McDonald, 1998). There was not much new in this story, or any other news coverage of other 1998 stadium conferences, which is significant in itself: PK has been unusually successful in apparently getting its regional PK rallies onto the media's routine list of story subjects for a sustained period of time; on the other hand, however, media coverage of PK rallies of 1998 wasn't any different from media coverage of regional rallies in 1997, despite dramatic news—both good and bad—in the interim. The first four rallies in 1998 were held in Detroit, Little Rock, Los Angeles and Fresno. In most cases, the newspapers only briefly mentioned the layoffs and subsequent recalling or rehiring of Promise Keepers national staffers. The anticipated drop in attendance turned up as a theme in much of the coverage (especially advance stories), as did PK's finances and sometimes other issues.

For instance, a proposal to overturn a law legalizing casinos took center stage in the weeks leading up to the Detroit rally (DeHaven, 1998). The issue was whether anti-gambling forces should be given free rein to solicit signatures at this gathering of 40,000 men and other opposing sides should be kept out. The issue of homosexuality also was resurrected in Michigan papers' coverage of the conference (Brand-Williams, 1998); that PK was restarting its conference schedule despite some financial challenges was barely covered. Arkansas papers, leading up to the Little Rock rally, focused more on PK itself, but the advance stories seemed similar to those published prior to Stand in the Gap (Fewer Promise Keepers, 1998). If there was any negative coverage, it centered on the predicted drop in attendance from previous events. Even when the *Arkansas Democrat-Gazette* asked, "Who are these weirdos?" (Find Out for Yourself, 1998), it then challenged readers to find out for themselves more information about PK. Coverage in Los Angeles was surprisingly subdued, with coverage of the Memorial Stadium event emphasizing the number of men expected and those attending, the estimated 16,000 local accountability groups, and the organization's plans for the future.

The Fresno conference received very different media coverage that indicated more excitement about, and anticipation of, the event. The *Bee* ran several features (McCartney, 1998, and others) leading up to PK's fourth stadium conference including one featuring two local pastors' efforts at racial reconciliation. A *Bee* reporter added, "The president of Promise Keepers gave Christian men their marching orders for the new millennium" (Taylor, 1998c). Only brief mention was made of the atheists who protested outside the stadium. Fresno was also the location of the Chosen Women Revival, a gathering of Christian women similar in some ways to PK, but not affiliated with it. Having both events to cover, Fresno newspapers had the opportunity to compare and contrast them, which they did. But one story (Taylor, 1998a) reported that a lack of local interest might have forced planners to move the rally to a smaller venue, and another (Taylor, 1998b) focused on how the 30,000 registrations fell far short of expectations. Overall, however, media coverage of stadium events in early 1998 was extremely similar to that during 1997.

As 1998 went on, it became increasingly obvious that, despite Stand in the Gap, PK had returned to being the big event of the day in a city-near-you, but not the big event in the nation. Even the layoff and rehiring of PK staff received relatively little attention in the nation's print media. And NOW's announcement received almost no attention, despite NOW's newsworthy claim that the layoff and rehiring constituted a hoax, a strategic "fundraising scheme to fool the media ... nothing more than a cynical fundraising ploy, reminiscent of Oral Roberts' assertion that God would call him home if supporters didn't send $7 million to his ministry."

So, is PK merely a shooting star in the media sky, seen brightly but only briefly during the 1997 Washington prayer rally? Or, did PK have as much power or more than ever in 1998, at a time when a strong and favorable public image was necessary to convince thousands to send in money and keep it alive? That is an important question—one that, when answered, might tell us more about the power, or pointlessness, of establishing a certain type of relationship with the media.

PK Leaders' Reactions to Coverage

Despite PK's overwhelmingly favorable coverage, PK participants (see Allen, this volume) and executives have often complained anyway. For instance, *The Wall Street Journal* (Shiflett) reported in October 1994 that "in fact, [PK president] Mr. [Randy] Phillips is amazed by the steadily improving reception his organization is enjoying. 'When we started out,' he says with some understatement, 'the media coverage wasn't always so friendly.'" (Apparently Phillips wanted PK's media coverage "always to be friendly.") McCartney has been bitter about media coverage he received in various stages of his career (McCartney, 1995, 1997a), and other conservative Christian leaders who have spoken at PK events or who have been supportive of PK regularly criticize America's mass media (see Allen, this volume) in speeches, television appearances, fundraising letters and other forums.

But complaints by PK leaders or members that PK received negative coverage generally do not take into account how PK's media coverage compares with that of either current or past religious or social movements, or evangelical denominations generally. And such complaints also do not take into account what PK was or was not doing that would affect its own media coverage. For instance, a *Christianity Today* article (Rabey, 1996) included this disclaimer: "PK did not respond to numerous requests to be interviewed for this story," and it has not been the only article about PK that does not include an official comment when one was or probably was sought (Chengelis, 1996).

Was PK uncooperative or inept in dealing with media because it didn't have staffers with media savvy, or because PK apparently was becoming wildly successful without extensive media coverage, or because of McCartney's (1995, pp. 53–54, 292) history with the media? The answer is not important from the perspective of reporters and editors trying to publish or broadcast stories.

And one of the most unusual aspects of PK's media coverage is that at least some of the negative media coverage PK has received has been the fault of either PK or one of its leaders, such as McCartney. Stammer's article (1996c) in *The Los Angeles Times*, for instance, included this:

> Some Caucasian men who attended last year's Coliseum conference complained afterward that they resented suggestions that they were racist.
> "It didn't come across right," said one white regional officer who was there. "I don't think the speakers thought about what they were really talking about. They were sawing off their own logs talking about how bad things were."
> [PK national spokesman Steve] Chavis acknowledged that Promise Keepers may have pushed "too hard" when it implored participants to seek forgiveness for the sin of racism.

McCartney (1997a), in his much-cited *Policy Review* article, admitted, "We realize that [stadium] conferences might produce a lot of heat, but not much light" and, in his second autobiography, explained, "After the white-knuckle excitement and adrenaline wore off, many who sported PK t-shirts, made vows of purity and lifted hands in worship returned home to resume their carnal, less-than-promise-keeping lifestyles" (quoted in A.D. Banks, 1997). PK spokesman Jim Jewell added, "You just can't fill up stadiums forever. The only way that this will have a lasting impact is if it becomes grounded in local churches involved in the community. It needs to change devotion and faith into a lifestyle and commitment to social change" (Cimons and Zeuthen, 1997). Such statements by PK leaders and spokesmen are commendable for their candor, but when media quote them, both media and PK should be aware that the news media are acting like the ancient bearers of bad news.

The deepest self-inflicted wound of all for PK, if not McCartney's first autobiography, *From Ashes to Glory*, was his second, *Sold Out*. Held for release after Stand in the Gap because McCartney (according to his "literary" agent) "wanted to help men have a tool to process their own spiritual growth," the second book went "into greater detail about McCartney's long battle with alcoholism and the troubles in his marriage" (Murphy, 1997)—just in case Americans hadn't realized after his first book what a "jerk to his own family, a clueless hypocrite" (Waddle, 1997) McCartney was. Media coverage of *Sold Out* concentrated, not surprisingly, on the parts of the book written by McCartney's wife, Lyndi, who admitted to depression, dramatic weight loss, social isolation, anger at her husband's sudden religious conversion, and thoughts of suicide, all after he started Promise Keepers. She also resented her husband's obsession with PK so much that she considered him a hypocrite for asking other men to commit to their families while he was still not doing so himself. But there was more to come. In late October 1997, as Bill McCartney's promotion of his new book was getting into full swing, it was disclosed in *The New York Times* that he had had an extramarital affair more than 25 years earlier—and that the McCartneys had chosen to leave that episode out of their book.

In addition to news coverage that did or might reflect poorly on McCartney or PK, there also has been much coverage whose interpretation depends on what assumptions and attitudes about PK—or Christianity generally—one brings to reading it. For example, *Christian Century* (Smith, 1994) described PK as follows:

> Amazingly absent from Promise Keepers' literature and presentations are many of the elements familiar to followers of the evangelical world. There is little if any political labeling. "Liberals," either political or theological, are not paraded for ridicule. There is scant evidence of the fundamentalists' nonnegotiable principles of faith. Descriptions of Christian belief are framed in broad rather than narrow terms. It would, apparently, be possible to endorse evolution and still be a Promise Keeper.

Given the history and convictions of its leaders, who represent a relatively narrow band of theological opinion, it is not likely that they have significantly modified their beliefs or are less willing to proclaim them. Rather, this at least silent liberalism seems to betoken a conscious retreat on the part of the evangelicals in order to keep the appeal of the "message to men" as broad as possible.

IMPROVING MASS MEDIA'S COVERAGE OF PROMISE KEEPERS

From the vantage point of other U.S. men's organizations or even the Million Women March (the media coverage of which was fairly summed up as "nothing, zip, nada, zero" [Baye, 1997]), it must seem as though Promise Keepers has received a huge amount of media attention. After all, Promise Keepers is far from the first or only men's movement in the United States. The National Organization for Men Against Sexism (formerly National Organization for Changing Men) was formed many years ago, as were "men's rights" groups such as Men's Rights Association and Men's Rights Incorporated. But these organizations have never received much media attention. Traditional men's fraternal organizations, such as the Masons, Elks, Moose, Odd Fellows, Shriners, Eagles and others also receive almost no media coverage, despite their involvement in charities and public events, and their often enormous financial resources (see Rich and de los Reyes, this volume).

PK is only one of many national Christian men's organization, some of which predate PK—such as the Christian Business Men's Committee, which was founded during the Great Depression. Others include, but are not limited to, Christian Men's Network, Dad's University, National Center for Fathering, Career Impact Ministries, Business Life Management, Men Reaching Men, Fathers and Brothers, Dad the Family Shepherd, the Southern Baptist Convention Brotherhood Commission's Men's Ministries (Rabey, 1996), and CatholicMen Fellowships (Schoch, 1996). None of these organizations receives much media coverage either, and there have been few if any attempts by news media to compare and contrast PK with the other men's ministries.

The mythopoetic men's movement (see Clatterbaugh, 1990), whose de facto leader is Robert Bly, gained widespread attention in late 1990 and 1991, when Bly's book, *Iron John*, became a bestseller, followed by Sam Keen's *Fire in the Belly*. Other mythopoetic leaders, such as James Hillman, Michael Meade, Shepherd Bliss and others received notice for their books, speeches or other public activities (Kimmel, 1995). In the early 1990s, hundreds of thousands paid for "wild man weekends," supported "men's centers" in major cities, and bought books and tapes addressing male gender issues. Mythopoetism was covered by myriad newspaper and magazine articles during 1990, 1991 and the first half of 1992, before media coverage slowed to a trickle—where it has remained ever since (Claussen, 1996). The Million Man March, held in Washington in 1995, also was extensively covered at the time. But again, local and national media have provided almost no follow-up coverage of its long-term effects, which have included the mobilization of black men to become more involved in community affairs in places such as Kansas City, MO.

So how did Promise Keepers obtain a place on the nation's media agenda seemingly so quickly and easily? Well, it did and it didn't. Other than extensive coverage in its early years in Denver's *Rocky Mountain News* and *Denver Post* due to PK's launch by McCartney, PK received very little media coverage until the second half of 1994 (Claussen, 1996), and almost all of the early coverage was in either local and regional newspapers or small-circulation magazines. But coverage increased dramatically in the second half of 1994, in part because elite national media such as *The Los Angeles Times*, *The Washington Post* and *The New York Times* finally noticed PK, followed by most other elite national print and broadcast media by mid–1995. This pattern is typical (Grey, 1966), but PK's public relations firm took credit for this."'Promise Keepers was a nonentity five years ago,' says Lawrence Swicegood of the DeMoss Group in Atlanta. 'We've had it for 2½ years, and it is one of the largest religious organizations in the country'" (Rourke, 1997).

But despite the fact that PK has received much more media coverage than most religious organizations or social movements, the news media's coverage of PK still has been woefully incomplete. The majority of academic writing about Promise Keepers places the organization in the history of American evangelical or even fundamentalist organizations, with the phenomena discussed most often ranging from Billy Sunday (Bruns, 1992) and Muscular Christianity, to the Social Gospel organization Men and Religion Forward Movement, to the Moral Majority and the Christian Coalition.

U.S. journalists could do the same. How does Promise Keepers fit into the Third—or depending on how one is counting, the Fourth— Great Awakening (McLoughlin, 1978), assuming one doesn't believe that this latest Awakening has been over for several years? (Why did media portray PK as part of a Christian revival [Stammer, 1996a] at almost the moment it reported that U.S. church attendance had hit an 11-year low after five years of decline? [Stammer, 1996b].) How is Promise Keepers related to, similar to or different from the Christian Coalition, or the Moral Majority (see Quicke and Robinson, this volume)? Why do academics compare and contrast PK with Muscular Christianity (Vance, 1985) or the Men and Religion Forward Movement? Which Christian denominations are officially cooperating with PK and why? What about the more liberal Christians (see Stodghill, 1997) and more conservative Christians (see Eastland, 1997) who are skeptical or even hostile to PK? What is the response of Catholics to PK (see Feuerherd, 1996)? Why is Promise Keepers yet another new religious movement (NRM, to academics) in a country that has had so many others during the past 30 years? How should we account (as did Dart's article in the May 6, 1995, *Los Angeles Times*) for the fact that PK's leaders are largely fundamentalist or Pentecostal/charismatic (see Chrasta, this volume), although most PK followers are not? Does PK take men away from involvement they would otherwise have in local churches (see Tyson, 1997)? What is the role of, and how effective are, the men's small, local accountability groups (see Woodard, 1997)? Media regularly interview other religious organizations' apostates, but what about men who have attended PK events or read PK literature and become disappointed, angry or otherwise dissatisfied? Beyond the usual question of whether PK leaders have ultimately political goals, what about PK participants' objections to the Religious Right political organizations (Lape, 1996; Leo, 1997)? What is the relationship between PK and various charismatic Christian women's movements, which "beneath the surface ... [have] a surprisingly feminist desire for independence and respect" (McDonald, 1997)? And, contrary to what PK critics might ask, why—as compared with other Religious Right organizations—does PK address abortion and homosexuality so rarely? Is it because conservative positions on those issues are taken as givens, or is it because those issues are considered too political and might produce fissures in PK, not to mention less positive press coverage (Eastland, 1997)? American journalists could have been asking all of these questions and many others for several years but almost none have. Surely one reason is that few American journalists are experts on religion, and especially not about the history of religion; one former reporter who was, Mark Silk, didn't even cover religion for the whole time he was at *The Atlanta Journal & Constitution*. Perhaps if more reporters were knowledgeable about religion, the news media would stop its habit of proclaiming—every three or four years—a return to faith in the United States (Marquand, 1996).

Alternately, American journalists might be situating Promise Keepers as part of a larger men's movement in the United States. The media might want to look at what is probably the most unusual aspect of Promise Keepers, considering that it is neither a fraternal nor a liberal organization: its strong advocacy of close male friendships in a culture in which close male friendships (Janssen, 1994)—not the superficial ones most American men have, if they have any at all—are rare due to homophobia, competitiveness, poor communication skills and other factors. But such stories (see Bruni, 1996) are rare. Media might be comparing and contrasting PK with the mythopoetic men's movement (Baum [1997] called PK the "stepson" of mythopoetism), the Million Man March, and various other profeminist men's, men's studies and men's rights organizations and philosophies. But again, this has been uncommon (Religion News Service, 1996b, made a halfhearted attempt), surely at least partially because few (if any) American journalists are experts about male gender and sexuality issues.

Or Promise Keepers might have been covered—fairly or not—as constituting a reaction to feminism. Reporters might have been examining PK, mythopoetism, the Million Man March and perhaps other groups, and comparing and contrasting the groups themselves and the circumstances surrounding their emergence, with some period of feminism (not necessarily the early years of the early 1960s). But when PK and feminism have been discussed at all in the general-interest (i.e. not explicitly feminist publications) mass media, the issue has as often been framed as the National Organization for Women reacting to PK, as if NOW speaks for all feminists or even all women; note, in particular, Suzanne Fields' (1997) *Washington Times* column, which began: "The National Organization for Women is looking for a fight, and they've picked it with God-fearing Christians. That's a bigoted ms.-take." And while attention has been given to PK men's wives who are happy with their husbands' involvement, essentially no attention has been given to PK men's wives, girlfriends, daughters, mothers and sisters who are unhappy, or who think PK is too simplistic (see Smith, 1996; Winner, 1999). Attention also has only rarely been given (see "Suburbia Seeks Salvation," 1997) to PK men and/or their wives who explicitly reject PK teachings vis-à-vis marital roles. Lipsyte (1997) noted, "I'd become a Promise Keeper myself if McCartney dropped the gender war and started a class war."

The mass media might be covering PK's racial reconciliation efforts more deeply, including why PK seems to avoid words "like integration and equality" (Stodghill, 1997) and, in particular, concentrating more on the reactions it receives from average black Americans and the continued difficulty of mandating an end to racism (Goodstein, 1997). But again, with few exceptions (Hamblin, 1996), media coverage of any but PK's claims is superficial (DeParle, 1996) to nonexistent.

The mass media might well be covering gay men who attend Promise Keepers events (Hannaham, 1996; Leo, 1997, quoting *The Washington Blade*), not only gay men who protest PK, and PK men who reject PK's official position on homosexuality. But, apparently, no story published in any publication in America through mid-1998 has tackled this angle in any detail.

Media have provided apparently no in-depth coverage of PK's plan to expand abroad; as of June 1997, PK had affiliates in Canada, Australia and New Zealand, and was "developing relationships with men's groups in 40 countries in all" (Kennedy, 1997). But, generally, Americans must read Canadian magazines (Philips, 1997) to learn anything about PK's Canadian operations. Scandale (1997) joked that, as PK goes global, "They have no idea what they're in for when they encourage thousands of Germans to hug Team Denmark. There's going to be a lot of crying, but absolutely no hugging." But how PK is received overseas is not only a serious question, but an interesting story.

Finally, the mass media could try covering PK as a sort of cultural phenomenon—religious revival as cultural fad, or as yet more groupthink in our only partially well-educated and profoundly anti-intellectual country (Hofstadter, 1963; Wood, 1996). This would have prompted questions, among others, about whether PK men were practicing what they were preaching, and why attendance at regional PK events dropped off so significantly in 1997. (McCartney [1997b] has blamed whites' reaction to the racial conciliation theme, but it may simply have been boredom; as van Leeuwen wrote [1997], "Like going to a Billy Graham crusade, once you've been to one PK rally you've pretty much been to all of them.") But the mass media have particularly wanted to avoid questioning anyone's motives, sincerity or intelligence. Among the few exceptions, Raab (1996) went too far in comparing a PK event to a Nazi rally in his article, "Triumph of His Will," and Hitchens (1997) amused only himself by calling PK "Mass Millerite Madness," "Moral Majority Manipulation," "Mellow Musings on the Mall," and "Another Prick in the Wall." King (1997), despite her whimsical reporting on a stereotypical Southerner named Earl, has been essentially alone in asking more serious questions in the conservative *National Review*:

> All right, so I'm a cynic. That's better than being a desperate idealist like most of my fellow conservative columnists, who let themselves be persuaded that PK's gospel according to the T-shirt signaled the ultimate victory for family values. When will we learn that religion does not a conservative make, nor atheism a liberal? Like all people driven by emotion, PK could be swung like a lariat; the Right is in trouble if we think that 700,000 weeping men is good news in an era that is already close to rule by hysteria. Whatever happened to our traditional distrust of the mob?
>
> I also reject the view put forth by several gleeful conservative pundits that PK dealt a fatal blow to radical feminism. After three decades of male bashing, what is there to gloat about in the spectacle of 700,000 men curdling with guilt and begging for forgiveness? It sounds like successful brainwashing to me.

Media also might be covering PK as big business (Torry, 1997), despite its non-profit status. Swomley (1996) observed, "Promise Keepers is preeminently a commercial enterprise. This commercial trademark appears on the tracts and books which are for sale in the huge tents set up next to the meeting sites. Dozens of cash registers in the so-called Ministry Booths ring up sales in the hundreds of thousands of dollars. Credit card transactions are welcomed. In addition to the religious literature, they offer for sale a wide variety of merchandise. This includes ball caps, T-shirts, sweat shirts, lapel pins, cassettes, CDs and other types of souvenirs—all of which bear the PK logo." And after all, not every non-profit organization spends about $200 million in two years (1996 and 1997), fires part of its staff, then decides to dramatically cut its revenues, then lays off its entire staff, and then rehires the staff. With non-profit organizations, and churches in particular, being big businesses in the United States, this was a great business story by journalistic standards. But the media, with few exceptions, have not covered this story either.

CONCLUSIONS

Why has PK received almost entirely positive coverage (complaints from some PK men who want the media to be even bigger cheerleaders notwithstanding)? First, as has been shown, the mass media's coverage of Promise Keepers has been superficial year after year. This is partly because few reporters who cover evangelical organizations, gender issues, or social movements are truly knowledgeable about their subject matter. Second, perhaps conservative Christians are now seen by many media workers as part of the status quo, rather than as a threat to it; a majority of today's journalists say that religion is important in their own lives (Dart & Allen, 1994). Third, perhaps media workers have a difficult time questioning an organization that is public, Christian, anti-racist and espouses racial reconciliation; rapidly grew in popularity, causing men to renew family and community commitments; and denies that it is sexist. Promise Keepers also says very little about homosexuality or abortion—unlike fundraising letters mailed and some speeches made by various Religious Right leaders who often act as though homosexuality has had more negative consequences for American society than poor parenting, racism, sexism, poverty, illiter-acy, crime, anti-intellectualism and poor schools, children's (and adults') easy access to guns, prisons that fail to rehabilitate, political apathy, thedeclining work ethic, or the country's superficial, overly-materialistic consumerism.

Fourth, it is possible that the media were "primed" by their experience covering mythopoetism to cover PK more positively. In other words, media might have given mythopoets less or more negative coverage (for example, see Ferguson, 1992) on the basis that some thought the group was an anomaly, and that men's issues really weren't of any importance in society. But when PK emerged, media workers might have realized that Men's Movements and men's issues weren't limited to one organization, philosophy or theme and therefore must have broader support and be more important.

Fifth, one wonders to what extent the news media may be writing neutral to positive articles about PK at least in part to avoid the feedback they would receive from readers in PK. Novosad (1996), for instance, reported, "The newspaper that ran the controversial Promise Keepers article received protest calls for more than two weeks after it appeared and subsequently ran a column indicating the callers were right, the paper should not have devoted so much space to the protesters."

Sixth, perhaps some media workers were unaware of how conservative PK is, and would have written or edited stories differently had they known. Seventh, perhaps media workers believe that the state of society has become so grim that an organization such as PK—even if media workers don't agree with all of the ways in which it has framed social problems, causes, consequences and solutions—can only do more good than harm. Greenberg (1997), for instance, wrote:

> How will the Promise Keepers fit into this historical pattern [of revivals]? "By their fruits ye shall know them." Before judging, or even better, instead of judging the Promise Keepers right now, perhaps their critics can explain how they themselves would propose to lift the standards of American society—and do it without running the grave risk of invoking moral values.

Eighth, the news media simply seem to find it difficult to negatively cover national organizations or events-oriented organizations, especially those that have top public relations advisers, as PK now does. One must wonder if PK would be receiving a substantial, growing amount of news coverage if it had a magazine, books and tapes, and local chapters, but no large public events. It is doubtful under those circumstances that PK would receive much, if any, news coverage.

Ninth, perhaps PK fared better because the mythopoets' message was more "ambiguous, unfinished, and versatile" (van Zoonen, 1996) than PK's, and because of the differences in their names: the obscure, academic-sounding word, "mythopoetic," versus the clear, positive "Promise Keepers" (McCombs and Shaw, 1993).

In any case, the fact also remains that no matter how favorable media coverage of PK has been, PK men are never quite satisfied with it. As Allen (this volume) and others (Maus, 1990) have shown, ultimately this does not seem to be related to anything the mass media do or don't do, but primarily because PK men apparently distrust and dislike the mass media no matter what they do. Nowhere was this more evident than in an article by Eric Frazier (1997), the religion reporter at the *Charleston Post and Courier*. If one reporter at a newspaper could be assumed to be friendly to religion, it would be the religion reporter. And if any part of the country could be assumed to be friendly to PK, it would be a state such as South Carolina. But PK men grilled Frazier anyway:

> What church did I attend, they asked. What did I think of Promise Keepers? Their intentions were obvious: They wanted to know if I

stood for this great movement or against it. (I'm sure the fact that I was a reporter from the ever-questioning, left-leaning, Godless media made me spiritually suspect in their eyes.)

References

Banks, A.D. (1997, November 28). Bill McCartney bares his soul in new book. *The* (Raleigh) *News and Observer*, E3.

Banks, S. (1997, October 10). Life as we live it: Must strong men be such a threat? *The Los Angeles Times*, E1.

Baum, M.D. (1997, November 14). "Iron John" Bly will speak for Dismas House appeal. *The Chattanooga Times*, B6.

Baye, B.W. (1997, October 30). Black women are people of value. *The* (Louisville) *Courier-Journal*, 13A.

Bly, R. (1990). *Iron John: A book about men*. Reading, MA: Addison–Wesley.

Brand-Williams, O. (1998, May 14). Promise Keepers return: Thousands expected at Christian conference as group faces fire from gays, minorities. *The Detroit News*, C1.

Briggs, J.B. (1992). *Iron Joe Bob*. New York: The Atlantic Monthly Press.

Bruni, F. (1996, September 22). In the arena of faithful, joyful noise and prayer. *The New York Times*, 1/43.

Bruns, R.A. (1992). *Preacher: Billy Sunday and big time American evangelism*. New York: Norton.

Butler, M., & Paisley, W. (1978). Magazine coverage of women's rights: What does "she" mean? *Journal of Communication 28*(1), 183–186.

Cantor, M.G. (1990). Prime-time fathers: A study in continuity and change. *Critical Studies in Mass Communication 7*, 275–285.

Chengelis, A.S. (1996, September 15). U-M game report. *The Detroit News*, E6.

Cimons, M., & Zeuthen, K. (1997, September 30). Participants, doubters ponder premise of Promise Keepers movement: As huge gathering nears, leaders of Christian group consider ways to broaden impact. Critics fear a return to restrictive roles for women. *The Los Angeles Times*, A5.

Clatterbaugh, K. (1990). *Contemporary perspectives on masculinity: Men, women, and politics in modern society*. Boulder, CO: Westview Press.

Claussen, D.S. (1996). *United States print mass media coverage of two men's movements: Robert Bly, Iron John, and the mythopoets, and Bill McCartney and the Promise Keepers*. Unpublished master's thesis, Kansas State University, Manhattan.

Claussen, D.S. (ed.) (1999). *Standing on the Promises: The Promise Keepers and the Revival of Manhood*. Cleveland: Pilgrim Press.

Coakley, J.J. (1986). *Sport in society: Issues and controversies*. St. Louis, MO: Times Mirror/Mosby.

Conason, J., Ross, A., & Cokorinos, L. (1997, October 7). The Promise Keepers are coming: The third wave of the Religious Right. *The Nation 263*, 11–19.

Connell, R.W. (1990). *Love fast and die young: The construction of masculinity among young working-class men on the margin of the labour market.* Unpublished manuscript, Department of Sociology, Macquarie University (Australia).
Conniff, R. (1997, November). Invasion of the Promise Keepers. *Progressive 61,* 10.
Craig, S. (ed.) (1992). *Men, masculinity, and the media.* Newbury Park, CA: Sage Publications.
Daniels, G.L. (1998, March). *Praying portrayals: How newspapers covered the Promise Keepers "Stand in the Gap" rally.* Paper presented to the Newspaper Division, AEJMC Southeast Colloquium, New Orleans, La.
Dart, J. (1995, May 6). Promise Keepers, a message to L.A. men conference: Gathering at the Coliseum includes 15 hours of events designed to spread the group's belief in traditional father-husband duties. About 70,000 are expected to attend. *The Los Angeles Times.*
Dart, J., & Allen, J. (1994). *Bridging the gap: Religion and the news media.* Nashville, TN: Freedom Forum.
DeCelle, D. (1996, July 3). Among the Promise Keepers: A pastor's reflections. *Christian Century 113,* 695–697.
DeHaven, J. (1998, May 11). Casino foes look for new life: Coalition counts on Promise Keepers rally for support as petition drive loses steam. *The Detroit News,* D1.
DeParle, J. (1996, August 4). The Christian right confesses sins of racism. *The New York Times,* 4/5.
Diaz, G. (1996, December 29). Playing by God's rules. *The Orlando Sentinel,* C6.
Duncan, M.C., Messner, M.A., & Williams, L. (1990). *Gender stereotyping in televised sports.* Los Angeles: The Amateur Athletic Association of Los Angeles.
Eastland, T. (1997, October 20). Promise Keepers and the press. *The Weekly Standard,* 17.
Fejes, F.F. (1992). Masculinity as fact: A review of the empirical mass communication research on masculinity. In S. Craig (ed.), *Men, masculinity, and the media.* Newbury Park, Calif.: Sage Publications.
Ferguson, A. (1992, January). America's new man. *The American Spectator 25,* 26–33.
Feuerherd, P. (1996, October 25). Not your momma: Promise Keepers, an all-male Protestant evangelical group. *Commonweal 123,* 31.
Fewer Promise Keepers than expected to show at War Memorial Stadium. (1998, May 21). *Arkansas Democrat-Gazette,* E8.
Fields, S. (1996, December 26). Dealing with moral issues from the gut. Los Angeles Times Syndicate column, published Dec. 26 in the *Tampa Tribune,* December 29 in the *Fort Worth Star-Telegram* (Editorial section, p. 8) and other newspapers.
Fields, S. (1997, September 1). Enough of NOW. *The Washington Times,* A21.
Find out for yourself. (1998, May 23). *Arkansas Democrat-Gazette,* B8.
Frazier, E. (1997, October 12). Promises, promises: The Promise Keepers movement draws out enthusiastic crowds publicly, but the true test of the

movement's spiritual force will be tried privately in homes. *The* (Charleston) *Post and Courier*, E13.

Fulwood, S. III (1997, October 5). Though united by faith, personal quests drew many: For one man, going to the rally meant expressing his Christianity openly. For others, attendance was a civic duty. *The Los Angeles Times*, A24.

Gilbreath, E. (1998, May). A time of reckoning. *New Man*, 22–24.

Gingold, A. (1991). *Fire in the john: The manly man in the age of sissification.* New York: St. Martin's Press.

Goodman, W. (1997, October 6). Day of prayerful messages for the crowd on the mall. *The New York Times*, E3.

Goodstein, L. (1997, September 29). For Christian men's group, racial harmony starts at the local level. *The New York Times*, A12.

Gray H. (1986). Television and the new black man: Black male images in prime-time situation comedy. *Media, Culture & Society 9*, 223–242.

Greenberg, P. (1997, October 22). Promise Keepers part of America's longstanding reform tradition. *The* (Charleston) *Post and Courier*, A17.

Grey, D.L. (1966). Decision-making by a reporter under deadline pressure. *Journalism Quarterly 43*, 419–428.

Hamblin, K. (1996, June 25). A patronizing promise. *The Denver Post*, B-07.

Hannaham, H. (1996, October 1). Losers, weepers. *Village Voice 41*, 31.

Hitchens, C. (1997, October 27). Another march, another prick in the wall. *The Nation 265*, 9.

Hofstadter, R. (1963). *Anti-intellectualism in American life.* New York: Knopf.

Hoynes, W., & Croteau, D. (1989). *Are you on the "Nightline" guest list?* New York: Fairness & Accuracy in Reporting.

Janssen, A., & Weeden, L.K. (eds.) (1994). *Seven promises of a Promise Keeper.* Colorado Springs, CO: Focus on the Family Publishing.

Jolliffe, L. (1989). Comparing gender differentiation in the *New York Times*, 1885 and 1985. *Journalism Quarterly 66*, 683–691.

Jolliffe, L. (1996). The disposable sex: Men in the news. In P.M. Lester (ed.), *Images that injure: Pictorial stereotypes in the media.* Westport, CT: Praeger.

Keen, S. (1991). *Fire in the belly: On being a man.* New York: Bantam Books.

Kennedy, J.W. (1997, June 16). Promise Keepers goes global. *Christianity Today 41*, 58.

Kimmel, M. (1995). *The politics of manhood: Profeminist men respond to the mythopoetic men's movement (and the mythopoetic leaders answer).* Philadelphia: Temple University Press.

King, F. (1997, November 10). The misanthrope's corner. *National Review 49*, 68.

Lape, H.N. (1996, Sepember 29). On Promise Keepers, don't play to fears [letter to the editor]. *The New York Times*, 4/14.

The last punching-bag (1997, October 1). *The Richmond Times-Dispatch*, A10.

Leo, J. (1997, November 3). Men behaving well. *U.S. News & World Report 123*, 16.

Lieb, T. (1991). *Ms.-ing the news: Mass media coverage of women's issues and the feminist movement, 1963–1977.* Unpublished doctoral dissertation, University of Maryland—College Park.

Lipsyte, R. (1997, October 12). Of owners, coaches, Promise Keepers and today's new sports order. *The New York Times*, 8/6.
Lucal, B. (1995). The problem with "battered husbands." *Deviant Behavior: An Interdisciplinary Journal 16*, 95–112.
Luebke, B. (1989). Out of focus: Images of women and men in newspaper photographs. *Sex Roles 20*(3-4), 121–133.
Marquand, R. (1996, December 31). America taps religious roots in year of spiritual questing. *The Christian Science Monitor*, 1.
Maudlin, M.G. (1992, Oct. 5). Spiritual fads and evangelistic opportunities: I am man, hear me roar. *Christianity Today 36*, 73.
Maus, M. (1990). Believers as behavers: News coverage of evangelicals by the secular media. In Q.J. Schultze (ed.), *American evangelicals and the mass media: Perspectives on the relationship between American evangelicals and the mass media.* Grand Rapids, MI: Academie Books/Zondervan Publishing House.
McCartney, B. (1995). *From ashes to glory, 2nd ed.*, Nashville: Thomas Nelson Inc.
McCartney, B. (1997a). Promise makers. *Policy Review 85*, 14–19.
McCartney, B. (1997b). *Sold out: Becoming man enough to make a difference.* Dallas: Word Books.
McCartney, B. (1998, June 5). *The Fresno Bee*, B9.
McCartney, B., et al. (1992). *What makes a man? 12 promises that will change your life.* Colorado Springs, CO: Navpress Publishing Group.
McCombs, M.E., & Shaw, D.L. (1993). The evolution of agenda-setting theory: 25 years in the marketplace of ideas. *Journal of Communication 43*(2), 58–66.
McDonald, D.F. (1998, June 19). Promise Keepers. *NBC NewsChannel* script, Charlotte, NC.
McDonald, M. (1997, October 6). My wife told me to go. *U.S. News & World Report 123*, 28.
McLoughlin, W.G. (1978). *Revivals, awakenings, and reform: An essay on religion and social change in America, 1607–1977.* Chicago: The University of Chicago Press.
Meyers, R. (1980). *An examination of the male sex role model in prime time television commercials.* ERIC Document Reproduction Service No. ED 208 437.
Minkowitz, D. (1995, November/December). In the name of the father. *Ms. 6*, 64–71.
Murphy, C. (1997, November 1). After the big rally, head of Promise Keepers brings out 2nd autobiography. *The Washington Post*, B8.
Novosad, N. (1996, August). God squad. *Progressive 60*, 25.
Parsons, D. (1997, October 5). There isn't anything wrong with keeping a promise. *The Los Angeles Times*, B1.
Phillips, A. (1997, October 6). Christian men on the march. *Maclean's 110*, 52–53.
Pollitt, K. (1997, October 27). The promised land. *The Nation 265*, 13.
Postman, N., Nystrom, C., Strate, L., & Weingartner, C. (1987). *Myths, men and beer: An analysis of beer commercials on broadcast television.* Falls Church, VA: AAA Foundation for Traffic Safety.
Promise Keepers to lay off paid staff (1998, March 11). *Christian Century 115*, 254–255.

Raab, S. (1996, January). Triumph of his will. *GQ 66*, 110–117+.
Rabey, S. (1996, April 29). Where is the Christian men's movement headed? Burgeoning Promise Keepers inspires lookalikes. *Christianity Today 40*, 46–49, 60.
Religion News Service (1996a, Feb. 24). Revival group preaches racial unity; Evangelism. *The Los Angeles Times*.
Religion News Service (1996b, August 24). Promise Keepers eclipsing secular men's groups; Christian gatherings attract millions, while myth-oriented, pro-feminist and fathers' rights movements lag far behind. *The Los Angeles Times*, B4.
Risen, J. (1997, October 5). Christian men hold huge rally on D.C. mall; Promise Keepers crowd reaches historic proportions in day of prayer and pledges. Fundamentalists stream in from across the country for multiracial gathering. *The Los Angeles Times*, A1.
Robinson, G.J. (1978). Women, media access and social control. In L.K. Epstein (ed.), *Women and the news*. New York: Hastings House Publishers.
Rosin, H. (1997, October 27). Promise weepers. *The New Republic 217*, 11–12.
Rourke, M. (1997, January 18). Big names in religion use a little PR to reach the masses. *The* (Memphis) *Commercial Appeal*, A11.
Scandale, F. (1997, October 26). He said, she said. *The Denver Post*, E-2.
Schoch, D. (1996, January 28). Putting faith in God's game plan: Catholic men gather for a super Saturday of sharing. *The Los Angeles Times*, B1.
Seyfarth, S. (1992). Arnold Schwarzenegger and Iron John: Predator to protector. *Studies in Popular Culture 15*(1), 75–81.
Shiflett, D. (1994, Oct. 12). Dads vs. the devil. *The Wall Street Journal*, A1.
Shor, F. (1993). Contrasting images of reconstructing manhood: Bly's Wild Man versus Spielberg's Inner Child. *Journal of Men's Studies 2*(2), 109–128.
Skelly, G., & Lundstrom, W. (1981). Male sex roles in magazine advertising, 1959–1979. *Journal of Communication 31*(4), 52–57.
Smith, C.C. (1994, Sept. 7–14). Message to men. *Christian Century 111*, 805–806.
Smith, L. (1996, July 21). Real life: '90s family; Men can't be good dads if moms block the way. *The Los Angeles Times*, E3.
Snyder, H.A. (1994, Nov. 14). Will Promise Keepers keep their promises? *Christianity Today 38*, 20–21.
Solomon, N. (1996, August 6). Promise Keepers gains reverential coverage. *The Arizona Republic*, B7.
Spalding, J.D. (1996, March 6). Bonding in the bleachers: A visit to the Promise Keepers. *Christian Century 113*, 260–265.
Spilka, B., Lacey, G., & Gelb, B. (1979). Sex discrimination after death: A replication, extension and a difference. *Omega Journal of Death and Dying 10*(3), 227–233.
Stammer, L.B. (1996a, January 20). Many American Christians believe Kingdom of God is near. *The Dallas Morning News*, 4G.
Stammer, L.B. (1996b, March 2). Church attendance falls to 11-year low; Head of survey says findings contradict claims by some denominations of a widespread revival. *The Los Angeles Times*, B4.

Stammer, L.B. (1996c, December 7). Promise Keepers dodges skeptics in dropping bid for Rose Bowl rally: Critic says move was made to avoid hearing on male supremicist views. Men's group claims higher calling. *The Los Angeles Times*, B4.
Stammer, L.B., & Granberry, M. (1997, October 3). D.C. rally draws men on a mission. *The Los Angeles Times*, A1.
Steinfels, P. (1997, October 18). Beliefs. *The New York Times*, B5.
Stodghill, R. II (1997, October 6). God of our fathers. *Time 150*, 34–40.
Strate, L. (1992). Beer commercials: A manual on masculinity. In S. Craig (ed.), *Men, masculinity, and the media*. Newbury Park, CA: Sage Publications.
Suburbia seeks salvation. (1997, October 11). *The Economist 354*, 30.
Swanson, N. (1997, October 15). A report from the Promise Keepers' Washington gathering. *Flagpole*, 6–7.
Swomley, J. (1996, September/October). Cashing in for Christ. *Humanist 56*, 39–41.
Taylor, J.G. (1998a, April 22). Promise Keepers may pick Fresno rally site next week. *The Fresno Bee*, B3.
Taylor, J.G. (1998b, June 5). Promise Keepers praying for last-minute increase; Organizers hope to draw more than the 30,000 registered men. *The Fresno Bee*, B6.
Taylor, J.G. (1998c, June 7). Promise Keepers get new orders: Group president tells 23,000 men to get set for millennium rally. *The Fresno Bee*, B1.
Tompkins, J. (1994). Saving our lives: Dances with Wolves, Iron John and the search for a new masculinity. In M. Torgovnick (ed.), *Eloquent obsessions: Writing cultural criticism*. Durham, NC: Duke University Press.
Torry, S. (1997, September 29). Promise Keepers success also measured in dollars: Group has rapidly become a big business. *The Washington Post*, A1.
Tyson, A.S. (1997, October 6). Why men throng rallies, but not pews. *Christian Science Monitor 89*, 11.
Vance, N. (1985). *The sinews of the spirit: The ideal of Christian manliness in Victorian literature and religious thought*. Cambridge, United Kingdom: Cambridge University Press.
van Leeuwen, M.S. (1997, October 22). Mixed messages on the mall. *Christian Century 114*, 932–934.
van Zoonen, E.A. (1996). A dance of death: New Social Movements and mass media. In D.L. Paletz (ed.), *Political communication in action: States, institutions, movements, audiences*. Cresskill, NJ: Hempton Press, Inc.
Waddle, R. (1997, November 23). How trial and error yielded the top Promise Keeper. *The* (Nashville) *Tennessean*, 2D.
Wanta, W., & Leggett, D. (1989). Gender stereotypes in wire service sports photos. *Newspaper Research Journal 10*(3), 105–114.
Wilgoren, J. (1997, October 5). Southern Californians flock to join brethren at national revival: Men from skid row's L.A. mission, suburban churchgoers journeyed to Promise Keepers' rally. Van Nuys pastor Jack Hayford emceed the event. *The Los Angeles Times*, A24.

Winner, L.F. (1999). Kept women. In Claussen, D.S. (ed.), *Standing on the promises: The Promise Keepers and the revival of manhood*. Cleveland: Pilgrim Press.
Winners & Losers (1997, October 13). *Time 150*, 17.
Wolf, R. (1995, Aug. 8). Men at work—on the power of prayer: Growing movement shows husbands, fathers new way. *USA Today*.
Wood, D.N. (1996). *Post-intellectualism and the decline of democracy: The failure of reason and responsibility in the twentieth century*. Westport, CT: Praeger.
Woodard, J. (1997, April 7). A popular men's movement under fire. *Alberta Report/Western Report 24*, 44.
Woodward, K.L. (1994, Aug. 29). The gospel of guyhood. *Newsweek 124*, 60–61.

Conclusion

Will the Promises Be Kept?
by Robert D. Linder

The main charge to historians is to make sense out of the past. The editor has asked me, as a historian, to discuss the meaning of the essays contained in this volume, identify the main insights which I believe they have revealed, and bring this discussion to an appropriate conclusion. It is a daunting challenge because the foregoing contributions come from scholars in a wide variety of disciplines with a diversity of viewpoints. Nevertheless, with a baseball umpire's mandate to "call 'em as I see 'em," I will proceed with my appointed task by summarizing the collection, highlighting several chapters that I believe to be outstanding contributions to the purpose of the volume, note what I see as problems with some of the essays, and briefly discuss the main issues raised by the various authors.

Some of the pieces in this book complement each other nicely (e.g., Quicke/Robinson, Balmer and Brickner), others contradict each other (e.g., Lundskow and Cole), and a few both complement and contradict each other simultaneously (e.g., Waters, Allen and Claussen). The result is not only intellectually healthy and mentally stimulating but also at times makes the head spin! Moreover, several of the articles themselves will invite the kind of verbal and rhetorical analysis to which some of them have subjected the Promise Keepers (PK) verba and dicta. Most of all, this collection illustrates the fact that PK has invited this attention because it has been the fastest growing and most dynamic religious movement in the United States today and is well on its way to being the movement most heavily covered by the mass media, and most intensely scrutinized by scholars.

Summary of Main Points

This collection of essays accomplishes the general purpose of the book to present a wide variety of ideas and opinions about PK in diverse styles, with a variety of viewpoints, and from the perspective of several disciplines. Although a little weak in terms of numbers of representatives from history and political science, the contributors do, in fact, represent these disciplines along with journalism/mass communication, sociology, speech communication and sport science, as well as American and women's studies. Especially prominent are scholars involved in various aspects of communications studies. PK leaders will be interested and perhaps amused to learn that a large segment of their stadium crowds have been communications researchers and freelance reporters scrutinizing their rhetoric.

In any case, the contributors are primarily academics trying to understand and explain the PK movement from a scholarly perspective. Scholars are by nature critical. However, in this volume, the scholars are of two kinds: critics and friendly critics, and their perspectives are fairly easy to identify. Their two basic types of critiques, in turn, give the collection a nice balance, with most of the essays falling somewhere between the undisguised hostility of the National Organization for Women at one end of the socio-political spectrum (NOW website) and the hammer blows of fundamentalist Phil Arms at the other (Arms, 1997). In any event, the interdisciplinary approach of this volume is bound to have broad appeal to a wide reading public.

This collection will leave three lasting impressions on readers. First, there is both more and less to PK than meets the eye. Every essay takes a peek into some corner of the movement, raising questions concerning what is going on there, some with a more powerful analytical flashlight than others. Nevertheless, all reveal aspects of this Christian men's movement that need attention but which have been hitherto largely neglected by scholarly research. Moreover, with the impressive PK "Stand in the Gap" rally in Washington, DC, on October 4, 1997, and the publication of PK leader Bill McCartney's latest book (*Sold Out*, 1997), and with plans for more stadium events in the near future, there is reason to expect that the movement will receive increasing attention from the public, the press and politicians. This interest will be heightened by breaking events during this volume's gestation period: a new free admission policy for stadium events, financial difficulties at PK headquarters, plans (now cancelled) to hold rallies on the steps of every US state capitol on January 1, 2000, and a grandiose vision for global expansion (Kennedy, 1998, p. 29).

Second, it seems evident that PK is a genuine Christian grassroots movement, with all the strengths and weaknesses of such dynamic action groups which originate outside of normal power centers. The very fact that it was born in Boulder, CO, far away from the great media concentrations on the two coasts, is in itself a remarkable feature of the movement. As journalist Gustav Niebuhr of the *New York Times* noted in his profile of the PK movement on the day before the Washington rally in October 1997, the fact that a football coach from the heartland could build such a large religious movement was evidence that Christian energy was now coming from "outside traditional institutions." Moreover, it was employing methods and insights that had largely escaped denominational leaders and other members of the American religious establishment (Niebuhr, 1997, p. A1).

McCartney transferred his considerable organizational and communications skills from the football field to the religious arena with marked success. However, he seemed at first to be unaware of the higher stakes and their consequently more intense scrutiny as he gradually shifted his primary focus from sports and entertainment to religion. To make matters more interesting and complicated, McCartney was and is no theologian. He soon found that some questioners and critics tested his theological sophistication, and he has spent increasing amounts of time with people whom he believes can help him with this blindspot. Because of his initial lack of theological finesse, and other, more personal, reasons, he was reluctant in the early days of the movement to deal at length with the media. However, he soon found that this did not help his cause.

Moreover, McCartney is an intelligent individual who gives every indication of being educable in terms of furthering his movement without compromising its basic goal of re-establishing integrity among those American males who profess to be followers of Jesus Christ. Therefore, the story of the movement as it has unfolded since its foundation in 1991 has been one of stumbling forward, with indications of increased understanding of how to deal with the media and the general public (see esp. Waters' chapter for evidence). In so doing, McCartney has become the leader of a major religious revival that, as now constituted, stands primarily in the holiness-pentecostal-charismatic tradition. It is not clear if it will continue in this vein. It is clear that McCartney senses that it needs to be more broadly evangelical if he is to accomplish his goals, and he seems to be moving in that direction. In all of this, he is more of a Luther than a Calvin. Just as Martin Luther was the fomenter and main symbol but not the systematic theologian of the Protestant Reformation of the 16th century, so McCartney has been the fomenter and main symbol but hardly the systematic theologian of the PK movement in the 1990s. The Coach has yet to find his Calvin.

Third, these essays make it clear that both PK and its opponents see the movement as part of the "culture wars" that erupted in the U.S. in the 1980s (J.D. Hunter, 1991, pp. 52–64). This struggle to define basic American values after the breakup in the 1920s of the previously dominant Protestant moral consensus, and the moral shifting sands that followed, exacerbated by the political and social turmoil of the 1960s, has left the nation searching for a new national moral concord. One recent response has been to resort to "multiculturalism," an often ill-defined term that usually is popularly interpreted as meaning "live and let live" while respecting everybody's culture.

But, as sociologist James Davison Hunter points out, most Americans have not been satisfied with this attempt to patch up American society. Moreover, the debate is not about opinions or attitudes toward specific issues but over fundamentally different concepts of moral authority (J.D. Hunter, 1991, pp. 49–52). Therefore, PK cannot be understood solely as a part of the history of religious awakenings in the U.S. but needs to be placed in the context of the late 20th-century effort to define the meaning of America itself—what it has been in the past, what it is now, and what it aspires to be in the future (Wuthnow, 1989, pp. 3–18). As several of the foregoing essays have emphasized (e.g., Kelley and Allen) and all have pointed out, both the leaders and the rank-and-file of the PK movement are aware of this conflict and are determined, with the help of God, to win it. In order to comprehend how important this larger historical context is for understanding this movement, it is well to keep in mind that PK is a part of the largest single group of religious Americans: evangelical Christianity, a well-educated segment of the population, with increasing wealth and political influence at its disposal (Marsden, 1984, pp. vii–xix; Noll, 1994, pp. 8–9). In short, what Promise Keepers do matters!

Highlights

As most reviewers of published collections of essays usually remark at some point in their critiques, the articles in this volume are uneven in form, content and value. This, no doubt, will be said of this book, despite the best efforts of the editor to impose some kind of intellectual order, and precisely because Claussen has deliberately set out to allow the various contributors the freedom to speak for themselves from within their own disciplines. Also, some of the writers, in my judgment, have contributed better written, better researched and better balanced studies than others.

In these terms, I believe that Lundskow, Beal, Balmer and Brickner have made the most valuable contributions to this book. Moreover, it seems to me that the last three chapters by Waters, Allen and Claussen are dynamite, especially in terms of what they claim to have discovered about the internal workings of the PK movement in the context of its coverage by the mass media.

Using a sensitive and well-developed interview protocol and questionnaire, sociologist Lundskow conducted 22 intensive interviews with PK men and five with PK wives. He defined his terms, set forth his methodology and explained his goals, all with great care and attention to detail. Moreover, he was forthright and honest with his interviewees about his intentions. In particular, he wanted to find out what PK men think and feel about life, religion, the family and themselves. He also attempted to discover how much of official PK doctrine they internalize, to what extent they alter it, and how much satisfaction they receive from their PK experiences. In particular, he wanted to know how much authoritarianism the movement displayed, especially among the rank-and-file.

His investigation yielded carefully-stated and well-articulated conclusions that are important for an understanding of the movement: (1) it is not a virulent authoritarian movement that threatens the rights of others; (2) participation in the small group meetings at the local level is the most important aspect of being a PK adherent; (3) the movement contains many positive and humanitarian aspects that complement its elements of a soft patriarchy; and (4) PK adherents are conservative on most issues but seem to have no desire to develop public policy or laws based on their religious values. Lundskow's essay is well-written and clear, and he himself is probably as objective as a scholar can be about such a dynamic, controversial group. In short, his work is nicely written and a model of sound scholarship.

Beal's essay stands out because it is a hard-hitting and openly feminist critique of one of the most important features of the PK movement, namely, its use of sport as a means of promoting its program. Her analysis focuses on three ways in which sport is utilized to support a patriarchal ideology: (1) using it as a demonstration of masculine qualities that are linked with a superior kind of leadership; (2) utilizing it as a means to rally men around male superiority; and (3) using sport images and metaphors to conjure mental images of male superiority.

With this focus, Beal correctly identifies PK's concern for what it perceives to be the ethical decay of American society. However, in tracing the roots of that concern, she fails to distinguish between the more broad category of "evangelical" and the more narrow one of "fundamentalist," and does not seem to be aware of the basic holiness-pentecostal-charismatic roots of the movement. Her case would be strengthened and her understanding broadened if she realized that all fundamentalists are evangelicals but not all evangelicals are fundamentalists. Moreover, although fundamentalists and holiness-pentecostal-charismatic Christians share much in common, they disagree on several key doctrines, such as the meaning of the gifts of the Spirit, which make the PK strain of evangelicalism more flexible than fundamentalism.

These few problems aside, she clearly illustrates why feminists have legitimate concerns about PK efforts to reestablish male leadership as a solution to social problems, fearing that this could easily result in the dismissal of the leadership that women have exercised in this area in recent years. In this instance, she may not fully understand PK's theology of male leadership; for example, it consistently claims that it does not seek male privilege. On the other hand, she exposes a great deal of silliness in the writings of PK supporters, especially in the publications of authors Gary Smalley and John Trent. For instance, in *What Makes a Man* (McCartney et al., 1992), Smalley and Trent introduce three shining examples of men who kept their promises: Jesus Christ, Douglas MacArthur and Babe Ruth. Beal notes the irony of using the hard-living Ruth as a role model for men dedicated to moral, spiritual and sexual purity. Although the Babe was one of the greatest baseball players of all time, he was also a major league womanizer and boozer who may or may not have kept his legendary promises to his fans. Jesus and perhaps MacArthur pass muster as "promise-keepers," but Ruth belongs on another list.

In a related article, Balmer writes with grace and charm to argue that PK uses militarism and altheticism, especially athletics, to combat feminism. Many will argue with some of his sweeping generalizations (e.g., "The biggest social revolution in American history began in 1963 with the publication of *The Feminine Mystique*, by Betty Friedan"), but none will deny the power of his prose or the provocation of his main points. As do several other contributors, Balmer points out that the women's movement and the concomitant sexual revolution touched off fears among evangelical Christians that these developments eventually would destroy the traditional family. Consequently, many evangelical leaders blamed feminism for the social ills of the age, which led to widespread attempts to reestablish the Victorian ideals of feminine spirituality and domesticity.

The most telling part of Balmer's essay is his analysis of what has been heretofore a central focus of PK emphases and activities: the sports arena—the one place in modern American life where feminism has not had much impact. He goes on to recite the consonance between sports and spirituality, especially in terms of an orderly universe and perceived male values. He concludes that McCartney commonly utilizes traditional Christian metaphors of athleticism and militarism, the latter complemented by football values, to overcome feminism, all in the guise of a benevolent patriarchalism.

Balmer may over-emphasize the sports component of PK culture but he certainly provides food for thought for any concerned citizen, including the PK leadership. If movement leaders are serious about making men more sensitive in dealing with their families, their neighbors, and society as a whole, they may want to reconsider this apparent overuse of military and athletic metaphors. It is true that the Bible uses similar figures of speech ("spiritual warfare," I think, rather than "militarism," contrary to Balmer's terminology—but most certainly athletic imagery) but not excessively. Christians historically have believed that behind the current cosmology lies a great struggle between good and evil. However, the New Testament nowhere authorizes Christian believers to be violent or to ignore the teachings of Jesus concerning love, peace and spirituality. In any case, Balmer clearly demonstrates that PK leaders have used sports venues and metaphors to reach men, and that they have used this means to communicate with their constituency in a place of camaraderie amidst familiar surroundings. Whether this in turn has provided them, as Balmer suggests, with a social cocoon is problematical.

Based on an impressive piece of fresh research, Brickner's essay provides the reader with what is by far the most interesting and insightful interpretation in this volume, and it seems to me that he is on to something. Using clever metaphors and imagery, he claims that PK represents a third and new kind of 20th-century evangelicalism. In contrast to the "traditional" evangelicals (modeled on the work of Billy Graham, who emphasizes personal salvation) and the "new" evangelicals (exemplified by Jerry Falwell and Pat Robertson, who stress some form of political activism), the Promise Keepers are the product of a new strain of historic evangelical Christianity that Brickner labels "social" evangelicalism.

After carefully identifying the three main tenets of evangelicalism (conversion, biblicism and activism), Brickner proceeds to make his case. In so doing, he is sophisticated in his approach and, most important, aware of differences with the evangelical camp. Further, he understands that there are traditional and new evangelicals associated with PK. However, he argues that, in the combination of the two, PK has come to embody this new strain of modern evangelical Christianity.

He notes that the majority of PK can be categorized as traditional evangelicals, although they are often more charismatic than most believers in mainstream evangelical Christianity. Moreover, he points out that a number of new evangelicals—such as James Dobson, Bill Bright and Pat Robertson—support PK, and that therein lies a problem for the new movement. New evangelicals and PK share a common concern over many "moral and social evils," including the unjust treatment of the poor and disadvantaged, racism, abortion on demand, pornography, euthanasia, totalitarianism, atheism, moral relativism, evolution, and encroachment on family rights and personal liberty. Many people see this as a mixed bag of concerns that could translate into political action. However, PK has repeatedly stressed that it is not interested in curing these moral and social evils by political means but by attacking the root cause: spiritual decay. Therefore, it has chosen to concentrate on improving the spiritual quality of men's lives, and through them society as a whole.

After a careful analysis of PK literature, using reasoned argumentation, Brickner concludes that PK has no political agenda. Could PK activity and concerns have a political impact? Of course, he responds, but it does not seem likely that PK will become political activists because the essential nature of the movement is social, rather than personal or political. He goes on to explain that the PK message is not grounded in the new evangelicalism and its concern for political action—at least not at the present. The announced current intention of PK leaders is to remain morally and socially engaged with society without adopting what could be construed as a right-wing political stance.

Finally, the last three essays in the volume (Waters, Allen and Claussen) bring extraordinary insights to bear on the PK movement, and should be read together as a sub-unit of this book. Waters discusses how PK has used the mass media to its own advantage, Allen argues that the Promise Keepers evince a deep-seated hostility toward the media, and Claussen shows how media coverage of PK events has been basically even-handed and fair. On the surface, these three articles seem to contradict each other to some extent. On the other hand, they also provide valuable insights into how PK has regarded and dealt with the media over the years since its inception.

Waters focuses on the massive PK "Stand in the Gap" rally held in Washington on October 4, 1997, and shows how the PK leadership used the services of a professional public relations firm to frame press attention and set an agenda calculated to increase the probability of receiving favorable media coverage of the event. Allen penetrated PK at the grassroots and attended stadium events to engage in what he described as "participant observation research" in order to study the attitude of PK at all levels toward the media. He claims that nearly every individual Promise Keeper with whom he had contact bitterly complained about the media because of what was perceived to be misreporting of PK's true intentions. Moreover, he explains this antagonism on the basis of an intractable dualistic worldview held by nearly all Promise Keepers, an outlook that makes it difficult for them to see any good in the people they consider to be "enemies" and "outsiders." Then, on the basis of extensive and highly sophisticated research, Claussen reveals that, contrary to popular opinion, PK received consistently positive coverage by the media in the period 1992–1996.

Can all three of these scholars be correct? Do PK leaders shrewdly manipulate the mass media for their own purposes, while they and the rank-and-file simultaneously complain bitterly about media misreporting of their movement? And on what basis do these complaints rest if, as Claussen reveals, media coverage of PK events as been fundamentally positive in the past? Perhaps the answer lies in the fact that even though media reporting on the whole has been even-handed, some coverage has been hostile, especially that coming from the more left-wing segments of the press. Moreover, and perhaps more helpful in understanding this matter, Claussen's essay offers some insight into the problem when he explains the basic journalistic approach to covering a story such as that of the PK movement. He points out that nearly all PK stories follow a standard pattern based on established norms and practices. For about two-thirds of a standard article, the reporting is neutral and factual. This is followed by one or two negative paragraphs, often interpretative in nature, and then the story is capped with a positive conclusion. It is possible that Promise Keepers, like most Americans, are unaware of this pattern and, because of widespread popular distrust of the news industry, coupled with their predisposition to view the world in terms of good and evil, fairly naturally single out the negative section of any given story and interpret the story as a whole as an attack on their movement.

Apart from the fact that these three essays require careful reading and a bit of reflection in order to resolve apparent contradictions, some readers will have problems with Allen's methodology. Although not spelled out in detail, a large part of his research seems to be based on infiltration of the PK movement without revealing his true intentions. For example, he informs the reader that he once posed as a PK lay volunteer to obtain information. Others will wonder how accurate his direct quotations are if he did not electronically record them.

Issues Raised for Consideration

The essays in this volume raise a number of important issues that merit serious consideration by all those who are concerned with the goals, activities and future growth of the PK movement. Some of them deserve a book of their own. Assuming that the movement's leaders are people of good will, perhaps they will learn more than anybody else from these essays.

First and foremost, there is the matter of gender equality. Without questioning the sincerity of the PK leadership, it appears that researchers have uncovered some ambivalence concerning how the movement regards gender roles in society. There seems to be little doubt, as several authors have pointed out, that the modern American male lives with considerable confusion concerning gender roles. In this respect, PK appears to be making a genuine effort to help resolve this confusion.

It seems clear that PK participants are not cavemen and have no intention of keeping all women barefoot, pregnant and in the kitchen. It is also evident that they regard the female spouse as a true companion in a sacred relationship. Moreover, large numbers of women apparently agree with PK efforts to make their marriage partners more responsible, caring human beings. On the other hand, PK leaders need to resolve what appears to be tension in the movement concerning their view of the role of women in the marriage relationship and in society at large. Do they advocate mutual submission or something like what some have described as a "soft patriarchy" (van Leeuwen, 1997, p. 11)? Perhaps talk of "servant leadership" is the best they can do in the light of their biblical mandate, and they simply will have to live with this tension. However, they might be able to put to rest some of the nagging criticism of the movement if they can come to a theological understanding of the key New Testament passage over which many stumble, namely, Ephesians 5:21–33. This passage can be and has been interpreted in several different ways, including mutual submission and male servant-leadership. In this respect it is too bad that no theologians were included in this volume in order to help clarify this question.

Whatever the case, there is no doubt that PK needs to give this issue more thought. Perhaps the most telling criticism of current PK thinking on this point comes from friendly critics Douglas and Rebecca Merrill Groothuis.

After noting PK's concerns for the pain that African-Americans and other minorities have experienced from racism in the past and their progressive views on this subject, the Groothuises (1998, p. 24) observe:

> It is good that PK men are learning to hear, without criticism or judgment, the hurt that their minority brothers have felt in a white-dominant society. It is a shame that PK men are not also learning to hear, uncritically and nonjudgmentally, the pain that women of all races have experienced in a male-dominant church and society.

Second, there is the charge that PK has a right-wing political agenda. Several authors express this fear that, in their view, means a return to pre-feminist days and perhaps even the imposition of a patriarchal theocracy on the United States. Kelley, in particular, has pointed out how these critics link the PK movement to the New Religious Right (NRR) and its political goals.

On the one hand, there is some justification for these fears in that NRR leaders such as Pat Robertson and James Dobson have endorsed PK and provided some financial support for the movement. In addition, PK rallies have featured various speakers from Dobson's Focus on the Family, and Focus on the Family does have a conservative political agenda. Gutterman's criticism of the fact that PK leaders seem to have embraced what is commonly called civil religion also merits consideration because civil religion certainly has profound political implications. There is a certain irony here for these leaders do not seem aware that they are practicing civil religion and, like most Americans, tend to confuse Christianity with the national public religion (Pierard and Linder, 1988, pp. 20–25 and pp. 284–298). Further, Gutterman is convinced that the effort of PK leaders to combat racism is really done for the sake of unity rather than justice, another blindspot of which they may not be fully aware.

On the other hand, Quicke/Robinson and Lundskow present arguments to show that PK does not now have a political agenda and has no interest in political activism. Lundskow, in particular, presents compelling evidence that, although conservative in their views on many issues, Promise Keepers differ from the NRR in that they do not want to become political activists nor impose anything resembling a theocracy on the nation. This has been buttressed by McCartney's clear denial of any political aspirations on the part of PK in an interview on CNN's "Larry King Live," on October 7, 1997, shortly after the much-publicized mass rally in Washington. When King queried: "You are not political at all?" McCartney responded with a blunt "no." King probed further: "Not—you couldn't call yourself conservative or liberal or middle of the road? That has nothing to do with the agenda?" McCartney replied: "We don't believe that is where the answers are. We believe these are heart issues. We believe that if a man's heart is wrong, he's not going to be able to solve his problems. But if his heart is right, it's going to lead him to solutions" (CNN transcript, 1997, p. 7).

Therefore, it seems that PK, indeed, does not intend to become directly involved in politics, especially partisan politics. However, there are always the lingering questions of homosexuality and abortion, which McCartney emphasized in the early days of the movement. Apparently, the Coach has decided to relegate his convictions concerning homosexuality more to private life and has muted his pronouncements concerning abortion. Homosexuality is clearly a sensitive subject and statements concerning it easily can be misunderstood. Abortion is another matter, and probably needs to be depoliticized altogether, removing it from the political categories that make it a "conservative" or "liberal" issue.

There are also icebergs ahead of the good ship Promise Keepers in terms of personal friendships; interlocking interests with and geographic proximity to some conservative Christian groups with political agendas, like Focus on the Family, located in nearby Colorado Springs; and financial lines to certain organizations that are clearly identified with what Brickner identifies as the politically active "new evangelicals."

Also related to the political posture of PK is the constant need to distinguish between prophetic, pastoral and priestly ministries that groups like PK can perform. Most Christians consider it appropriate for Christian leaders and organizations to engage in prophetic and pastoral ministries, which are represented by calls for repentance and the need for spiritual consolation, respectively. Prophetic and pastoral functions are distinct from a priestly ministry that usually involves stroking political elites and affirming the country's "chosenness" and national mission. Thus far, PK seems solidly in the pastoral tradition while, in the main, avoiding priestly proclivities. The only danger in this area may be in their seeming inability to tell the difference between Christianity and civil religion, pointed out by Gutterman, which can lead to being coopted to support questionable enterprises by shrewd politicians. Further, they may want to consider expanding their prophetic vision. Calling individuals and nations to repent, shun evil and establish justice has long been a mainstay of the Judeo-Christian tradition.

Third, there is issue of the evangelical context of the movement and what this means in terms of PK's public face. Several of the contributors have pointed out that it is impossible to understand PK apart from the American evangelical tradition, and the great national spiritual awakenings of the past that made evangelicalism a major force in US history. Here, and at other places in these essays, definitions and the correct use of terminology becomes important. The words revival, revivalism, and awakenings (not to mention fundamentalism, evangelical, evangelicalism, evangelism, charismatic and right-wing) have been tossed about with considerable abandon in these essays. In this regard, the distinction made by historian William G. McLoughlin is important to any understanding of the place of PK in American history. According to McLoughlin, one of the leading authorities on the subject, revivals alter the lives of individuals, while awakenings change the worldview of an entire people or culture (McLoughlin, 1959, p. xiii). PK is obviously in the revival business. It remains to be seen if it is major contributor to a Third Great Awakening in American history. Historians of the future will have to determine whether or not Americans today are living in such a period.

Further, it is important to note that PK's mission statement places it squarely in the evangelical Christian tradition. The two primary marks of evangelicalism (the historian's term used to describe the particular kind of historic evangelical Protestantism that emerged in the 18th century and that stressed the classical Reformation doctrines of biblical authority, salvation by faith in Christ through grace alone and the church, along with a new emphasis on a personal experience of the grace of God expressed in such terms "new birth" or "conversion to Christ") have always been the urge to convert people to Jesus Christ and the urge to improve individuals and society (McGrath, 1995, 53–87 and Dayton and Johnston, 1991). PK is no exception. It is, of course, the second urge that makes many feminists nervous because they are not certain where this determination to alter society will take the nation. Historically speaking, evangelical Christianity in America has been consistently on the side of progressive reform (e.g., see Dayton, 1976; Smith, 1980). This progressive emphasis is not as clear in the current revivals as it has been in the past.

Moreover, as now constituted, the PK movement exhibits a bent toward the pentecostal-charismatic wing of the modern evangelical movement. As noted by Chrasta and several other contributors, much of the leadership, including McCartney himself, is charismatic Christian. This factor tends to make PK more flexible and more open to all denominations, including Roman Catholics, than are other branches of the evangelical movement (H.D. Hunter, 1990, pp. 241–244). Therefore, PK stresses only core evangelical beliefs and allows for individual participants to fill in the details. This aspect of the PK movement has been highlighted by Lundskow and Brickner, and, in their judgment, makes PK less likely to fall prey to right-wing political activists. This view makes sense but things could change if PK leaders are not careful to keep partisan politics out of their movement. In any event, PK can be best understood and can best understand itself in its evangelical context.

Fourth and last, there is the question of the role and personality of Coach Bill McCartney himself in the PK movement. These essays make clear that he is a man of considerable integrity, ability and intelligence who possesses outstanding organizational skills. They also make it readily apparent that he runs PK like a football team with himself as head coach. And just as he was a highly successful coach, so he has been a highly successful leader of PK.

But it is equally evident that, as noted previously, McCartney is an individual who thinks a great deal about his mission to promote integrity in the lives of Christian men, and is willing to change when he sees a clear reason to do so when that change does not affect his basic mission (Quicke/Robinson; Abraham, 1997, pp. 16–31; and Alsdurf, 1998, p. 32).

Several contributors (e.g., Eidenmuller, Stewart, Gutterman, Beal and Balmer) also stress how McCartney's football background has affected the way PK delivers its message. Most of these scholars believe that this emphasis on sports language and imagery demonstrates the inherent male prejudice and propensity for violence that permeates the movement. As for McCartney, sports metaphors come easily to his lips precisely because of his football background. Moreover, the sports mania in modern America, no matter what its root cause, makes it a natural and compelling venue to connect with males in order to discuss spiritual matters with them. Only McCartney and his associates can judge whether or not sports and military metaphors are appropriate for use in reaching men for Jesus Christ and in persuading them to be men of integrity who are sensitive to the hurting people of the world.

A Concluding Unscientfic Postscript (With Apologies to Søren Kierkegaard)

Thus, readers of these essays can infer that PK are loving and prone to violence, deceptive and courageous, dangerous and benign, well-intentioned and calculating, thoughtful and ignorant, old-fashioned fundamentalists and new-fangled evangelicals, narrow in outlook and open to new ideas and techniques, shrewd manipulators of the media and bungling ideologues, not to mention cultural leaders and cultural misanthropes. When PK leaders and adherents read these pages they will be better informed, maybe even inspired, and perhaps a bit angered, perplexed and amused. In any case, there is much here for all who are concerned with this subject to ponder and discuss.

It is clear from the foregoing that PK is a complex movement that defies simple categorization. On the other hand, PK is and must be studied because the stakes are high and nobody today is certain where America is going. Given thoughtful and sensitive leadership and favorable circumstances, PK could be a major factor in helping to change the fabric of American society for in a positive way. Given another kind of leadership and the collapse of the American economy, the movement could be deflected into channels different from its stated purposes and become a tool of political extremism.

As far as relations with the media and people of diametrically opposed ideology are concerned, there will always be a certain amount of tension, especially in a free society (emphasized by Healey). Moreover, it is the nature of religion in general and evangelical Christianity in particular periodically to challenge the culture in which it dwells. The religious dimension is really the bottom line in any analysis of this movement. The media coverage and post-rally analysis of the Washington "Stand in the Gap" gathering in October 1997 was extensive and thoughtful. Ellis Cose in his *Newsweek* commentary on the event noted that many critics were concerned that PK might go political and support some partisan right-wing figure or cause. Viewing the rally first-hand led Cose to believe that the main aim of the PK movement was to spark a spiritual revival, and that this made the question of whether or not PK is a political group irrelevant. While believing that it was inevitable that far-right political groups would try to tempt PK to support them, he (1997, p. 31) concluded:

> But the Promise Keepers' aspirations, as it is quick to acknowledge, go well beyond the political. And if its critics were being honest, most would admit that that is precisely what bothers them: not just the potential for political activism, but the in-your-face religiosity of a group that makes no apologies for its unquestioning and particular relationship with God, and that is actively seeking converts.

That is the crux of the matter, and that is the real reason for the tension, and that is quintessentially American!

What do these essays reveal, then, concerning the question of whether the Promise Keepers are "good news," as one article claimed, or "dupes and reactionaries," as another article called PK adherents. The answer is multiple and tentative. Does the PK movement represent "good news" for Americans? The answer is yes, at least for large numbers of people who have been touched by the movement. Are its adherents "dupes," self-deceived or used by others for some end other than that which they believe they are seeking? The answer is that they do not think so and that they do not seem to be at present, but they could be. If they are to be an independent voice in the public square, representing the virtues which they espouse—trust in Christ, male integrity and responsibility in the home and society, moral and sexual purity, love for family, church and other humans—then they will have to take special pains to involve themselves routinely in self-examination and self-criticism in order to avoid being captured by Brickner's politically-minded "new evangelicals." Are they "reactionaries," rigid conservatives who want to turn the social clock back to the first century or the Middle Ages, or at least to 19th-century America? The answer is that it depends on one's viewpoint. And such verdicts are always relative in the sense that nobody knows how the future will judge the present. PK participants obviously do not see themselves as reactionaries except perhaps in the sense that they want to restore what they believe are the better moral values of the past. Insiders are convinced that they can and will improve the quality of life of Christian families by adhering to their program—and, as a consequence, improve the general social health of the nation in the process. Critics obviously do not share these views and fear that the success of the PK movement is but a prelude to an attempt to force women back into more traditional modes based on male superiority.

These essays illustrate that PK is a powerful national movement, a thought that cheers some while scaring others. In any case, it seems to me that Promise Keepers are the masters of their own destiny, and will continue to change lives or self-destruct according to the measure of their own wisdom or their own folly. They have the best chance of succeeding if they live up to their own standards and continue to be open to the voices of their friendly critics.

Will the promises be kept? Will Bill McCartney keep his promise to remain non-partisan in politics? Will he continue to pursue social justice, even for women? Will the men who attend the rallies keep their promises? Only the future words and deeds of Coach McCartney and his millions of followers can determine the answers to these queries. In the end, all of these questions and issues will be decided not by theory but by action.

Surely there is a Hollywood movie in all of this. As they say in the communications business, stay tuned!

References

Abraham, K. (1997). *Who are the Promise Keepers?: Understanding the Christian men's movement.* New York: Doubleday.

Alsdurf, P.E. (1998, May 18). McCartney on the Rebound. *Christianity Today 42,* 26–28, 30–32.

Arms, P. (1997). *Promise Keepers: Another Trojan horse.* Houston, TX: Shiloh Publishers.

CNN transcript. The idea behind Promise Keepers. (1997, October 7). *Larry King Live.* Transcript # 97100701V22.

Cose, E. (1997, October 13). Promises ... Promises. *Newsweek 130,* 28–31.

Dayton, D.W. (1976). *Discovering an evangelical heritage.* New York: Harper & Row Publishers.

Dayton, D.W., & Johnston, R.K. (eds.). (1991). *The variety of American Evangelicalism.* Knoxville, TN: University of Tennessee Press.

Groothuis, R.M., & Groothuis, D. (1998, February). Women keep promises, too! *Christian Ethics Today,* 17–25.

Hunter, H.D. (1990). Charismatic Movement. In D.G. Reid, R.D. Linder, B.L. Shelley, & H.S. Stout (eds.), *Dictionary of Christianity in America* (pp. 241–244). Downers Grove, IL: InterVarsity Press.

Hunter, J.D. (1991). *Culture wars: The struggle to define America.* New York: Basic Books.

Kennedy, J.W. (1998, May 18). Up from the ashes? *Christianity Today 42,* 29.

Marsden, G.M. (1984). The evangelical denomination. In George M. Marsden (ed.), *Evangelicalism and modern America* (pp. vii–xix). Grand Rapids, MI: Eerdmans.

McCartney, B., et al. (1992). *What makes a man?* Colorado Springs, CO: Focus on the Family.

McCartney, B. (1997). *Sold out: Becoming man enough to make a difference.* Dallas, TX: Word Publishing.

McGrath, A.E. (1995). *Evangelicalism and the future of Christianity.* Downers Grove, IL: InterVarsity Press.

McLoughlin, W.G. (1959). *Modern revivalism: Charles Grandison Finney to Billy Graham.* New York: The Ronald Press Company.

National Organization for Women (NOW) website. Available at: http://www.now.org

Niebuhr, G. (1997, October 3). Religious rally in capital is a test of faith. *The New York Times,* p. A1.

Noll, M.A. (1994). *The scandal of the evangelical mind.* Grand Rapids, MI: Eerdmans.

Pierard, R.V., & Linder, R.D. (1988). *Civil religion and the presidency.* Grand Rapids, MI: Zondervan.

Smith, T.L. (1980). *Revivalism and social reform: Protestantism on the eve of the Civil War.* Baltimore: The Johns Hopkins University Press.

van Leeuwen, M.S. (1997, November/December). Weeping warriors. *Books & Culture,* 9–11.

Wuthnow, R. (1989). *The struggle for America's soul: Evangelicals, liberals, and secularism.* Grand Rapids, MI: Eerdmans.

About the Contributors

L. Dean Allen II is a Ph.D. candidate in Social Ethics and Sociology of Religion at Boston University's Division of Religious and Theological Studies.

Randall Balmer, Ph.D., is Ann Whitney Olin Professor of Religion at Barnard College, Columbia University.

Becky Beal, Ed.D., is Assistant Professor in the Department of Sport Science at the University of the Pacific.

Bryan Brickner, Ph.D., is the author of *The Promise Keepers: Politics and Promises* (Lexington Books, 1999).

Michael J. Chrasta, Ph.D., finished his doctorate in 1998 at the University of Texas at Dallas.

Dane S. Claussen, Ph.D., is Assistant Professor of Communication and Mass Media at Southwest Missouri State University in Springfield. He is also President/Principal of American Newspaper Consultants, Ltd., and Editor of the *Industrial Marketing Practitioner*, a monthly newsletter.

Robert A. Cole, Ph.D., is Assistant Professor of Speech Communication at State University of New York at Oswego.

Donald Deardorff II, Ph.D., is Assistant Professor of English at Cedarville (Ohio) College.

Michael Eidenmuller, Ph.D., is Assistant Professor of Speech Communication at Northwestern State University of Louisiana.

Tanya Erzen is a Ph.D. candidate in American Studies at New York University.

David S. Gutterman is a Ph.D. candidate in Political Science at Rutgers University.

Billy Hawkins, Ph.D., is Assistant Professor of Physical Education and Sport Studies at the University of Georgia.

Kevin Healey is an M.A. candidate in Sociology at Rutgers University.

Colleen E. Kelley, Ph.D., is Associate Professor in the Division of Humanities and Social Sciences at Pennsylvania State University at Erie.

About the Contributors

Robert D. Linder, Ph.D., is Professor of History at Kansas State University, and Senior Research Fellow at The Centre for the Study of Australian Christianity, Robert Menzies College.

Michael A. Longinow, Ph.D., is Associate Professor of Journalism at Asbury College.

George Lundskow, Ph.D., is assistant professor of sociology at Grand Valley State University.

Andrew Quicke, M.A., is Associate Professor and Chairman of the School of Cinema-Television at Regent University, and a Ph.D. Student at the Open University.

Guillermo de los Reyes, Ph.D., is Professor of International Relations and History at the University of the Americas, Puebla, Mexico, and a lecturer at the University of Pennsylvania.

Janet Lynn Reynolds, Ph.D., is Assistant Professor of Communication at Pepperdine University.

Rodney A. Reynolds, Ph.D., is Professor and Director of the Masters Studies Program in the College of Communication and the Arts at Regent University.

Paul J. Rich, Ph.D., is Professor of International Relations at the University of the Americas, Puebla, Mexico, and a Fellow of the Hoover Institution at Stanford University.

Karen Robinson, M.L.S., M.A., is Associate Librarian at Regent University.

Robert A. Stewart, Ed.D., is Professor of Communication Studies and Associate Dean of Arts and Sciences at Texas Tech University.

John Suk, Ph.D., is Editor of *The Banner*, an independent biweekly magazine for the Christian Reformed Church, and a former pastor in Sarnia, Ontario, and Ann Arbor, Mich.

Ken Waters, Ph.D., is Associate Professor of Journalism at Pepperdine University.

Index

Abbey, Edward 201, 202
abortion 9, 17, 64–66, 97, 117, 134, 156, 196, 243, 296, 299, 314, 318
Abraham, Ken xiii, 8–9, 13, 18, 29, 34, 39, 42, 44, 52, 87, 89, 143, 151, 320 322
accountability groups xvii, 106
Acker, J. 34, 39
Adams, J.L. 39
Addams, Jane 50
Adorno, T. 58, 73
African Americans 45, 70, 86–87, 166, 178, 182–193, 211, 255, 275, 285, 317; *see also* Race and PK
Alcoholics Anonymous 243
Allen, H. 30, 39
Allen, J. 256, 266, 299, 302
Allen, L. Dean II xvii, 24, 27, 69, 176, 269–280, 284, 292, 300, 308, 311, 314–316, 325
Alliance for Revival & Reformation (previously Coalition on Revival) 210–212
Allyn, A. 39
Alsdurf, P.E. 320, 322
Altemeyer, B. 59, 73
American Civil Liberties Union (ACLU) 9, 96, 288
American Federation of Labor-Congress of Industrial Organizations (A.F.L.-C.I.O.) 288
Arkansas Democrat-Gazette 291, 302

Arkansas newspapers 290, 291, 302
Arms, Phil xii, 309, 322
Arnold, Peter 258, 263–266
Arterburn, Stephen 240–241
Asbury, Francis 45, 46
Asbury College 22
Asbury Park [NJ] *Press* 287
Asian Americans 87, 178; *see also* race and PK
Assemblies of God 10, 21, 23, 177
atheism 210, 298, 314
atheists 122, 291
Athletes in Action International 92, 195, 287
Atlanta Journal-Constitution 296
Aunese, Sal 96, 97
authoritarianism 56–75
Avila, Jim 262, 266
Awana Clubs, 194
Azusa Pacific University 209

Baird, Robert 45, 183, 192
Bakhtin, M.M. 113, 130
Balmer, Randy vii, xiv, xvi, 1–5, 22, 27, 194–203, 228, 235, 308, 311, 313, 320, 325
Banks, A.D. 293, 301
Banks, Sandy 289, 301
Baptists 177, 178, 180, 211, 294; *see also* Southern Baptist Convention Brotherhood Commission's Men's Ministries
Barr, J. 233, 235
Barthes, Roland 134
Barton, B. 48, 52

Barton, John 138, 151
Bateson, M.C. 33, 39
Bauer, Gary 289
Baum, M.D. 296, 301
Baye, B.W. 294, 301
Beal, Becky xiii, 58, 73, 106, 111, 153–163, 311–312, 320, 325
Beavis and Butthead 85
Bebbington, D.W. 205, 213
Beckler, Lori 241, 253
Bederman, Gail 49, 50, 51, 52, 195, 202
Beecher, Henry Ward 43
Belliveau, Gregory 87, 89
Beltrame, J. 264, 266
Bendroth, M.L. 196, 197, 203
Bercovitch, Sacvan 135, 148, 151
Berg, T. 251–253
Billy Graham Evangelistic Association 211; *see also* Graham, Billy
Birnbaum, J.H. 10, 16, 18
Bizzell, P. 130
Blackaby, Henry 170–171, 173
Bledstein, Burton J. 47, 49, 52
Bliss, Shepherd 294
Blue, Ronald 209
Bly, Robert xiii, 30–33, 38–39, 201, 294, 301; *see also Iron John*; mythopoetism
Bohan, D.H. 229, 235
Boleman-Herring, Elizabeth A.R. vii
Boles, J.B. 183, 192
Boone, K. 228, 230, 233–235

327

Boone, Kathryn 242
Boone, Bishop Wellington 117, 130, 165, 168, 173, 211, 242
Boorstin, Daniel 47, 52
Bosmajian, H. 234-235
Boulder CO 92-93, 97, 98
Brand-Williams, O. 290, 301
Branham, William 21
Breaking Down the Walls see race and PK
Brickner, Bryan W. xiv, xvi, 204-214, 308, 311, 313-314, 319, 321, 325
Bridgewater, Mary Ann 241
Bridgman, H.A. 43, 52
Briggs, Joe Bob 287, 301
Bright, Bill 133, 134, 135, 151, 155, 210, 213, 215, 241, 314
Bright, Cheri 241, 242, 253
Brinkley, Harold 177
Brod, Harry 130
Brokaw, Tom 262
Brown, K.M. 228, 235
Bruce, S. 7, 18
Bruni, F. 296, 301
Bruns, R.A. 295, 301
Bruyn, S.T. 216, 225
Bryan, William Jennings 50
Bryant, David 170-173, 209
Bryson, L. 158, 162
Buber, Martin 136, 151
Buchanan, Pat 197
Bundy, Al 85
Burke, Kenneth 91, 100, 103, 104, 164-167, 171-172, 173, 226, 227, 234-235
Burnard, T. 38, 39
Bush, George 15, 147
Business Life Management 294
Butler, M. 282, 301
Bynum, Pierre 210

C-SPAN 175
Cable News Network (CNN) 263-264, 266, 289, 317-318
Calvary movement xiv, 22-23, 24, 240
Calvin, John 310
Calvinism 45
Cameron, Glen T. vii
Campbell, Joseph 30, 38
Campus Crusade for Christ 15, 133, 155, 194-195, 210, 241, 243, 252
Cantor, M.G. 282, 301
Caputo, John 129, 130
Career Impact Ministries 294
Carnes, Mark 36, 37, 40, 49, 52, 78, 89
Carter, Jimmy 196, 205
Case, Carl D. 3, 48, 53
Castaneda, Carlos 37
Catholics and Catholic Church 9, 13-14, 22, 24, 44, 60, 177, 178, 243, 294-295, 319
Centennial Olympic Park see Olympic Park (Atlanta) bombing
Charleston [SC] Post and Courier newspaper 300
Chavis, Steve 93, 100, 292
Cheney, G.E. 91, 100
Chengelis, A.S. 292, 301
Chosen Women Daughters of the King 238-254, 291
Chrasta, Michael J. xiv, 20-28, 296, 319, 325
Christian Business Men's Committee 294
Christian Century 18, 43, 54, 203, 285-286, 293
Christian Coalition xiv, 7-19, 65, 72, 195, 295; see also Reed, Ralph
Christian Men's Network 155, 294
Christian Service Brigade 194
Christian Woman 241
Christianity Today 212, 241, 270, 284-286, 292
Church of the Foursquare Gospel 21, 23
Cimons, M. 293, 301
civil rights movement 150, 255
Clairmont, Patsy 248, 253
Clark, Steve 22
Clarkson, F. 204, 211, 213, 230, 231, 233, 235
Clary, Pat 240
Clatterbaugh, Kenneth 82,
83, 84, 87, 89, 99, 100, 114-115, 130, 294, 301
Claussen, Dane S. vii-viii, xii-xiv, 15, 30, 35, 40, 49, 53, 69, 73, 96, 101, 176, 181, 233, 256, 266, 269, 279, 281-307, 308, 311, 314-315, 325
Clay, A. 276, 279
Clergy Conference for Men 164-174
Clinton, Bill 264
Clinton, Hillary Rodham 197
CNN see Cable News Network
Coakley, J.J. 58, 73, 158, 162, 283, 301
Coalition on Revival (later Alliance for Revival and Reformation) 210-212
Cokorinos, L. 20, 24, 28, 204, 211-213, 230, 236, 289, 301
Cole, Edwin Louis 131, 155, 209, 218, 274-275, 279
Cole, Robert A. xv, 113-132, 325
Coleman, R.E. 21, 27
Colorado, University of (Boulder) 9, 92-98, 154, 161, 195, 206-207, 270
Colorado for Family Values 212
Colorado Springs, Colorado 92
Colson, Charles W. "Chuck" 209, 213, 272-273; see also Prison Fellowship Ministries
Columbia Broadcasting System (CBS) 263-264
Combs, J. 227, 236
communism 197, 210
Compassion International 92
Conant, R.W. 48, 53
Conason, J. 20, 24, 28, 204, 211-213, 230, 236, 289, 301
Concerned Women for America 196, 199
Concerts of Prayer International 209
Connell, R.W. 59, 73, 283, 302

Index

Conniff, R. 287, 302
Cooper, M. 227, 235
Cooper, Rodney 147, 151
Cooperman, J. 103, 111
Cose, Ellis 117, 130, 321–322
Coulter, T.T. 59, 74
Cousineau, P. 38, 40
Cox, Henry 177, 181
Craig, Steve 282, 302
Crane, Stephen 166, 173
Crites, Stephen 134, 151
Croteau, D. 283, 303
Crouch, Stanley 182, 192
"Culture wars" 1, 20, 102, 271, 310; *see also* Hunter, John Davison
Curl, J.S. 37, 40
Curry, T. 158, 162

Dad the Family Shepherd 294
Dad's University 294
Dager, A.J. 99, 101
Dallas Cowboys 200
Dallas Theological Seminary 25, 28
Daniels, George L. vii, 287–288, 302
Danile, J. 37, 40
Dart, J. 115, 130, 256, 266, 296, 299, 302
Darwin, Charles 122
David and Goliath 167, 169, 171
Dayton, D.W. 196, 203, 319, 322
Deardorff, Donald II xv, 76–90, 325
DeBerg, B.A. 196, 203
DeCelle, D. 285, 302
DeHaven, J. 290, 302
Democrats 178, 288
DeMoss, Mark 34
DeMoss Group 257, 295
Denmark 297
Denton, Robert E. 91, 101, 114, 116, 131
Denver Post 290, 295
DeParle, J. 297, 302
Detroit 290
Detroit Free Press 290
Diamond, S. 57, 73, 155, 156, 161, 162
Diaz, G. 287, 302
Diles, D. 269, 280

Disney [Studios] 176
Dittes, James 83, 89
Dobson, James 92, 93, 155, 209, 217, 240, 257, 289, 314, 317
Dole, Bob 270
Dong, Larry 285
Doughney, M. 234, 236
Douglass, Frederick 185, 191–192
Doty, W.G. 33, 39–40
Dubbert, J.L. 35, 39, 40, 81, 89
Duquesne University 22
Dumenil, L. 35–36, 40
Duncan, M.C. 283, 302
Durkheim, Emile 31
Dyson, David 32

Eagles 30, 294
Easthope, A. 81, 89
Eastland, Terry 287–289, 295–296, 302
The Economist 297, 306
ecumenicalism xvi, 175–181
Eidenmuller, Michael E. vii, xiv, xv, 91–101, 320, 325
Eliade, M. 38, 40
Elkins, S.M. 183, 192
Elks 30–31, 38, 294
Enroth, R.M., 21, 22, 28
Entman, R. 256, 266
Entner, Sandi 88, 89
Episcopalians 288
Equal Partners 32
Ericson, E.E. 21, 28
Erzen, Tanya xvi, 238–254, 325
Escobar, Gabriel 261, 264, 266
Evangelical Free Church members 177
Evans, E. 20, 28
Evans, H.R. 35
Evans, Tony 25, 26, 28, 103–104, 106, 112, 124, 130, 144–145, 151, 156, 164, 166, 169, 171–173, 200, 203, 209, 221, 230, 236
evolution 69, 293, 314
Exodus International 143, 243, 246
Exodus narrative 133–152
Eysenck, H.J. 59, 74

Fackre, G. 205, 213
Falwell, Jerry 7, 68, 204, 205, 260, 314
Fan into Flame *see* Clergy Conference for Men; pastors
Farrakhan, Louis xiii, 276; *see also* Million Man March
Farrar, Steve 277–279
Fathers and Brothers 294
Fellowship of Christian Athletes 3, 8, 195
Fejes, Fred F. 282, 302
feminist analysis xv, 76, 104, 107–111, 142–143, 153–163, 251, 312–313, 319
Ferguson, A. 299, 302
Ferguson, M. 35, 40
Feuerherd, P. 295, 302
Fields, Suzanne 287, 297, 302
Fimrite, R. 198, 203
finances 5, 11–12
Finney, Charles 43
Fish, Stanley 135, 151
Fitzgibbons, Chris 250
Flagpole 288
Focus on the Family 15, 92, 155, 196, 209, 217, 240, 243, 252, 317–318
Folkenflik, D. 264, 268
Forsey, H. 82, 89
Fort Worth Star-Telegram 287
Fosdick, Harry Emerson 3, 48, 53
Foss, S.K. 107, 111
Foster, H. 35, 40
Four Weddings and a Funeral 86
Fowler, R.B. 205, 213
Frame, R. 210, 211, 213
Frank, D. 194, 203
Franklin, J.H. 182, 183, 192
Franklin, P. 95, 101
Frazier, Eric 300–303
Freemasons *see* Masons
Frenkel-Brunswik, E. 58, 73
Fresno CA 290–291
Fresno Bee 291
Freud, Sigmund 122
Friedan, Betty 197, 313

Friedman, Thomas L. 197, 203
friendship and PK xvii, 82–83, 123, 126, 289, 296
Frisbee, Lonnie 22–23, 27
From Ashes to Glory see McCartney, Bill
Fromm, E. 58–59, 66, 74
Full Gospel Businessmen 24
Fulwood, S. III 288, 303

Galtung, J. 216, 225
Gambling and PK 290
Gamson, W.A. 256, 266
Gantry, Elmer 263
Garlington, Joseph 211
Gates, Bill 62
Gaultiere, W. 120, 130
gay men xv, 1, 2, 17, 57, 67, 69, 76, 97, 117, 143, 215, 219–221, 224–225, 231, 290, 296–297; *see also* homosexuality
Gelb, B. 283, 305
Genovese, E.D. 183, 192
Georgia newspapers 288
Gergen, David 262, 267
Germany 122, 297
Gerner, George W. 10, 14, 18
Gideons 51
Gilbreath, E. 57, 74, 115, 130, 290, 303
Gilmore, W.J. 46, 53
Gingold, A. 287, 303
Gitlin, Todd 256, 267
Gladden, Washington 50, 53
Glass, Bill 195
Goals of PK 4, 196
Goeringer, C.F. 211, 213
Goodfellas 86
Goodman, Walter 289, 303
Goodstein, Laurie 258, 267, 287, 297, 303
Gordon, H. 264, 267
Graham, Billy xvi, 25, 204, 205, 211, 240, 257, 273, 298, 314
Graham, Franklin 209
Granberry, M. 288, 306
Grave, L. 243, 253
Gray, H. 282, 303
Gray, J. 58, 74, 154, 162
Great Awakenings 2, 20, 137–138, 145, 262, 295, 311, 319
Green, Martin 34, 40
Greenberg, Paul 300, 303
Greene, M.S. 260, 267
Grey, D.L. 295, 303
Griffin, Clyde 78, 89
Griffin, C.L. 107, 111
Griffith, Marie 247, 253
Griffith, S. 108, 111, 154–157, 159–162
Grimstead, Jay 210
Groothuis, Douglas 265, 267, 316–317, 322
Groothuis, Rebecca Merrill 265, 267, 316–317, 322
Gruen, Dietrich 147, 152, 280
Gulf War 147
Guliksen, Kenn 23
Gutterman, David S. xv, 133–152, 317–318, 320, 325

Habecker, E.B. 83–84, 87, 89
Habitat for Humanity 257
Hagendoorn, A. 59, 74
Hagin, Kenneth Jr. 182
Hahn, D. 231, 234, 236
Halbrook, B. 278, 280
Hale, Chip 264, 267
Hall, D.E. 57, 74
Hall, Stuart 82, 89
Hall, T.C. 46, 53
Hamblin, K. 297, 303
Hancock, J. 95, 101
Handy, R.T. 20, 28
Hannaham, H. 297, 303
Hanson, J. 256, 267
Hardenbrook, W.M. 44, 49, 53
Harrell, D. 24, 28
Harris, T. 182, 192
Harvard University 198
Hatch, Nathan O. 45–46, 53
Hawkins, Billy xvi, 182–193, 325
Hawley, J.S. 228, 236
Hayford, Jack 167–168, 170, 173, 209
Head, J. 265, 267
Healey, Kevin xvi, 215–225, 320, 325
Hedron, Mari 251
Hefly, James C. 195

Hegel, Georg Wilhelm Friedrich 122
Henderson, J.L. 31, 40
Henningsen, G.A. 39, 40
Herdrich, J. 242, 253
Heritage Foundation 212
Heritage Keepers 241
Hertzke, A.D. 205, 213
Herzberg, B. 130
heterosexism *see* homosexuality
Hetherly, M. 9, 17, 18, 231, 233, 236
Hicks, R. 120, 123, 130
Higgs, R.J. 186, 192
Hill, E.V. 211
Hillman, James 294
Hispanic Americans 87, 178; *see also* race and PK
Hitchens, Christopher 298, 303
Hitler, Adolf 122, 219
Hocken, P. 23, 24, 28
Hoffer, R. 115, 130, 270, 280
Hofstadter, Richard 298, 303
Holbrook, B. 270, 280
Holiness 2
Holy Roman Empire 36
homosexuality 9, 35, 57, 64–65, 67, 69, 76, 92, 97, 117, 128, 143, 156–157, 212, 215, 219–221, 224–225, 228, 231, 243–247, 249, 251–252, 260, 263–264, 288, 290, 296–297, 299, 318; *see also* gay men; Lesbian Avengers
Horner, B. 275, 280
Horrocks, Roger 85, 89
Hoynes, W. 283, 303
Hughes, J. 264, 267
Hughes, T. 48, 53
Hunter, John Davison 102, 107, 109–111, 201, 203, 271–274, 278–280, 310–311, 319, 322; *see also* "Culture Wars"
Huntington, Samuel P. 138–139, 151
Hussein, Saddam 147
Hybels, Bill 131, 209

Independents 178
Ingham, Mary 32, 40

Index

Inglehart, R. 38, 40
Ingraham, Laura 259, 267
Inman, C.C. 83, 90
Innerst, C. 16, 18
internal operations of PK xvii
International Bible Society 92
international expansion of PK xvii, 192, 297
International Sunday School Committee 51
Internet 118, 178–181, 217–225
Ireland, Patricia 232, 236, 259–261, 263, 264, 267, 288; *see also* National Organization for Women
Iron John xiii, 1, 30, 32, 33, 39, 201, 294; *see also* Robert Bly
Jackson, D. 264, 267
Jackson, Earl 14
Jackson, Jesse 288
Jackson, Larry 131
James, William 172, 173
Janssen, A. 111, 130, 225, 303
Janssen, J. 59, 74
Jesus movement xiv, 21, 24
Jewel, Jim 293, 301
Jews 9–10, 14, 60, 88, 288
John XXIII, Pope 176
Johnson, Barbara 242–243, 246, 248, 250, 253
Johnson, Dave 161
Johnson, H. 115, 131
Johnston, R.K. 319, 322
Jolliffe, Lee 282, 303
Jones, C.E. 44, 53
Jones, J. 260, 267
Jordan, Michael 200
Jordan, Winthrop D. 183, 184, 192
Journal of Sport & Social Issues 153–163
journalists *see* mass media
Joyful Journey conference 238
Jurji, E.J. 176, 181

Kaminer, W. 146, 151
Kansas City MO 295
Karl, Jonathan 264, 267
Kaufman, M. 114, 130–131, 157, 162, 183, 192

Kavoori, Anandam P. vii
Keeler, B. 258, 267
Keen, J. 232, 236
Keen, Sam 82, 89, 294, 303; *see also* mythopoetism
Kehrein, Glen 168
Kelley, Colleen E. xvi, 226–237, 311, 317, 325
Kemp, K.W. 51, 53
Kennedy, G. 110, 111
Kennedy, J.W. 297, 303, 309, 322
Kennedy, T. 87, 89
Kerston, K. 233, 236
Kertzer, D.I. 32, 40
Kidd, B. 158, 162
Kierkegaard, Søren 129
Kimbrell, Andrew 81, 89
Kimes, S. 240, 243–244, 247, 251, 253
Kimmel, Michael S. 15, 18, 20, 28, 57, 74, 76, 89, 114–115, 120, 131, 157, 162, 183, 192, 204, 212–213, 230–231, 236, 294, 303
Kimmel, Tim 131
King, F. 298, 303
King, Larry 317–318
King, Martin Luther, Jr. 150, 216
Kneisly, L. 234, 236
Knights of Columbus 194
Knights of Pythias (Pythians) 29, 30
Koppel, Ted 263, 267
Korean War 200
Krebs, D.L. 216, 225
Kuhlman, Kathryn 21
Kuhn, C.M. 51, 53
Kuhnhenn, J. 264, 268
Kurth, Karen 242
Kurtz, H. 8, 18
Kuwait 147

Lacy, G. 283, 305
LaHaye, Beverly 199; *see also* Concerned Women for America
Lape, H.N. 296, 303
Latin America 243, 253
Latourette, K.S. 43, 53
Leave it to Beaver 72
Lederer, G. 59, 74
Leete, F.D. 52, 53
Legacy Ministries 209

Leggett, D. 283, 306
Lenin [Vladimir I. Ulyanov] 122
Leo, John 14, 18, 296–297, 303
Leonard, T.G. 49, 53
Lesbian Avengers 56, 264, 288; *see also* homosexuality
Levinson, D.J. 58, 73
Lezynski, J. 244, 250, 253
Liberals United 275
Lieb, Thom 281, 303
Liddy, G. Gordon 197
Lifton, R. 234, 236
Limbaugh, Rush 197
Lincoln, C.E. 183, 192
Lindelof, B. 240, 253
Linder, Robert D. vii, xvii, 308–323, 326
Lindsay, Gordon 23
Lions Club 36
Lipset, S.M. 175, 181
Lipsyte, R. 297, 304
Little Rock AR 290
Long, Denise 197
Longinow, Michael A. xv, 42–55, 326
Loose, C. 258, 267
Loritts, Crawford, Jr. 209
Los Angeles 290–291
Los Angeles Times 286, 287, 288, 292
Luebke, B. 283, 304
Lucado, Max 167, 173, 181
Lucal, B. 283, 304
Lundskow, George N. xv, 56–75, 311–312, 317, 319, 326
Lundstrom, W. 282, 305
Luther, Martin 310
Lutherans 177
Lynn, Barry 263

MacArthur, Douglas 159, 312–313
MacIntyre, Alasdair 134, 151
MacKay, John 176
Mafia 36
magazine coverage *see* mass media; *individual magazine titles*
Mahan, A.T. 48, 53
Mahoney, Pat 210
Majors, Richard 86, 89
March for Jesus 211

March on Washington 150
Marquand, R. 296, 304
Marsden, G.M. 46, 48, 54, 311, 323
Martin, Ralph 22
Marty, Martin E. 47, 49, 54, 181
Marx, H.L. 176, 181
Marx, Karl 122
Masons and other fraternal men's organizations xv, 1, 29–41, 43, 49–50, 78–79, 294
mass media xvii, 1, 25, 69–70, 96–98, 117, 125, 149, 153–154, 231–232, 234, 255–307, 309–310, 314–316, 320–321
Mathews, D.G. 45, 54
Mattingly, Terry 104, 111
Mattox, W.J., Jr. 105, 111
Maudlin, M.G. 284, 304
Maus, M. 300, 304
Maxcy, D.J. 255, 267
Maxwell, J. 13, 18
Maxwell, John 166, 168, 170, 174
McCartney, Bill 1–3, 8–9, 21–22, 24–29, 43–44, 59, 68–69, 92–99, 101, 105, 116, 123, 131, 139–144, 146, 149, 151, 154, 161, 164–168, 174, 182, 190–192, 195–196, 198, 201, 205–208, 210, 212–214, 217–218, 224, 229–230, 232–233, 236, 257, 260–261, 263, 269–270, 276–278, 280, 282, 284–286, 289–293, 295, 298, 304, 309–310, 313, 317–320, 322
McCartney, Kristi 96
McCartney, Lyndi 285, 293
McCombs, Maxwell 256, 267, 300, 304
McCoy, Connie 240, 243, 253
McCracken, G. 59, 60, 74
McDonald, D.F. 290, 304
McDonald, M. 104, 111, 296, 304
McGee, M. 227, 236
McGrath, A.E. 319, 322
McIntyre, Mark 258, 260, 265, 267
McKinney, George 131

McLoughlin, W.G. 43–44, 49–51, 54, 137–139, 151, 295, 304, 318–319, 323
McPheeters, J.C. 45, 54
Meade, Michael 294
Media see mass media
Meet the Press 149
Meeus, W. 59, 75
Meloen, J.D. 59, 74
Meltzer, B.N. 38, 40
Men and Religion Forward Movement xv, 3, 17, 49–51, 79, 195, 295; *see also* Social Gospel
Men Behaving Badly 85
Men Reaching Men 294
Men's Rights Association 294
Men's Rights Incorporated 294
Messner, Michael A. 57–58, 74, 83, 84, 90, 114, 131, 157–158, 162, 183, 193, 283, 302
Methodism 44, 45
Methodists 177, 288
Meyers, R. 282, 304
Michigan, University of (Ann Arbor) 94
Michigan newspapers 290
Miles, R. 186, 193
military: and PK 12, 277; metaphors 147–148, 159, 194–203, 218, 222–224, 241, 277, 313
Miller, D.E. 23, 28
Miller, L. 43, 54
Miller, Perry 138, 152
Milling, T.J. 264, 267
Million Man March xiii, 124, 255, 258, 265, 276, 281, 287, 289, 295–297
Million Woman March 294
Minerth Meier Clinics *see* New Life Clinics
Minkowitz, Donna 33–34, 57, 75, 262, 285, 304
Miranda, Jesse 166, 170–171, 174, 209
Mishler, E.G. 60, 75
Missouri, University of (Columbia) 290
Modigliani, A. 256. 266
Moen, Matthew 7–8, 17, 18
Moen, S. 276, 280
Moltmann, J. 136, 152

Moody, Dwight Lyman 3, 48
Moody Bible Institute 209
Moore, L.R. 255, 267
Moore, William D. 36, 40
Moose, Loyal Order of 30, 294
Moral Majority xiv, 7, 13, 65, 205, 295; *see also* Falwell, Jerry
Moreno, S. 264, 267
Morrison, Henry Clay 45, 54
Mosmiller, T. 115, 120, 131
Moss, A.A. 182, 192
Mott, Frank Luther 47, 54
Mozart, Wolfgang Amadeus 37
Ms. 201, 262, 285
Murphy, Caryle 261, 264, 268, 293, 304
Murrin, J.M. 198, 203
Muscular Christianity xv, 1–3, 51, 57, 195, 295; *see also* Billy Sunday
mythopoetism xi, 1, 30, 38, 114, 157–158, 281, 294–296, 299–300; *see also* Bly, Robert; *Iron John*; Keen, Sam

Nakamura, D. 264, 268
The Nation 289
National Association of Evangelicals 20
National Center for Fathering 294
National Endowment for the Arts 10, 16
National Institute on Biblical Inerrancy 211
National Organization for Men Against Sexism (NOMAS) (formerly National Organization for Changing Men) 294
National Organization for Women (NOW) xiv, 2, 9, 15, 56, 104, 226–227, 230–237, 250, 255, 259–262, 264–266, 268, 288, 291, 297, 309, 323; *see also* Ireland, Patricia
National Religious Broadcasters 209
National Review 298

Index

Native Americans 31, 87; see also race and PK
Navigators 92
Nazarenes 177
NBC NewsChannel 290
Needleman, Jacob 176
Neill, M. 115, 131
Nelson, M.B. 161, 162
Network of Evangelical Women in Ministry 240
Neuman, W.L. 60, 75
New Age movement 34–35, 210
New Covenant 23
New England Fellowship 20–21
New Life Clinics 240
New Man xiii, 116, 118, 155, 161
New Republic 10, 289
New York Times 282, 287–289, 293, 295, 309
New York Yacht Club 36
Newman, D.M. 215, 225
newspaper coverage *see* mass media; *names of individual newspapers, reporters and columnists*
Newsweek 285
Niebuhr, Gustav 29, 32, 34, 40, 262, 268, 309–310, 323
Nietzsche, Friedrich 122
Nightline 263
Nimmo, D. 227, 236
1920s 196, 310
Nix, S.D. 177, 181
Nixon, Richard M. 209
Noll, M.A. 46, 54, 311, 323
Nord, David Paul 46, 54
North American Free Trade Agreement (NAFTA) 197
North, Oliver 197
Notre Dame, University of 22
Novosad, Nancy 76, 90, 299–300, 304
Nystrom, C. 282, 304

O'Connor, E.D. 22, 23, 28
Odd Fellows 29, 30, 43, 294
Oldfield, D.M. 18
Oliver, G. 279, 280
Oliveto, F. 276, 280

Olympic Park (Atlanta) bombing 275
Omi, M. 186, 193
Operation Rescue 65, 212
Oriard, M. 78, 90
Orlando Sentinel 287
Osherson, S. 80, 90
Ostling, R.N. 230, 236
Otto, M. 264, 268

Paisley, W. 282, 301
Palinkas, L.A. 105, 111
Pardun, Carol J. vii
Parents and Friends of Lesbians and Gays (PFLAG) 246
Parsons, D. 288, 304
pastors xv, 13, 26, 164–174, 178, 289
Patton, Cindy 251, 253
Pederson, Duane 21, 28
People for the American Way 288
Perkins, John 211
Perot, H. Ross 197
Perrin, R.D. 24, 28
Peters, J.W. 38, 40
Pew Research Center 15, 18
Pharr, Suzanne 73, 75
Phillips, A. 9, 18, 297, 304
Phillips, Holly 143–144, 152, 229, 236, 262–263
Phillips, Randy 8, 21, 24, 96, 101, 116, 143, 217–218, 233, 259, 262–264, 269, 276, 280, 292
Pierard, R.V. 317, 323
Pierce, John N. 3, 48, 54
Polanyi, Michael 46, 54
Policy Review journal 292–293
Politics 7–19, 65–66, 72, 314, 317, 321
Pollitt, Katha 226, 233, 237, 288, 304
Porter, Bishop Phillip 139
Portland [ME] Press Herald 287
Postman, Neil 282, 304
postmodern religion xv, 91–101
Powell, Colin 147
Power Team for Christ 195
Praise Keepers 240
Prentiss, John, Jr. 198

Presbyterians 177, 288
Priester, D. 276, 280
Princeton University 198
Prior, K. 33, 40
Prison Fellowship Ministries 209, 272
Promise Keeper: Living a Life of Integrity 177, 181
Promise Reapers 116, 241
Proudfoot, W. 228, 236
Puritans 148, 165
Putney, C. 30–31, 40
Pythians *see* Knights of Pythias

Quicke, Andrew xiv, 7–19, 295, 308, 317, 320, 326

Raab, Scott 108, 111, 161, 163, 209, 214, 286, 298, 305
Raajmakers, Q. 59, 75
Rabey, S., 13, 18, 270, 280, 292, 294, 305
race and PK xvi, 9, 13–14, 17, 70–71, 76–77, 86–87, 103, 124, 141, 147, 166–167, 177, 182–193, 206, 215, 261, 276–278, 297, 314, 317; *see also* African Americans; Asian Americans; Hispanic Americans; Native Americans
Ralston, R. 275, 280
Rambo motion pictures 85
Rauschenbusch, Walter 51
Rayman, P.M. 216–225
Reagan, Michael 197
Recer, J. 231, 237
Red Men, Improved Order of 30, 32, 38
Reed, Ralph 10, 14–16, 18, 182, 195, 203, 289; *see also* Christian Coalition
Reeves, B. 248, 253
Reid, Russ *see* Russ Reid Agency
Religion News Service 284, 296, 305
Rendell, J. 44, 54
Republicans 10, 17, 178
Reyes, Guillermo de los xiv, 29–41, 294, 326
Reynolds, J. Lynn xvi, 175–181, 326
Reynolds, L.T. 38, 40

Reynolds, Rodney xvi, 175–181, 326
Rice, J.R. 196, 203
Rich, Paul xii, 29–41, 294, 326
Richardson, Bobby 195
Richmond Times Dispatch 284, 303
Ricoeur, Paul 146, 152
Risen, J. 288, 305
ritualized resistance 76–90
Rivera, J. 264, 268
Robbins, Raymond 50
Roberts, Oral 21, 291
Roberts, Wes 166, 174
Robertson, Pat xvi, 7, 13, 16–17, 204–205, 209–210, 257, 260, 314, 317
Robinson, Doug 80, 90
Robinson, G.J. 281, 305
Robinson, Karen xiv, 7–19, 295, 308, 317, 320, 326
Rocky Mountain News 295
Romano, M. 264, 268
Rosin, H. 10, 19, 289, 305
Ross, A. 20, 24, 28, 204, 211, 212, 213, 230, 236, 289, 301
Rotundo, E. Anthony 30, 32, 36, 41, 46–47, 54, 77–78, 90
Rourke, Mary 295, 305
Rudy, K. 143, 152
Ruppe, Steve 258–261, 268
Russ Reid Agency 257, 262–263, 265–266
Russia 122
Ruth, Babe 159, 312–313
Ryle, James 8, 21, 131

Sahagun, L. 58, 75
St. Jude's Hospital 257
Salvation Army 194
Samaritan's Purse 209
Samuelson, R.J. 197, 203
Sandhill Farm (Missouri) 82
Sanford, R.N. 58, 73
Santa Fe New Mexican 287
Scalia, Justice Antonin 272–273
Scandale, F. 297, 305
Schatzman, L. 59, 75
Schlafer, D. 164, 174, 289
Schneider, A.G. 45, 54
Schneider, L. 244, 245, 253

Schoch, D. 294, 305
Schultze, Q. 257, 268
Schwarzkopf, Gen. Norman 147
Scopes "Monkey Trial" 196
Scotland 48
Segal, L. 34, 41
Seib, Gerald xiii
700 Club 210, 248; *see also* Robertson, Pat
Seven Promises 9, 44, 84, 116, 118, 127, 177, 206, 208, 229
Seven Promises of a Promise Keeper 154–157, 199, 215, 217, 218, 221, 274, 277, 279
Seyfarth, S. 283, 305
Shakespeare, William 113
Shapiro, J.P. 57, 75, 115, 131
Shaw, Donald L. 256, 267, 300, 304
Shedd, C.P. 51, 54
Sheldon, Charles 3, 48–49, 54, 195
Shiflett, D. 269, 284, 280, 292, 305
Shor, F. 283, 305
Shrine 34, 294
Silk, Mark 296
Simpson, Homer 85
Skelly, G. 282, 305
Smalley, G. 119, 131, 145, 147–148, 152, 159, 199–200, 203, 209, 312, 323
Smith, C.C. 293, 305
Smith, Chuck 21–23, 26–28
Smith, Craig A. 91, 101, 114, 116, 131
Smith, David R. 83, 84, 86, 90
Smith, Fred B. 48, 50, 54
Smith, Gary Scott 17, 19, 49, 54, 79, 90, 195, 203
Smith, Gipsy 50
Smith, L. 297, 305
Smith, S. 115, 130, 270, 280
Smith, T.L. 45, 54, 319, 323
Snyder, H.A. 212, 214, 305
Sobran, J. 231, 237
Social Gospel movement xiii, 49, 51, 295; *see also*

Men and Religion Forward
Solomon, N. 284, 305
Southern Baptist Convention Brotherhood Commission's Men's Ministries 294
Spalding, J.D. 286, 305; *see also* Baptists or Baptists and PK
Spatula Ministries 246
Spilka, B. 283, 305
sports: and Christianity 78; and PK xv, 3, 68, 93–99, 105–107, 146, 153–163, 187, 188, 194–203, 206–208, 230, 273, 285, 289, 310, 313, 319–320
Stammer, L.B. 156, 163, 288, 292, 295, 305–306
Stampp, K.M. 183, 184, 193
Stand in the Gap 4, 11, 13, 26, 56–57, 82–85, 87, 115, 124, 139–140, 142, 144, 150, 175, 181, 210–211, 230, 255–268, 273, 276, 278, 284, 287–291, 293, 309, 315, 321
Stecker, Chuck 12
Steinfels, P. 289, 306
Stelzle, Charles 50
Stewart, Charles J. 91, 101, 114, 116, 131
Stewart, Robert A. xv, 102–112, 320, 326
Stipe, Tom 24
Stodghill, R. II 103, 112, 237, 261, 268, 274, 280, 295, 297, 306
Stoltenberg, John 231, 233, 237
Stouffer, A.H. 265, 268
Stowell, Joseph M. 166, 209
Strate, L. 282, 304, 306
Strauss, A.L. 59, 75
Student Volunteer Movement 48
Suitable Helpers 240–241
Suk, John D. xiii, 164–174, 326
Sullivan, F.A., 22, 28
Sunday, Billy xv, 3, 51, 57, 194, 289, 295; *see also* Muscular Christianity

Sunde, D. 275, 280
Swaggert, the Rev. Jimmy 68
Swanson, Neil 288, 306
Sweet, L.I. 46, 55
Sweet, W.W. 44, 55
Swicegood, Lawrence 295
Swift, Jonathon 166
Swindoll, Chuck 167, 169–170, 174
Swomley, John 8, 11, 13, 19, 76, 90, 298, 306

Tall Cedar 38
Tampa Tribune 287
Tapia, A. 87, 89
Tarkowski, E. 210, 211, 214
Taylor, G.R. 37, 41
Taylor, J.G. 291, 306
Taylor, Tim 85
Teitcher, A. 92, 96, 101
television coverage *see* mass media
Terzian, Philip 261, 268
Thailand 243, 253
Thomas, Cal 265, 268
Thompson, C.W. 264, 268
Thompson, F.L. 49, 55
Thompson, K. 115, 131
Thoreau, Henry David 47
Tiger, L. 34, 41
Time magazine 274, 288, 307
Tippencott, S. 245, 248, 254
Tiribassi, Becky 248
Title IX 197
Tocqueville, Alexis de 173, 183, 185, 193
Today's Family 209
Todd, J.T. 27
Toledo, E. 232, 237
Tomorrow, Tom 287
Tompkins, J. 283, 306
"Toronto Blessing" 24
Torry, S. 261, 268, 298, 306
Trent, J. 119, 131, 145, 147–148, 152, 159, 312, 323
Tuchman, Gaye 256, 268
Tucker, D. 276, 280
Turner, Victor 45
Tyson, A.S. 260, 268, 296, 306

United Nations 197

Unitarian Universalist Church 219, 288
U.S. News & World Report 288
Urban Alternative 209; *see also* Evans, Tony

Vachon, B. 22, 28
Valentine, Harry 210
van Biema, D. 57, 75, 115, 132
Vance, N. 295, 306
van Hesteren, F. 216, 225
van Leeuwen, M.S. 76, 79, 90, 144, 152, 229–230, 237, 284, 298, 306, 316, 323
van Zoonen, E.A. 300, 306
Veterans of Foreign Wars (VFW) 200
Vietnam War 195, 255
Vineyard movement xiv, 8, 21, 23, 24, 44
Visser, L. 59, 74
Vollebergh, W. 59, 75

Waddle, R. 293, 306
Wagenheim, J. 132, 156, 161, 163
Wagner, C.P. 28
Wagner, David 9, 19
Wagner, E. Glenn 131, 147, 152, 277, 280
Walker, K. 115, 132
Wall Street Journal 286, 292
Wallis, Jim 150, 152
Walsh, Shelia 248
Walzer, M. 136, 152
Wanta, Wayne 283, 306
Wardell, Dave 3, 8, 93, 98, 101, 195
Warren, David 85, 86, 88, 90
Washington, Raleigh 87, 131, 166, 168, 171, 174
Washington Blade newspaper 297
Washington Post 265, 268, 288, 295
Washington newspaper 297
Watergate 209
Waters, Ken xvi, 69, 176, 233, 255–268, 269, 308, 310, 311, 314–315, 326
Watson, J. 12, 19
Watson, Matthew 15–16

Watts-Ditchfield, J.E. 51, 55
Wayne, K.H. 48, 55
Weaver, David H. 69, 75
Weaver, R. 227, 237
Weber, Bruce 155, 163
Weber, Stu 142–143, 152
Wehmeyer, Peggy 263, 268
Weiner, B. 33, 41
Weingarter, C. 282, 304
Wells, Thelma 248, 249, 254
Westword 96, 269
White, B. 48, 55
White, H. 134, 152
Whitson, D. 158, 163
Whittinghill, Al 131
Wickersham, Dave 195
Wilcox, C. 205, 214
Wilgoren, J. 288, 306
Wilhoit, G. Cleveland 69, 75
Wilkerson, Bruce H. 141, 152
Wilkerson, David 22, 23
Williams, L. 283, 302
Willis, P. 158, 163
Willis, R. 41
Wilson, G.D. 59, 74
Wilson, P.B. 239, 244–250, 254
Wilson, Woodrow 46
Wimber, John 8, 21, 23–24, 26–28
Wimber, T. 95, 101
Winant, H. 186, 193
Wind, R. 27
Winner, Lauren F. 297, 307
Winthrop, John 148–149
Wolf, R. 284, 307
women 17, 33–34, 99, 108, 119–124, 128, 199, 221–224, 226–254, 316; *see also* National Organization for Women; Women's Christian organizations
Women of Faith 238–254
Women Today International 241
women's Christian organizations xvi, 238–254
Wood, Donald N. 298, 307
Wood, F. 183, 184, 185, 193
Wood, Julia T. 83, 90

Woodard, J. 43, 55, 296, 307
Woods, W.J. 17, 19
Woodstock 263
Woodward, K.L. 115, 132, 285, 307
Word of God community 22
World Impact 209
World Vision 241, 257
World War II 200
World Wide Web *see* Internet
Worthington, Al 195
Wright, J. Elwin 20–21
Wuthnow, R. 22, 28, 103–104, 112, 311, 323

Yale University 198
Yonkman, Todd 168, 174
Young Men's Christian Association (YMCA) 48, 50, 51, 198
Youth for Christ 92
Yows, S.R. 256, 268

Zeuthen, K. 293, 301
Zweir, R. 205, 214

CANISIUS COLLEGE LIBRARY

3 5084 00368 1536

BV 960 .P76 2000

The Promise Keepers

DATE DUE

GAYLORD — PRINTED IN U.S.A.

CANISIUS COLLEGE LIBRARY
BUFFALO, N.Y.